Achaemenid Imperial Administration in Syria-Palestine and the Missions of Ezra and Nehemiah

SOCIETY
OF BIBLICAL
LITERATURE

DISSERTATION SERIES

Number 125

Achaemenid Imperial Administration
in Syria-Palestine and the Missions
of Ezra and Nehemiah

by

Kenneth G. Hoglund

Kenneth G. Hoglund

Achaemenid Imperial Administration in Syria-Palestine and the Missions of Ezra and Nehemiah

Scholars Press
Atlanta, Georgia

Achaemenid Imperial Administration in Syria-Palestine and the Missions of Ezra and Nehemiah

Kenneth G. Hoglund

Ph.D., 1989
Duke University

Advisor:
Eric M. Meyers

Library of Congress Cataloging in Publication Data

Hoglund, Kenneth G.
Achaemenid imperial administration in Syria-Palestine and the missions of Ezra and Nehemiah / Kenneth G. Hoglund.
p. cm. — (Dissertation series ; no. 125)
Thesis (Ph.D.)—Duke University, 1989.
Includes bibliographical references.
1. Palestine—History—To 70 A.D. 2. Jews—History—586 B.C.-70 A.D. 3. Syria—History—To 333 B.C. 4. Achaemenid dynasty, 559-330 B.C. 5. Bible. O.T. Ezra—History of Biblical events. 6. Bible. O.T. Ezra—History of contemporary events. 7. Bible. O.T. Nehemiah—History of Biblical events. 8. Bible. O.T. Nehemiah—History of contemporary events. I. Title. II. Series: Dissertation series (Society of Biblical Literature) ; no. 125.
DS121.65.H64 1992
933—dc20 92-26311
CIP

Printed in the United States of America
on acid-free paper

CONTENTS

TABLES

ABBREVIATIONS

AASOR	*Annual of the American Schools of Oriental Research*
AJA	*American Journal of Archaeology*
AJP	*American Journal of Philology*
AJSL	*American Journal of the Semitic Languages*
BA	*Biblical Archaeologist*
BASOR	*Bulletin of the American Schools of Oriental Research*
BCE	Before the Common Era
ca.	circa
CBQ	*Catholic Biblical Quarterly*
CP	*Classical Philology*
CQ	*Classical Quarterly*
HTR	*Harvard Theological Review*
HUCA	*Hebrew Union College Annual*
IEJ	*Israel Exploration Journal*
JANES	*Journal of the Ancient Near Eastern Society*
JAOS	*Journal of the American Oriental Society*
JARCE	*Journal of the American Research Center in Egypt*
JBL	*Journal of Biblical Literature*
JCS	*Journal of Cuneiform Studies*
JEA	*Journal of Egyptian Archaeology*
JNES	*Journal of Near Eastern Studies*
JSOT	*Journal for the Study of the Old Testament*
JTS	*Journal of Theological Studies*
PEQ	*Palestine Exploration Quarterly*
PJB	*Palästinajahrbuch des deutschen evangelischen Instituts für Altertumswissenschaft*
SBL	Society of Biblical Literature
VT	*Vetus Testamentum*
VTSupp	*Supplements to Vetus Testamentum*
TAPA	*Transactions of the American Philology Association*
ZAW	*Zeitschrift für die alttestamentliche Wissenschaft*
ZDPV	*Zeitschrift des deutsches Palästina-Veriens*

ACKNOWLEDGMENTS

A dissertation of the complexity and scope of the present work could not have been attempted without the support and assistance of a number of individuals. At the head of those who should be recognized are the members of the author's dissertation committee, especially its chair Professor Eric M. Meyers. His close attention to all aspects of the presentation prevented innumerable errors and vagaries. Also deserving acknowledgment is a former member of the committee, Professor Allen Zagarell, now of the faculty at Western Michigan University. His close questioning of the social implications of the conditions prevailing in the mid-fifth century brought many issues into sharper focus.

Assistance on a variety of matters has been freely rendered by Professors Jack Sasson and John Van Seters of the University of North Carolina, Chapel Hill, Professor Ronald Sack of North Carolina State University, Professor Joan Bigwood of Victoria College, Professor Edwin Yamauchi of the University of Miami, Ohio, and Professor Christopher Tuplin of the University of Liverpool.

Some of the materials used in the archaeological arguments of this dissertation are unpublished and have been made available to me by several individuals. The late Professor Yigal Shiloh was most helpful in discussing the Persian period evidence from his City of David excavations. Nancy Lapp of the Pittsburgh Theological Seminary and Professor Steven Derfler of Hamline University were also helpful in sharing information on the excavations at Shechem and Nahal Yattir, respectively.

Gratitude is also due to the the Israel Archaeological Survey and Yehudit Ben-Michael for assistance in accessing and examining the ceramic materials collected in the 1967 archaeological survey of the occupied territories.

An expression of thanks is owed to the Office of the Dean of the Graduate School at Duke University for a dissertation travel grant in 1986 that helped to defray some of the costs associated with the field research conducted in Israel.

My understanding of the biblical narratives in Ezra-Nehemiah has been largely shaped by interacting with the work of two talented scholars, Professor Hugh Williamson of Cambridge University and Professor Tamara Eskenazi of the Hebrew Union College, Los Angeles. I am indebted to both for their willingness to share their insights with me.

In the process of preparing the dissertation for publication Professor James VanderKam of the University of Notre Dame rendered invaluable help in suggesting a number of corrections. Also my distinguished colleague Professor Fred L. Horton, Jr. of Wake Forest University rescued several computer files from certain oblivion, saving days of labor.

In many ways, the interaction with my fellow graduate students over various matters regarding the postexilic period was as useful as my own research. Dr. Julia O'Brien, Rev. James Christoph, and Dr. Stephen Goranson have, in their own ways, taught me a great deal.

Finally, this volume would have been impossible without the support, encouragement, and patience of my wife Karen. It is only fitting that this work be dedicated to her, a small reward for sacrifices she has made to allow me to work on it.

1

Introduction

When Cyrus the Great captured the city of Babylon in 539 BCE, the Achaemenid dynasty came into possession of the entirety of the Neo-Babylonian empire, including Syria-Palestine. A new imperial system now controlled the Near East and was to continue its domination for the next two centuries. This new system represented a melding of older styles of Near Eastern imperial rule with Achaemenid innovations, creating a dynamic political structure capable of varied application in the newly conquered territories.

For the Levant on the western fringes of this empire, the shift from Neo-Babylonian to Achaemenid rule ultimately resulted in widespread changes in the social and cultural patterns of the societies of Syria-Palestine. While at first this process may have been imperceptible, by the mid-fifth century BCE there was a marked enlargement of influence in local Levantine affairs by the imperial administration.

For much of Syria-Palestine, there is a lack of written documentation for the period of Persian domination, and inferences regarding the social and political developments of the period must be drawn from the combined analysis of Greek historical accounts and archaeological evidence. The situation is considerably better, however, in the case of the post-exilic Israelite community where the biblical work of Ezra-Nehemiah provides a window into the fifth century. Pervading the narratives is a consciousness that changes took place in the mid-fifth century that had profound implications for the community as a part of the imperial order.

In the self-consciousness of the Restoration community, the missions of Ezra and Nehemiah delineate a new phase in Achaemenid involvement in the province's local affairs. With theological concerns in the forefront of the compilation of the narratives found in Ezra-Nehemiah, the missions of these two personalities are portrayed largely as their activities lend themselves to such interpretation. Still, there is the explicit recognition that their missions are undertaken with royal authority and some of their activities are presented as the fulfillment of a larger imperial purpose. Though problematical, the chronology presented in Ezra-Nehemiah places both reformers in the mid-fifth century. As a consequence, the missions of Ezra and Nehemiah must be related to the larger imperial concerns of the Achaemenid empire in Syria-Palestine during this period in order to comprehend the transformation of the Restoration community as the result of these missions.

The administrative changes of the mid-fifth century in the Levant did not occur in a vacuum of political and social development. Rather, these changes partook to a certain degree of administrative techniques that had been adopted and refined as the result of preceding imperial experience. To understand this process of development, it is necessary to survey briefly the emergence and consolidation of the Achaemenid empire for the decades prior to the end of the first quarter of the fifth century BCE, roughly extending to the end of the reign of Darius I (522-486 BCE). The developments of this period, particularly as they relate to the administration of Syria-Palestine, suggest a strong continuity with earlier imperial systems and structures.

The fall of Babylon in 539 BCE to the advancing army of Persia under the command of Cyrus was both the termination of a long process of empire building and the beginning of a new extension of Persian control to the west.[1] The drive toward an empire by conquest had begun with Cyrus' inheriting the preexisting Median empire following the capture of the Median king Astyages around the year 550/549 BCE.[2] Though its internal structure at the time of its incorporation into Cyrus' growing holdings is poorly documented, Diakonoff has suggested a strong resem-

[1] For the date of Cyrus' conquest of Babylon, see Richard A. Parker and Waldo H. Dubberstein, *Babylonian Chronology 626 B.C.-A.D. 45.* Studies in Ancient Oriental Civilization No. 24 (Chicago: University of Chicago Press, 1942), 11-12.

[2] Richard N. Frye, *The History of Ancient Iran.* Handbuch der Altertumswissenschaft Abt. 3, Teil 7 (Munich: C.H. Beck, 1984), 91-92.

blance to later Achaemenid forms.[3] In contrast, Harmatta has utilized linguistic evidence to suggest the Median state was a developed bureaucratic system in contrast to the less developed Achaemenid kingdom.[4] The absence of clear documentation prohibits any certain conclusion beyond the acknowledgment that some Median precedents influenced the conception of empire and the form of administration undertaken by Cyrus.[5]

Following the absorption of the Median empire, Cyrus apparently undertook a far-ranging campaign across the Tigris River westward into Asia Minor in 547. He eventually captured the Lydian monarch Croesus and gained control of the Lydian kingdom.[6] Leaving the consolidation of his Anatolian holdings to his trusted subordinates, Cyrus returned to the Median capital of Ecbatana, although it is possible that he spent some time expanding the empire eastward.[7]

The campaign to conquer Babylon entered the field in 539 BCE, but it is not evident when the first preparations for this conquest were undertaken.[8] George Cameron has argued that a fragmentary portion of the Nabunaid Chronicle records the army of Persia entered the Diyala region in the month of Addan (March) in 539. Since the Chronicle places Cyrus' entry into Babylon on October 12, 539, there would seem to be an inex-

---

[3] I.M. Diakonoff, "Media," in *The Cambridge History of Iran. Volume 2: The Median and Achaemenian Periods,* ed. I. Gershevitch (Cambridge: Cambridge University Press, 1985), 134-39.

[4] J. Harmatta, "The Rise of the Old Persian Empire - Cyrus the Great," *Acta Antiqua Academiae Scientarum Hungaricae* 19 (1971):3-15.

[5] See Pierre Briant, "La Perse avant l'Empire (un état de la question)," *Iranica Antiqua* 19 (1984):96-100; Heleen Sancisi-Weerdenburg, "Medes and Persians: To What Extent was Cyrus the Heir of Astyages and the Median Empire?," *Persica* 10 (1982):278.

[6] Frye, *History of Ancient Iran,* 92-93; J.M. Cook, "The Rise of the Achaemenids," in *The Cambridge History of Iran. Volume 2: The Median and Achaemenian Periods,* ed. I. Gershevitch (Cambridge: Cambridge University Press, 1985), 211-13. There is some controversy on the exact interpretation of the Nabunaid Chronicle at this point, for which see J. Cargill, "The Nabonidus Chronicle and the Fall of Lydia," *American Journal of Ancient History* 2 (1977):97-116.

[7] Frye, *History of Ancient Iran,* 93.

[8] There is no reason to adopt the suggestion of Bogdan Skladanek that all of Cyrus' campaigns to this point were directed toward cutting off Babylon from the supplies of its outlying imperial holdings; "The Structure of the Persian State (An Outline)," in *Acta Iranica. Première Serie. Commemoration Cyrus* (Leiden: E.J. Brill, 1974), 117-18. The Anatolian campaign of Cyrus was more likely the natural extension of the preceeding Median empire since the Medes and Lydians had struggled together earlier; see Pierre Briant, "La Perse avant l'Empire," 86-87.

plicable delay in Cyrus' campaign over the summer.[9] Cameron relates this delay to an account by Herodotus of Cyrus having his army dig a number of canals along the Diyala River (1.189). Citing the survey of archaeological sites in the Diyala region by Robert Adams, Cameron concluded that the evidence for an increased population density in this region during Achaemenid times supports the plausibility of an improvement in field irrigation.[10]

Cameron's hypothesis is suggestive of two important aspects of this formative stage in Achaemenid imperial practice. First, there is the propagandistic value of such actions that contrasted the preceding Neo-Babylonian royalty's disregard for the welfare of the state with Cyrus' concern to insure prosperity. Doubtless this improved Cyrus' appeal to the fractured leadership of Babylon and demonstrated his willingness to conform to traditional Babylonian conceptions of the proper role of a sovereign.[11] Second, such an action requiring a considerable investment of labor for little in the way of immediate return is indicative of an Achaemenian interest in the long-term economic viability of conquered territories. This attention to the renewal of agricultural production in the Diyala region reflects an effort to insure a constant flow of surpluses into the imperial system from such rural areas and a concern with the economic interaction of territories under imperial control.

The collapse of Babylonian resistance to Cyrus and his army and the resulting fall of the city into Persian hands was a pivotal event in world history. Cyrus entered the city on October 29, 539 BCE and promptly declared a state of "peace," marking the respect extended to the fallen city.[12] Not only did one of the ancient world's great urban centers fall into Persian hands, but Cyrus now came into possession of the Neo-

[9] George C. Cameron, "Cyrus the 'Father', and Babylon," in *Acta Iranica. Première Serie. Commemoration Cyrus* (Leiden: E.J. Brill, 1974), 45-46. Cameron's suggestion is based on a new reading of Rev. III:3 of the Chronicle, a reading accepted by A.K. Grayson, *Assyrian and Babylonian Chronicles.* Texts from Cuneiform Sources Volume V (New York: J.J. Augustin, 1975), 282.

[10] Cameron, "Cyrus the 'Father'," 46-47. The survey data referred to is Robert Adams, *Land Behind Baghdad: A History of Settlement on the Diyala Plains* (Chicago: University of Chicago Press, 1965).

[11] As suggested by Cameron, "Cyrus the 'Father'", 47-48; see also the suggestion by M.A. Dandamaev, *Persian unter der ersten Achämeniden* (Wiesbaden: Reichert, 1976), 97-98 that the blocking of eastern trade routes by the Persians led to an alliance of merchants and priests in favor of Cyrus.

[12] Frye, *History of Iran,* 94; Svend Pallis, "The History of Babylon 538-93 B.C." in *Studia Orientalia Ioanni Pedersen* (Hauniae: Einar Munksgaard, 1953), 276.

Babylonian empire and its extensive holdings in Syria-Palestine.[13] There is ample evidence to conclude that at its inception the new Achaemenid administration of Babylon sought to retain the same economic, political, and social conditions that had prevailed under the Babylonian kingship.[14]

For the outlying districts, especially those in the Levant, there appears to have been little administrative change in the transition from Neo-Babylonian to Achaemenid rule. Indeed, in the Achaemenid organizational structure the entire Neo-Babylonian empire came under the rule of a single satrap placed over "Babylon and Beyond the River."[15] This organizational division suggests that until the status of Syria-Palestine was redefined at a later date, Achaemenid rule in the Levant maintained the same patterns as prevailed under Neo-Babylonian domination.[16]

Since the newly emergent Achaemenid empire incorporated the Neo-Babylonian empire as a whole into its administrative system, the character of Neo-Babylonian rule in the Levant and its effect on the region prior to 539 BCE constitute an important prelude to Persian domination. Regrettably, the available documentation of the imperial system of the Neo-Babylonian empire is scarce. Few texts pertain directly to the administration of imperial territories in the west, and the economic tablets that might provide a reflection on the interaction with outlying territories number in the thousands, making a synthetic analysis still unattainable.[17] What documentation is available suggests that the Neo-Babylonian empire adapted in part the structures, terminology, and territorial divisions of the preceding Assyrian empire.[18] Consequently, before

---

13 Frye, *History of Iran*, 95; J.M. Cook, *The Persian Empire* (NY: Schocken Books, 1983), 32-33; Cook, "The Rise of the Achaemenids," 212; A.T. Olmstead, *History of the Persian Empire* (Chicago: University of Chicago Press, 1948), 59.

14 See particularly the discussion in Olmstead, *History of the Persian Empire*, 70-85.

15 Frye, *History of Iran*, 113-14; A.F. Rainey, "The Satrapy 'Beyond the River,'" *Australian Journal of Biblical Archaeology* 1 (1969), 52. The Neirab archive, often cited as evidence of continuity between Neo-Babylonian and Achaemenid rule in the Levant, may not relate to this issue at all. See the discussion of these texts below.

16 Cook, *The Persian Empire*, 41; Aharoni, *The Land of the Bible*. 2nd ed., 408.

17 See, for example, the comments of Paul Garelli, "Les empires mésopotamiens" in *Le Concept d'Empire*, ed. Maurice Duverger (Paris: Presses Universitaires de France, 1980), 42-43; and Ronald Sack, *Amel-marduk, 562-560 B.C.: A Study Based on Cuneiform, Old Testament, Greek, Latin and Rabbinical Sources*. Alter Orient und Altes Testament-Sonderreihe Bd. 4. (Neukirchen: Verlag Butzon & Nercker Kevelaer, 1972), 33-35.

18 Paul Garelli and V. Nikiprowetzky, *Le Proche-orient asiatique: Les empires Mésopotamiens, Israel* (Paris: Presses Universitaires de France, 1974), 157-59; Aharoni, *The Land of the Bible*, 2nd ed., 408.

evaluating the possible Neo-Babylonian rule of the Levant, it would be advantageous to examine in outline the Assyrian imperial system, particularly as it relates to the imperial territories in Syria-Palestine.

The Assyrian empire had its foundations in a series of ever-widening conquests moving from the north Mesopotamian plateau outward. By the reign of Tiglath-Pileser III in the second half of the eighth century BCE, Assyria had managed to subdue most of the surrounding kingdoms and to exact considerable tribute from smaller states fearful of Assyria's might.[19] The strain of the constant mustering of seasonal armies combined with the challenge to Assyrian hegemony in northern Syria presented by the Urartian kingdom led to considerable military and administrative reforms under Tiglath-Pileser III (745-727 BCE). The Assyrian monarch initiated a policy of subdividing conquered territories into provincial districts, each with an administrative head (*bel paḫati*) and several military commanders (*rab kisri*), as well as its own provincial military force. The provincial administration was responsible for collecting various agricultural taxes as well as insuring the conscription of troops from the province, some of whom served in the provincial military force, while others went on to serve in the Assyrian army proper.

The end result of this structure was the permanent occupation of conquered territories and their incorporation into a specialized administrative structure with powers of enforcement. The empire also gained a standing army, ready to advance on any provincial trouble spot and to insure the regular delivery of tribute from surrounding vassal states.[20] This is in contrast to earlier Assyrian practices of establishing vassal kings in conquered territories, maintaining preexisting geopolitical boundaries, and emphasizing the collection of tribute (*mandattu*) as the primary economic benefit of imperialistic expansion to the central administration.[21]

---

19 Georges Roux, *Ancient Iraq*. 2nd ed. (Harmondsworth: Penguin Books, 1982), 278-82; William W. Hallo and William Kelly Simpson, *The Ancient Near East: A History* (NY: Harcourt Brace Jovanovich, Inc., 1971), 130.

20 On the reforms of Tiglath-pileser III, see Roux, *Ancient Iraq*, 282-86, 320-21; H.W.F. Saggs, *The Might That Was Assyria* (London: Sidgwick & Jackson, 1984), 85-87; Garelli, "Les empires mésopotamiens," 26-27. On the organization of provincial responsibilities, see J.N. Postgate, *Taxation and Conscription in the Assyrian Empire*. Studia Pohl: Series Maior 3 (Rome: Biblical Institute Press, 1974), 218-33.

21 See Garelli, "Les empires mésopotamiens," 26-27; Garelli and Nikiprowatzky, *Le proche-orient*, 231-34; Roux, *Ancient Iraq*, 263-67; Herbert Donner, "The Separate States of Israel and Judah," in *Israelite and Judean History*, John H. Hayes and J. Maxwell

The transformation of the Assyrian imperial system under Tiglath-Pileser III also brought with it the systematic application of mass deportations of conquered populations. Though occasionally attested in the ancient Near East prior to Tiglath-Pileser's reign, no previous imperial system utilized this technique of rule on such an extensive basis.[22] Estimates of the total number of individuals deported under Assyrian imperial rule range between four and five million, indicating not only the extensive use of the practice but also suggesting the economic and political impact of such deportations upon the imperial system as a whole.[23]

The technique of mass deportations provided the Assyrian imperial system with a multifaceted policy of considerable importance. The deportation of a conquered population effectively destroyed the ability of that group to resist Assyrian domination by removing it from its ideologically significant homeland. The deportees, often settled in depopulated areas or along strategic borders, became an ethnic minority within their new regions and thus were more apt to remain loyal to the empire in order to enjoy imperial protection.[24]

Aside from motivations rooted in maintaining political control over a subjected population, there were considerable economic benefits to be gained by the technique of mass deportations. Those deported from an ancestral homeland and resettled in some other part of the empire constituted a land-tied population. While not reduced to a condition of total slavery, these deportees as individuals and as a population were not allowed to leave their agrarian responsibilities in their new settlements.[25] While it is true that deported populations had access to arable lands, this access was controlled and dictated by the central administration of the

---

Miller, eds., (Philadelphia: Westminster Press, 1977), 416-18. On the nature of *maduttu*, see Postgate, *Taxation and Conscription*, 119-21.

[22] Roux, *Ancient Iraq*, 284; Bustenay Oded, *Mass Deportations and Deportees in the Neo-Assyrian Empire* (Wiesbaden: Dr. Ludwig Reichert Verlag, 1979), 1-2, 42-3.

[23] Bustenay Oded, "Mass Deportations in the Neo-Assyrian Empire—Facts and Figures," *Eretz-Israel* 14 (1978):62-68 [Hebrew].

[24] Bustenay Oded, "Mass Deportation in the Neo-Assyrian Empire—Aims and Objectives," *Shnaton* 3 (1978-79):159-73 [Hebrew]; Oded, *Mass Deportations and Deportees*, 41-67.

[25] Oded, *Mass Deportations and Deportees*, 91-99; see also J.N. Postgate, Review of Bustenay Oded, *Mass Deportations and Deportees in the Neo-Assyrian Empire*, *Bibliotheca Orientalis* 38 (1981):636-37; W.G. Lambert, Review of Oded, B., *Mass Deportations and Deportees in the Neo-Assyrian Empire*, *Society for Old Testament Study Booklist* (1981):41. For a somewhat more cautious approach in interpreting the evidence, see G. van Driel, "Land and People in Assyria: Some Remarks" *Bibliotheca Orientalis* 27 (1970):168-75.

empire.[26] As such, this condition was tantamount to a kind of serfdom and had corollaries in earlier ancient Near Eastern practices.[27] While the precise modern terminology for this condition has been debated, the term 'dependent population' is to be preferred due to its neutral connotation in comparision with other suggested terms as regards differential rights and privileges granted to this social class versus native Assyrians.[28]

The use of dependent populations as agrarian workers provided the Assyrian empire with a constant supply of laborers for the agrarian base of the empire. This base was vital to imperial survival, not only by insuring supplies of foodstuffs to the burgeoning urban centers of Assyria and the imperial provinces, but also by providing an expanding base for the agrarian-tied taxation system.[29] The various taxes assessed on cultivated fields (*šibšu* and *nusāhu*) were the means for supporting the specialized administrative structure of the empire and constituted the basic resource collected for the central administration.[30] Consequently, the use of mass deportations and resettlements of conquered peoples was a policy essential for maintaining the Assyrian imperial system.

An example of the means by which the Assyrians used to incorporate conquered territories into the empire can be seen in the case of the northern kingdom of Israel. In 758 BCE Tiglath-Pileser III undertook a

---

26 Oded, *Mass Deportations and Deportees*, 98-99. It is obvious that in deporting and resettling vast numbers of peoples, the empire served notice that it ultimately owned conquered territories and that deportees retained access to an agrarian territory only through the good graces of the empire. Thus Oded's suggestion made without support that such lands eventually became private property seems untenable. Of course, this does not help in determining the alienability of lands held by remnants of the conquered population left in an ancestral homeland.

27 I. M. Diakonoff, "Slaves, Helots and Serfs in Early Antiquity," in *Wirtschaft und Gesellschaft im Alten Vorderasien*, eds. J. Harmatta and G. Komoroczy, Nachdruck aus den Acta Antiqua Academiae Scientarum Hungaricae 22 (Budapest: Akademiai Kiado, 1976), 45-78.

28 Oded, *Mass Deportations and Deportees*, 79-81; also see the discussions in G. Komoroczy, "Landed Property in Ancient Mesopotamia and the Theory of the So-called Asiatic Mode of Production." *Oikumene* 2 (1978):20-21; J. N. Postgate, Review of Bustenay Oded, 637; and V. A. Jakobson, "The Social Structure of the Neo-Assyrian Empire" in *Ancient Mesopotamia: Socio-Economic History*, I. M. Diakonoff, ed. (Moscow: Nauka Publishing House, 1969), 289-93.

29 J. N. Postgate, "The Economic Structure of the Assyrian Empire," in *Power and Propaganda: A Symposium on Ancient Empires*, Mogens Trolle Larsen, ed., Mesopotamia 7 (Copenhagen: Akademisk Forlag, 1979), 214-15.

30 Postgate, "Economic Structure," 205; see also Postgate, *Taxation and Conscription*, 174-99.

punitive expedition against Hamath in Syria. With the threat of Assyrian conquest so imminent, Samaria offered tribute to the Assyrian king and became a vassal state.[31] In 734 a new Assyrian campaign was launched into the Levant, this time directed along the Levantine coast toward the Philistine cities as far south as Gaza. It is possible that this move was designed both to cut off trade relationships with Egypt and to gain control of trading centers along the coast. Portions of the kingdom of Israel, lost earlier to a Syrian kingdom ruled from Damascus, were reorganized into distinct provinces.[32]

Sometime during this period, a Syro-Ephraimite alliance launched an attack against neighboring Judah, seeking to compel Ahaz, the Judean monarch, to join in a revolt against Assyria. Instead, Ahaz asked for relief from the Assyrian king, and in 733-732, Tiglath-Pileser destroyed the kingdom of Damascus, splitting its former territory into several smaller provinces and deporting a number of citizens.[33] The Northern Kingdom saw a change of monarchs, the pro-Assyrian Hoshea coming to the throne (2 Kings 15:30), thus sparing Samaria itself from certain destruction. Israel, now a puppet state, continued to offer tribute to Tiglath-Pileser and his successor, Shalmaneser V (727-722 BCE).[34]

After a brief rule, Hoshea attempted to revolt and Shalmaneser entered the Levant to quash the rebellion in 722.[35] After the capture of the

---

31 See Siegfried Herrmann, *A History of Israel in Old Testament Times.* Revised and enlarged edition (Philadelphia: Fortress Press, 1981), 243-46; Benedkt Otzen, "Israel under the Assyrians," in *Power and Propaganda: A Symposium on Ancient Empires,* ed. Mogens Trolle Larsen, Mesopotamia 7 (Copenhagen: Akademisk Forlag,1979), 253; J. Maxwell Miller and John H. Hayes, *A History of Ancient Israel and Judah* (Philadelphia: Westminster Press, 1986), 322-23.

32 Otzen, "Israel under the Assyrians," 254-55; Bustenay Oded, "The Phoenician Cities and the Assyrian Empire in the Time of Tiglath-pileser III," *ZDPV* 90 (1974):38-49. For the reorganization of Israelite territories, see Emil Forrer, *Die Provinzeinteilung der assyrischen Reiches* (Leipzig: J. C. Hinrichs, 1920), 59-62.

33 Miller and Hayes, *A History of Ancient Israel and Judah,* 331-32; Hayim Tadmor, "The Southern Border of Aram," *IEJ* 12 (1962):114-22; Bustenay Oded, "Observations on Methods of Assyrian Rule in Transjordania After the Palestinian Campaign of Tiglath-Pileser III," *JNES* 29 (1970):179-83.

34 Miller and Hayes, *A History of Ancient Israel and Judah,* 332-34; Herrmann, *A History of Israel,* 248-49; Otzen, "Israel under the Assyrians," 257. On the distinction between a vassel state and what is termed here a 'puppet state,' see Morton Cogan, *Imperialism and Religion: Assyria, Judah and Israel in the Eighth and Seventh Centuries B. C. E..* SBL Monograph Series, 19 (Missoula: Scholars Press, 1974), 42.

35 It is probable that Hoshea's rebellion was not an isolated act, but was done in conjunction with a general rebellion in the Levantine states; see Miller and Hayes, *A History of Ancient Israel and Judah,* 334-36; Otzen, "Israel under the Assyrians," 256-57.

capital, the Assyrians deported a number of the citizenry and resettled them in Assyria proper (2 Kings 17:6). Sargon II, who succeeded Shalmaneser in the course of the campaign to vanquish Samaria, boasted in his annals that he deported 27,290 people from the region. He also claimed, "I repopulated Samaria more than before, and put into it peoples from the countries which I had conquered."[36] There is also clear evidence that not all those captured in the fall of Samaria were reduced to a condition of dependency. Some of the professional military personnel of the Northern Kingdom were placed as a functional unit in the royal army of Assyria.[37] Samaria was reduced from a puppet state to a province within the Assyrian empire with an Assyrian governor and continued to receive populations of deportees from other parts of the empire up through the reign of Ashurbanipal (668-627 BCE).[38]

For an example of Assyrian imperial administration after the consolidation of a province, one can turn to the region of Nippur located in the ancient Akkadian heartland. The province was under the rule of a governor and served as a garrison for the imperial army.[39] The landscape around the city was divided by a number of canals that served to delineate parcels of land. Some of these parcels were royal estates owned by members of the royal family. Others, at least by the Neo-Babylonian period, seem to have been in the hands of private individuals and to have functioned as large estates with settlements of deportees from various parts of the empire constituting the work force.[40] The individuals who held these estates may have received the lands either as the result of hereditary holdings or through the well-attested practice of royal grants

---

36 The Annals of Sargon II as translated in Stephanie Dalley, "Foreign Chariotry and Cavalry in the Armies of Tiglath-pileser III and Sargon II," *Iraq* 47 (1985): 36. The translation is of a passage from a prism of Sargon II originally published by C.J. Gadd, "Inscribed Prisms of Sargon II from Nimrud," *Iraq* 16 (1954):173-201. See also Hayim Tadmor, "The Campaigns of Sargon II of Assur," *JCS* 12 (1958):33-39.

37 Stephanie Dalley, "Foreign Chariotry and Cavalry," 31-48.

38 Miller and Hayes, *A History of Ancient Israel and Judah*, 337-39; Oded, *Mass Deportations and Deportees*, 66; Herbert Donner, "The Separate States of Israel and Judah," 433-34.

39 Ran Zadok, "The Nippur Region During the Late Assyrian, Chaldaean and Achaemenian Periods" *Israel Oriental Studies* 8 (1978):273-74. It is possible that because of the favorable attitude this region demonstrated toward Assyria, it received a more respectful treatment as a province and thus may reflect the most optimal conditions of imperial existence.

40 Zadok, "The Nippur Region," 326-27; Oded, *Mass Deportations and Deportees*, 66, 86.

to imperial officials.[41] The resulting picture is of a prosperous, well-integrated system of agricultural production, all regulated and taxed by the imperial authorities.

While the dominant impression of Assyrian interests in maintaining the empire highlights the role of agrarian production, it should be noted that this was only one portion of the larger system of benefits derived from the imperial system.[42] For example, once the Assyrians entered the Levant, great interest was evident in gaining access to the Phoenician seaports in order to control the exchange of goods with the western Mediterranean.[43] This desire was not only evident in the initial campaigns in the Levant by Tiglath-Pileser III but in subsequent efforts by the Assyrian monarchs to control the Phoenician coast.[44] The whole question of the importance of exchange to the imperial structure of Assyria still requires analysis before any certain conclusions can be reached.[45]

Before completing the consideration of the Assyrian imperial system, one last factor for consideration relates to the relationship of the provincial authorities to the central imperial administration. One of the great strengths of the Assyrian system was its extreme centralization: all provincial officials reported directly to the king.[46] As an example, in one text an official in charge of a subdistrict (a *rab ālāni* of Sippar who appar-

---

[41] See, for example, Zadok, "The Nippur Region," 292-93. On possible hereditary ownership in this period in Babylonia, see J.A. Brinkman, *Prelude to Empire: Babylonian Society and Politics, 747-626 B.C.* Occasional Publications of the Babylonian Fund, 7 (Philadelphia: University Museum, 1984), 74-75; also Postgate, "The Economic Structure," 214. For royal land grants, see J.N. Postgate, *Neo-Assyrian Royal Grants and Decrees.* Studia Pohl: Series Maior 1 (Rome: Biblical Institute Press, 1969).

[42] Postgate, "The Economic Structure," 206-07.

[43] Oded, "The Phoenician Cities and the Assyrian Empire," 38-49; see also the extensive discussion by Susan Frankenstein, "The Phoenicians in the Far West: A Function of Neo-Assyrian Imperialism," in *Power and Propaganda: A Symposium on Ancient Empires,* ed. Mogens Trolle Larsen, Mesopotamia 7 (Copenhagen: Akademisk Forlag, 1979), 263-94.

[44] Bustenay Oded, "The Relations Between the City-States of Phoenicia and Assyria in the Reigns of Esarhaddon and Ashurbanipal," in *Studies in the History of the Jewish People and the Land of Israel,* Volume 3, eds. B. Oded et. al., (Haifa: University of Haifa, 1974), 31-42 [Hebrew].

[45] Postgate, "The Economic Structure," 198-99, 207; see also the analysis offered by N.B. Jankowska, "Some Problems of the Economy of the Assyrian Empire," in *Ancient Mesopotamia: Socio-Economic History,* ed. I.M. Diakonoff (Moscow: Nauka Publishing House, 1969), 253-76.

[46] Postgate, "The Economic Structure," 193; Roux, *Ancient Iraq,* 313-20; Saggs, *The Might That Was Assyria,* 147-51.

ently supervised a territorial division called a *qannus)* wrote to the king to report on the collection of grain taxes in his area.[47]

The result of such a policy of centralization was the creation of a group of imperial servants whose positions were maintained by their constant loyalty to the king. Consequently, with the exception of Babylonia, which was treated as a special case in the imperial system, there are no records of revolts led by the provincial administrators seeking autonomy from the empire.[48] This policy also had implications beyond the political structures of the empire. In treating all of the empire as ultimately the king's domain, there was no need to differentiate among the various ethnic groups being deported and resettled in the empire. All the evidence suggests that while distinctions may have been drawn in terms of their legal classification, no rights or privileges were denied dependent populations solely on the basis of their ethnic character. Efforts were made to integrate all peoples into the imperial system as subjects of the Assyrian king under the watchful eye of the provincial administration.[49]

Returning to the Neo-Babylonian empire, this new entity had its origins during a protracted period of Assyrian weakness that allowed Nabopolassar (626-605 BCE) to take the throne of Babylon and declare himself king. By 616 BCE, the Babylonians under the command of their new monarch launched a campaign up the Euphrates River, receiving tribute from peoples who had formerly been loyal subjects of the Assyrian empire.[50] In 612 BCE, a coalition of Median and Babylonian forces attacked Nineveh, the seat of the Assyrian imperial administration, and sacked the city, effectively bringing to a sudden end one of the world's most powerful imperial systems.[51] While the effort to find the causes behind this collapse continues, it is sufficient to note here that the

---

47 J.V. Kinnier Wilson, *The Nimrud Wine Lists: A Study of Men and Administration at the Assyrian Capital in the Eighth Century B.C.* (London: British School of Archaeology in Iraq, 1972), 16-17, citing ND 2452.

48 J.A. Brinkman, "Babylonia under the Assyrian Empire, 747-627 B.C.," in *Power and Propaganda: A Symposium on Ancient Empires,* ed. Mogens Trolle Larsen, Mesopotamia 7 (Copenhagen: Akademisk Forlag, 1979), 238-39.

49 Jakobson, "The Social Structure," 294; Oded, *Mass Deportations and Deportees,* 44, 86.

50 Roux, *Ancient Iraq,* 343-46; D. J. Wiseman, *Chronicles of Chaldaean Kings (626-556 B. C.)* (London: British Museum, 1961), 6-12.

51 Roux, *Ancient Iraq,* 346-47; Wiseman, *Chronicles of Chaldaean Kings,* 16-17; and Saggs, *The Might That Was Assyria,* 119-21.

effective maintenance of Assyrian imperial rule had ceased some years before the final destruction of Nineveh.[52]

In the course of the campaign against Nineveh, the Assyrian monarch Ashur-uballit managed to escape to Harran on the upper Euphrates. Apparently in an effort to head off a possible Assyrian resurgence in the west, Nabopolassar made an expedition into the upper Euphrates region in 611, collecting spoils and forcibly subjecting those regions along the border with Harran.[53] By 610 BCE, a combined Medean and Babylonian attack forced Ashur-uballit and his forces out of Harran and the city fell into Babylonian hands. Before retreating, Nabopolassar stationed a garrison there to protect against future attempts by the Assyrian forces to enter the Euphrates valley.[54] This fear was well-founded as demonstrated in 609 when the Assyrian forces returned to lay siege to the city, only to give up after about two months.[55]

The containment of the Assyrian threat of resurgence proved of little comfort to Babylonian concerns over security since a new power was spreading into the Levant. With the gradual dissolution of the Assyrian imperial hold on outlying territories, the Egyptian monarchy saw an opportunity to move into the Levant. Sometime in the last half of the seventh century, the Egyptian king Psammetichus I (664-610) attacked the Levantine port of Ashdod and took the city. This not only gave Egypt access to a major coastal port, but allowed it to control traffic along the Coastal Highway, the primary route for commerce along the eastern Mediterranean coast.[56] In 609, apparently in response to pleas from the

---

[52] Saggs, *The Might That Was Assyria,* 117-19. There is the continuing question of Scythian involvement in the fall of Assyria, a matter which allows no easy solution. For a recent overview and proposal, see A. R. Millard, "The Scythian Problem," in *Orbis Aegyptiorum Speculum: Glimpses of Ancient Egypt, Studies in Honour of H. W. Fairman,* eds. John Ruffle, G. A. Gaballa, and Kenneth A. Kitchen (Warminster: Aris & Phillips, 1979), 119-22.

[53] Wiseman, *Chronicles of Chaldaean Kings,* 17-18; Roux, *Ancient Iraq,* 347.

[54] Wiseman, *Chronicles of Chaldaean Kings,* 18-19.

[55] Wiseman, *Chronicles of Chaldaean Kings,* 19-20; Saggs, *The Might That Was Assyria,* 120.

[56] Herodotus, *Histories,* 2.157; see also Alan Gardiner, *Egypt of the Pharaohs: An Introduction* (London: Oxford University Press, 1964), 357; Friedrich Karl Kienitz, *Die politische Geschichte Ägyptens vom 7. bis zum 4. Jahrhundert vor der Zeitwende* (Berlin: Akademie Verlag, 1953), 16-17; and Alan B. Lloyd, "The Late Period, 664-323 B. C." in *Ancient Egypt: A Social History,* ed. B.G. Trigger (Cambridge: Cambridge University Press, 1983), 337-38. Anthony Spalinger, "Psammetichus, King of Egypt, II," *JARCE* 15 (1978):49-57 would put Egyptian operations along the Coastal Highway as beginning in the last quarter of the seventh century BCE. Abraham Malamat has

Assyrians for assistance against Nabopolassar, his son Necho II (610-595) mobilized a large force and began to move northward up the Coastal Highway intending to engage the Babylonians at the Euphrates. Judah, one of the former Assyrian vassal states, intercepted the Egyptian forces at the Megiddo pass in an effort to prevent Assyrian redomination of Syria-Palestine. The Judean king Josiah was slain by the Egyptian forces and Necho continued on to encounter the Babylonian troops at Carchemish.[57] Until the decisive battle of Carchemish in 605 BCE, the Egyptians held hegemony over the Levantine region.

The brief intrusion of Egyptian control into Syria-Palestine took place in the vacuum of Assyrian imperial rule. While the precise beginnings of the dissolution of Assyrian power in the Levant cannot be determined, it is clear that by 616 BCE Egypt was acting as an ally of Assyria.[58] There are no grounds to support the contention of some that Egypt had been given the Assyrian provincial territories upon entering an alliance with Assyria.[59] During this period of shifting imperial control, the Judean monarch Josiah (639-609 BCE) appears to have expanded Judean influence both westward and northward. While the exact extent of this influence is controverted, it is apparent that some portions of the Assyrian province of Samerina were incorporated into the state of Judah.[60] The ability of a nominal Assyrian vassal like Judah to appropri-

---

suggested that Psammetichus also dominated the Assyrian province of *Magiddu* encompassing the Jezreel Plain and Galilee; "The Twilight of Judah: In the Egyptian-Babylonian Maelstrom, " *VTSupp* 28 (1975): 125.

57 2 Kings 23:29-30. On the strategy behind Josiah's move, see Abraham Malamat, "The Last Wars of the Kingdom of Judah," *JNES* 9 (1950): 219-20; and "The Last Kings of Judah and the Fall of Jerusalem," *IEJ* 18 (1968):137-38. In all probability it did not signal a Judean desire to enter into alliance with Babylonia as argued by Saggs, *The Might That Was Assyria,* 120.

58 Babylonian Chronicle BM 21901, line 10 mentions the Egyptian army in actions with the Assyrians against Babylonia in this year; Wiseman, *Chronicles of Chaldaean Kings,* 12, 54-55.

59 For example, see Spalinger, "Psammetichus, King of Egypt II," 51; Cogan, *Imperialism and Religion,* 72 note 36. Such a transfer of imperial territories from Assyrian rule to another would be unprecedented in Assyrian practice. See also Anthony Spalinger, "Egypt and Babylonia: A Survey (c. 620 B. C. - 550 B. C.)," *Studien zur Altagyptischen Kultur* 5 (1977): 224 where effective Egyptian control over Syria is used as an argument against the plausibility of such a transfer of authority. It seems nonsensical to claim that the Egyptians committed themselves to military responsibilties in exchange for territories they already controlled.

60 See the general discussion in Bustenay Oded, "Judah and the Exile," in *Israelite and Judaean History,* John H. Hayes and J. Maxwell Miller, eds. (Philadelphia: Westminster Press, 1977), 465-66. A recent, and properly cautious, handling of the

ate portions of the former Assyrian provincial territories highlights the complete collapse of the Assyrian provincial system by the last quarter of the seventh century.

During the ensuing Egyptian domination of the Levant, what little evidence exists suggests that the various Levantine territories reverted to the patterns of hereditary rule that had prevailed for centuries prior to the emergence of the Assyrian empire. This development would have been in keeping with the larger scheme of Egyptian imperial administration. Even at the height of the expansion of the New Kingdom, Egypt knew of no differentiated political and economic provincial system. Rather, Egyptian overseers worked with local rulers to exact tribute and corvee laborers, the enforcement of imperial rule coming from Egyptian troops garrisoned at strategic cities like Beth-Shean.[61] Similarly, no differentiated political and economic system for administering the Levant is in evidence from the time of Psammetichus or Necho II.[62]

One piece of evidence for this pattern of governance from the general period, the Aramaic "Letter of Adon," has a Philistine king using the language of vassalship in a communication to the Egyptian pharaoh

---

topic can be found in Miller and Hayes, *A History of Ancient Israel and Judah,* 401. The more expansive view of those territories under Judaean control formed on the basis of finds of *lmlk* seals must be revised in the light of more recent excavations that clearly locate the *lmlk* corpus in the reign of Hezekiah and not Josiah. For the earlier perspective, see especially H. Darrell Lance, "The Royal Stamps and the Kingdom of Judah," *HTR* 64 (1971): 315-32 and Abraham Malamat, "Josiah's Bid for Armageddon: The Background of the Judean-Egyptian Encounter in 609 B. C.," *JANES* 5 (1973): 270-74. For the redating of the *lmlk* seals, see David Ussishkin, "The Destruction of Lachish by Sennacherib and the Dating of the Royal Judean Storage Jars," *Tel Aviv* 4 (1977): 28-60; and most recently, Othmar Keel, "Ancient Seals and the Bible," *JAOS* 106 (1986): 310. Aharoni's "maximalist" understanding of Josiah's influence is based on a naive reading of 2 Chronicles 34:6-7, and has no supporting archaeological evidence; *The Land of the Bible,* rev. ed., 401-03.

61 B. J. Kemp, "Imperialism and Empire in New Kingdom Egypt," in *Imperialism in the Ancient World,* P. D. A. Garnsey and C. R. Whittaker, eds. (Cambridge: Cambridge University Press, 1978), 43-45; David O'Connor, "New Kingdom and Third Intermediate Period, 1552-664 BC," in *Ancient Egypt: A Social History,* B. G. Trigger, ed. (Cambridge: Cambridge University Press, 1983), 206-09.

62 Lloyd, "The Late Period, 664-323 BC," 337-40; Mary Francis Gyles, *Pharaonic Policies and Administration, 663 to 323 B.C.* (Chapel Hill: The University of North Carolina Press, 1959), 89-90. See Miller and Hayes, *A History of Ancient Israel and Judah,* 383-85 for a brief summary of the political history of this period of Egyptian domination.

appealing for military assistance.[63] A more ambiguous incident is the replacement of Jehoahaz as the Judean monarch with his elder brother Jehoiakim (2 Kings 23:31-35). While this can be interpreted as simply the replacement of a pro-Babylonian vassal with a pro-Egyptian one, and thus in continuity with previous Assyrian policy toward Judah, another interpretation is more satisfactory. Given an armed revolt by the previous Judean monarch, Josiah, opposing Egyptian pretensions to control over the Levantine region, one would expect the Egyptian monarch to respond to Judah with severity and to reduce its status from that of a vassal state to a province, if the Assyrian model of imperial administration were being followed. The fact that Necho retained the hereditary line of kingship in Judah, even taking steps to place the eldest of Josiah's sons on the throne, is suggestive of the Egyptian determination to control subject territories through the domination of hereditary sources of power rather than through the imposition of new governing structures.[64]

Consequently, for the several decades of Egyptian imperial domination of the Levant following the Assyrian retreat from this region, there was a break with the previous Assyrian imperial system of administration. This break not only represented a disruption of the Assyrian pattern of sub-dividing traditional geopolitical units and using a specialized category of imperial servants to administer those provincial territories, but also represented the reinstitution of traditional patterns of hereditary rule.[65] Without presenting evidence to the contrary, it is therefore

---

63 See, for example, J. A. Fitzmyer, "The Aramaic Letter of the King Adon to the Egyptian Pharaoh," *Biblica* 46 (1965): 43-44, 55, reprinted in *A Wandering Aramean: Collected Aramaic Essays*. SBL Monograph Series No. 25 (Chico, CA: Scholars Press, 1979), 239-40; and Bezalel Porten, "The Identity of King Adon," *BA* 44 (1981): 48-50. Another possible source for this Egyptian preference to work through hereditary kingship is a text from the fifty-second year of Psammetichus I (612 BCE). In describing the labors of the kings of the Phoenicians to produce goods for the Egyptian court, the text claims, "their chiefs were subjects of the Palace, with a royal courtier placed over them, and their taxes were assessed for the Residence, as though it were in the land of Egypt" (cited in K. S. Freedy and D. B. Redford, "The Dates in Ezekiel in Relation to Biblical, Babylonian and Egyptian Sources," *JAOS* 90 [1970]: 477). The Egyptian term translated here as "royal courtier" (*smr)* has no specific governmental function. For the text, see Émile Chassinat, "Textes provenant du Serapeum de Memphis," *Recueil de Travaux* 22 (1900): 166. For a discussion of the term *smr,* see R. O. Faulkner, *A Concise Dictionary of Middle Egyptian* (Oxford: The Griffith Institute, 1962), 229.

64 On Jehoiakim's vassalage to Necho, see Freedy and Redford, "The Dates of Ezekiel," 478.

65 The clearest example of this pattern is Sidon in Phoenicia. An Assyrian vassal state, Sidon's king was killed and the territory reduced to a province with an

improbable to argue as some have done that the Neo-Babylonian or Achaemenid imperial administrative systems in the Levant simply continued previous Assyrian patterns.[66]

The Egyptian hegemony over the Levant was broken in 605 BCE with the Babylonian victory over the Egyptian forces at the battle of Carchemish. The total defeat of the Egyptians left the Levant open to the further advance of the Babylonian army under the command of Nabopolassar's son and heir apparent. The Babylonian records summarized this action by stating, "at that time Nebuchadnezzar conquered the whole area of the Hatti country."[67] Apparently the Babylonian crown prince stayed in the Levant for a time, though the exact place and duration is uncertain.[68] Following the death of Nabopolassar, Nebuchadnezzar made a hasty return to Babylon to ascend to the throne and contain any internal opposition to his reign. By 604 BCE, he was back in the west to demand the presentation of tribute and the swearing of loyalty from the various kings of the region.[69]

This series of military maneuvers in the Levant began a process of coalescing imperial control over the region. Despite their detailed

---

Assyrian governor in the reign of Esarhaddon (680-669 BCE). Yet an inscription early in the reign of Nebuchadnezzar II (605-562 BCE) mentions a "king of Sidon" among captive officials in the Babylonian court. The Serapeum text of Psammetichus I (664-610 BCE) dated to 612 BCE mentions the Phoenician leaders as being under Egyptian control. At a minimum, Egypt allowed Sidon to reestablish a native monarchy, perceiving such a political structure as suited to its imperial goals. For Esarhaddon's campaign against Sidon, see Roux, *Ancient Iraq,* 300-301; Bustenay Oded, "The Relations Between City-States," 35-42; and the account of Esarhaddon on "Prism A"; see the translation of column i, 9-54 by A. L. Oppenheim in "Babylonian and Assyrian Historical Texts" in *Ancient Near Eastern Texts Relating to the Old Testament,* Third edition, ed. by J. B. Pritchard (Princeton: Princeton University Press, 1969), 290-91. For the presence of a king of Sidon in the court of Nebuchadnezzar, see Istanbul prism 7834, Column V, line 25, found in Babylon. The prism was published in Eckhard Unger, *Babylon: Die Heilige Stadt nach der Beschreibung der Babylonier* (Berlin: Walter De Gruyter, 1931), 286. An English translation may be found in Oppenheim, "Assyrian and Babylonian Historical Texts," 308.

66 Particularly Albrecht Alt and his followers who contend that Samaria retained its provincial capital status from 721 BCE well into the period of Achaemenid control. A more detailed presentation and critique of this viewpoint will appear in Chapter 2.

67 On the battle of Carchemish in general, see Roux, *Ancient Iraq,* 348-49; Saggs, *The Greatness That was Babylon,* 147; Wiseman, *Babylonian Chronicles,* 23-25. The quotation is from BM 21946, l. 8 published in Wiseman, *Babylonian Chronicles,* 68-69.

68 Wiseman makes the plausible suggestion that Riblah functioned as the military headquarters of Nebuchadnezzar, though this can only be inferred from the pattern of his later western campaigns; *Babylonian Chronicles,* 26.

69 BM 21946, ll. 13, 16-17, published in Wiseman, *Babylonian Chronicles,* 68-69.

accounting of the months in which the campaigns began and the major victories achieved by the Babylonian forces, the available chronicles are vague concerning the structural steps taken by Nebuchadnezzar to insure continuing imperial administrative control over the area. When the Babylonian forces are said to march through "Hatti-land," they take "tribute (*bilat*)" from the surrounding rulers.[70] Such characterizations seem, on the surface, to describe little more than quick raids for the acquisition of booty. The presence of the kings of the region presenting themselves to Nebuchadnezzar and bearing tribute is suggestive of the establishment of a vassalage system along the lines of the previous Egyptian rule of the Levant, though this can only be inferred from the failure of the Babylonian Chronicles to speak of more specific means to administer the newly conquered territories.[71]

The vagueness of the Babylonian Chronicles regarding Nebuchadnezzar's efforts to consolidate control over the Levant is symptomatic of a basic problem in trying to analyze the administrative structure of the Neo-Babylonian empire. Despite the oft-repeated assertion that "the general lines of Assyrian policy continued to be carried out" in the conquered territories, there is scant evidence on which to base such conclusions.[72] Several Assyriologists have noted just how little direct evidence has been preserved regarding the administration of the empire and the intercommunication between the provincial authorities and the royal court.[73] Consequently, before drawing any conclusions as to the form of Neo-Babylonian imperial administration, it is necessary to consider the meager literary evidence that does exist.

One piece of evidence for the form of Neo-Babylonian imperial administration is the above-mentioned Aramaic "Letter of Adon." This correspondence between a Palestinian king, probably in Ekron, and the Egyptian pharaoh uses the language of vassalship to appeal for military

---

[70] For example, BM 21946, l. 13, l. 17, rev. l. 13, and l. 24.

[71] The presentation of "tribute (*bilat*)" to the Babylonian king is also usually associated with formal vassalage relationships; see s.v. *The Assyrian Dictionary of the Oriental Institute of the University of Chicago, Volume 2 "B"*, ed. A. L. Oppenheim et al. (Chicago: The Oriental Institute, 1965), 234-35.

[72] Saggs, *The Greatness That was Babylon*, 261; for similar assessments, see the references in note 18 above.

[73] For example, Garelli and Nikiprowetzky, *Le proche-orient Asiatique*, 158-59, and A. L. Oppenheim, "Neo-Assyrian and Neo-Babylonian Empires," in *Propaganda and Communication in World History Volume 1: The Symbolic Instrument in Early Times*, eds. Harold D. Lasswell, Daniel Cerner, and Hans Speier (Honolulu: University Press of Hawaii, 1979), 137.

assistance against the Babylonians.[74] Though the exact historical context in which the letter was written remains unresolved, there is little question that the communication was made under dire circumstances, King Adon facing certain conquest without Egyptian intervention.[75] To this end, the closing lines of the letter reflect an appeal to the Pharaoh's self-interest in maintaining the king of Ekron, and report that the "commander" of the troops of Babylon has placed a "governor in the land" (*pḥh bmtʾ*). While the verb connecting the "commander" with the phrase "governor in the land" is missing, most interpreters have assumed from the context that the appeal is suggesting that the Babylonians are replacing local vassals of the Egyptian pharaoh with a "governor."[76] The term *pḥh* ("governor") is the Aramaic equivalent of the Assyrian term *bel pāḫāti,* suggesting that just as the Assyrians appointed a *bel pāḫāti* to administer conquered territories, the Neo-Babylonians employed the same form of differentiated imperial post to administer those territories it gained by conquest.[77]

A second piece of evidence is provided by the Wadi Brisa inscription of Nebuchadnezzar II.[78] Erected in a strategic pass through the Lebanon mountains, the inscription records Nebuchadnezzar's military operations in Phoenicia in the late seventh or early sixth century.[79] Following the usual Neo-Babylonian practice of portraying his military campaigning as a service to the gods, Nebuchadnezzar claims Marduk desired Lebanon "over which a foreign enemy was ruling and robbing its riches." The text

---

[74] The identification with the king of Ekron is almost certain in light of the new Demotic evidence offered by Porton, "The Identity of King Adon," 43-45.

[75] See particularly Fitzmyer, *A Wandering Aramean,* 231-32 for the various dating schemes that have been proposed.

[76] See, for example, the comparative translations of H. L. Ginsberg, J. A. Fitzmyer, and J. C. L. Gibson in Porten, "The Identity of King Adon," 37.

[77] For the linquistic equivalency, see Rosenthal, *A Grammar of Biblical Aramaic,* 58. See also C. F. Jean and J. Hoftijzer, *Dictionnaire des inscriptions semitiques de l'Ouest* (Leiden: E. J. Brill, 1965), 226 s.v. *pḥh.*

[78] The text and a German translation appears in F. H. Weissbach, *Die inschriften Nebukadnezars II im Wadi Brisa und am Nahr el-Kelb.* Wissenschaftliche Veröffentlichungen der Deutschen Orient-Gesellschaft Heft 5 (Leipzig: J. C. Hinrichs, 1906). The English translation utilized here is by A. L. Oppenheim, "Babylonian and Assyrian Historical Texts," 307. See also Paul-Richard Berger, *Die neubabylonischen Königsinschriften des ausgehenden babylonischen Reiches (626-539 a. Chr.).* Altes Orient und Altes Testament Band 4/1 (Neukirchen-Vluyn: Butzon & Bercker Kevelaer, 1973), 316-18.

[79] For a description of the pass and a possible historical setting of the inscription, see A. T. Olmstead, *History of Palestine and Syria to the Macedonian Conquest* (New York: Charles Scribner's Sons, 1931), 512-14.

goes on to claim, "its people were scattered, had fled to a far (away region)." The king claims that the country was made joyful by his military campaigning, an action that removed the enemy in its entirety. Furthermore, "all its scattered inhabitants I collected and brought together."[80] The text speaks of elaborate actions taken to insure the flow of cedars and mulberry wood to Babylon, and then states, "I made the inhabitants of the Lebanon live in safety together and let nobody disturb them."

While no specific administrative structure is mentioned in this inscription, what is significant is the attention given the disposition of native populations as the result of Nebuchadnezzar's campaign. The foreign "enemy" has been variously interpreted, and is usually assumed to refer to the Egyptians.[81] However, the term employed, *amelu nakru,* is found in contemporaneous Babylonian royal inscriptions as a generic term with no specific referent.[82] Consequently, there is no compelling need to see the "scattering" of the population, or the "robbing" of their riches, as anything more than a generalized discrediting of previous rulers. However, the text's indications that the Babylonians were concerned to return native populations to the regions they formerly inhabited do demonstrate that the manipulation of populations to maintain control over a conquered territory was part of imperial policy. In the specific case of the Wadi Brisa inscription, Nebuchadnezzar's claim to have "collected" and "gathered together" those who had been scattered may indicate the use of force to manipulate these populations.

A third piece of evidence often cited for the structure of Neo-Babylonian imperial rule is a prism recovered from Babylon that provides a listing of members of Nebuchadnezzar's court.[83] Though not dated, the text seems to deal with the establishment of responsibilities for

---

[80] Oppenheim translates, "all its scattered inhabitants I led back to their settlements (lit.: collected and reinstalled)." For *pahāru* having the sense of "be brought together," see Wolfgang von Soden, *Akkadisches Handwörterbuch,* Band II M-S (Wiesbaden: Otto Harrassowitz, 1972), 810-11.

[81] See, for example, Miller and Hayes, *A History of Israel and Judah,* 384.

[82] See s.v. *The Assyrian Dictionary of the Oriental Institute of the University of Chicago. Volume 11 N, part I* (Chicago: The Oriental Institute, 1980), 194.

[83] For a transcription, transliteration and a translation into German of the prism, see Unger, *Babylon,* 282-94. An English translation by A. L. Oppenheim appears in "Assyrian and Babylonian Historical Texts," 307-8. See also Berger, *Die neubabylonischen Königsinschriften,* 59 for a description of the prism and 313 for further references of studies on this text.

various officials, suggesting a date early in the monarch's reign.[84] Along with various overseers of the palace operations, the text mentions "governors (*amelurab* and *amelubel pāḫāti*)" over various districts and urban centers around Babylon, as well as "officials" in the same area.[85] Also noted as present in the court are the kings of Tyre, Gaza, Sidon, Arvad, and Ashdod.[86]

Though there is some ambiguity regarding the purpose of the text, it clearly does not provide any information regarding provincial administration in the conquered territories. The various administrative officials listed are in charge of Babylonian territories, not regions in the former Assyrian or Levantine homelands. Moreover, the presence of Levantine kings in Nebuchadnezzar's court provides no clarification on whether their royal powers have been subsumed under an imperial official or if they have been replaced by a more quiescent member of the dynastic line.

The condition of the Levant upon the conquest of Babylon by Cyrus appears to have possessed some form of differentiated administrative structure that was installed over the western holdings of the Neo-Babylonian empire. This may be assumed on the basis of the Letter of Adon, as well as the biblical evidence recounting the appointment of Gedaliah to oversee Babylonian interests in the territory of Judah after the fall of Jerusalem in 587 and the execution of King Zedekiah (2 Kings 25:22-4; Jeremiah 40:11; 41:2). While the phraseology of Gedaliah's being "appointed" is ambiguous, there are some indications that this office incorporated at least some of the courtly elements associated with the monarchy.[87] Thus Gedaliah may be seen as an example of the effort to involve native aristocratic personnel in the consolidation of control over a newly conquered region.

Regrettably, there are no textual sources to illumine the period following Gedaliah's assassination (2 Kings 25:25-6; Jeremiah 41:2-18),

---

84 Col. iii, line 33: "I ordered the following court officials....to take up position," seems to imply the initiation of their service to the crown.

85 Following Oppenheim, who notes that the group lu E.BAR does not equal *sagnu;* "Assyrian and Babylonian Historical Texts," 308 n. 10.

86 Col. v, lines 23-7.

87 P. R. Ackroyd, "The History of Israel in the Exilic and Post-Exilic Periods," in *Tradition and Interpretation: Essays by Members of the Society for Old Testament Study,* ed. G. W. Anderson (Oxford: Clarendon Press, 1979), 324-25. Particularly significant are the "king's daughters" in Jeremiah 41:10 who are with Gedaliah in Mizpah. On Gedaliah's brief administration, see Miller and Hayes, *A History of Ancient Israel and Judah,* 421-24; and Oded, "Judah and the Exile," 476-80.

though the long-lived policy under both the Assyrians and Babylonians of keeping conquered geopolitical entities intact as administrative sub-units makes it doubtful that the Babylonians would have subsumed the territory of Judah under the imperial administration in Samaria.

In terms of the social and economic structure of the territories under Neo-Babylonian domain, there are no ready indications of the extent to which the imperial system intruded into local affairs. While some studies have been done of the distinctive aspects to Neo-Babylonian society in the imperial heartland, there are no similar syntheses of conditions in the imperial periphery due to the lack of documentation.[88]

In the specific case of Judah, the problems are intertwined with the divergent biblical accounts of the extent of the deportation process enacted by the Babylonians. Some have taken the biblical accounts to suggest that the Neo-Babylonian empire established vast agricultural estates in the territory of Judah and that those inhabitants who may have been left behind were assigned to provide the labor for these enterprises.[89] Others, noting the biblical references to the Babylonian redistribution of land holdings to the peasantry (for example, Jeremiah 39:10), have argued that the traditional kinship-based system of land ownership was deliberately abolished by the Neo-Babylonian empire.[90] Neither explanation can offer strong evidence that such a radical reorganization of the means of agrarian production in a conquered territory was an intentional aim of the Babylonian imperial system, and both can only selectively appeal to the biblical evidence.[91] There may be

---

[88] See particularly J. Klima, "Beiträge zur Struktur der neubabylonischen Gesellschaft," in *Compte Rendu de l'ouzième Rencontre assyriologique Internationale* (Leiden: Nederlands Instituut voor het Nabije Oosten, 1964), 11-21.

[89] See, for example, J. N. Graham, "Vinedressers and Plowmen: 2 Kings 25:12 and Jeremiah 52:16," *BA* 47 (1984):55-8.

[90] This is particularly the argument of Heinz Kreissig, *Die Sozialökonomische situation im Juda zur Achämenidenzeit.* Schriften zur Geschichte und Kultur des Alten Orients 7. (Berlin: Akademie Verlag, 1973), 20-9. On some of the problems with this understanding, see J. P. Weinberg, "Probleme der Sozialökonomischen Struktur Judäas vom 6. Jahrhundert v. u. z. bis zum 1. Jahrhundert u. z.," *Jahrbuch für Wirtschaftsgeschichte* 1973:248-49.

[91] The varying biblical traditions on the numbers taken into exile by the Babylonians are nicely summarized in Miller and Hayes, *A History of Ancient Israel and Judah*, 417-20. Given the strong literary parallels between the accounts in 2 Kings and Jeremiah regarding the alleged redistribution of land to the peasantry, there is little probability that they are independent witnesses. A more comprehensive assessment of this literary relationship and the role this mention plays in both

some hope that in the future the data from the material culture of the very brief phase of Neo-Babylonian domination will assist in clarifying the extent to which imperial concerns shaped the local social order.

It is in this larger stream of imperial developments in the Levant that one of Cyrus' most renowned actions must be understood, namely granting the Judean exiles permission to return to Jerusalem. As several recent studies have demonstrated, Cyrus was neither an innovator nor a particularly benign imperial ruler, but was following precedents established during the Assyrian empire for the control of regionalized populations.[92] It is in the presentation of this decree in Ezra 1:1 that the redactor's program becomes most apparent: Cyrus did not act out of "secular" political concerns, but "Yahweh stirred up the spirit of Cyrus" to accomplish the return of the exiles.[93] As will be seen, for the redactor of the materials in Ezra-Nehemiah, the political realities of life under the empire are submerged in favor of this theocentric understanding of the postexilic community's destiny.

From the shadowy accounts preserved in the biblical narratives of this first return, the numbers of exiles who actually resettled in Jerusalem and its vicinity were few. The community was under the guidance of Sheshbazzar, an individual who is given the title of "governor (*peḥah*)" in Ezra 5:14.[94] While the precise role of this office is far from certain, the fact that the biblical traditions remembered him as a Judean aristocrat (Ezra 1:8) should be taken as favoring an administrative office of considerable status.

Cyrus' sudden decease in 530 BCE and the accession of Cambyses to the throne apparently caused little change in the Levantine imperial territories.[95] Perhaps the most significant aspect of Cambyses' rule was the renewal of a campaign to conquer Egypt, a goal of Cyrus' that never

---

narratives needs to be made before attempting to use these accounts in reconstructing the social history of the postexilic period.

[92] See especially Amelie Kuhrt, "The Cyrus Cylinder and Achaemenid Imperial Policy," *JSOT* 25 (1983):83-97 and R. J. van der Spek, "Did Cyrus the Great Introduce a New Policy towards Subdued Nations? Cyrus in Assyrian Perspective," *Persica* 10 (1982):278-83.

[93] On the first six chapters of Ezra as the distinctive contribution of the redactor, see H. G. M. Williamson, "The Composition of Ezra i-vi," *JTS* new series 34 (1983):1-30.

[94] On Sheshbazzar's governorship, see Carol L. Meyers and Eric M. Meyers, *Haggai, Zechariah 1-8*. Anchor Bible. (Garden City, NY: Doubleday & Co., 1987), xxxiv; and Williamson, *Ezra, Nehemiah*, 17-19.

[95] On the death of Cyrus, see Cook, *The Persian Empire*, 37.

came to fruition. The effort against Egypt was part of a deliberate Achaemenid policy to control the only power left in the Near East capable of opposing the empire. At some point early in 525 BCE, Cambyses assembled a massive land force along the Levantine coast and marched southward along the coastal highway and into Egypt.[96] Aided by political uncertainty within Egypt, Cambyses was successful and by the end of the year controlled the Nile Valley.

The importance of securing Egypt for the Achaemenids is highlighted by the fact that Cambyses chose to stay in Egypt for three years, consolidating control over the ancient kingdom while also attempting to expand the imperial holdings to the south and west.[97] There is no evidence that any similar attention was paid to the Levantine holdings. In 522 BCE word of a revolt back in Persia reached Cambyses, and he began a swift journey back when he was apparently assassinated.[98]

After a brief period of instability, Darius I (522-486) took the Achaemenid throne, despite the fact that he apparently did not belong to the royal dynasty.[99] The political confusion in Persia and the questions that must have arisen regarding the legitimacy of Darius' rule led to revolts throughout the empire. For the first year, the new monarch faced rebellions on multiple fronts, but within a year and a half of his accession Darius had quashed these uprisings and ruled as the uncontested "Great King."[100]

Possibly as the result of this experience of the fragility of the empire, early in his reign Darius embarked on an ambitious program of strengthening the structure of administering the empire. The system that emerged had the configuration familiar from a number of Greek writers: satraps ruled over large territorial entities that had little resemblance to previous geopolitical divisions, "governors" administered regionalized provinces that usually represented the former boundaries of past kingdoms, and military commanders assumed responsibilities for imperial

---

96 Olmstead, *History of Palestine and Syria,* 559-60 has the expeditionary force assembling at Acco, an unlikely possiblity at this time. However, some Phoenician port (Byblos or Tyre) further north may have been the staging point for the attack on Egypt.

97 On the campaigns of Cambyses, see Cook, *The Persian Empire,* 46-49; Frye, *History of Ancient Iran,* 97-8; and Olmstead, *History of the Persian Empire,* 86-93.

98 On the mysterious death of Cambyses, see the excellent summation of Frye, *History of Ancient Iran,* 98.

99 On the lineage of Darius I, see Cook, *The Persian Empire,* 74.

100 On Darius' success in putting down the revolts that accompanied his accession, see the summation in Cook, *The Persian Empire,* 52-7.

forces stationed in the conquered territories. An intricate network of officials emerged who were assigned various responsibilities on a provincial level, some apparently reporting directly to the court while others reported through the governor or satrap who was their immediate supervisor.[101] As will be seen below, these structural changes were only part of a series of innovations designed to integrate more completely the political and the social order of a conquered territory into the imperial system.

The structural changes that directly related to the Levantine holdings are somewhat ambiguous, but it appears likely that the entire Levant was part of the satrapy of "Beyond the River," with smaller regions being administered by various levels of "governors."[102] Some have interpreted the evidence from Herodotus and other sources as indicating that the entire Neo-Babylonian empire was reconstituted into a single administrative district governed by a satrap of "Babylon and Beyond the River," Babylon being removed from this arrangement following uprisings in that city upon the accession of Xerxes to the Achaemenid throne in 486 BCE.[103] Others believe the urban center of Babylon proper, as well as the surrounding countryside, were established as an administrative division separate from Beyond the River.[104] The degree to which either arrangement may have impacted the Levant is unclear, but presumably as a separate entity, Beyond the River would have enjoyed greater prominence in the imperial system.

As for the remnants of the Judean kingdom and those who had returned to the territory during the reign of Cyrus, Darius' policies marked a major change in the nature of the community. After a period of stagnation and opposition, Darius gave the orders for the continuation of the rebuilding of the Temple in Jerusalem (Ezra 6:6-12) with the

---

101 On the rudiments of the imperial system established by Darius, see now the excellent summation by Tuplin, "The Administration of the Achaemenid Empire," 111-13."

102 On the extent of the satrapy "Beyond the River," see Meyers and Meyers, *Haggai. Zechariah 1-8*, xxxii-xxxiv; and the very useful study of Rainey, "The Satrapy 'Beyond the River,'" 51-78.

103 Rainey, "The Satrapy 'Beyond the River'," 54-5.

104 For the historical background to these problems, see George C. Cameron, "Darius and Xerxes in Babylon," *AJSL* 58 (1941):318-19. The Behistun inscription of Darius lists Babylon apart from "Athura," or 'Beyond the River," leading to speculation that Babylon had been separated from 'Beyond the River' following the revolt against Darius; Cook, *The Persian Empire*, 77. The suggestion has been made that these various listings are not administrative districts but majority ethnic groups within the administered regions; see George Cameron, "The Persian Satrapies and Related Matters," *JNES* 32 (1973):47-56.

assistance of the revenues from the district.[105] More importantly, it was apparently under Darius' initiative that the "governor" Zerubbabel was appointed over the district and brought with him members of the exilic community from Babylon. Zerubbabel was a member of the Davidic line (1 Chronicles 3:19), and the appointment of such an individual as the chief political authority within the old boundaries of the former kingdom of Judah marked a definite change in the imperial attitude toward the region. Certainly by this point one may talk of Yehud as a district within the Achaemenid system and as an autonomous administrative unit.[106]

This new influx of fiscal support from the imperial government and the returning exiles from Babylon led to the prophetic anticipation of a restoration of the Judean community's fortunes, reflected in the prophetic books of Haggai and Zechariah.[107] As such, the postexilic community in Yehud may well be termed the "Restoration community," since the biblical narratives present the administration of Zerubbabel as focusing on the restoration of the temple cultus in anticipation of the rewards this action would bring to the community (Zechariah 1:17; 8:9-13).[108]

It is also at this time that tensions begin to emerge between the Restoration community and elements of the population to the north (Ezra 4:1-3). While some have attempted to interpret this antagonism as a prelude to the Jewish-Samaritan schism of later times, there is no warrant for such a perspective since the actual origin of Samaritanism lies several centuries later.[109] Given the number of Yahwistic names among the governors of Samaria and the delegation from Bethel that comes to Jerusalem for an authoritative instruction (Zechariah 7:1-6), it is apparent

---

105 On the importance of this event for both Achaemenid rule and the history of the Restoration community, see Ackroyd, "Israel in the Exilic and Post-exilic Periods," 331-32; and Williamson, *Ezra, Nehemiah*, 82-3.

106 On the importance of Zerubbabel as a signal of the administrative independance of Yehud, see Eric M. Meyers, "The Persian Period and the Judean Restoration: From Zerubbabel to Nehemiah," in *Ancient Israelite Religion: Essays in Honor of Frank Moore Cross*, eds. P. D. Hanson, D. McBride and P. D. Miller (Philadelphia: Fortress Press, 1987), 509-10.

107 See Meyers and Meyers, *Haggai, Zechariah 1-8*, xl-xliv; and Meyers, "The Persian Period and the Judean Restoration," 510.

108 For the classic statement of this approach to understanding the biblical sources, see Peter R. Ackroyd, *Exile and Restoration: A Study of Hebrew Thought of the Sixth Century B. C.* (Philadelphia: Westminster Press, 1968), 145-47, 163-64, and 175-76. See also Meyers, "The Persian Period and the Judean Restoration," 513-14.

109 See especially Frank M. Cross, "Aspects of Samaritan and Jewish History in Late Persian and Hellenistic Times," *HTR* 59 (1966):201-11.

that Yahwism retained a strong presence north of Jerusalem. If this condition were true, then the desire to worship at the new temple in Jerusalem may have represented a potential loss of political control by the Samarian authorities, leading to their opposition and resistance.[110]

The return of some of the Judean exiles to Jerusalem was not an isolated act of favor by the imperial court, but part of a larger strategy in the Levant. This can be seen in the evidence of the Neirab archive, a collection of tablets recovered from a site southeast of Aleppo in the 1920s. The archive consists of a set of loan transactions involving barley and silver, inscribed on 27 cuneiform tablets. Most who have studied the contents have concluded that these tablets represent a family archive.[111] Recently Israel Ephᶜal has made a convincing argument that these tablets were not written in Syria at all but represent accounts written in Babylonia and carried with an ethnic group to Neirab.[112] Most pertinent to his point is the line in text 17 that gives the location of the transaction as "the town of the Neirabeans that is on the Bel-aba-user canal."[113] There is little doubt that this indicates a community of Neirabeans living in Babylonia as an identifiable ethnic enclave. The last dated tablet in the collection is from the year 521 BCE, approximately the time of Zerubbabel's appointment as governor of Yehud and the return of members of the exilic community. Thus while members of the Judean exilic community are being moved back into the region around Jerusalem, members of the Neirabean exile are similarly moving back to north Syria.

---

110 For a general discussion along these lines, see Carl Schultz, "The Political Tensions Reflected in Ezra-Nehemiah" in *Scripture in Context: Essays on the Comparative method,* eds. C. Evans, W. Hallo and J. White (Pittsburgh: Pickwick Press, 1980), 221-44. This matter will be returned to in Chapter 5. Throughout the current work, the pre-Mount Gerizim temple inhabitants of Samaria are termed "Samarians," the term "Samaritans" being reserved for the population in the area following the foundation of Samaritanism. This follows a suggestion by John Macdonald, "The Discovery of Samaritan Religion," *Religion: Journal of Religion and Religions* 2 (1972):143-44. Macdonald bases his argument on the philological impossibility of rendering the Hebrew *shōmrōnîm* as anything other than "inhabitants of Samaria," or "Samarians."

111 The Neirab tablets were originally published in P. Dhorme, "Les Tablettes babyloniennes de Neirab," *Revue d'assyriologie et d'archéologie Orientale* 25 (1928):53-82. A very helpful analysis of their contents may be found in F. M. Fales, "Remarks on the Neirab Texts," *Oriens Antiquus* 12 (1973):131-42.

112 Israel Eph'al, "The Western Minorities in Babylonia in the 6th-5th Centuries B. C.: Maintenance and Cohesion," *Orientalia* n.s. 47 (1978):84-87.

113 Dhorme, "Les tablettes babyloniennes de Neirab," 63. See also the comments of Ephᶜal, "The Western Minorities in Babylonia," 85.

A further illustration of the extent of Darius' efforts to restructure the Achaemenid imperial system can be found in his activities related to Egypt. As with much of the empire, Egypt revolted when Darius took the throne. Control over the Nile Valley was regained around 519 BCE, and Darius appointed a commission to codify the laws that were in effect in Egypt at the end of the reign of Amasis (ca. 526).[114] At approximately the same time, Darius sent a collaborator named Udjahorresnet to Sais to restore the "House of Life," or scribal institution, associated with a temple complex there.[115] Udjahorresnet's various undertakings on behalf of the Achaemenid court are recorded in an inscription on his mortuary statue. Through the portrayal of this activity, and through the very vocabulary he uses to describe Darius and his actions in Egypt, Udjahorresnet emphasizes Darius' fulfillment of the traditional ideals of Egyptian kingship.[116] The same effort at legitimizing Darius' rule can be seen in his codification of those laws in effect in the reign of Amasis, and not those in effect during the rule of Cambyses. In other words, Darius is appealing to the legal customs of the last native Egyptian ruler and enacting those as part of the imperial administration of Egypt.

Darius was succeeded on the Achaemenid throne by Xerxes I (486-465 BCE), a transition in power that was marked by revolts in Babylon and Egypt, though the Egyptian uprising at this time was fairly minor.[117] Some have suggested that events connected with the Babylonian revolt

---

114 On the date for the order by Darius to codify Egyptian law, see the discussion in Frye, *History of Ancient Iran,* 104; Peter Frei/Klaus Koch, *Reichsidee und Reichsorganisation im Perserreich* (Göttingen: Vandenhoeck & Ruprecht, 1984), 14-5; and Edda Bresciani, "The Persian Occupation of Egypt," in *The Cambridge History of Iran. Volume 2: The Median and Achaemenian Periods,* ed. Ilya Gershevitch (Cambridge: Cambridge University Press, 1985), 507-08. A helpful overview of Darius' effort may be found in N. Reich, "The Codification of the Egyptian Laws by Darius and the Origin of the 'Demotic Chronicle'," *Mizraim* 1 (1933):178-85.

115 On Udjahorresnet's biographical text, see Alan B. Lloyd, "The Inscription of Udjahorresnet: A Collaborator's Testament," *JEA* 68 (1982):166-80; and the English translation with some commentary in Gardiner, *Egypt of the Pharaohs,* 366-68. An important discussion of the physical layout of the text on Udjahorresnet's statue may be found in Ursula Rössler-Köhler, "Zur Textkomposition der naophoren Statue des Udjahorresnet/Vatikan Inv.-nr. 196," *Göttingen Miszellen* 85 (1985):43-54.

116 Lloyd, "The Inscription of Udjahorresnet," 174-5. On other efforts to legitimize Darius' rule over Egypt, see K. M. T. Atkinson, "The Legitimacy of Cambyses and Darius as Kings of Egypt," *JAOS* 76 (1956):170-72. The Egyptian ideological background to Udjahorresnet's inscription is largely ignored in the recent study by Joseph Blenkinsopp, "The Mission of Udjahorresnet and Those of Ezra and Nehemiah," *JBL* 106 (1987):409-21.

117 Cook, *The Persian Empire,* 99; and Frye, *History of Ancient Iran,* 126.

had dire implications for Persian attitudes toward the Levant, an issue that will be discussed in detail below. In general, once the revolt in Babylon was quashed, Xerxes' attention was more directed toward affairs in Anatolia and the war with Greece than in Levantine affairs, and it was not until the mid-fifth century and the reign of Artaxerxes I that a new concern with the western imperial holdings was evident.

The Transformation of the Restoration Community in the Mid-fifth Century

It has become commonplace in writing on the history of Israel to see the mission of Ezra and its attendant developments as marking a major point of departure from Israel's previous expressions of its self-consciousness as a community. Throughout the works of biblical scholars of the nineteenth and twentieth centuries, this departure or transformation, though receiving slightly varied interpretations, has been retained as a benchmark in the political, social and religious development of Israel.

In the beginnings of the critical historiographic movement in biblical studies in the second half of the nineteenth century, there was a widespread emphasis on the results of Ezra's mission as reformulating the postexilic community. For example, Heinrich Graetz in his landmark *History of the Jews* termed Ezra's mission a "transformation" of the Restoration community, characterizing Ezra as the founder of "the new religious and social order of things" in the postexilic community.[118] For Graetz, this transformation was the direct result of Ezra's role as a promulgator of a new understanding of the Mosaic Torah, including an extension of that Torah to cover a total ban on intermarriage.[119]

In a parallel treatment, Heinrich Ewald also stressed Ezra's transformational role in bringing a "firm constitution" to the Restoration

---

118 Heinrich Graetz, History *of the Jews. Volume 1: From the Earliest Period to the Death of Simon the Maccabee (135 B. C. E.).* Translation of the 1870 German edition by Bella Lowy. (Philadelphia: The Jewish Publication Society of America, 1891), 363, 365-66. In its original German edition, Graetz's *History* appeared from 1861-75. For Graetz's importance in the emergence of critical historiography, see John H. Hayes, "The History of the Study of Israelite and Judean History." In *Israelite and Judean History,* eds. John H. Hayes and J. Maxwell Miller. (Philadelphia: Westminster Press, 1977), 61 and Salo W. Baron, *History and Jewish Historians: Essays and Addresses,* compiled by Arthur Hertzberg and Lan A. Feldman. (Philadelphia: The Jewish Publication Society of America, 1964), 263-75.

119 Graetz, *History of the Jews. Volume 1,* 364-67. Graetz saw the new emphasis on Torah as an idea originating in the exilic community in Babylon and expounded by Ezra.

community "which, in its essential features, it could never again abandon."[120] In Ewald's estimation it was Ezra's extension of Torah observance to include the banning of intermarriage that marked the reformulation of the postexilic community, just as it had for Graetz.[121]

The historiographic concern with Ezra's mission as a major transformation of the Restoration community reached a new clarity of expression in the studies of Julius Wellhausen. Working within a larger concern with the historical experience of the Israelite community, Wellhausen became convinced that the religious institutions of ancient Israel had undergone a process of development that was reflected in the literary remains of the Hebrew Bible. The result of his efforts to reconstruct this development was the monumental *Prolegomena to the History of Israel,* the first installment in a sweeping reappraisal of the course of Israel's social and religious development.[122]

One of Wellhausen's central concerns was the place of the legal traditions of Israel that regulated the institutionalization of Israelite faith, the so-called Priestly Code. Unlike several earlier writers, Wellhausen's analysis of the various sources behind the Pentateuch led him to conclude that the priestly materials reflected the latest stage in the composition of the Pentateuch as a whole.[123] Though conceding earlier materials were present within the Priestly Code, Wellhausen tied the promulgation

---

120 Heinrich Ewald, *The History of Israel. Volume V: The History of Ezra and of the Hagiocracy in Israel to the Time of Christ,* trans. J. Estlin Carpenter. Second edition (London: Longmans, Green, and Co., 1880), 129. Carpenter's translation is of the German edition of 1864-68. On Ewald's importance in the development of the critical study of the history of Israel, see Hayes, "The History of the Study of Israelite and Judean History," 59-61.

121 Ewald, *The History of Israel. Volume 5,* 139-47. It should be noted that Ewald's critical study of the Pentateuchal legislation had concluded that the bulk of Israel's legal traditions had come into existence in the period of the Monarchy. Thus, before the exile, the Law was already an existent ideal, though one rarely attained; *The History of Israel,* 133-34.

122 The general literature on the development of Wellhausen's thought and the impact his views have had on Old Testament studies is too vast to be summarized here. For more recent summaries of the impetus behind the *Prolegomena,* see Rudolf Smend, "Julius Wellhausen and his Prolegomena to the History of Israel," *Semeia* 25 (1982):11-15; John H. Hayes, "Wellhausen as a Historian of Israel," *Semeia* 25 (1982):41-4; and John Rogerson, *Old Testament Criticism in the Nineteenth Century: England and Germany* (Philadelphia: Fortress Press, 1985), 260-65. On the institutional focus of Wellhausen's approach, see most recently Moshe Weinfeld, "Bible Criticism," In *Contemporary Jewish Religious Thought,* eds. Arthur A. Cohen and Paul Mendes-Flohr. (New York: Charles Scribner's Sons, 1987), 35-40.

123 See in particular the discussion of Rogerson, *Old Testament Criticism,* 262-64.

and enforcement of this legal material in regulating Israelite worship and practice to the missions of Ezra and Nehemiah. He emphasized that the mention of Ezra's skill "in the law of Moses (Ezra 7:6)" was a reference to the completed Priestly Code itself.[124]

In Wellhausen's conception of the legal character of the Priestly Code, with its stipulations for individual observance of regulations regarding diet, ethnic and ritual purity, there was a fundamental change in the religious orientation of ancient Israel. Whereas the creative impetus of the religious experience of Israel found free expression prior to this legislation, the introduction of the written body of law resulted in the stultification of religious innovation and the emergence of Judaism as a "narrow shell" seeking to fend off foreign influence.[125] Thus, though he argued the point on a different basis than preceding historians of Israel, Wellhausen was in agreement with them in seeing that Ezra's mission of legal reform, especially in its proscriptions against intermarriage, indelibly transformed the postexilic community.

The anti-Semitism inherent in Wellhausen's position has often been commented upon, and the overall context of Wellhausen's work within continental Protestant biblical scholarship in its day suggests this attitude was more a product of theological lineage than personal intention.[126] Still, Wellhausen's basic reconstruction of the development of Israelite institutions and the particular thesis that the emergence of Judaism was the result of the legal reforms of Ezra has exerted a broad influence on studies in the postexilic period.

This Wellhausenian inheritance continues to dominate the historical understanding of contemporary biblical scholarship, as can be seen in several examples of recent treatments of the postexilic period. In the last edition of John Bright's influential *A History of Israel,* while Nehemiah initiates an important process of transforming the Restoration community, it is Ezra who is elevated to heroic proportions: "It was Ezra who reconstituted Israel and gave her faith a form in which it could survive through the centuries."[127] This reconstitution took two distinctive forms, according to Bright. The first was the reorganization of the entire com-

124 Julius Wellhausen, *Prolegomena to the History of Ancient Israel.* Trans. W. Robertson Smith. reprint edition (Cleveland: Meridian Books, 1965), 404-9. See also Wellhausen's articles on "Israel" that appeared in the Ninth edition of *Encyclopedia Britannica,* reprinted in this edition of the *Prolegomena,* 496-97.

125 Wellhausen, *Prolegomena to the History of Ancient Israel,* 425.

126 See particularly Lou H. Silberman, "Wellhausen and Judaism," *Semeia* 25 (1982):75-82.

127 Bright, *A History of Israel,* 389.

munity on the basis of its adherence to Pentateuchal legislation.[128] The second was to reconstitute the community's own self-identity by means of the ban against intermarriage with the surrounding ethnic groups.[129] In Bright's view, these two steps laid the groundwork for the community to exist as a "definable entity" within the Achaemenid empire, a desirable end given the upheavals in the western imperial territories during the mid-fifth century. The ban on intermarriage and the promulgation of a fuller corpus of legislation, both aims of the missions of Ezra and Nehemiah, led to the transformation of the community and the emergence of Judaism as a distinct religious system.[130]

A very similar line of approach is taken in J. Alberto Soggin's *A History of Ancient Israel.*[131] Here, the transformation of the community is accomplished by a series of reforms enacted on all levels of communal life: cultic, civil and everyday.[132] Soggin sees the missions of both Ezra and Nehemiah as reflecting an effort to "bring some order" to the region in light of continuing troubles in the mid-fifth century.[133] This order was accomplished by the ban on intermarriage and the institutionalization of "the law of the God of Heaven" that Ezra brought with him. As a result of the actions of both reformers, the Pentateuch became not only the normative rule for the religious life of the community, but gained additional stature as the civil law enforced by the imperial authorities.[134]

A final example is the influential essay of the German biblical scholar Klaus Koch, who contended that the importance of Ezra for the postexilic period cannot be overestimated. Koch contends that as an imperial official, Ezra "succeeded in moving the apparatus of a huge empire" for the Restoration community.[135] He did this by promulgating the Priestly Code as an imperial official, and in this manner established

---

[128] Bright, *A History of Israel,* 388-89. He bases his reconstruction on the thesis that Nehemiah 9-10 represents a transposed narrative and that the concept of a meeting of the entire group to reconstitute itself in conformity with Pentateuchal legislation belongs to the mission of Ezra. As will be discussed below, this transposition is unwarranted.

[129] Bright, *A History of Israel,* 386-88.

[130] Bright, *A History of Israel,* 380 and 390.

[131] J. Alberto Soggin, *A History of Ancient Israel.* Trans. John Bowden. (Philadelphia: Westminster Press, 1984).

[132] Soggin, *A History of Ancient Israel,* 276.

[133] Soggin, *A History of Ancient Israel,* 273.

[134] Soggin, *A History of Ancient Israel,* 280.

[135] K. Koch, "Ezra and the Origins of Judaism." *Journal of Semitic Studies* 19 (1974):195.

"God's law as obligatory by governmental decree."[136] Part of this larger legal reform effort involved the ban on intermarriage, which Koch interprets as "cultic separation," borrowing its distinctive terminology from both priestly and Holiness concerns.[137] This successful effort to redefine the postexilic community in terms of an "ethnic group in a defined territory" became one of the foundational components of later Judaism.[138]

These examples suffice to demonstrate that the basic thrust of contemporary critical reconstructions of the postexilic period share the same Wellhausenian view of the mission of Ezra. In this view, the postexilic community was transformed as the result of Ezra's promulgation of the Priestly Code as a legislative standard to be enforced by the imperial authorities. Part of that same promulgation was a new understanding of the Pentateuchal laws to mandate a ban on intermarriage with those outside of the community. While Wellhausen may have been correct in seeing Ezra as the beginning of the enforcement of the Priestly Code, there is no direct evidence from the narratives of Ezra-Nehemiah that such a promulgation was part of either reformer's mission. And, as a number of recent commentators have demonstrated, there is no unequivocal method to determine the character of the "law of the God of Heaven" that Ezra enforced within the community.[139] In sum, the view of Wellhausen and those who follow him that the Restoration community was transformed as the result of the authoritative enforcement of the Priestly Code is based on factors extrinsic to the biblical narratives of Ezra-Nehemiah.

This observation leads naturally to the second factor credited in the critical reconstruction of the postexilic period with transforming the Restoration community, namely the ban on intermarriage. Here, both those who came before Wellhausen and those who have come afterward agree that the community is being redefined in exclusively ethnic terms. According to many of those who follow this line of thought, the new definition of membership in the community resulted in a transformation of the Restoration community and a new self-awareness of themselves as a distinctive element within the Achaemenid empire.

---

136 Koch, "Ezra and the Origins of Judaism," 197.

137 Koch bases this argument on the use of the forms of *bdl* in Ezra-Nehemiah; "Ezra and the Origins of Judaism," 180.

138 Koch, "Ezra and the Origins of Judaism," 197.

139 For example, see the comments of H. G. M. Williamson, *Ezra, Nehemiah.* Word Biblical Commentary, 16 (Waco, TX: Word Books, 1985), xxxvii-xxxix.

On the subject of the ban against intermarriage, it is apparent that both Ezra and Nehemiah strenuously sought to use their authority to oppose intermarriage. That this regulation represents an extension of the Pentateuchal laws opposing intermarriage among the Canaanites has also been made plain by a number of recent studies.[140] Indeed, it is only in this mid-fifth century setting that Israel encounters such a limitation on personal relationships.

For the ideology of the redactor of Ezra-Nehemiah, the issue of intermarriage is directly related to the issue of obedience to divine ordinance. In repeated expressions in Ezra-Nehemiah, intermarriage is characterized as a "guilt (*ʾāšām*)" of the community.[141] In Nehemiah 13:27 intermarriage is seen as acting "treacherously" against God, that is, as an act of willful rebellion against the divine order. Not surprisingly, some scholars have followed the redactor's lead and have interpreted the ban on intermarriage in purely religious terms.[142] Such an interpretation fails to explain why it is that two imperial officials are the ones seeking the enforcement of such a law within the community, and why such a legal innovation should emerge within the mid-fifth century.

In several places in the narratives of Ezra-Nehemiah, the issue of intermarriage is inextricably linked to the idea of membership in the community, the clearest example being in Ezra 10:8. Here, the penalty for not attending the meeting of the "assembly (*qāhāl*)" appointed to deal with the intermarriage issue is banishment from the "assembly." Thus the ban on intermarriage is an integral element in one's remaining part of the community.

A number of scholars have noted the unique terminology employed in the narratives of Ezra-Nehemiah relating to group identity. The phrase that appears in Ezra 10:8, the "assembly of the Exile (*qāhāl haggôlāh*)," is one such example. Others include simply "the assembly," or "the exile," or more elaborate labels such as "the assembly of those who returned from the captivity" (Nehemiah 8:17). As Sara Japhet has pointed out, the existence of several geographically removed populations of Judean exiles led to the issue of community identity that became a central concern for

140 See especially Shaye J. D. Cohen, "From the Bible to the Talmud: The Prohibition of Intermarriage." *Hebrew Annual Review* 7 (1983):23-39; David J. A. Clines, "Nehemiah 10 as an Example of Early Jewish Biblical Exegesis." *JSOT* 21 (1981):111-17; and David Bossman, "Ezra's Marriage Reform: Israel Redefined." *Biblical Theology Bulletin* 9 (1979):32-8.

141 For example, Ezra 9:6, 9:15, and 10:10.

142 F. C. Fensham, "Some Theological and Religious Aspects in Ezra and Nehemiah." *Journal of Northwest Semitic Languages* 11 (1983):65-6.

the narratives of Ezra-Nehemiah.[143] These rather similar labels were the primary means for the narratives of Ezra-Nehemiah to mark the identity of the community, and as such constitute a technical vocabulary that is not used outside of these narratives within the biblical corpus.[144] In that the issue of intermarriage is apparently bound up in the definition of who may belong to the "assembly of the exile," it can be concluded that the ban on intermarriage was seeking a new means to define the Restoration community. As such, Graetz and those who followed him were correct in perceiving that the ban on intermarriage resulted in a transformation of the Restoration community.

The fact that the intermarriage issue is linked to communal self-identity within the postexilic community is vital for establishing boundaries to any analysis of the transformation of the postexilic community in the mid-fifth century. It also provides an important criterion to utilize in evaluating the relevance of other biblical materials to the transformation of the postexilic community, materials that lay outside of the narratives of Ezra-Nehemiah. For example, in a recent essay Alexander Rofé has tried to make the argument that since portions of Trito-Isaiah (Isaiah 54-66) seem to criticize the Jerusalemite priesthood for acts of idolatry with language similar to Ezra's denunciation of priests involved in intermarriage, the context of Trito-Isaiah's prophetic activity is the same mid-fifth century setting.[145] Rofé goes on to draw parallels to some of the social and political conditions reflected in Ezra-Nehemiah from Trito-Isaiah, and argues that both works are addressing the same concerns, and thus emerge at the same time. However, in no place do the prophecies contained in Trito-Isaiah address the issue of communal identity with the same technical vocabulary utilized in Ezra-Nehemiah. Nor, for that matter, does Trito-Isaiah ever raise the matter of intermarriage and communal identification. Accordingly, it seems rather doubtful that Trito-Isaiah can be confidently situated in the same mid-fifth century context as the missions of Ezra and Nehemiah.

---

[143] Sara Japhet, "People and Land in the Restoration Period," in *Das Land Israel in biblischer Zeit,* ed. G. Strecker. Göttinger theologische Arbeiten, 25 (Göttingen: Vandenhoeck und Ruprecht, 1983), 104-6.

[144] Japhet, "People and Land in the Restoration Period," 112-13; and Hubertus Vogt, *Studie zur nachexilischen Gemeinde in Esra-Nehemia* (Berlin: Dietrich Coelde, 1966), 96-8.

[145] Alexander Rofé, "Isaiah 66:1-4: Judean Sects in the Persian Period as Viewed by Trito-Isaiah." In *Biblical and related Studies Presented to Samuel Iwry,* eds. Ann Kort and Scott Morschauser (Winona Lake, IN: Eisenbrauns, 1985), 213-14.

The same can be said of the book of Malachi, where the issue of intermarriage appears to be directly relevant (Malachi 2:11). However, the language of Malachi is redolent with the traditional covenantal terms for idolatry, and in the specific instance of the marriage to "the daughter of a foreign god," it is not at all certain if this is a reference to intermarriage or the worship of a goddess. Given the covenantal language of the book as a whole and the possibility that the book is structured along the form of a covenant, it would be most consistent with the context of the verse to interpret Malachi 2:11 as a reference to idolatrous practices.[146] In addition, there is no indication that the practices of 2:11 have caused the community to lose its identity, and Malachi does not contain any of the distinctive vocabulary of the Restoration community encountered in Ezra-Nehemiah.

In sum, the Restoration community was transformed by the missions of Ezra and Nehemiah in their promulgation of an innovative ban against intermarriage. This transformation had at its core the redefinition of the community, and thus is closely linked to a technical vocabulary of the community that appears only in these narratives. Since this is a unique situation within the biblical canon, there are no other passages in the biblical literature that can provide additional data on the nature and form of this transformation.

Method and Interpretation of the Biblical Sources

The only sources for reconstructing the missions of Ezra and Nehemiah are contained in the biblical book of Ezra-Nehemiah. The complexity of the biblical narratives and the uncertainties regarding the events of the period of Achaemenid domination in the Levant have engendered a series of questions regarding the literary form of these narratives and their veracity as historical documents. The basic questions have revolved around four interrelated issues, namely, the relationship of Ezra-Nehemiah to the Chronicler's history, the unity of the narratives

---

[146] Provisionally, see Beth Glazier-McDonald, "Intermarriage, Divorce, and the *bat-ʾēl nēkār*," *JBL* 106 (1987):603-11. Glazier-McDonald admits to Malachi's use of language more appropriate to the condemnation of idolatry, but wants to read the "marriage to the daughter of a foreign god" on both a literal and symbolic level. Given the failure of Malachi to address the larger concerns of communal self-identity in relation to intermarriage, it seems that Malachi's protest is in relation to another issue altogether. For an argument similar to Glazier-McDonald, see W. J. Dumbrell, "Malachi and the Ezra-Nehemiah Marriage Reforms," *Reformed Theological Review* 35 (1976):42-52.

in Ezra-Nehemiah, the chronological order of the two reformers, and the nature of the various sources underlying the narratives.

Over the last century, biblical scholars have offered a bewildering variety of methods for approaching these questions and have proposed an equally bewildering array of solutions. It is not the purpose of this work to review in detail the various proposals and counter-proposals that have marked the debate over these questions. Rather, since the manner in which one resolves these issues strongly affects the way one utilizes the narratives in any historical reconstruction, it is necessary to state briefly the means of resolving the questions used in this presentation and the implications of such means for the interpretation of Ezra-Nehemiah.

Regarding the first issue, the relationship of Ezra-Nehemiah to the Chronicler's history, the very distinctive phraseology and orthography shared between these two books have led many to assume a unity in authorship.[147] However, over the last few decades a growing number of studies have highlighted the differences in ideology between Ezra-Nehemiah and 1 & 2 Chronicles.[148] Moreover, the linguistic similarities that led to the assumption of a common authorship between these two works can be seen as a reflection of the changes in Hebrew during the postexilic period rather than a sign of shared origin.[149]

For the present study, the independence of Ezra-Nehemiah from 1 and 2 Chronicles is presumed, based on the studies regarding the ideological and historiographical differences noted above. However, the first six chapters of Ezra-Nehemiah reflect a somewhat intermediate character. For example, Williamson has provided a detailed analysis of Ezra 3 arguing for its dependence on the Chronicler's version of the building of the First Temple (2 Chronicles 3-5). Williamson's conclusion was that while Ezra 1-6 as a whole showed some signs of dependency on 1 and 2 Chronicles, it also presented concepts at variance with the ideology of

---

[147] For example, see C. C. Torrey, *The Composition and Historical Value of Ezra-Nehemiah.* Beihefte zur Zeitschrift für die Alttestamentliche Wissenschaft 2. (Giessen: J. Ricker, 1896), 35-42; L. Batten, *The Books of Ezra and Nehemiah.* International Critical Commentary. (Edinburgh: T. & T. Clark, 1913), 1-2; Wilhelm Rudolph, *Esra und Nehemia samt 3. Esra.* Handbuch zum Alten Testament, 20. (Tübingen: J. C. B. Mohr, 1949),xxii-xxiv; Otto Eissfeldt, *The Old Testament: An Introduction.* Trans. Peter R. Ackroyd. (New York: Harper & Row, 1965), 530-31; and Jacob M. Myers, *Ezra. Nehemiah.* The Anchor Bible, 14. (Garden City: Doubleday & Co., 1965), lxviii-lxx.

[148] See particularly Sara Japhet, "The Supposed Common Authorship of Chronicles and Ezra-Nehemiah Investigated Anew," *VT* 18 (1968): 330-33.

[149] Japhet, "The Supposed Common Authorship," 371.

the Chronicler. Thus, he assigned the origin of Ezra 1-6 to a "priestly revisor" who, it is hypothesized, was responsible for a light redaction of 1 and 2 Chronicles.[150]

While some possible connections between Ezra 1-6 and the Chronicler's history must be taken into account, so too must the literary and thematic relationships between Ezra 1-6 and the remainder of the narratives of Ezra-Nehemiah. For example, the abortive attempt to rebuild the walls of Jerusalem noted in Ezra 4:7-23 serves to highlight the transformation of imperial attitudes towards the Restoration community in the time of Nehemiah. As will become clearer in the discussion of the unity of the narratives of Ezra-Nehemiah, there are significant reasons to conclude that Ezra 1-6 is inextricably interrelated to the remainder of Ezra-Nehemiah. This factor leads to the conclusion that whatever relationship these chapters may have to the Chronicler's history, it is more the function of a process of redaction than of authorship.[151] Thus, while limited portions of Ezra 1-6 may share a relationship with the Chronicler's history, these chapters as a whole are the work of the author of Ezra-Nehemiah.

The issue of the unity of the narratives of Ezra-Nehemiah is, on the surface, a simpler matter to resolve. As has been noted by a number of scholars, in the earlier Masoretic texts of the work, Ezra and Nehemiah are combined together, and the Masoretic notations treat the two parts as a unity.[152] Apparently, it was not until the promulgation of the Vulgate

---

[150] Williamson's entire study is worthy of careful consideration. H. G. M. Williamson, "The Composition of Ezra i-vi," *Journal of Theological Studies* N.S. 34 (1983): 1-30.

[151] Suggesting some form of relationship between Ezra 1-6 and 1 and 2 Chronicles raises the difficult issue of the date of 1 and 2 Chronicles, or the dates of the various levels of compilation if one choses a multiple-author model. For the present study, 1 and 2 Chronicles is viewed as a basicly unified composition of an early third century BCE date. Ezra-Nehemiah gives every evidence of having been completed by the end of the fifth century BCE. There is some evidence of a subsequent redaction of 1 and 2 Chronicles, and Williamson may well be correct in seeing the action of this redactor as extending over both biblical books. For the general issue of the dating of 1 and 2 Chronicles, see H. G. M. Williamson, *1 and 2 Chronicles*. New Century Bible Commentary. (Grand Rapids: Wm. B. Eerdmans, 1982), 15-17 and the literature cited there.

[152] On the unity of the narratives in Ezra-Nehemiah, see Eissfeldt, *The Old Testament*, 541-42; Myers, *Ezra.Nehemiah*, xxxviii; D. J. A. Clines, *Ezra, Nehemiah, Esther*. New Century Bible Commentary. (Grand Rapids: Wm. B. Eerdmans, 1984), 2-4; and H. G. M. Williamson, *Ezra, Nehemiah*. Word Biblical Commentary, 16. (Waco, TX: Word Books, 1985), xxi-xxiii.

that this work was split into two parts, and transmitted within various language groups as a "Book of Ezra" and a "Book of Nehemiah." Despite the consensus of scholarly opinion that these two works were intended to stand as one unified composition, many commentators have persisted in treating the structure of the narratives as two independent units.[153] This approach has obscured the interdependency of the narratives and the overall thematic point of the work.

In a recent dissertation on the literary character of Ezra-Nehemiah, Tamara Eskenazi has attempted to articulate not only the extensive intertwining of themes and motifs in the narratives; she has also been able to demonstrate conclusively the unified nature of the narratives as a whole.[154] More importantly, her analysis has clarified the central thrust of the narratives, that of showing the Restoration community itself as the fulfillment of Cyrus' decree in Ezra 1 to rebuild the "house of God." Since much of the present work is dependant on her analysis of the literary character of Ezra-Nehemiah, a brief summation of her presentation is in order.

In Eskenazi's analysis, the primary concern of the author is the importance of the communal efforts in response to the stimulus of Ezra and Nehemiah. This intentionality is manifested in a number of ways, such as the repeated list of community members in Ezra 2 and Nehemiah 7.[155] The deemphasis of the heroic and the placement of the community in the foreground of the narratives serve to stress the community as an identifiable entity and the sphere in which the deity undertakes to restore the theological ideal of Israel. This restoration is not achieved merely by the reestablishment of the Second Temple in Jerusalem, but by the community taking upon itself a strict obedience to the Torah (Nehemiah 8-9) as interpreted by Ezra and Nehemiah. The Restoration community itself is presented as having realized the ideal of the "House of God" that Cyrus in Ezra 1 decrees to be established in Jerusalem.[156] This final achievement by the community is marked by the author's repeated treatment of the entire walled enclosure of Jerusalem as a sacred precinct, from the stationing of Levites to guard the city gates

---

153 For example, see Clines, *Ezra, Nehemiah, Esther*, 31-2.

154 Tamara Eskenazi, *In An Age of Prose: A Literary Approach to Ezra-Nehemiah*. Society of Biblical Literature Monograph Series 36. (Atlanta: Scholars Press, 1988). I am indebted to Prof. Eskenazi for allowing me to use an unpublished version of this work prior to its appearance.

155 Eskenazi, *In An Ege of Prose*, 48-50; 88-95.

156 Eskenazi, *In An Age of Prose*, 104-09.

(Nehemiah 12:25) to a sacral procession along the tops of the newly erected walls (Nehemiah 12:31-43). This sacral character of the walled city is further affirmed by the narrator's claim that the procession on the walls stood "in the House of God" (Nehemiah 12:40). Thus the community, by its obedience to the Torah, has transformed itself and the walled enclosure of Jerusalem into a single sacral realm, fulfilling the prophetic ideal of a holy people dwelling in a holy city.[157]

Eskenazi's study has reaffirmed the integrity of the narratives of Ezra-Nehemiah as a whole by elucidating the careful interweaving of the themes of the Temple's reconstruction and the city's refortification. In this light, the materials in chapters 1-6 of Ezra, particularly the troublesome chronological intrusion of Ezra 4:6-23, are vital introductions to the process of the community's realization of the "House of God." Consequently, whatever similarities exist between Ezra 1-6 and 1 and 2 Chronicles are presumably the result of an editorial process and not a sign of varying hands in compiling the narratives of Ezra-Nehemiah.[158]

Moreover, Eskenazi's sensitivity to the literary clues of the author's intentionality has revealed the essentially theological purpose behind the composition of these narratives. While the work as a whole is rooted in a social and political reality, the author is not seeking so much to communicate that reality as to make evident the theological import of the community's being tranformed and pervaded by divine sanctity through its obedience to the reforms of Ezra and Nehemiah. Thus any effort to utilize portions of the narratives of Ezra-Nehemiah for reconstructing the conditions of the mid-fifth century must evaluate the degree to which the author's intentionality has shaped the content of these narratives.

Turning to the question of the chronological order of the missions of Ezra and Nehemiah, perhaps more debate has revolved around this issue than any other in the study of these narratives. There has long been general consensus that the author of Ezra-Nehemiah has created a strong sense of sequential action from the opening of the narratives to their

---

157 Eskenazi, *In An Age of Prose*, 120-26.

158 Within the previous studies of 1 and 2 Chronicles, there has been considerable debate over the evidence for a series of expansions on the Chronicler's original narrative. If some stage of expansion is posited, then there is the possibility that the redaction of Ezra 1-6 was part of the same phenomenon. Such a stage of redaction would have been subsequent to the completion of 1 and 2 Chronicles and prior to its incorporation into the biblical canon. The entire issue is of more complexity than can be readily handled here. For an excellent overview of the debate over the nature and extent of a subsequent redaction to 1 and 2 Chronicles, see Williamson, *1 and 2 Chronicles*, 12-15.

close. Thus by placing the mission of Ezra prior to the narratives regarding Nehemiah, the author has intended to place Ezra's reforms prior to those of Nehemiah. For both reformers, date formulas are given with reference to a Persian monarch named "Artaxerxes." For Ezra, his mission is dated to the "seventh year of Artaxerxes (Ezra 7:8);" and for Nehemiah, his mission is reported to have begun in the twentieth year of Artaxerxes (Nehemiah 2:1). Since there were three Persian monarchs bearing the name "Artaxerxes," it is possible that some chronological confusion may have occurred, thus the need to determine which Artaxerxes is being referred to.

Of the two reformers, the chronological framework for Nehemiah has received near universal support from scholars. The discovery of the Elephantine papyri in 1906 provided a critical piece of data for the dating of Nehemiah's mission. Among these materials were two copies of a letter written from Elephantine to Jerusalem in the year 408 BCE (Cowley No. 30 and 31). The letter is addressed to Bagoas, the governor of Yehud, and notes that a copy of the letter had been sent to one of the sons of "Sanballat, the governor of Samaria."[159] Sanballat, the governor of Samaria, is mentioned frequently in the narratives dealing with Nehemiah's mission as a constant adversary (for example, Nehemiah 3:33-4; 4:1-2 [Eng. 4:7-8]; and 6:1-2). If one of his sons was governing Samaria in 408 BCE, it can be assumed that Sanballat himself must have held the office of governor at some earlier time. The Persian monarch named Artaxerxes that would be closest in time to the last quarter of the fifth century was Artaxerxes I, who reigned from 465 to 424 BCE. Thus, if Sanballat and Nehemiah were contemporaries and Nehemiah served under a monarch named Artaxerxes, then the only possible identification of this king would be Artaxerxes I.

Since the biblical narratives claim that Nehemiah began his mission in the twentieth year of Artaxerxes, this would place the year as 445 BCE. Also, in Nehemiah 5:14 the reformer's first term as governor is said to have extended from the twentieth to the thirty-second year of Artaxerxes, which would place Nehemiah as governor over Yehud from 445 to 433 BCE. These data are consistent with what can be known from the Elephantine papyri for the time period of Sanballat's governorship. As a consequence, the dating of Nehemiah's mission to the third quarter

[159] A. Cowley, *Aramaic Papyri of the Fifth Century B. C.* (Oxford: Clarendon Press, 1923), 108-22.

of the fifth century has received broad acceptance among biblical scholars.[160]

In the last decade, this consensus has been challenged by Richard Saley who is concerned to correlate the account of Josephus regarding the foundation of the temple at Mount Gerizim (*Antiquities* 11.297-328) with the chronology of the succession of high priests found in Nehemiah 12:1-26.[161] Arguing for the extensive use of papponymy among the various inherited offices of leadership in the Persian imperial territories of Yehud and Samaria, Saley concludes that the biblical evidence correlating Nehemiah's mission and the governorship of Sanballat of Samaria and a high priest in Yehud named Eliashib (Nehemiah 3:1,20; 13:4,7) could be referring to a period under either Artaxerxes I or Artaxerxes II (404-358). Noting the account of the expulsion by Nehemiah of one of the sons of the high priestly line due to his intermarriage with the line of Sanballat (Nehemiah 13:28), Saley argues this individual is Manasseh, the same person noted by Josephus as having been driven from Jerusalem and subsequently founding the temple at Gerizim. Since Josephus places these events during the reign of Artaxerxes II, Saley claims that Nehemiah's mission should be dated to the twentieth year of Artaxerxes II, not Artaxerxes I, or the year 384 BCE.[162]

While Saley's hypothesis is intriguing, in the final analysis it fails to provide certain evidence of its central assumption, namely that papponomy was prevalent not only in the governor's line of Samaria, but also in the line of the high priesthood of Jerusalem.[163] Not only is this assertion made without evidentiary support, but in the case of the high priestly line seems to go contrary to the biblical evidence itself (such as the list of

160 H. H. Rowley, "Nehemiah's Mission and Its Background." In *Men of God: Studies in Old Testament History and Prophecy.* (London: Thomas Nelson & Sons, 1963), 234-35.

161 R. Saley, "The Date of Nehemiah Reconsidered." In *Biblical and Near Eastern Studies in Honor of William Sanford LaSor,* ed. G. Tuttle (Grand Rapids: Wm. B. Eerdmans, 1978), 151-60.

162 Saley, "The Date of Nehemiah Reconsidered," 160-63.

163 This same criticism was made by Ralph Klein in commenting on Saley's arguments as presented in his unpublished dissertation; Ralph Klein, "Ezra and Nehemiah in Recent Studies." In *Magnalia Dei. The Mighty Acts of God: Essays on the Bible and Archaeology in Memory of G. Ernest Wright,* ed. Frank M. Cross, Jr. (Garden City: Doubleday & Co., 1976), 371-72. The finds from the Wadi Daliya reportedly contain several letters of a Sanballat, governor of Samaria, who served during the reign of Artaxerxes III (358-338 BCE). While this is clear evidence of some papponymy in the line of the governor of Samaria, the extension of this practice over multiple generations of imperial functionaries in the Levant as envisioned by Saley is unwarranted.

the high priestly line in Nehemiah 12:10-11) without explaining why that evidence should be rejected. This critical failure in Saley's hypothesis makes it clear that there is every reason to continue to place Nehemiah's mission under the reign of Artaxerxes I.

Regarding the dating of the mission of Ezra, there is no similar, generally accepted, chronological framework due to the varying ways scholars have sought to resolve the literary problems associated with the various options for dating his mission. In following the plain implication of the narratives themselves, that Ezra's mission preceded that of Nehemiah, then Ezra's mission took place under Artaxerxes I beginning in the year 458 BCE. This position, often termed the traditional view, has been called into question on the basis of two primary issues.

First, despite the fact that their missions would have overlapped, the narratives place Ezra and Nehemiah together in only two places (Nehemiah 8:2 and 12:36), both of which may be harmonistic insertions.[164] Second, despite the importance of the intermarriage issue in the mission of Ezra, Nehemiah finds the same circumstances prevalent during his mission a short time later (Nehemiah 13:23-29). In the view of many critics, Nehemiah's having to address the same issue without reference to Ezra's earlier reforms aimed at the same problem makes little historical sense. They would prefer to see Ezra's mission taking place under Artaxerxes II, and thus his opposition to intermarriage coming a generation or two after Nehemiah's earlier reforms.[165] The supposition of such critics is that the author of Ezra-Nehemiah was confused as to the monarch being referred to in the date formulas and simply coalesced both reformers under Artaxerxes I.[166]

The present work is not the place to review extensively the arguments and counter-arguments that have been put forward to support either chronological arrangement. However, a few general observations may be offered to indicate the position adopted here. First, despite all the debate, no critic has shown the priority of Ezra to be impossible. While there are certainly problems associated with the traditional view, the issues raised in placing Ezra prior to Nehemiah can be explained.

---

164 For example, see Rudolph, *Esra und Nehemia,* 198; Myers, *Ezra.Nehemiah,* xxxvi; Clines, *Ezra, Nehemiah, Esther,* 16-17; and Williamson, *Ezra, Nehemiah,* xliv, 368.

165 For example, see Batten, The *Books of Ezra and Nehemiah,* 28-30; and Rowley, "The Chronological Order of Ezra and Nehemiah," 162-64.

166 For example, Myers, *Ezra.Nehemiah,* lii; and the comments of Clines, *Ezra, Nehemiah, Esther,* 18-20 in summarizing the views of a number of writers on this topic.

Secondly, the various lines of argument that have been adduced for placing Ezra after Nehemiah tend to trade historical problems for literary problems. It is generally thought that the solemn covenant ceremony in Nehemiah 9 has more to do with Ezra than Nehemiah, thus most critics who place Ezra after Nehemiah also consider Nehemiah 9 to be misplaced.[167] If the author of Ezra-Nehemiah were simply confused, then the current placement of Nehemiah 9 becomes difficult to explain.

Thirdly, the discovery of new epigraphic evidence relating to the line of governors over Yehud has led a number of scholars to conclude that the traditional view of Ezra's priority makes for a better fit with this evidence than assuming the priority of Nehemiah.[168] Consequently, a number of recent works on the chronological order of these two reformers have reaffirmed the traditional view of Ezra's priority.[169]

Finally, as will be seen in the course of analyzing the content of the mission of Ezra in the perspective of the requirements of imperial rule over a subject territory, the traditional view makes the most sense of the relationship between Ezra's reforms and those of Nehemiah. Particularly in the case of the issue of intermarriage, an imperial system tends to precede major transformations in the socio-economic structure of a governed territory by legal reforms. In this light, Ezra's juridical role makes more sense as an action that preceded the more directly administrative role of Nehemiah. Consequently, the present work will follow the traditional order of the missions of Ezra and Nehemiah, seeing Ezra as coming in 458 BCE and Nehemiah in 445 BCE.

On the issue of the various sources that may, or may not, underlie the narratives, there is a wide diversity of opinion on what sources may have been utilized and to what extent the author has modified these materials in the course of piecing together the narratives. To begin with, it is necessary to differentiate the various categories of potential sources that have been alleged to be present in Ezra-Nehemiah. For the purposes of this discussion there are three basic groups of materials to be evaluated, namely a Nehemiah Memoir (usually seen as Nehemiah 1:1-

---

[167] On this literary question, see particularly the discussion of Myers, *Ezra.Nehemiah*, xlii-xlviii; and Clines, *Ezra, Nehemiah, Esther*, 189-190 summarizing the views of others.

[168] See particularly Frank M. Cross, Jr., "A Reconstruction of the Judean Restoration." *JBL* 94 (1975):4-18; and S. Talmon, "Ezra and Nehemiah (Books and Men)." In *Interpretor's Dictionary of the Bible. Supplement*, ed. K. Crim (Nashville: Abingdon Press, 1976), 325.

[169] See the summation in Edwin Yamauchi, "The Reverse Order of Ezra/Nehemiah Reconsidered." *Themelios* 5 (1980):7-13.

7:73; 11:1-36; 12:31-43; and 13:4-31), an Ezra Memoir (usually seen as underlying Ezra 7-10 and Nehemiah 8-9), and a series of official imperial documents and letters of authorization that appear in the narratives (especially in Ezra 1-6 and 7:11-26).[170] Other scholars have suggested somewhat more refined classifications, but these three categories cover the basic aspects of the discussion.

Taking the Nehemiah Memoir first, it has been common in the study of the narratives of Ezra-Nehemiah to assert that the first person style in much of the materials dealing with Nehemiah marks the use of some form of recounting of his activities by the reformer himself.[171] This somewhat ambiguous attribution received far more precision in the work of Sigmund Mowinckel who compared the form and style of these narratives to various royal inscriptions from the ancient Near East in an effort to provide a form-critical basis for determining what portions of these narratives were from Nehemiah's hand, and what portion may have been supplied by the author of the book as a whole.[172]

Mowinckel's comparative data was further refined by Gerhard von Rad who found in Egyptian biographical inscriptions of the Late and Persian periods (664-300 BCE) strong parallels in form and style to the basic contents of the Nehemiah Memoir.[173] However, such parallels provide little indication for the original role of the Memoir prior to its adaptation by the author of Ezra-Nehemiah. There is little in the materials ascribed to the Memoir that would fit either a royal testament or a mortuary inscription.[174]

This is in essence where Ulrich Kellermann begins his major study of the Nehemiah Memoir. Following his critique of the earlier suggestions for the first person narratives, Kellermann contends the memoir has its closest parallels to the "prayer of the accused," similar to that found in

---

170 A similar tripartite approach may be found in Rudolph, *Esra und Nehemia,* xxiii-xxiv and Williamson, *Ezra, Nehemiah,* xxiii-xxxiii. Additional elements that may represent other sources are the various lists in the narratives.

171 Rudolph, *Esra und Nehemia,* xxiv; Myers, *Ezra.Nehemiah,* LI-LII; Clines, *Ezra, Nehemiah, Esther,* 4-6; and Williamson, *Ezra, Nehemiah,* xxiv-xxviii.

172 Sigmund Mowinckel, *Studien zu dem buche Ezra-Nehemiah.* Volume 2. Skrifter utgitt av det Norske Videnskaps-Akademi I. Oslo II. Hist.-Filos. Klasse Nu Serie, 5 (Oslo: Universitetsforlaget, 1964-65), 50-86.

173 Gerhard von Rad, "Die Nehemia-Denkschrift," *ZAW* 76 (1964):176-87.

174 See particularly the helpful summary and discussion of Clines, *Ezra, Nehemiah, Esther,* 4-5 and the comprehensive criticisms of Ulrich Kellermann, *Nehemia: Quellen, Überlieferung und Geschichte.* Beihefte zur Zeitschrift für die alttestamenliche Wissenschaft, 102 (Berlin: Alfred Töpelmann, 1967), 76-88.

Psalm 5.[175] Thus he conceives of the Memoir as having been a formal appeal to God for vindication following some charge that had been alledged against Nehemiah. Kellermann's position, like those before it, also leaves a number of unresolved problems, as several critics have pointed out.[176] Hugh Williamson has attempted to resolve these issues by appealing to the possibility of extensive alteration of these materials by the author of Ezra-Nehemiah or a subsequent redactor, but Williamson's own position can be criticized for its failure to demonstrate that such alterations did, in fact, take place.[177]

The most helpful suggestion made to date regarding these materials is that of Eskenazi. After a careful consideration of the narrative forms in Ezra-Nehemiah from the perspective of the work's literary unity, she concludes that the shift from a third person narrative to a first person narrative is not an indication of the utilization of a distinct source. Rather, she presents several arguments for interpreting this shift as a deliberate literary device by the narrator to involve the reader in the unfolding drama of events.[178] This is not to suggest that the author of the narratives has simply created the accounts of Nehemiah from nothing, but that whatever source the author used in creating the narratives as we have them, the narratives themselves provide no clues from which one may reconstruct a first person document attributable to Nehemiah.

This assessment of the Nehemiah Memoir has significant implications for the determination of the second possible source, the so-called "Ezra Memoir." Portions of the narratives dealing with Ezra's reforms also use a first person style (mainly in Ezra 7:27-9:15), leading a number of scholars to assume that some form of personal account underlies these narratives, an Ezra Memoir.[179] This conclusion has been soundly criticized by others on a variety of grounds, the most common being that it is impossible to find any stylistic grounds for distinguishing these narratives from other narratives in Ezra-Nehemiah outside of their first person format.[180]

One issue that has not been incorporated in the discussion is the substantial literary and ideological continuity between portions of the

---

175 Kellermann, *Nehemia*, 84-88.

176 For example, see the criticisms of J. A. Emerton, Review of Nehemia: *Quellen, Überlieferung und Geschichte.* by U. Kellermann. *JTS* ns 23 (1972): 173-77.

177 Williamson, *Ezra, Nehemiah*, xxv-xxvii.

178 Eskenazi, *In An Age of Prose*, 129-34.

179 See Rudolph, *Esra und Nehemia*, 165-67; Myers, *Ezra. Nehemiah*, XLVIII-XLIX; and Clines, *Ezra, Nehemiah, Esther*, 6-7.

180 See especially Kellermann, *Nehemia*, 56-69.

narratives identified as the Nehemiah Memoir and the Ezra Memoir. For example, in Ezra 7:28 the first person narrative explains the royal favor toward Ezra by exclaiming that "the hand of the LORD my God was upon me." Similarly, the first person narrative in Nehemiah 2:8, the monarch's favor is due to "the good hand of my God that was upon me." C. C. Torrey, who noted other parallels in literary style between the Ezra Memoir and the Nehemiah Memoir, concluded that the Ezra Memoir was a secondary composition based, in part, on the preexisting wording of the Nehemiah Memoir.[181] Eskenazi's literary approach to these narratives provides a more satisfactory solution in regarding these first person accounts, like the materials that surround them, as coming from the hand of the author. Consequently, while there may be some authentic source behind the narratives regarding Ezra, as there may have been behind the narratives dealing with Nehemiah, in their present form it is not possible to use the first person narratives of Ezra-Nehemiah to isolate such an "Ezra Memoir."

The last group of possible sources in Ezra-Nehemiah are various official documents, mainly located in Ezra 1-6 but including the letter from Artaxerxes commissioning Ezra in Ezra 7:11-26. Here, as with a number of issues relating to the character of the narratives in Ezra-Nehemiah, the debate has been protracted and the options put forth by various authors have been numerous. In general, the comparison of the form and contents of these various documents with actual Achaemenid documents has given little cause to question the general authenticity of these citations in the narratives.[182] This general conclusion does not preclude the potential for editorial insertions, abridgements, or other alterations of an authentic document in order to shape it to fit the larger context of the narratives.

One of the more exhaustive studies of the imperial documents in Ezra-Nehemiah was undertaken by Bezalel Porten. Though lacking a clear sense of the unity and literary coherence of Ezra-Nehemiah, Porten was able to show that the documents in Ezra 1-6 were largely unaltered by a subsequent editor. However, the letter of Artaxerxes commissioning Ezra (Ezra 7:11-26) showed too many literary parallels to the earlier documents for Porten to accept it as being quoted without redaction. Rather, he argued that the author of the narratives in Ezra 7 had taken an authentic commission and structured it along the lines of the earlier documents in order to create the impression of Ezra fulfilling the

---

181 Torrey, *The Composition and Historical Value of Ezra-Nehemiah,* 14-29.

182 Clines, Ezra, *Nehemiah, Esther,* 9; and Williamson, *Ezra, Nehemiah,* xxiii-xxiv.

imperial concerns and mandates expressed in these other documents.[183] While such shaping is a distinct possibility, it would seem strange for an author or editor to handle the earlier documents with care, and then largely revamp the commission in Ezra 7. Rather, it seems more likely that the overall letter quoted in Ezra 7 reflects an actual commissioning of Ezra, and as a more detailed analysis will show, a subsequent hand has interjected elements to shape the document to the larger literary purposes of the narratives of Ezra-Nehemiah.

To summarize, for this study Ezra-Nehemiah is taken to be a work distinct from the Chronicler's History and possessing a strong literary unity, despite the various stylistic and form critical components contained within the work. The author's presentation of the chronological order of Ezra preceding Nehemiah is taken to reflect the actual historical order of the reformers while acknowledging there are historical difficulties with this position. Moreover, due regard must be given to the role of the author in shaping the narratives, and thus efforts to use stylistic and form critical criteria to isolate various sources underlying the narratives may be misdirected. Rather, an understanding of the author's art suggests that there is no certain way to classify the sources relating to the missions of Nehemiah and Ezra as deriving from some form of "memoirs." Finally, the various imperial documents that appear in the opening chapters of Ezra are taken to be authentic, though in some instances alterations may have been introduced to seat them more clearly within the narrative flow. Thus Ezra-Nehemiah as a work is a form of history, albeit a tendentious history, that reflects a selective recounting of the political and social conditions of the mid-fifth century BCE.

Any effort to utilize the narratives of Ezra-Nehemiah in reconstructing the historical setting of Achaemenid imperial policy must explicitly deal with this characteristic of the narratives. The derivation of historical information from these materials can be only accomplished by comprehending the narratives from the perspective of the author's larger intentionality, thus discerning the degree of shaping and adaptation that has altered their contents. By means of such a careful analysis of these materials, a plausible understanding of their historical value can be achieved.

As has been seen, the emergence and consolidation of Achaemenid imperial rule over the Levant was not marked by a particularly sharp break from the previous imperial rule of the Neo-Babylonian empire. It was not until the reign of Darius I and his reorganization of the

183 Bezalel Porten, "The Documents in the Book of Ezra and the Mission of Ezra." *Shnaton* 3 (1978-79):174-96 [Hebrew].

Achaemenid imperial administration that a major departure can be discerned; yet even at that time there were few structural changes in the administration of Yehud as an autonomous district. Moreover, the degree of continuity from the Assyrian empire to the Achaemenid is striking in the employment of various techniques to maintain imperial control over a subject territory.

It is not until the mid-fifth century that the biblical narratives provide a reflection of some form of transformation of the Restoration community, a transformation brought about by the missions of two imperial officials, Ezra and Nehemiah. This dramatic change in the administration of Yehud is linked with the specific injunctions against intermarriage. The essential issue in trying to account for this transformation is to comprehend what factors led to the commissioning of Ezra and Nehemiah and how their missions were shaped by the requirements of the Achaemenid empire.

2

THE HISTORY OF RESEARCH

The biblical tradition relates a major transformation of the Restoration community in the fifth century to the missions of Ezra and Nehemiah. This same biblical tradition is silent, however, on the conditions that gave rise to the transformation and that largely shaped the direction of the missions. The motivations behind the Persian monarch's commissioning of either Ezra or Nehemiah are hardly hinted at in the narratives, leading subsequent interpreters to suggest varying social and political considerations as the causation for the work of these two figures. Several recent authors have attempted to articulate models for explaining this transformation with varying degrees of success, as will be seen below. None of these proposals, however, provides a fully satisfactory explanation of these missions within what can be observed of Persian administrative practices in Syria-Palestine.

The Alleged Catastrophe of 485 BCE

One of the most innovative efforts to provide an explanation for the fifth-century transformation of the Restoration community was devised by Julian Morgenstern. For a period encompassing over three decades, Morgenstern repeatedly argued that a major catastrophe had befallen the Restoration community as a consequence of an abortive revolt.[1] The mis-

[1] Morgenstern's first published suggestion for the disaster of 485 appeared in 1938 ("A Chapter in the History of the High-priesthood—Concluded," *AJSL* 55 [1938]: 375) and his last published essay on the subject appeared in 1970 ("Isaiah 61,"

sions of Ezra and Nehemiah, in Morgenstern's scheme, represent an effort by the Persian court to restore the vitality of a province devastated by this catastrophe.

While elements of Morgenstern's proposal appear in a variety of seemingly unrelated studies, the basic argument and the evidence for it appeared in the late 1950s and early 1960s in a series of three articles.[2] He began his argumentation by highlighting Nehemiah's reaction in Nehemiah 1:4 to news that the walls of Jerusalem were in ruins. He argues it is "inconceivable" that Nehemiah's reaction would have been caused by the destruction of the city by Nebuchadnezzar in 586 BCE.[3] Furthermore, he notes that some biblical evidence suggests that Jerusalem was prosperous and flourishing by the end of the sixth century. He cites the references to "ceiled houses" in Haggai 1:4 and the imagery of Psalm 48, which he dates to the late sixth to early fifth century, as reflecting the "wealth and grandeur" of the city prior to Nehemiah. He concludes that between this time of prosperity and the report to Nehemiah of Jerusalem's dire condition, some "catastrophe" must have struck the city. Efforts to recover from this event were unsuccessful, and when the report of the continuing decay of the city reached Nehemiah, he was "keenly, bitterly disappointed."[4]

Morgenstern then turns his attention to the book of Lamentations where he finds some reflection on this catastrophe. To Morgenstern, the mention of Edom in Lamentations 4:21 clearly argues against understanding the work as a meditation on the destruction of Jerusalem in 586 since Edom was an ally of Judah at that time. Consequently, the despoiling of Jerusalem portrayed in Lamentations must relate to some campaign against the city after 586, a destruction in which Edom and other surrounding peoples participated.[5]

With the concept of an alliance of neighboring nations devastating Jerusalem and led by Edom, Morgenstern proceeds to muster a vast array of anti-Edomite prophetic passages as well as pronouncements

---

HUCA 40-41 [1969-70] :117-19). There is no indication of any substantial modification of his views over the course of his essays on this subject. Morgenstern derived some of his ideas from S. A. Cook, "The Age of Zerubbabel" in *Studies in Old Testament Prophecy*, ed. H. H. Rowley (Edinburgh: T. & T. Clark, 1950), 34-35.

[2] "Jerusalem—485 B.C." *HUCA* 27 (1956):101-79; "Jerusalem—485 B.C. (continued)" *HUCA* 28 (1957):15-47; and "Jerusalem—485 B.C. (concluded)" *HUCA* 31 (1960):11-29.

[3] "Jerusalem—485 B.C.," 101-02.

[4] "Jerusalem—485 B.C.," 104-05.

[5] "Jerusaelm—485 B.C.," 106-08.

against other surrounding nations and argues that these are insertions from the postexilic period. Furthermore, these insertions do not relate to various continuing problems with surrounding peoples over a period of time; rather they recount one specific action, undertaken by all these named peoples in concert.[6] In Psalms as well, Morgenstern finds indications of his projected catastrophe, Psalm 79 presenting "the simplest and most immediate picture" of the event.[7]

Acknowledging that the evidence he has adduced provides only a general dating for the catastrophe, Morgenstern goes on to seek more specific evidence for the date of the event. He finds it in the letter to the Persian monarch Artaxerxes I in Ezra 4:7-23 in which the king is asked to order a halt to an effort at rebuilding the walls of Jerusalem. His Samarian officials claim that if he would check the "records of your fathers" he would find the city had a history of rebellions. Morgenstern argues that it is "hardly likely" that such records included revolts under the Neo-Babylonian and Assyrian kings. Moreover, the use of "your fathers" in Ezra 4:15 must be taken literally and thus refers to both Darius I and Xerxes.[8] Assuming that Zerubbabel had rebelled sometime during the reign of Darius I, that leaves a need for a revolt during the reign of Xerxes. Furthermore, as Morgenstern reconstructs the events surrounding the alleged revolt of Zerubbabel, a revolt that he places during the construction of the Second Temple, rather than razing the Temple in punishment for the revolt, the Persian authorities sponsored its completion. This action served to support a "universalistic" party within the community that was in opposition to a more "nationalistic" group that had fomented the revolt. Since the Temple was not destroyed during this revolt under Darius I and the Book of Lamentations depicts the spoliation of the Temple, he concludes that the proposed catastrophe must have occurred during the reign of Xerxes.[9]

Morgenstern thus understands the sequence of events as beginning with the death of Darius I in 486 BCE. The "nationalistic" party attempted to seat a new Judean monarch on the throne (a figure whom Morgenstern identified as "Menahem").[10] The local imperial authorities

---

6 "Jerusalem—485 B.C.," 109-16.

7 "Jerusalem—485 B.C.," 117-47.

8 "Jerusalem—485 B.C.," 155-58.

9 "Jerusalem—485 B.C.," 162-63.

10 "Jerusalem—485 B.C.," 166-67, 170-71. Morgenstern concluded the king's name was Menahem from Isaiah 51:12-13, which he claimed was an answer to Lamentations; "Jerusalem—485 B.C. (continued)," 17-18.

wrote an "accusation" against the Judean community to the Persian court, recorded in Ezra 4:6, that exposed the revolt. The new king, Xerxes, was faced with internal conflicts regarding his succession and with a "serious rebellion" in Egypt. Rather than deal with the Judean revolt in person, Xerxes gave the surrounding nations "permission to form a coalition against Judah" and attack Jerusalem. The Restoration community was unable to defend itself, and Jerusalem was invaded, its walls torn down, and the Temple destroyed. Among those nations spearheading the attack, the Edomites were particularly merciless, earning the vilifications of numerous prophetic oracles. A number of Judeans were captured and "sold to the Greeks for resale in the slave-markets of the western world."[11]

In the devastated region a series of ideological changes took place. The lack of a temple brought an end to centralized worship and a diminution in the status of the Levitical priesthood. The synagogue as an institution emerged, as well as "more or less divergent patterns of religious belief and worship," marking the origins of Jewish sectarianism.[12] The successor to Xerxes, Artaxerxes I, sent Ezra "to restore the Temple structure and revive its sacrificial cult." This marked change in Achaemenid attitudes toward the Restoration community was in part the result of the Egyptian revolt of the mid-fifth century, which threatened Artaxerxes' hold on the western empire.[13] Ezra was accompanied by priests of the Zadokite line and together they sought to impose a program of "particularism and separatism" upon the community. After Ezra's successful rebuilding of the so-called Third Temple, a group of exiles undertook the unauthorized refortification of the city reported on in Ezra 4:7-23 in the Artaxerxes' correspondence and halted by the provincial authorities.[14]

It was the failure of this effort to rebuild the walls that caused Nehemiah such anguish when the news in Nehemiah 1:4 reached him. Using the rather general request of repairing the city gates to receive Artaxerxes' permission to rebuild the city (Nehemiah 2:3), Nehemiah undertook with speed the restoration of the city walls to prevent interference from the provincial authorities in Samaria. He was also con-

---

11 "Jerusalem—485 B.C.," 171-74; see also Morgenstern's "The Dates of Ezra and Nehemiah," *Journal of Semitic Studies* 7 (1962):1 for a condensed restatement of his reconstruction, as well as "Isaiah 61," 117-19.

12 "Jerusalem—485 B.C. (concluded)," 17-20.

13 "Jerusalem—485 B.C. (concluded)," 23, n. 2.

14 "Jerusalem—485 B.C. (concluded)," 23-28.

cerned that his appointment as governor over Judah, which resulted in the "curtailment" of administrative power over the province by Sanballat and his staff, had created an atmosphere of jealousy.[15] Nehemiah's successful refortification and repopulation of the city led to the economic recovery of the Restoration community, now regulated by the Zadokite program of Ezra.[16]

For Morgenstern, the missions of Ezra and Nehemiah are the result of conscious, and in the specific case of Nehemiah, more properly unintended, efforts by the Persian court to rectify the devastation left by the catastrophe of 485 BCE. As such, these missions are a complete reversal of Achaemenid imperial attitudes towards the Judean community, a change stimulated perhaps by external political developments.

Despite the wide-ranging scope of Morgenstern's proposals and the importance of the topics he has sought to illuminate, his reconstruction of Judean history has yet to receive a substantive critique. It can be argued that his views have been largely ignored since he does not merit even a footnote in most of the recent works on the history of the period.[17] Of the few works offering some criticisms of Morgenstern's views, the problems that are highlighted either misunderstand Morgenstern's reconstruction or are so generalized as to offer little in the way of a relevant case against his views. For example, in an essay analyzing the Babylonian revolt against Xerxes in 484 BCE, de Liagre Böhl argued that there was not enough time for Xerxes to lead a campaign against Jerusalem in 485 and then return to suppress the revolt in Babylon. Consequently, to de Liagre Böhl, the campaign against Jerusalem in 485 never took place.[18] This, however, has no real bearing on Morgenstern's reconstruction since Morgenstern saw little, if any, direct Persian military involvement in the attack on Jerusalem, and certainly never advocated a scenario in which the Persian monarch led the forces against the city.[19]

In another critique of Morgenstern, Geo Widengren has claimed that Morgenstern's reconstruction can be rejected because it is built on biblical texts that can be explained on other grounds and because it posits

---

15 "Jerusalem—485 B.C.," 163-65.

16 "Jerusalem—485 B.C. (concluded)," 28-29.

17 For example, Bright, *A History of Israel;* Noth, *The History of Israel;* Herrmann, *History of Israel in Old Testament Times;* and Jagersma, *A History of Israel in the Old Testament Period.*

18 F. M. Th. de Liagre Böhl, "Die babylonischen Prätendenten zur Zeit des Xerxes," *Bibliotheca Orientalis* 19 (1962): 114.

19 See Morgenstern, "Jerusalem—485 B.C.," 132-34, 150, 171-72. I am indebted to James Christoph for this asssessment of de Liagre Böhl's argument.

several major events that receive no scriptural notice.[20] While Widengren's first point is true as far as it goes, it does not address the question of which explanation is more plausible or what criteria may be employed to reject Morgenstern's interpretation in favor of some alternative suggestion. As for Widengren's second point, one need only note that many have assumed Zerubbabel led an abortive revolt against the Persians, although there is no narrative recounting of such a dramatic event.[21] Indeed, for the postexilic period as a whole there are only a few explicit biblical narratives, making it necessary to exercise a certain liberty in extracting what little evidence does exist. In this light, Widengren's case against Morgenstern's proposal fails to offer substantive reasons for the wholesale rejection of the alleged catastrophe.

While it is not the purpose of this work to offer a comprehensive critique of Morgenstern's reconstruction, it is necessary to attempt a response that pinpoints several critical deficiencies in his proposal. Specifically, the reconstruction of a catastrophe in 485 BCE can be shown to be based first: on a selective and inadequate use of biblical evidence for the economic conditions of Jerusalem prior to 485; secondly, on a misinterpretation of several passages in Ezra; and thirdly, on an implausible understanding of Persian administrative policies toward Yehud and its neighbors. The untenability of Morgenstern's thesis can be further revealed in its failure to correlate with archaeological evidence that has emerged subsequent to the early 1970s.

Morgenstern presupposes that by the time of the completion of the Second Temple, Jerusalem was a prosperous urban center. He bases his argument on his dating of Psalm 48 to the period between 516-485 BCE, and Haggai 1:4, both texts which, he contends, demonstrate the wealth of the city.[22] His dating of Psalm 48 is arrived at by a highly subjective consideration of "the spirit of quiet confidence and security," which he finds would not have fit the preexilic age of Israel.[23] In contrast, he sees the period of the Second Temple (516-485 BCE in Morgenstern's dating) as a period in which the Temple would have enjoyed the "passsionate regard of the vast majority of the population, not merely of Judaea proper."[24]

---

[20] Widengren, "The Persian Period," 526. Widengren is restating in a more concise form the arguments of H. H. Rowley, "Nehemiah's Mission and its Background," 238-42.

[21] See, for example, Bright, *A History of Israel,* 372; Herrmann, *History of Israel in Old Testament Times,* 304-5.

[22] "Jerusalem—485 B.C.," 102-05.

[23] Julian Morgenstern, "Psalm 48," *Hebrew Union College Annual* 16 (1941), 18-25.

[24] "Psalm 48," 25.

This was also, he contends, the time that "Jerusalem had been restored to the state of a truly imposing city, with palaces, towers and a wall, precisely as this Ps. records."[25] Thus the circularity of Morgenstern's use of Psalm 48 is clear: it dates to the Second Temple because it portrays a prosperous Jerusalem, and Jerusalem was prosperous at this time because Psalm 48 indicates such a state.[26]

With regard to Morgenstern's use of Haggai 1:4, here he is selective in his use of evidence for the economic conditions of the Restoration community in Haggai and Zechariah and interprets the verse out of context. Morgenstern admits that several texts in Zechariah portray the difficult economic conditions facing the postexilic community in the late sixth century, but he brushes these aside by pointing out that the prophet anticipated the rapid recovery of Jerusalem once the Temple was rebuilt.[27] He does not make reference to other passages in Haggai (for example, 1:11, 2:16-17) that paint the same somber picture of conditions in Jerusalem as those from First Zechariah. Moreover, the expression in Haggai 1:4 is intended to contrast the unfinished Temple with the completed homes of the residents of Jerusalem: there is no implication in the use of the term *sĕpûnîm* that those homes are luxuriously appointed as Morgenstern implies.[28] In sum, Morgenstern has provided no real evidence for the purported wealth and grandeur of Jerusalem prior to 485 BCE. Without such evidence, one must reject his contention that the report of the city's condition recorded in Nehemiah 1:4 marks some sudden change in Jerusalem's fortunes.

Morgenstern relies on the correspondence between Artaxerxes I and his provincial officials preserved in Ezra 4:7-22 to date his proposed catastrophe. He contends that it is necessary to read the reference to the archives of the "fathers" of Artaxerxes (Ezra 4:15) as denoting those kings who immediately precede him, namely Darius I and Xerxes. Thus the record of rebellions by Jerusalem (Ezra 4:15, 19) does not refer to the period of Assyrian and Babylonian domination, but to the time of the actual "fathers" of Artaxerxes, the reigns of Darius I and Xerxes.[29] However, Morgenstern does not give due regard to the symbolic value of the term "father" for establishing legitimacy of rule.

---

[25] "Psalm 48," 26.

[26] See for example Morgenstern's use of the date of Psalm 48 in "Two Prophecies from 520-516 B.C.," *Hebrew Union College Annual* 22 (1949), 399-400.

[27] Morgenstern, "Jerusalem—485 B.C.," 102.

[28] See Meyers and Meyers, *Haggai, Zechariah 1-8*, 23-4.

[29] "Jerusalem—485 B.C.," 157-59.

In an earlier discussion, the efforts undertaken by the early Achaemenid monarchs to appear as the legitimate inheritors of Mesopotamian and Egyptian kingship were highlighted. As a further illustration of this tendency, all of the Achaemenid kings included the phrase "the great king" in their titulary, a phrase employed by the Assyrian monarchs several centuries earlier as part of their titulary proclaiming their right to imperial rule.[30] Furthermore, when the Achaemenid monarchs in their own inscriptions referred to their predecessors on the throne, it was either through the employment of standard genealogical formula (e.g., "Artaxerxes, son of Xerxes the king, of Xerxes son of Darius the king") or by direct reference to their genealogical relationship to their predecessors (e.g., "son" or "grandson").[31] There are no royal texts where an Achaemenid king refers to several generations of actual predecessors as his "fathers" as Morgenstern would interpret the term in Ezra 4:15.[32] Thus, to interpret Ezra 4:15 as being restricted to Artaxerxes I's immediate lineage is to ignore the symbolic value of the term for legitimizing the Achaemenid monarch's reign over the ancient Near East.

In addition, a careful reading by Morgenstern of the correspondence preserved in Ezra 4:7-22 would have revealed the untenability of his interpretation of the term "fathers." In Ezra 4:19-20, Artaxerxes reports on the results of his search of the archives and notes the extended history of Jerusalem's rebellions against monarchs. He further remarks that "mighty kings" have been over Jerusalem when ruling the entire Levantine region. Some commentators have had problems in determining the precise group this phrase refers to, in part because they have overlooked the function Artaxerxes' letter is fulfilling in the narrative.[33] The Persian monarch is seeking to justify the order he will be giving to his provincial administrators. They are to use whatever means are necessary to put a stop to the rebuilding of Jerusalem's walls, because that city

---

30 For the Achaemenid inscriptions, see Kent, *Old Persian,* 116-57. For some Assyrian examples chosen at random, see Daniel David Luckenbill, *Ancient Records of Assyria and Babylonia* (Chicago: University of Chicago Press, 1927), vol. 2, 25, 39 (Sargon); 370, 372 (Assurbanipal).

31 Kent, *Old Persian,* 153, texts A^1I and A^1Pa. In the latter text, Artaxerxes I calls himself the "grandson" (Old Persian *xsayaθiyahya)* of Darius, a convention followed by many Achaemenian royal texts (see 181 for references).

32 In one text of Artaxerxes II (A^2Sa), Darius I is referred to as the "great-great-grandfather" to the king; Kent, *Old Persian,* 154.

33 See, for example, the works cited in Fensham, *The Books of Ezra and Nehemiah,* 75-76 as arguing for a reference to the Davidic line of kings in this text.

has a long history of rebelling against "kings." Moreover, these rebellions have been directed at "mighty kings" who have administered the city as part of a larger Levantine territory, or in other words, against kings seeking to keep the city within a larger imperial structure encompassing the Levant. Thus, these "mighty kings" are imperial rulers, and since there is no use of genealogical terms in 4:20 to link them to Artaxerxes, they are presumably non-Achaemenids, namely the Assyrian and Neo-Babylonian kings who administered the Levant as part of an imperial system. Though their argumentation differs in some respects from what is presented here, this has been the conclusion of several recent commentators on Ezra 4:19-20.[34] Consequently, if in the course of checking the archives of his "fathers," Artaxerxes found evidence of Judean rebellions against Assyrian and Neo-Babylonian kings, the term "fathers" must incorporate a longer royal lineage than simply Darius I and Xerxes.

The final argument against Morgenstern's reconstruction relates to several critical assumptions regarding Persian imperial practice upon which his theory is to a large extent dependent. First, Morgenstern has the Persians using Moabite, Ammonite, Edomite, and other troops as surrogates to quell the nationalistic rebellion in Jerusalem. In all the sources for Achaemenid military campaigns, there is not a single instance where the Persians employed other armies to enforce the imperial order.[35] The use of such surrogates would conceptually remove the effectiveness of the enforcement of the imperial order from the central administration of the empire, thus weakening the hold of the central administration over outlying territories. Moreover, the large-scale coalition encompassing most of the peoples of the Levant that Morgenstern envisions as opposing Jerusalem would have the same basic constitution as the coalition of Levantine states that opposed the Assyrians and Neo-Babylonians at various points in the histories of those empires. The encouragement of such a coalition for imperial goals would run the considerable risk of having the same coalition turn against the empire in revolt, just as they had repeatedly opposed earlier empires. Consequently, it seems most unlikely that the Persian court would have suppressed a Judean revolt using surrogates, an action that would make the central

---

[34] For example, Fensham, *The Books of Ezra and Nehemiah,* 76; Clines, *Ezra, Nehemiah, Esther,* 81; Williamson, *Ezra, Nehemiah,* 63. In an earlier phase of commentaries, Galling, *Die Bucher der Chronik, Esra, Nehemia,* 198 also came to this conclusion.

[35] For a brief overview on Persian military organization, see Cook, *The Persian Empire,* 101-07.

imperial administration look ineffectual. Moreover, utilizing a force composed of surrounding peoples to punish Jerusalem, peoples who in the past had formed coalitions to oppose the imperial schemes of previous eastern powers, created the possibility of another Levantine alliance opposing imperial rule.

In addition to these considerations that weigh heavily against the reconstruction proposed by Morgenstern, the extensive amount of information from archaeological research subsequent to Morgenstern's publications casts even further doubt on its plausibility. The excavations of Kathleen Kenyon revealed a wall around the eastern edge of Jerusalem of an approximate mid-fifth century date built along a rock scarp. Kenyon associated this wall with the activities of Nehemiah, and she found no evidence of an intervening defensive system in this area dating from the period between the destruction of the city in 586 and the arrival of Nehemiah.[36] The more extensive excavations along the same eastern side of the City of David under the direction of Yigal Shiloh has also failed to encounter any fortification system that dates to the period between the destruction of the city in 586 and the refortification of the city under Nehemiah. In addition, the Persian period remains (stratum 9) provide no evidence of a break in continuity or of widespread evidence of destruction consistent with the catastrophe Morgenstern posited for 485 BCE.[37] Thus, from Jerusalem itself, there is none of the physical evidence one might expect if the city had suffered the alleged destruction integral to Morgenstern's proposal.

Outside of Jerusalem, new research in Transjordan has made it possible to reconstruct the broad outlines of the region's culture history. For example, the excavations at the probable site of Bozrah, the Edomite capital, have shown that the city was destroyed shortly after the fall of Jerusalem to the Babylonians, possibly in a later campaign by Nebuchadnezzar in 582 BCE. The devastation indicated by the archaeological remains accords well with the prophetic declarations against Edom for its transgressions against Judah.[38] Furthermore, the available evidence

---

36 Kathleen Kenyon, *Jerusalem: Excavating 3,000 Years of History* (London: Thames and Hudson, 1967), 111-12.

37 Oral communication with Prof. Yigal Shiloh. I am indebted to Prof. Shiloh for discussing the unpublished Persian period materials from the City of David with me. For a preliminary report on some of these findings, see Yigal Shiloh, *Excavations at the City of David I (1978-1982).* Qedem: Monographs of the Institute of Archaeology, 19. (Jerusalem: Hebrew University of Jerusalem, 1984), 29.

38 Crystal-M. Bennett, "Excavations at Buseirah (Biblical Bozrah)" in *Midian, Moab and Edom: The History and Archaeology of Late Bronze and Iron Age Jordan and North-west*

for living conditions in Edom during the Persian period would suggest that it was incapable of raising much of a military force to join in Morgenstern's alleged coalition as a major protagonist.[39]

For Moab as well, the widespread destruction of urban sites, possibly the result of a Neo-Babylonian conquest of the region, disrupted any ability to maintain national identity. Recent surveys have noted the relative scarcity of Persian period occupation in the region.[40] Such evidence suggests that by the early fifth century, neither Edom nor Moab would have been in a position to field a military force against Jerusalem. The evidence also points to the devastation of Edom in the sixth century as the event referred to by biblical pronouncements against Edom for its role in the spoliation of Jerusalem and the Temple. This would place such an attack on Jerusalem considerably before Morgenstern's 485 BCE date for the Edomite action.

In sum, there are strong arguments against Morgenstern's reconstruction of a catastrophe in 485 BCE, ranging from his own unchecked utilization of biblical sources to the absence of any archaeological indication that such a catastrophe as he envisions ever affected the postexilic community. Consequently, the context for the missions of Ezra and Nehemiah must be sought elsewhere.

The Alleged Disturbances at the End of the First Quarter of the Fifth Century

In a second hypothesis not unrelated to Morgenstern's proposal, a number of scholars have suggested that all or a portion of the Levant was affected by widespread disturbances near the end of the first quarter of the fifth century. These disturbances are reportedly attested by archaeological evidence at a variety of sites in Palestine. Though not directly linked to the missions of Ezra or Nehemiah, those who advocate this hypothesis clearly intend it to provide a partial explanation for the background of unrest in the Levant that encouraged Achaemenid officials to consider taking extraordinary steps to insure the loyalty of those populations in this region.

Arabia, eds. John F.A. Sawyer and David J.A. Clines, JSOT Supplementary Series 24 (Sheffield: JSOT Press, 1983), 16-17.

39 J.R. Bartlett, "From Edomites to Nabataeans: A Study in Continuity," *PEQ* 111 (1979): 58-9, 65-6.

40 J.R. Bartlett, "The Moabites and Edomites" in *Peoples of Old Testament Times*, ed. D.J. Wiseman (Oxford: Clarendon Press, 1973), 242-43; J. Maxwell Miller, "Archaeological Survey of Central Moab," *BASOR* 234 (1979): 50-51.

This alternative explanation for the transformation of Achaemenid administration in the Levant arises from an observation made by G. Ernest Wright as the result of his excavations at Tell Balaṭah (Shechem). In discussing the fragmentary archaeological remains of the Persian period at Shechem (Stratum V), Wright noted that these remains point to an end of Persian period occupation around 475 BCE:

> That age is a dark one as far as the history of Palestine is concerned, and we simply do not know what happened. We know that Bethel, Gibeon and Gibeah have pottery similar to the local wares of Stratum V, and all four sites may have had their history interrupted in the same period.[41]

Wright's simple remark on possible stratigraphic correlations between Shechem and other sites in the Samarian hillcountry took on a darker tone in the hands of his interpreters. Yohanan Aharoni, for example, spoke of "a time of great disturbances in Palestine," citing the studies of Wright and Morgenstern.[42] Ephraim Stern, in his 1969 dissertation on the Persian period, noted that a number of towns in the southern part of Samaria and in the territory of Benjamin were also destroyed in the Persian period. These include Shechem, Bethel, Tell el-Ful, Tell en-Naṣbeh and Gibeon.[43] He went on to conclude:

> The cities in the territory of Benjamin and in the southern part of Samaria were laid waste in approximately 480 B.C....The group of Palestinian cities which were destroyed or whose occupation ceased at this time are all situated in a limited area of the centre of the country. We have no way of connecting their destruction with any known event, and can only assume that it was a partial destruction which took place during a war between neighboring provinces like the one threatened by Judah's neighbors in the days of Nehemiah, or a local rebellion suppressed by the Persian authorities.[44]

---

41 G. Ernest Wright, *Shechem: The Biography of a Biblical City* (New York: McGraw-Hill Book Co., 1965), 167.

42 Yohanan Aharoni, *The Land of the Bible: A Historical Geography*, trans. A. F. Rainey (Philadelphia: The Westminster Press, 1967), 358. See also Yohanan Aharoni, *The Land of the Bible: A Historical Geography*, revised and enlarged edition, ed. and trans. A.F. Rainey. (Philadelphia: The Westminster Press, 1979), 412. Also, A. F. Rainey, "The Satrapy 'Beyond the River'," 74, n. 29: "It is clear that this was a time of great disturbances in Palestine...."

43 Ephraim Stern, *Material Culture of the Land of the Bible in the Persian Period 538-332 B.C.* (Warminster: Aris & Phillips, 1982), 253. This is the revised and updated English edition of his 1969 dissertation in Hebrew, accepted at the Institute of Archaeology, Hebrew University, Jerusalem.

44 Stern, *Material Culture*, 254.

In a later publication, Stern again returned to this theme:

> ...a large number of towns which had been spared the destruction wrought upon Judea at the fall of the monarchy were destroyed about a hundred years later (about 480 BCE). No historical explanation was found for this destruction, though it may be assumed that it occurred in connection with some minor war, such as that which threatened Judea in the days of Nehemiah.[45]

The presumption of some widespread disturbance at the end of the first quarter of the fifth century has also found its way into recent commentaries on Ezra-Nehemiah, despite the fact that the proposed dates of these archaeological strata do not match the chronology presented in Ezra-Nehemiah. Hugh Williamson, for example, in discussing the "accusation" in Ezra 4:6, notes:

> It is known that just prior to Xerxes' accession Egypt rebelled against her Persian overlord, obliging Xerxes to pass through Palestine during 485 B.C. Perhaps this explains the archaeological evidence for disturbances at a number of sites at this time....It is tempting, though ultimately conjectural, to link this accusation against the Jews with these events, though their specific cause remains unknown.[46]

While the proponents of this hypothesis (notably Aharoni and Stern) have not explicitly tied this assumption of large-scale disturbances directly into a perceptible change in Persian attitudes toward the portion of the Levant, such an implication is inescapable. Particularly as employed by Aharoni, the possibility of wide disturbances in Palestine during the first few years of Xerxes' reign is seen as providing some evidence of Morgenstern's argument for a major change in the social and political development of Yehud at this time.[47] Any unrest requiring concerted military action to quell, whether such unrest was localized or more pervasive, would be reported to the Persian court. Such notoriety would also, in all likelihood, result in some administrative adjustments

---

[45] Ephraim Stern, "The Archaeology of Persian Palestine," in *The Cambridge History of Judaism. Volume One: Introduction—The Persian Period,* eds. W. D. Davies and L. Finkelstein (Cambridge: Cambridge University Press, 1984), 114.

[46] H. G. M. Williamson, *Ezra, Nehemiah,* 60. Wright reported as early as 1965 that the latest fragment of imported Greek pottery from stratum V at Shechem is dated to c. 480 BCE; see *Shechem,* 167. Ezra 4:6 purports to record an incident in the first year of Xerxes, i.e. 485 BCE.

[47] For a similar understanding of Aharoni, see Widengren, "The Persian Period," 526.

to insure the continued stability of the region. Consequently, this hypothesis needs to be assessed in order to understand the Persian imperial background to the missions of Ezra and Nehemiah.[48]

In analyzing the suggestion of an archaeologically attested general disturbance at the close of the first quarter of the fifth century, it should first be noted that the proponents of this view have gone beyond the the boundaries of the evidence they propose to utilize. The simultaneous terminations of Persian period strata at these sites does not suggest the same event caused these terminations as envisioned by the hypothesis.

Nor, for that matter, can the ends of these strata be unequivocally attributed to a violent destruction. Both these aspects must be successfully demonstrated to conclude from this evidence that a wider cultural disturbance of some kind has occurred. Moreover, there is now sufficient evidence to bring into question the proposed synchronic relationship among these strata that proponents of the hypothesis have asserted. Consequently, the proposal of a time of "great disturbance" during this period can be shown to be an unwarranted exaggeration of Wright's original, and provisional, observation.

Wright's interpretation of the evidence from Shechem, for example, is subject to modification. As Wright himself noted, stratum V at Shechem was encountered in only two excavation areas (fields VII and IX). In one of these two areas (field IX) the excavations revealed a line of debris at the top of stratum V, suggesting to Wright that "the occupation was terminated by fire during Persian times."[49] Wright based his dating for stratum V on Nancy Lapp's preliminary study of the imported black- and red-figured wares found in the various loci attributed to the stratum.[50] The entire range of ceramic evidence for stratum V has recently been published by Ms. Lapp.[51] While she retains the basic dating for stratum V proposed by Wright, several additional factors question both the

---

48 For a situation that might provide an approximate analogy to what would be expected in an imperial response to such disturbances, see the adjustments made in Achaemenid rule in Babylon after the revolt in 482 BCE; Rainey, "The Satrapy 'Beyond the River,'" 57.

49 Wright, *Shechem,* 167. See also the chart and discussion of Shechem's stratification in L.E. Toombs, "The Stratification of Tell Balaṭah (Shechem)," *BASOR* 223 (1976):57-59.

50 Wright, *Shechem,* 167; Nancy Lapp, "Appendix 7: Some Black- and Red-figured Attic Ware" in *Shechem,* 238-41.

51 Nancy L. Lapp, "The Stratum V Pottery from Balaṭah (Shechem)," *BASOR* 257 (1985):19-43.

means by which stratum V at Shechem ended, and the date for that terminus.[52]

In Lapp's new study of the ceramic evidence, section drawings from field IX are offered for the first time. In these representations of the excavated loci, a debris layer laced with charcoal is attributed to stratum IVB, a stratum which in field VII represents the first building activities of the early Hellenistic phase of the site.[53] Stratum IVB was dated by Wright from 331 to ca. 300 BCE on the basis of the ceramic and coin evidence found within this deposit.[54] If the debris in stratum IVB is that referred to by Wright, then it would seem to be subsequent to the termination of the Persian period stratum in field IX.[55] Also, the fact that no evidence of a similar "destruction" was found for the end of stratum V in field VII would suggest that this phase was simply abandoned over time, and not brought to a sudden end.[56]

New discoveries in the Shechem area also suggest that the relatively small sampling of stratum V may not tell the full story of the Persian period occupation in the area. Ephraim Stern has published the remains of a tomb some 1.5 kilometers northeast of Shechem that was accidentally discovered in 1976.[57] The contents of the tomb clearly possess a Mesopotamian affinity, leading Stern to conclude that the two individuals buried in the tomb were exiles from Mesopotamia.[58] Included in the burial goods were fragments of three Attic lekythoi,

---

[52] Lapp, "The Stratum V Pottery," 25.

[53] Lapp, "The Stratum V Pottery," 20, fig. 2.

[54] Wright, *Shechem,* 171-72; see also Toombs, "The Stratification of Tell Balaṭah," 58.

[55] It is unclear just what "lines of debris" Wright was making reference to; see *Shechem,* 167; cf. Lawrence E. Toombs and G. Ernest Wright, "The Fourth Campaign at Balaṭah (Shechem)," *BASOR* 169 (1963): 46 where the same expression is used. Nancy Lapp has indicated that there was no destruction debris noted in the field reports for field IX; Nancy Lapp, personal letter to the author.

[56] See the original discussion of stratigraphic problems related to stratum V in field VII in Toombs and Wright, "The Fourth Campaign," 37-38. Later sampling of a better preserved stratigraphic sequence in field VII also did not yield evidence of destruction; Robert J. Bull et. al., "The Fifth Campaign at Balaṭah (Shechem)," *BASOR* 180 (1965): 18. Nancy Lapp has confirmed that there was no destruction debris in field VII; Nancy Lapp, personal letter to the author.

[57] Ephraim Stern, "Achaemenian Tombs from Shechem," *Levant* 12 (1980):90-111. See also the Hebrew version of his report, "Achaemenid Tombs at Shechem," *Eretz-Israel* 15 (1981):312-30.

[58] "Achaemenian Tombs," 107-08.

which have been dated to the second quarter of the fifth century BCE.[59] The relative wealth of the tomb combined with its close proximity to Shechem would suggest that the tomb's owners were originally residents of the city, thus extending the length of the Persian occupation of Shechem into the mid-fifth century BCE. The conclusion, therefore, is that stratum V ended at Shechem several decades later than the date Wright provisionally assigned to it.[60]

Regarding the "destruction" of Tell el-Ful (Gibeah) at the end of the first quarter of the fifth century, the proponents of the time of "great disturbances" are guilty of a complete misreading of the relevant excavation reports. In a preliminary report on the excavations at Tell el-Ful, Paul Lapp noted that the fortress at the site was destroyed in the Iron II period, "presumably during Nebuchadnezzar's campaign of 597." In the latter half of the sixth century the site was extensively resettled. Lapp concluded that this resettlement phase of the site came to an end around 500 BCE and pointed out that "Gibeon, Bethel, and Shechem seem to have been abandoned about the same time."[61] In neither Lapp's 1965 report or the report on the earlier excavations at the site by Lawrence Sinclair is there any mention of destruction debris associated with the end of this phase of occupation.[62]

Indeed, in the final report on the Lapp excavations, this resettlement phase of the site (period IIIB) ended around the time of the first return of exiles to Jerusalem, circa 538 BCE. One of the primary reasons for this conclusion was the completed examination of the ceramic evidence, which showed a total absence of common Persian period ceramic forms from this phase and the presence of common, late Iron 2 wares. Again, as in the earlier reports, there was no mention of the presence of destruction debris at the close of this phase.[63] Thus, contrary to Stern's assertions,

---

[59] "Achaemenian Tombs," 101-02. There is also the possibility that Attic wares have a longer period of use due to their intrinsic high status as an imported item. Consequently, the use of Attic wares to provide so narrow a date range is problematical.

[60] "Achaemenian Tombs," 106-07. An even later Persian settlement may be indicated by a cache of Persian period ceramics found some 9 kms west of Shechem. This group, however, is far from homogeneous in date; Ephraim Stern and Yitzhak Magen, "A Pottery Group of the Persian Period from Qadum in Samaria," *BASOR* 253 (1984):9-27.

[61] Paul W. Lapp, "Tell el-Ful," *BA* 28 (1965):6.

[62] Lawrence A. Sinclair, *An Archaeological Study of Gibeah (Tell el-Ful).* AASOR 34-35 (1954-56). (New Haven: American Schools of Oriental Research, 1960).

[63] Nancy L. Lapp, ed., *The Third Campaign at Tell el-Ful: The Excavations of 1964.* AASOR 45. (Cambridge, MA: American Schools of Oriental Research, 1981), 39-40.

Tell el-Ful shows no evidence of having been destroyed in the Persian period; rather, the abandonment of the relevant phase of the site occurred approximately half a century before 475 BCE.

As was the case at Tell el-Ful, the evidence for a "destruction" at Bethel has also been misinterpreted by Stern and others. A destruction in the late Iron 2 period was reported by the excavators of the site, the layer of destruction debris being filled with fragments of ceramics of the sixth century BCE. However, no characteristic Persian forms were present in this phase.[64] In an evaluation of the ceramic materials from Bethel published in 1970, Paul Lapp concurred with this dating of the pottery evidence of the destruction debris and argued on the basis of several additional factors that the ceramics dated to a point just prior to the Persian conquest of Babylon.[65] The site apparently remained abandoned from the destruction of the late Iron II period until the fourth century BCE.[66] Thus, while Bethel was certainly destroyed, its demise predated the Persian period and is unrelated to the termination of Shechem stratum V.

In the case of Tell en-Naṣbeh, it is apparent that Stern has added a site to the list of cities "destroyed" at the close of the first quarter of the fifth century without cause. In his own discussion of the archaeological evidence of Persian period occupation at Tell en-Naṣbeh, Stern mentions neither a phase of Persian period occupation that ended around 480 BCE nor any evidence of a destruction during the entire Persian period.[67] Nor was any mention of a destruction of the site during the entire Persian period ever published by the original excavators of the site. Indeed, the ceramic evidence from several loci, cited by Stern in his own discussion

64 James L. Kelso, *The Excavation of Bethel.* AASOR 39. (Cambridge, MA: American Schools of Oriental Research, 1968), 38, 75.

65 Paul W. Lapp, "The Pottery of Palestine in the Persian Period" in *Archäologie und Altes Testament,* eds. Arnulf Kuschke and Ernst Kutsch, (Tübingen: J.C.B. Mohr, 1970), 181, n. 14. While Lapp does not identify this opinion as such, it is clearly a change from his earlier dating of this phase with the abandonment of Shechem; see Lapp, "Tell el-Ful," 6.

66 Kelso, *The Excavation of Bethel,* 58. See also James L. Kelso, "Bethel" in *Encyclopedia of Archaeological Excavations in the Holy Land,* Michael Avi-Yonah, ed. Volume 1 (Englewood Cliffs, NJ: Prentice-Hall, Inc., 1975), 193.

67 Stern, *Material Culture,* 31-2.

of the history of the site during this period, points to continuous occupation of the city well into the mid-fifth century BCE.[68]

The results of the excavations at Gibeon (el-Jib) for the Persian period are enigmatic at best, and certainly do not support the hypothesis of a general period of disturbance. The confusing nature of the evidence is due to the methodologically deficient manner in which the site was excavated and the manner in which the findings were published. As Paul Lapp concluded, the excavator "has not excavated stratigraphically, has failed to utilize pottery as a precise chronological tool, and has neglected to publish (or even save) vast quantities of material."[69] The excavation director, James Pritchard, concluded that most of the city was destroyed in 586 BCE when Gibeon's defensive system was destroyed and blocks from the city wall were used to intentionally fill a large circular stairwell leading to a source of water within the walls.[70] Pritchard also dated the last use of a series of silos (termed "the winery" by Pritchard) to the late Iron 2 period on the basis of his evaluation of the ceramics from this area.[71] In a carefully detailed review of this evidence, Paul Lapp demonstrated conclusively that a substantial amount of Persian period ceramic material was misidentified as Iron 2 in date by Pritchard, and that a significant early Persian settlement was present at Gibeon. Both Lapp and G. Ernest Wright pointed out numerous parallels to the ceramics of stratum V at Shechem, although it is probable that the Persian phase at Gibeon extended into the fourth century.[72] None of the Persian period

[68] Chester Charlton McCown, *Tell en-Naṣbeh. Volume 1: Archaeological and Historical Results* (Berkeley: Palestine Institute of Pacific School of Religion, 1947), 185. The later phase of stratum I was built over the city wall at several places, and the ceramics from this phase allow an acceptable range of 586-400 BCE for the occupation, with most of the materials coming from c. 575-450 BCE. See also the discussion of the dating of imported Greek wares from this phase on 175-78. Stern may have added Tell *en-Naṣbeh* to his list as the result of a serious misreading of a comment by Daniel Barag on what sites north of Jerusalem were inhabited after the destruction of Jerusalem in 586 BCE; see Barag, Review of *Winery, Defenses, and Soundings at Gibeon* by James B. Pritchard. *JNES* 26 (1967):143.

[69] Paul W. Lapp, Review of *Winery, Defenses, and Soundings at Gibeon* by James B. Pritchard. *AJA* 72 (1968):393.

[70] James B. Pritchard, *Gibeon, Where the Sun Stood Still: The Discovery of the Biblical City* (Princeton: Princeton University Press, 1962), 70-1, 163.

[71] James B. Pritchard, *Winery, Defenses, and Soundings at Gibeon.* Museum Monographs (Philadelphia: The University Museum, 1964), 17-23.

[72] Lapp, Review of *Winery, Defenses, and Soundings at Gibeon,* 391-92; G. Ernest Wright, Review of *The Water System of Gibeon* by James B. Pritchard, *JNES* 22 (1963): 211. Wright pointed out that the debris filling the stairway had a terminus date of ca. 550/500 BCE, but that some materials from the highest levels of the fill in this feature

evidence was recovered stratigraphicaly, and thus there is no evidence of a destruction or abandonment of the site during the entire span of its Persian habitation. Consequently, none of the evidence from Gibeon applies to the hypothesis of a period of social disturbances at the end of the first quarter of the fifth century.

In sum, outside of Shechem stratum V, there is no evidence from Tell el-Ful, Bethel, Tell en-Naṣbeh, or Gibeon of a destruction or abandonment at the end of the first quarter of the fifth century. Moreover, at Shechem itself, it is far from certain that the occupation of stratum V was brought to a violent end, or that it even ended around 475 BCE. The hypothesis that the period of ca. 480 to 475 BCE was marked by some form of widespread disturbance is totally devoid of evidentiary support and possesses no merit as an explanation for the transformation of the Restoration community in the fifth century.

The Political Reorganization Hypothesis

A third proposed explanation for the transformation of the Restoration community in the mid-fifth century was first advocated by the German scholar Albrecht Alt in 1934, and since that time it has gained wide currency.[73] Alt sought to understand the conflict between Jerusalem and Samaria as the result of a deliberate effort by the Persian court to reorganize the political administration of the province of Yehud by removing the territory formerly considered the kingdom of Judah from its previous oversight by the authorities of the provincial capital of Samaria. This new political entity was placed under the administration of a line of Jewish governors, of which Nehemiah was the first. According to such a view, this action provided the Restoration community with its first real independence under the Achaemenid empire and resulted in

---

had affinities with fourth-century materials. In Wright's opinion, the stairway was filled in the second half of the sixth century. While it is possible that this abandonment may have taken place early in the Persian period, it must be noted that this relates only to the abandonment of the inner-wall water system. There remains the question of the date of the Persian period settlement at Gibeon and its continuity during the period.

[73] The classic formulation of Alt's position is found in his essay "Die Rolle Samarias bei der Entstehung des Judentums," first published in *Festschrift Otto Procksch zum 60. Geburtstag* (Leipzig: A. Dekhurt & J.C. Hinrichs, 1934), 5-28. It was reprinted in Alt's *Kleine Schriften zur Geschichte des Volkes Israel,* Zweiter band (Munich: C.H. Beck, 1953), 316-37. All the following references will be to this later edition of the essay.

the transformation of community in the mid-fifth century attested to in the biblical materials.

Alt began his argument by pointing out the prominent role the city of Samaria played as a governmental center after the Assyrian conquest of the Northern Kingdom. Samaria was a self-sufficient governmental center, functioning as the capital of the Assyrian province of Samerina.[74] Moreover, it was customary in Assyrian practice to deport the upper classes of a population, and so Samaria became the recipient of such upper class groups from various parts of the Assyrian empire. These groups possessed administrative experience gained in their former territorial settings, and the Assyrians gave them administrative responsibilities in the province of Samerina.[75] Following the Babylonian conquest of Jerusalem in 586 BCE, the governance of Jerusalem and its surrounding territory was given to the Samarian ruling class.[76] Gedaliah, the Judean appointee of the Babylonians, served under Samarian oversight to administer the affairs of the remaining population after the deportation of the Judean upper classes.[77]

In Alt's understanding, this administrative pattern was retained when the Persians conquered the Neo-Babylonian empire. One piece of evidence Alt adduces to support this assumption is the account of Tattenai's inquiry into the rebuilding of the Temple, preserved in Ezra 5. Despite the official nature of Tattenai's visit, no leader of the Jerusalem community is evident. From this Alt concludes the Restoration community had no separate political administration but remained under Samarian jurisdiction.[78]

For Alt, this political order underwent a radical transformation with the mission of Nehemiah. While Alt provided no explanation for why Nehemiah is sent by the Achaemenid court to Yehud, he argued that the rebuilding of Jerusalem's walls marked the initial emergence of Jerusalem as a fully independent provincial center.[79] Nehemiah's exercise

---

[74] "Die Rolle Samarias," 318-20.

[75] "Die Rolle Samarias," 326-27.

[76] "Die Rolle Samarias," 328-29. Alt contended that portions of Judah were parcelled out to the surrounding provinces, the surviving remnants of the Levantine provincial system established during the period of Assyrian domination; 329, n. 1.

[77] "Die Rolle Samarias," 329, n. 2.

[78] "Die Rolle Samarias," 331-32.

[79] Alt notes that this is preserved in an unclear fashion; "Die Rolle Samarias," 336. For Alt, as for many who advocate this position, Nehemiah's mission preceeds Ezra's, thus there is little discussion of how Ezra may relate to this process of reorganization.

of authority, particularly in ordering the repopulation of Jerusalem (Nehemiah 11:1-2), pointed to a profound change in the relationship of Jerusalem to the surrounding territory.[80] The emergence of an independent Yehud brought about a crisis in the political relations between Samaria and Jerusalem, leading ultimately to the fracture between the peoples and the religious authorities of these two urban centers.

The original concept of a political reorganization of the Restoration community under Nehemiah as proposed by Alt has been slightly refined and further elaborated by several of Alt's students, the most notable being Kurt Galling and Martin Noth. Galling, following Alt's lead, argued that the Babylonians had placed the conquered territory of Judah under the supervision of imperial officials in Samaria.[81] With the Persian conquest of Babylonia, this arrangement remained unaltered. Thus, prior to the coming of Nehemiah, Yehud was governed by imperial officials situated in Samaria.[82] The mission of Nehemiah marks a major change in the Achaemenid administration of Yehud.

For Galling, Nehemiah's mission was the result of larger imperial concerns over security in the region, engendered by the mid-fifth century revolt in Egypt and the succeeding revolt by Megabyzos, the satrap of the region.[83] Nehemiah's actions in rebuilding the city wall of Jerusalem and in repopulating the city indicate he was the first "hyparch" of Yehud and that the Restoration community was now fully independent of the neighboring authorities.[84]

Another of Alt's distinguished students, Martin Noth, has also played a significant role in disseminating the political reorganization hypothesis. In his influential study of the history of Israel, Noth argued that Nehemiah's appointment as governor of Yehud "signified at the same time the constitution of Judah as an independent province."[85] This

---

[80] Alt uses the technical term "synoikismos" to characterize this development, referring to Rudolf Kittel's discussion of this point; "Die Rolle Samarias," 336-37, 337 n. 1. The appropriateness of this term for Nehemiah's actions will be discussed in chapter five of this work.

[81] Kurt Galling, "Assyrische und persische Präfekten in Geser," *PJB* 31 (1935): 86-87; and *Syrien in der politik der Achaemeniden bis zum Aufstand des Megabyzos 448 v. Chr.*, Der Alte Orient, 36. Band, Hefte 3/4. (Leipzig: J.C. Hinrichs, 1937), 33-34.

[82] Galling, *Syrien in der politik der Achaemeniden*, 34; Galling, *Studien zur Geschichte Israels*, 92 n. 3.

[83] *Syrien in der politik der Achaemeniden*, 45-47.

[84] Galling cites Nehemiah 5:14 as evidence, though he offers no definition for his understanding of the office of "hyparch"; *Syrien in der politik der Achaemeniden*, 44.

[85] Martin Noth, *The History of Israel*, second edition (New York: Harper & Row, 1960), 321.

political reorganization of Yehud immediately stimulated tension between Samaria and Jerusalem over Samaria's loss of political influence in the region. To Noth, this political reorganization was an unintended move on the part of the imperial authorities since the real goal of Nehemiah's mission was the restoration of Jerusalem as a functional urban center. Nehemiah, Noth contends, convinced Artaxerxes to agree to Yehud's independence "because it was a necessary condition for the proposed work of rebuilding the walls of Jerusalem."[86] He explains that Samarian distrust of Jerusalem stemmed from its past role as the location of the central sanctuary for the Israelite tribes. The reemergence of Jerusalem would have presented a serious rival to Samarian interests over the area. Consequently, for Nehemiah's restoration of Jerusalem to succeed, Jerusalem and its dependencies had to be free of Samarian governance.[87]

In summarizing Nehemiah's activity, Noth contended that his mission focused on the political concerns of Yehud, in keeping with the official nature of Nehemiah's office. His limited intrusion into the religious life of the community, namely his strictures against intermarriage and his closing of Jerusalem's gates on the Sabbath, are seen as representing the interests of the Babylonian exilic community and its concerns for Jewish identity in the midst of a pluralistic international setting.[88]

The more recent exponents of the political reorganization hypothesis have offered some significant adjustments and supplements to the position first formulated by Alt. Siegfried Herrmann, for example, has argued that given the intense rivalry between Samaria and Jerusalem, it is unlikely that Nehemiah came to Jerusalem possessing the full administrative powers of governor. Rather, the wide range of his authority gradually led to political independence for Yehud, Nehemiah possibly being made governor over a fully independent territory on his return from the court in 434/433 BCE (Nehemiah 13:6). Herrmann finds this change in the political status of Yehud reflected in the archaeological evidence of seal impressions bearing the legend "Yehud" and dating from the fourth century BCE.[89] Herrmann does not, however, provide a very satisfactory explanation for his contention that Nehemiah's initial mission was, on a

86 Noth, *The History of Israel*, 321-22.

87 Strangely, Noth offered no reason for the imperial interest in restoring Jerusalem outside of the influence of the Judean exiles in the east; *The History of Israel*, 323.

88 Noth, *The History of Israel*, 329-30.

89 Herrmann, *A History of Israel in Old Testament Times*, 312-13, 326.

political level, less than a full governorship. By his own admission, Herrmann notes that the rebuilding of Jerusalem's walls marked a major new stage in the city's status.[90] It is difficult to envision how Nehemiah could have brought about such a new status without possessing full administrative responsibilities over an independent Yehud.

Along very different lines, Ephraim Stern has argued in favor of Samaria's dominance over Yehud for only a portion of the period prior to Nehemiah's mission. In evaluating the archaeological evidence of the various classes of "Yehud" seal impressions, Stern argues that those seals bearing an Aramaic legend date from the end of the fifth to the fourth centuries BCE.[91] Since Stern assumes these seals have an official function, their chronological range as he understands it implies that Yehud as a distinct administrative entity did not exist until the period after Nehemiah. To this interpretation, Stern adds the evidence of another group of seal impressions of a more generic character, usually interpreted as having an official function and paralleled by impressions from other portions of the Achaemenid empire. Stern dates this group to the first part of the Persian period; and since they bear no legends traceable to a particular administrative district, he concludes that they suggest a more homogeneous administrative structure in the first stages of Persian rule in Palestine. Stern also concludes that these seals show that "there is no historical or archaeological evidence of the separate existence of a Jewish province in this period."[92]

With these archaeological interpretations in hand, Stern turns to the various biblical texts. He notes the governmental titles borne by both Sheshbazzar and Zerubabbel, and argues that at the time of the first return of exiles to Yehud there was an effort to establish an independent province. However, by the time Nehemiah enters the stage, there is a "political vacuum," suggesting the earlier effort was "short-lived."[93] Thus, both the biblical texts and the interpretation of the archaeological evidence he has offered suggest to Stern that Alt's hypothesis of a major

90 Herrmann, *A History of Israel in Old Testament Times,* 312.

91 Stern, *Material Culture,* 206.

92 Ephraim Stern, "History of Persian Palestine" in *The Cambridge History of Judaism. Volume One: Introduction—The Persian Period,* eds. W. D. Davies and L. Finkelstein, (Cambridge: Cambridge University Press, 1984), 82-83; *Material Culture,* 237.

93 "History of Persian Palestine," 82-83; Ephraim Stern, "The Province of Yehud: The Vision and the Reality," *Cathedra* 1(1977), 12-13.

political reorganization in Yehud under Nehemiah is substantially correct.[94]

In sum, Alt and those who have adopted his position see in Nehemiah's mission a major development in Achaemenid rule in Yehud. For Galling in particular, the Persian court, under the stimulus of external developments, perceived a need to reorganize the administration of Jerusalem and environs and sent Nehemiah as governor to establish the new provincial capital. For most of those who have advocated this hypothesis, the rebuilding of the walls of Jerusalem is seen as possessing particular significance in marking the old Judean capital as a fully independent urban center.

The hypothesis that the mission of Nehemiah marks a major reorganization of the imperial administration of Yehud has been the subject of several critical evaluations. Two of the most influential critiques have been the philological arguments of Morton Smith and Geo Widengren and the archaeologically based criticism of Nahman Avigad. Because these arguments are so often cited, it is of value to begin by examining some of the objections that have been raised against the hypothesis before offering additional grounds for rejecting the hypothesis as it has been expressed by its advocates.

In his larger study of the emergence of Jewish sectarianism, Smith devotes a separate section to discussing several of Alt's ideas relating to the emergence of the Samaritan movement, including Alt's essay on the origins of the tension between Samaria and Jerusalem.[95] Smith begins by emphasizing the hypothetical nature of most of Alt's suggested social and political conditions in Samaria during the periods of Assyrian and Babylonian dominance. He particularly questions the concept of upper-class exiles having administrative responsibilties in the Assyrian province of Samerina.[96]

Smith then turns to Nehemiah's defense of his official activities in which he claims he never ate the "food of the governor" (*leḥem hapeḥâh)* in contrast to "the former governors" (*hapaḥôt hāriʾšonîm*) who placed heavy burdens on the people (Nehemiah 5:14-15). Smith argues that Alt's

---

94 "History of Persian Palestine," 83; "The Province of Yehud," 14; Ephraim Stern, "Seal-impressions in the Achaemenid Style in the Province of Judah," *BASOR* 202 (1971):15-16.

95 Morton Smith, "Appendix: Alt's Account of the Samaritans," 193-201 in *Palestinian Parties and Politics that Shaped the Old Testament* (New York: Columbia University Press, 1971).

96 "Appendix," 193-95, especially 195.

contention that there were no governors in Yehud prior to Nehemiah would make Nehemiah's claim meaningless.[97] Smith also points to the fact that Zerubbabel bears the title "governor of Judah" in several places, and contends this title must convey the same implication of autonomous rule for Zerubbabel that Alt assumes was the case for Nehemiah.[98] Consequently, Smith finds it impossible for Nehemiah's mission to mark the first real independence of Yehud under imperial administration. He prefers to see Yehud as an independent province from the first return of exiles under Cyrus to the end of the Persian empire.

Smith's opposition to Alt relies largely on the understanding given to the term for "governor" (*peḥâh*) used of Nehemiah's predecessors and of Zerubbabel's office. This same argument has been adapted by Geo Widengren with the addition of several other philologically oriented elements. In response to Alt's contention that the book of Ezra contains no mention of an administrative office in Yehud equivalent to that of a governor prior to Nehemiah, Widengren points to an enigmatic term in Ezra 2:63. The word *tiršātāʾ* appears here, which Widengren argues was a loanword derived from a Persian term meaning "excellency." Such a term, he claims, would be used only of a governor in the fullest sense of an administrative official ruling over an independent district or province.[99]

Widengren also notes the use of the term *mĕdînâh* in several places in Ezra chapters 1-6, arguing that the term itself was used only of self-governing administrative units.[100] Consequently, if Yehud could be characterized as a *mĕdînâh* in the period prior to Nehemiah, Yehud must have been a self-governing unit in this same period. Hence, Widengren concludes that "there is no doubt that Judah from the beginning of the Persian period was given the status of a province by the Persian government."[101]

The criticism of Alt's hypothesis made by Nahman Avigad follows a very different line of approach. In the course of publishing an important cache of postexilic bullae and seals, Avigad argued for the official nature of these impressions and seals based on the appearance in the cache of

---

97 "Appendix," 195-96.

98 "Appendix," 196.

99 Widengren, "The Persian Period," 510. See also the discussion in Williamson, *Ezra, Nehemiah,* 27 and his extensive review of other suggestions for this term.

100 For example, Ezra 2:1; 4:15; 5:8; and 6:2. See also the discussion in F. C. Fensham, "*Mĕdînâ* in Ezra and Nehemiah," *VT* 25 (1975):795-97, and Williamson, *Ezra, Nehemiah,* 33.

101 Widengren, "The Persian Period," 510-11.

several seals belonging to officials identified as "the governor."[102] The collection, coming from an indeterminate place of origin though presumably near the Jerusalem area, is not capable of being dated stratigraphically or on the basis of materials found in association with the cache.[103] Instead, he offers an extensive paleographical analysis of the hoard, assigning the materials from the late sixth to the late fifth centuries BCE.[104]

Avigad then examines the implications of this cache for the postexilic history of Yehud, beginning with Alt's suggestion that the Restoration community did not possess full independence from Samaria until Nehemiah's mission.[105] Using the evidence of other jar-handle impressions as well as the bullae and seals of the hoard, Avigad proposes a list of governors over Yehud, starting with Sheshbazzar and extending to Nehemiah and beyond. Consequently, with the ability to reconstruct such a list, Avigad claims it is possible to provide a context for Nehemiah's defense that he had not taxed the people for his own benefit as the "former governors" had done (Nehemiah 5:15). Moreover, in that Nehemiah was apparently referring to individuals who had ruled immediately prior to the time he assumed his duties, Avigad argues that these individuals possessed the same administrative autonomy as Nehemiah possessed. Thus to Avigad, Alt's position that Samaria had administered Yehud prior to Nehemiah's coming is invalidated by the evidence of the various impressions and seals that allow for the reconstruction of a direct line of administration over Yehud extending from the time after Zerubbabel to Nehemiah.[106]

Both of these critiques of the political reorganization hypothesis, the philological arguments of Smith and Widengren and the archaeological argument of Avigad, have been more or less answered by supporters of the hypothesis. For example, Sean McEvenue has taken up the philological points raised by Smith and Widengren.[107] After restating the arguments of Alt, Smith, and Widengren, McEvenue examines the biblical use of the term *mĕdînâh* and argues that there is no evidence of the term

---

102 Nahman Avigad, *Bullae and Seals from a Post-exilic Judean Archive.* Qedem 4. (Jerusalem: The Institute of Archaeology of the Hebrew University, 1976), 5-7, 11-13, 30.

103 Avigad, *Bullae and Seals,* 30.

104 Avigad, *Bullae and Seals,* 15-20, 32.

105 Avigad, *Bullae and Seals,* 33-34.

106 Avigad, *Bullae and Seals,* 34-36.

107 Sean E. McEvenue, "The Political Structure in Judah from Cyrus to Nehemiah," *CBQ* 43 (1981):353-64.

assuming a new meaning in the postexilic period. Since its preexilic meaning was that of a "second-level administrative district," McEvenue rejects any suggestion of autonomy in the term's use in the postexilic period.[108]

McEvenue next undertakes a review of the biblical use of the term *peḥāh* and claims that any "further arguments which suppose a universal technical meaning for this term" are not consonant with the pattern of use evident in the biblical materials, both preexilic and postexilic. Hence, Smith's and Widengren's objections to the political reorganization hypothesis on the basis of Nehemiah's mention of "former governors" (Nehemiah 5:15) is invalid, and there is no evidence that any of the individuals prior to Nehemiah who bore this title acted as independent administrators. It was Nehemiah's actions in rebuilding the city wall and repopulating Jerusalem, in the view of Alt and McEvenue, that distinguished his authority from those who had preceeded him as *peḥāh*.[109] The response by McEvenue ends with a brief discussion of the term *tiršātāʾ*, noting both its limited biblical usage and the lack of any context in those places where it occurs. Consequently McEvenue rejects drawing any certain conclusions from the term. He concludes that while the biblical sources are "obscure" about the exact form of political authority that prevailed in Judah prior to Nehemiah, Alt's hypothesis of Samarian domination "remains the only proposal supported by probable arguments."[110]

In response to the interpretation of the archaeological evidence offered by Avigad, Ephraim Stern has generally accepted the official character of the bullae and seals and grants that they reflect continuity in the line of administration in Yehud. Where he differs from Avigad is in the dating and placement of several of the governors. Whereas Avigad wants to place several of the individuals named as governors prior to Nehemiah, Stern is of the opinion that they date later in the fifth century and should be placed following Nehemiah.[111] In this way, Stern retains the so-called governor gap between Zerubbabel and Nehemiah, and supports his modification of Alt's hypothesis in which Sheshbazzar and

---

108 McEvenue, "The Political Structure," 359-60.
109 McEvenue, "The Political Structure," 361-63.
110 McEvenue, "The Political Structure," 364.
111 Stern, "The Province of Yehud," 21 n. 25.

Zerubbabel could have ruled an independent Yehud, but no governors followed Zerubbabel until Nehemiah.[112]

Having reviewed these previous criticisms and the counter-arguments to them, it is possible to note several additional points in evaluating the plausibility of the political reorganization hypothesis. These points may be arranged under four basic categories. First, the philological evidence used both for and against Alt's hypothesis is in reality inconclusive and offers little ground to support either the political reorganization hypothesis or its obverse. Second, while the dating of the pertinent seal impressions and seals is far from secure, one of the seals published by Avigad is of major significance in resolving the issue of possible imperial administrators over Yehud between Zerubbabel and Nehemiah. Third, while Alt's hypothesis may provide a framework within which the conflict between Samaria and Jerusalem as reflected in Ezra-Nehemiah is understandable, there are several passages in these same narratives that are not consonant with the model of Samarian domination of Jerusalem prior to Nehemiah's mission. Fourth, there are numerous problems in seeking to reconcile the presumed conditions of the political reorganization hypothesis with known aspects of Achaemenid imperial policy or with the larger sweep of imperial practices in earlier periods in the Levant.

In examining the use of the evidence of linguistic referents to political offices in the postexilic period, it appears that Smith, Widengren, and McEvenue all commit a methodological error of central significance. The terms used, whether *peḥāh* in reference to an individual or *mĕdînâh* in reference to Yehud, occur in the framework of an imperial administrative structure. It is fundamentally wrong to seek to define these terms apart from their use within this larger imperial setting. McEvenue in particular commits a grave error in assuming that these terms as used in a preexilic or exilic context would possess the same semantic range in Achaemenid times.

The importance of this point is best seen in the form of an example. In the case of a very closely related term for political administration, H. W. F. Saggs has been able to show several semantic shifts from the period of Assyrian domination into Achaemenid times. These shifts affected not

[112] Stern, "History of Persian Palestine," 82-83. See also Peter R. Ackroyd, "Archaeology, Politics and Religion: The Persian Period," *The Iliff Review* 39 (1982):12-13 where the same point is made.

only the Akkadian term *šaknu* as it was used during this time but also affected the semantic range of its Hebrew cognate *sāgān*.[113]

In the case of *peḥāh*, there is broad agreement that the biblical term in its postexilic context functions as a cognate of the Akkadian phrase *bel piḫati*.[114] As was shown in the discussion of the early phases of Achaemenid imperial organization, varying levels of officials were given the title *bel piḫati*, just as varying levels of officials in the preceding Neo-Babylonian period had been termed a *bel piḫati*. If, in its larger imperial setting, *bel piḫati* possessed no connotations as to the hierarchical status of the title or the administrative autonomy of the bearer of the title, then it is not reasonable to assume that the Hebrew and Aramaic cognate *peḥāh* as used in the same imperial context would possess such connotations.

To a certain extent, this point vitiates the impact of the arguments of Smith and Widengren from the use of *paḥôt* in Nehemiah 5:15 that officials possessing the same autonomy of rule as Nehemiah governed prior to his mission. At the same time, this point invalidates McEvenue's contention that *peḥāh* possessed no technical meaning.[115] The term apparently had some specific administrative meaning: the issue at question is if that technical quality defined autonomy of rule or some other aspect of an individual's adminstrative function.

A similar situation is faced in dealing with the term *mĕdînâh*. In northwest Semitic, the term is derived from the root *dyn* and has something of the sense of "jurisdiction."[116] In a general governmental sense, a jurisdiction can apply to a variety of administrative responsibilities without connoting autonomy of administration. However, the issue under dispute is the possibility that within an Achaemenid imperial context, *mĕdînâh* possessed some more specific meaning. From the Aramaic papyri of the Persian period, it is clear that *mĕdînâh* was used to denote several levels of administrative responsibility, and thus did not possess an invariable sense of referring to an autonomous political unit. At the same time, it is also clear that in its imperial use it denotes a political adminis-

---

113 H. W. F. Saggs, "A Lexical Consideration for the Date of Deutero-Isaiah," *JTS* 10 (1959):84-87.

114 See, for example, Rosenthal, *A Grammar of Biblical Aramaic*, 58; Saggs, "A Lexical Consideration," 84 n. 1.

115 McEvenue, "The Political Structure," 363.

116 Max Wagner, *Die lexikalischen und grammatikalischen Aramaismen im alttestamentlichen Hebräisch*. Zeitschrift für die alttestamentliche Wissenschaft, Beihefte 96. (Berlin: Alfred Töpelmann, 1966), 72.

trative division of some level, contrary to McEvenue's contention that the term means nothing more than "region."[117]

In the case of the term *tiršātāʾ*, McEvenue is substantially correct in casting doubt on a possible derivation from a Persian word with the sense of "excellency." Several decades ago, R. H. Pfeiffer offered three separate etymologies for this term, originating from various postulated Persian words.[118] More recently, several authors have tried to make a case for *tiršātāʾ* being derived from a New Persian word meaning "to cut", implying either that Nehemiah was a eunuch or that the term was roughly equivalent to "the circumcised one."[119]

Moreover, there is no assurance that *tiršātāʾ* is a Persian loanword. Robert Wilson argued over a generation ago that *tiršātāʾ* represented a nominative form of the northwest Semitic root *ršh* that appears in contexts dealing with financial matters fitting Nehemiah's role in administering taxes.[120] This uncertainty surrounding the meaning of *tiršātāʾ* and the limited contexts in which the term appears in the biblical narratives preclude any certainty in its application either in support of or against the political reorganization hypothesis of Alt and his followers.

In summary, the various philological arguments have not succeeded in clarifying the form of political administration in Yehud prior to Nehemiah's mission. Particularly in dealing with the terms *peḥāh* and *mĕdînâh,* it is necessary to give more serious consideration to the way in which their connotations were modified under changing historical contexts and the technical nuance these terms possessed in their use in the Achaemenid empire. Also, before applying the Achaemenid meaning to these terms, one must address the issue of their literary setting in Ezra-

---

117 See A. Cowley, *Aramaic Papyri of the Fifth Century B.C.* (Oxford: Clarendon Press, 1923), 79-80; Charles F. Jean and Jacob Hoftijzer, *Dictionnaire des Inscriptions sémitiques de l'Ouest* (Leiden: E.J. Brill, 1965), 143. On the other hand, one can make a strong argument from Letter 6 of the cache published by G.R. Driver that *mĕdînâh* had the specific sense of self-governing administrative unit; *Aramaic Documents of the Fifth Century B.C.* Abridged and revised edition. (Oxford: Clarendon Press, 1957), 27-28 and the discussion on 16-17.

118 R. H. Pfeiffer, "Tirshatha," in *The Interpreter's Dictionary of the Bible,* ed. George A. Butterick et al., Volume 4 (New York: Abingdon Press, 1962), 652.

119 See Edwin M. Yamauchi, "Was Nehemiah the Cupbearer a Eunuch?" *ZAW* 92 (1980):136-37 and the literature cited there. See also Wilhelm Th. In der Smitten, "Der *Tirschataʾ* in Esra-Nehemia," *VT* 21 (1971):618-20.

120 Robert D. Wilson, "Tirshatha," in *The International Standard Bible Encyclopedia,* ed. James Orr et al., reprint of 1929 edition. Volume 5 (Grand Rapids, MI: Wm. B. Eerdmans, 1957), 2986-87.

Nehemiah and any implications the author of these narratives may have seen in their use.

Second, turning to the archaeological evidence of the various seal impressions, bullae, and seals presented by Avigad, it must be admitted that if the dating he has given to this evidence can be substantiated, then there is little question that the political reorganization hypothesis is fundamentally flawed. The paleographic arguments that Avigad has made in favor of a date prior to Nehemiah for some of this evidence is tenuous. The Aramaic scripts of the Achaemenid period are often a mixture of lapidary and cursive scripts, changing letter forms at varying rates over time.[121] Moreover, it is often the case that dating epigraphic materials possessing such differing styles is troublesome.[122] Consequently, reliance solely on paleography for the close dating of the epigraphic evidence put forth by Avigad is fraught with difficulty and is hardly conclusive when applied to the question of the form of political administration in Yehud prior to Nehemiah.[123]

Fortunately, paleography is not the only basis on which Avigad's evidence can be dated. As Eric Meyers has recognized, the seal belonging to Shelomith in the hoard published by Avigad is pivotal in confirming Avigad's reconstruction of the governors who administered Yehud prior to Nehemiah.[124] Meyers links the seal, which bears the legend "belonging to Shelomith, maidservant of Elnathan the governor," with the Shelomith of 1 Chronicles 3:19, the daughter of Zerubbabel.[125] Highlighting the remarkable occurrence of the name Shelomith in the Chronicler's list of Davidides, Meyers offers the plausible explanation that Shelomith was the means by which Elnathan attached himself to the line of Davidic succession in order to legitimize his rule as governor.[126]

---

121 See, for example, Larry G. Herr, *The Scripts of Ancient Northwest Semitic Seals.* Harvard Semitic Monographs Series No. 18. (Missoula, MT: Scholars Press, 1978), 7, especially his discussion of archaizing tendencies in the scripts of this period.

122 See Frank M. Cross, Jr., "Alphabets and Pots: Reflections on Typological Method in the Dating of Human Artifacts," *Maarav* 3 (1982):132 for the problems of dating scripts evolving at a slow rate, such as the Aramaic lapidary scripts of this period.

123 See, for example, the comments of Ackroyd, "Archaeology, Politics and Religion," 12-13 for this assessment of Avigad's dating.

124 Eric M. Meyers, "The Shelomith Seal and the Judean Restoration: Some Additional Considerations," *Eretz-Israel* 18 (1985):33*-38*; see also the comments in Meyers and Meyers, *Haggai, Zechariah 1-8,* 12-13.

125 Meyers, "The Shelomith Seal," 34*.

126 Meyers, "The Shelomith Seal," 35*. It should be noted that Avigad presents some substantial reasons for understanding the title "maidservant (*ʾāmāh*)" to denote a woman of noble birth; Avigad, *Bullae and Seals,* 11-13. Among this evidence is an

Elnathan, in marrying the daughter of Zerubbabel, became the full successor of Zerubbabel as governor in the late sixth century BCE. In that he ruled after Zerubbabel, Elnathan represents at least one figure who administered Yehud between Zerubbabel and Nehemiah, and the efforts he undertook to align himself with the Davidic line strongly argue for the autonomy of the office of governor in Yehud.[127] Consequently, Avigad's arguments in favor of a line of continuous rule from Zerubbabel to Nehemiah finds substantial verification in this consideration of the Shelomith seal. As was discussed earlier, the ability to reconstruct a line of territorial administrators between Zerubbabel and Nehemiah provides a crucial link in the administration of Yehud that weighs heavily against the conditions postulated in the political reorganization hypothesis.

Third, in terms of the biblical narratives themselves, there is strong reason to question the plausibility of the political reorganization hypothesis. As was mentioned, Alt seized upon the narrative of Tattenai's official inspection, preserved in Ezra 5, as evidence for the lack of an autonomous administration in Jerusalem prior to Nehemiah's arrival. The narrative does not mention Tattenai coming in contact with a governor, but this is hardly surprising given the tendency of Ezra-Nehemiah to downplay rulers of the Davidic line. Zerubbabel, who was in all probability the governor of Yehud at the time of Tattenai's visit, is usually placed in the background by the author of Ezra-Nehemiah.[128]

---

eighth century BCE tomb inscription from Siloam of a nobleman buried with his *ʾāmāh;* N. Avigad, "The Epitaph of a Royal Steward from Siloam Village," *IEJ* 3 (1953):137-52.

[127] Meyers and Meyers, *Haggai, Zechariah 1-8*, 12-15.

[128] See Sara Japhet, "Sheshbazzar and Zerubbabel Against the Background of the Historical and Religious Tendencies of Ezra-Nehemiah," *ZAW* 95 (1983):219-20; Clines, *Ezra, Nehemiah, Esther*, 27-28. Japhet's point is that the author of Ezra-Nehemiah has suppressed any Davidic ideology in order to throw the focus on the necessity for obedience on the part of the entire community. That Zerubbabel was governor at the time of Tattenai's visit is implied in Ezra 5:2 and 6:7. While the account in Ezra 5 provides no date formula for the correspondence, the overall impression is that Tattenai's inspection took place early in the reign of Darius, a context that seems particularly plausible given the fact that Darius was not of the direct line of Cyrus and Cambyses. Thus Tattenai may have undertaken an inspection tour of the outlying areas of the district of Eber Nari on behalf of Darius. Tattenai is known to have been a subordinate under the Satrap of Babylon and Eber Nari; A.T. Olmstead, "Tattenai, Governor of 'Across the River'," *JNES* 3 (1944):46. On Zerubbabel's importance in the rebuilding of the Second Temple, see Meyers and Meyers, *Haggai, Zechariah 1-8*, 250-54, 268-72.

Moreover, rather than act to stop the rebuilding of the Temple, Tattenai appears to assume the activity was authorized and simply reports on its progress to the court.[129]

It seems improbable that had Tattenai found this project underway without being under the direct supervision of a provincial authority, he would have responded in this way. The more plausible alternative is that some provincial figure was present, a figure the author of Ezra-Nehemiah has elected to suppress for the purposes of magnifying a specific theological perspective.

The account of Tattenai's investigation is not the only narrative in Ezra-Nehemiah that calls into question the presumed conditions of the political reorganization hypothesis. In Ezra 4 another series of letters are preserved from the reign of Artaxerxes I. Here, it is reported that a letter is sent to the Persian court from various administrative officials in Samaria reporting on an effort to rebuild the walls of Jerusalem. The king returns a letter specifying that the work is to cease, and the imperial officials are reported to have moved against Jerusalem to stop work on the walls.[130] Several points are pertinent to the question of provincial governance in this correspondance. First, the letter reporting on the wall building activity is sent from Rehum, identified as the *bĕʿel-ṭĕʿem*, and from Shimshai "the scribe," both of whom are said to "sit" in Samaria (Ezra 4:8-9, 17). The Aramaic *bĕʿel-ṭĕʿem* is representative of the Akkadian *bel ṭemi,* a term of uncertain technical meaning but clearly a significant administrative post in the imperial system.[131] Moreover, the use of the Aramaic *yātbîn* to indicate the location of these officials may reflect a technical sense of the location of governance, rather than the place of habitation.[132]

If, as Alt and his followers have contended Samaria was the only provincial center within the former boundaries of the unified kingdom of Israel, these elements make little sense. Why is the report of the wall

---

129 See the comments of Williamson, *Ezra, Nehemiah,* 76.

130 On the dating of this correspondence, see Rainey, "The Satrapy 'Beyond the River'," 62-63 and the larger discussion in Williamson, *Ezra, Nehemiah,* 62-63. Since Williamson's criticisms of Rainey's dating involve the events of the Egyptian Revolt of the mid-fifth century and its aftermath, these matters will receive more detailed consideration in chapter five of this work.

131 See Rosenthal, *A Grammar of Biblical Aramaic,* 58 and the very useful discussion of the term in Williamson, *Ezra, Nehemiah,* 54 and the entry on *ṭʿm* in Jean and Hoftijzer, *Dictionnaire,* 102.

132 See Jean and Hoftijzer, *Dictionnaire,* 112. The LXX tradition seems to confirm this interpretation, rendering *yātbîn* as *oikountas,* "manage".

rebuilding communicated to the court by the *bel ṭemi* and the "scribe" rather than the governor of Samaria? If Samaria was indeed over Jerusalem, why didn't these officials, or others, act within their appointed authority and stop the project before inquiring of the court if it was authorized?

Surely if the wall rebuilding was authorized by the court, the provincial authority over the district would have known. Instead, the narrative portrays the *bel ṭemi,* the "scribe," and their associates acting as though they are reporting on, and seeking authority over, an area that is not at the time under their jurisdiction. It is only after receiving direct authorization from the court that these officials proceed to intervene to halt the wall rebuilding (Ezra 4:23). All this suggests that, in fact, Samaria and those officials who governed out of Samaria, did not ordinarily possess jurisdiction over Jerusalem.

A fourth aspect to the political reorganization hypothesis that argues against its plausibility is the difficulty in reconciling the conditions presupposed by the hypothesis with Achaemenid imperial practices, or with pre-Achaemenid practices. As Morton Smith has argued, it seems highly unlikely that under the Neo-Assyrian or Neo-Babylonian imperial administration, upper class deportees from various places in the empire would have been given provincial responsibilities.[133] In all that is known of the status of deportees in the Neo-Assyrian empire, the scenario envisioned by Alt is rare, if not unexpected.[134]

Central to Alt's position is the assertion that following the fall of Jerusalem in 586 BCE, the Neo-Babylonian empire consolidated the former territory of the kingdom of Judah under Samarian administration. While little is known with clarity about the Neo-Babylonian imperial organization, as has already been discussed, it is apparent that when former kingdoms were conquered, the Neo-Babylonian empire treated these territories as discrete political units within the empire and maintained their territorial integrity. The kind of consolidation process assumed as the precondition of the political reorganization hypothesis is without parallel, and would seem to offer no advantage for administering the

133 Smith, "Appendix," 195.

134 See the discussion in Oded, *Mass Deportations and Deportees,* 104-07. While Oded notes the appearance of a number of foreign names among the *limmu* lists, it seems that in many of the examples he cites, those named are administering their territorial homelands, i.e. they are not deportees administering a territory that they had been settled in, the situation envisioned by Alt. There is, of course, the oft-debated methodological problem of assuming a foreign name necessarily denotes a foreigner, an assumption that Oded follows.

region. As has been argued, imperial practice under the Neo-Babylonian empire was characterized by the cooption of existing governmental structures and their transformation into imperial administrative mechanisms. The superimposition of administrative rule from an adjoining imperial territory onto a newly conquered territory as envisioned by Alt and his followers would constitute a major departure from what seems to have been a prevailing pattern in Neo-Babylonian practice.

Where the proponents of the political reorganization hypothesis have attempted to provide an important insight into Achaemenid imperial policy, it is interpreted within a framework devoid of comparative value. Those advocating a major transformation of rule in Yehud as the result of Nehemiah's mission have pointed to his rebuilding of the walls of Jerusalem as marking the city as an independent provincial capital. While it is entirely appropriate to highlight Nehemiah's wall building activity, the interpretation that this signifies the city has become an independent provincial capital is offered without examples of other urban capitals possessing walls in this period. In reality, the evidence suggests a considerably different interpretation for Nehemiah's activity. For example, for the entire Persian period Samaria apparently never possessed a city wall system, yet its status as a fully independent provincial capital is unquestioned.[135] The extraordinary character of Nehemiah's restoration of Jerusalem's city defenses also implies that it would have been impossible for this act to have been an incidental part of Nehemiah's mission as Martin Noth seems to have implied.

Even if it is granted that Nehemiah's mission marked the first independence of the Restoration community and the emergence of Yehud as an autonomous provincial district, the proponents of the political reorganization hypothesis have failed to explain satisfactorily what advantage this reorganization offered to the Achaemenid empire. The Achaemenid court would not have countenanced such a move unless it met some aspect of imperial political or strategic need. Of the proponents of the hypothesis, only Galling has tried to tie Nehemiah's activity into a larger imperial perspective. Yet even in Galling's work, no suggestion is offered as to how granting independence to Yehud resolved the prevailing insecurity in the region that he postulates for this period.[136] The creation of a new political unit within the Achaemenid imperial system,

---

[135] See Kathleen Kenyon, *Royal Cities of the Old Testament* (New York: Schocken Books, 1971), 132-34.

[136] See Galling, *Syrien in der politik der Achaemeniden*, 45-47.

therefore, requires some plausible explanation, and such an explanation has not been offered by either Alt or his followers.

In conclusion, there are no compelling reasons for adopting the political reorganization hypothesis, while there are strong reasons for rejecting it. There can be little doubt that from the reign of Cyrus on, Yehud was ruled by a continuous line of administrators bearing the title of *peḥāh*. While the title itself may be unclear, the fact that one individual between the administrations of Zerubbabel and Nehemiah, Elnathan, undertook measures to align himself with the Davidic line strongly suggests that the office of *peḥāh* bore considerably more importance than simply being a "commissioner" under Samarian oversight. Moreover, the narratives of Ezra-Nehemiah present several accounts that conflict with the political arrangements presupposed by the proponents of the hypothesis. Finally, given the difficulty in reconciling the central conditions postulated by the hypothesis with the prevailing patterns of imperial rule in the Levant, characteristic of both the Achaemenids and their predecessors, the hypothesis loses considerable plausibility. As a consequence, the view that the mid-fifth century transformation of the Restoration community was due to its new independence from Samarian domination can be rejected.

The Hypothesis that the Missions of Ezra and Nehemiah were an Imperial Inducement to Loyalty

The final proposal to be examined for explaining the transformation of the Restoration community in the mid-fifth century is perhaps more diffuse than the previous hypotheses, though it is fair to say that it is embraced by a far larger group of writers on the period. In its most basic form, this position sees the missions of Ezra and Nehemiah as an effort by the Achaemenid imperial authorities to engender continued loyalty on the part of the Restoration community.

Though no one writer can be credited with formulating the hypothesis, a number of prominent figures in Old Testament studies have given expression to this perspective. For example, H. H. Rowley, in seeking to explain why Artaxerxes I reversed his earlier prohibition against rebuilding the walls of Jerusalem by sending Nehemiah to undertake this very task, attributed the reversal to threatening conditions in the empire. He argued that as a personal servant of the king, Nehemiah's loyalty to the crown was unquestionable.[137]

In a synthetic study of the entire postexilic period, Jacob Myers advocated a similar understanding of Nehemiah's mission. In a review of the history of the disturbances in the Achaemenid empire during the mid-fifth century, he gave particular emphasis to the Egyptian Revolt of ca. 460 and the subsequent Megabyzos Revolt of ca. 448 BCE.[138] Against this background, Myers saw Nehemiah's mission as a shrewd combination of religious idealism and diplomatic expediency.[139] The rebuilding of Jerusalem's defensive wall system was not only Nehemiah's personal desire, but also dovetailed with the court's strategy to secure access to the Satrapy of Egypt along the strategic routes that ran through Jerusalem.[140] Thus Nehemiah was commissioned by the Achaemenid court because his mission insured a loyal and secure province on the southernmost boundary of a satrapy that had proven troublesome in the immediate past.

In a more concise discussion of these same points, Peter Ackroyd offered a parallel understanding of the imperial motives behind Nehemiah's mission. After noting the events of the Egyptian Revolt and the Megabyzos Revolt, Ackroyd commented:

> ...this makes it all the more intelligible that the Persian ruler should have seen fit to send Nehemiah to Jerusalem at just this moment of time. A loyal governor there, who owed his position to the personal favor of the Persian king, could be a valuable support for Persian control of the west. Judah was important for the approach roads to Egypt, and Egypt was a continuous source of anxiety.[141]

Consequently, for Ackroyd the mission of Nehemiah was in part conditioned by the Achaemenid court's desire to insure a loyal province along a strategic access point into Egypt.

---

137 H. H. Rowley, "Nehemiah's Mission and Its Background," 237-38. Rowley never offered a reason for why the wall rebuilding would have been needed in the first place.

138 J. M. Myers, *The World of the Restoration* (Englewood Cliffs, NJ: Prentice-Hall, 1968), 109-11.

139 Myers, *The World of the Restoration,* 111. See also Myers, *Ezra. Nehemiah,* xxxii-xxxiii.

140 Myers, *The World of the Restoration,* 113-15, 122-23.

141 Ackroyd, *Israel Under Babylon and Persia,* 175-76.See also Peter R. Ackroyd, *Exile and Restoration: A Study of Hebrew Thought in the Sixth Century B.C..* Old Testament Library. (Philadelphia: The Westminster Press, 1968), 141.

More recently, Geo Widengren has restated this same line of understanding. He argued that the Achaemenid court's commissioning of Nehemiah was not simply the bestowal of royal favor on a faithful servant.[142] He then reviewed the disturbances within the empire under Artaxerxes I's rule, starting with the widespread turmoil that reportedly occurred on the occasion of the accession of Artaxerxes. Widengren also noted the Egyptian Revolt of the mid-fifth century BCE and the Megabyzos Revolt that allegedly followed in its aftermath. Despite the eventual imperial triumph over these troubles, Widengren concludes that the disturbances "must have demonstrated how valuable it would be to the Persians to have a loyal province and reliable governor in the territory bordering on Egypt."[143] Out of these political and strategic considerations, Nehemiah was commissioned to refortify Jerusalem.

For many who have advocated dating the mission of Ezra to the traditional date of 458 BCE, similar connections are drawn between the turmoils of the period and the Achaemenid court's desire for a loyal populace in Yehud. For example, several decades ago Fritz Heichelheim contended that Ezra's commissioning by the court made sense only by relating his mission to the challenges to imperial control represented by the Egyptian Revolt and Athenian involvement in the revolt. Noting the appearance of Dor on the Delian League tribute lists for the period of 460-450 BCE, Heichelheim argued that Ezra's activity served to prevent further defections from Achaemenid control in Palestine.[144]

Heichelheim has not been alone in seeing Ezra's mission as an effort to insure continued Achaemenid control over the Levant. Anson Rainey claimed that Ezra's mission "may reflect an official attempt to assure the loyalty of various peoples in the province 'Beyond the River'," and pointed to the conditions of the Egyptian Revolt as the cause for imperial concerns over loyalty in the region.[145] J. L. Myers concluded that the "wide authority" of Ezra's commission was the result of Achaemenid anxiety over the disturbance presented by the revolt.[146] Most recently, Othniel Margalith has attempted to argue that Ezra's mission was an effort by the Persian court to insure a pro-Persian populace. Margalith

142 Widengren, "The Persian Period," 524.

143 Widengren, "The Persian Period," 528-29.

144 Fritz Heichlheim, "Ezra's Palestine and Periclean Athens," *Zeitschrift für Religions- und Geistesgeschichte* 3 (1951):251-53.

145 Rainey, "The Satrapy 'Beyond the River'," 62.

146 J. L. Myers, "Persia, Greece and Israel," *PEQ* 85 (1953):13.

contends, "From the point of view of the Persian king a strong pro-Persian Judea was a major threat to the Greek coastal lifeline."[147]

These same basic arguments are often encountered in a large body of current literature dealing with this period.[148] In most cases, the same pattern of argumentation is maintained. The assumption is made that the imperial authorities were concerned about security in the region because of the experiences of the Egyptian Revolt and its aftermath, the Megabyzos Revolt. As a response to this perception of insecurity in the region, the Achaemenid king allowed (or, as some have claimed, ordered) one or the other of the reformers to go to Yehud in an effort to insure a loyal populace in a strategic part of the empire.

The vagueness with which this explanation has been formulated makes the ability to offer a useful critique difficult. A basic aspect of the hypothesis centers on what each proponent understands by the idea of "loyalty," a term usually not defined. Without a clear sense of what it would mean for the Restoration community to be more "loyal," it is almost impossible to make a comprehensive assessment of the plausibility of this hypothesis. Nonetheless, there are several general observations that can be made regarding this explanation.

One critical element in the argument for the missions of Ezra and Nehemiah as an imperial attempt to induce loyalty in the Restoration community is the instability assumed for the mid-fifth century. For the convenience of analysis, this instability can be seen as having two implications. The first is that the disturbances of the period (the Egyptian Revolt and the Megabyzos Revolt) challenged imperial security in the places where these events occurred. The second implication is that as a consequence of this challenge, the strategic value of Yehud was raised in the perception of the imperial authorities, causing them to act in such as manner as to solidify imperial rule in Yehud. Despite the importance of these two implications, neither one has been demonstrated by the proponents of this explanation.

For a variety of reasons, the historical events of the Egyptian Revolt and its aftermath, including the alleged Megabyzos Revolt, have not

---

147 Othniel Margalith, "The Political Role of Ezra as Persian Governor," *ZAW* 98 (1986):111. Margalith's entire presentation is badly flawed by a number of undocumented and erroneous assumptions including the idea that Ezra held the office of governor, that the Philistine populations were allies of the Athenians, that the Athenians controlled the Levantine coast, and that "Judea" was targeted for imperial attention because of its traditional rivalry with the Philistines.

148 For example, see Williamson, *Ezra, Nehemiah,* xli.

received the critical attention of historians of Syria-Palestine.[149] As a case in point, the Megabyzos Revolt is reported by only one Greek historian of the period, Ctesias; and despite the factual conflicts between Ctesias' account and those of the other historians of the period, virtually every proponent of this hypothesis treats Ctesias' narrative as unquestioned historical fact.[150] The gravity of the Egyptian Revolt and its aftermath, and the extent to which these events actually destabilized imperial control in Egypt and contiguous territories, must be plausibly demonstrated before postulating a general atmosphere of insecurity or imperial anxiety in the region.

In addition to the need to show that these historical events presented the kind of challenge to imperial control assumed by this explanation, there is the corresponding need to demonstrate that the nature of this challenge directly affected the strategic value of Yehud. Several proponents of this explanation have made reference to the importance of the roads running through Yehud and leading into Egypt, but the mere existence of such routes is no guarantee that they were of strategic importance. For most of the historical periods of the Levant, the Coastal Highway or Via Maris served as the primary route into Egypt.[151] Since in the Persian period the Coastal Highway was never part of Yehud, it remains to be explained why the other routes running through Yehud had become of such interest, if indeed this is what happened.

As an illustration of the dilemma these two issues present to proponents of this hypothesis, one need only note that Egypt had revolted once before in the fifth century, early in the reign of Xerxes I.[152] At that time, there is no evidence to suggest that imperial control in the west was threatened, or that the Achaemenid authorities placed a new strategic value on Yehud. Consequently, it is not justifiable to propose the destabilization of imperial control in the west and an increased strategic role for Yehud as the consequence of the Egyptian Revolt of the mid-fifth century without further demonstration.

Another weakness in the hypothesis that the missions of Ezra and Nehemiah originated in an imperial effort to induce loyalty in the

149 This problem and its resolution are the focus of chapter three of this work where further discussion is offered on the limitations of past studies of the Egyptian Revolt and its aftermath.

150 For example, see Morton Smith, *Palestinian Parties and Politics,* 127; Ackroyd, *Israel Under Babylon and Persia,* 174-75; Widengren, "The Persian Period," 529; and Miller and Hayes, *A History of Ancient Israel and Judah,* 469.

151 Aharoni, *The Land of the Bible,* 45-54.

152 For a helpful overview of this incident, see Cook, *The Persian Empire,* 99-100.

Restoration community is the lack of a connection between the activities of these reformers and the proposed goal of their missions. The advocates of the hypothesis uniformly fail to demonstrate that such a linkage existed. Assuming that Ezra was sent by the Achaemenid court as the result of concern over instability in the region, the proponents of this view need to define how Ezra's mission would have contributed to engendering loyalty for the empire. For Nehemiah as well, there is the need to demonstrate how the rebuilding of Jerusalem's defensive system would have induced greater loyalty within the Restoration community. It should be noted that for Nehemiah's opponents, this very act signified a rebellion against imperial authority and did not connote deeper loyalty to the king (Nehemiah 2:19).

As a final comment, it may be said that if the missions of Ezra and Nehemiah were commissioned by the Achaemenid court to induce loyalty in Yehud, the narratives of Ezra-Nehemiah suggest that the reformers themselves were unaware of this goal. For example, in Ezra 9:8-9, in a prayer concerning intermarriage in the Restoration community, Ezra notes the status of the community as "bondsmen" under the Persian kings. And in the covenant ceremony of Nehemiah 9, at which Nehemiah is said to have been present (Nehemiah 10:1), the community is said to be "in great distress" because of the manner in which the Achaemenid kings exercise their authority (Nehemiah 9:37).[153] Such statements hardly seem conducive to engendering greater loyalty toward the empire.

In sum, the hypothesis that the missions of Ezra and Nehemiah represent an effort by the imperial authorities to induce greater loyalty in Yehud in the face of the destabilizing influences of the Egyptian Revolt and its aftermath is plagued by considerable uncertainties. Without a clearer understanding of the way in which the events of the period transpired and the implications these events had for strategic concerns in the Levant and Yehud in particular, it is impossible to judge the plausibility of this explanation. There are, however, indications in the narratives of Ezra-Nehemiah that suggest loyalty was not the central concern of the reformers themselves.

---

153 Because of the importance of this evidence for understanding the Restoration community's self-understanding of their status in the imperial system, these passages are discussed more fully in chapter six of this work.

The Requirements for a New Synthesis of Historical, Archaeological, and Biblical Evidence

In the previous sections, the major explanations for the transformation of the Restoration community in the mid-fifth century BCE were reviewed. As has been seen, these explanations are all, in varying degrees, inadequate. The factors that have revealed their inadequacy are varied and range from irreconcilability with archaeological evidence for the period to incompatibility with the narratives in Ezra-Nehemiah. Consequently, before attempting to formulate another explanatory hypothesis for the transformation of the mid-fifth century, it is only logical to begin by delineating the elements that such a hypothesis must address.

Given the validity of the biblical representation of Ezra and Nehemiah as imperial officials and the biblical self-consciousness of their missions as a decisive event in the experience of the Restoration community, it is critical to understand the motivation behind the commissioning of these two figures. The close timing between the missions of these figures strongly suggests that some condition (or conditions) prevalent in the mid-fifth century caused the imperial authorities to initiate these missions. As has already been suggested, the mid-fifth century was a period of considerable disturbance within the western holdings of the Persian empire, commencing with the Egyptian Revolt of ca. 460 BCE and not finding resolution until well into the 440's.[154]

As noted previously, proponents of both the political reorganization hypothesis and the hypothesis that the missions were an imperial inducement to loyalty have appealed to the Egyptian Revolt and its aftermath as the preconditions for the imperial interest in Yehud. Thus, it is apparent that any attempt to develop a new explanation for the transformation of the Restoration community needs to comprehend the circumstances and impact of the revolt and its aftermath.

Modern day knowledge of the events of the Egyptian Revolt is dependent on the reports of several Greek historians, some of which are preserved in second-hand, fragmentary form. Since these are literary sources (though some epigraphic materials may also be utilized in trying to understand the period), the methodology required to interpret these accounts consists of fairly standard historical criticism, the weighing and sorting of literary narratives on the basis of what is known of the

154 A concise summary of the events of this period can be found in Cook, *The Persian Empire,* 127-29.

author's veracity in general terms and evaluating accounts on the basis of what is known from other attestations. As will be explored in the next chapter of this work, to a certain extent this task has already been accomplished by generations of classical scholars. However, inner-disciplinary debates over several of the specific issues involved in the historiography of the revolt and its aftermath, combined with the limited perspective of those who have worked on these materials in the past, require a reexamination of these accounts with an eye toward the role the Egyptian Revolt may have played in altering Achaemenid rule in the West.

For the specific task of understanding the context within which Ezra and Nehemiah were commissioned by the Achaemenid court, it is necessary to examine the two aspects of the revolt that were noted in the discussion of the weaknesses of the hypothesis that their missions represent an imperial effort to induce greater loyalty in the Restoration community. First, attention must be given to the issue of how serious a challenge the revolt represented to imperial control over Egypt and the contiguous territories, including the Levant. Second, the available historical sources need to be assessed for any indications of circumstances that would have caused the Levant in general, and Yehud in particular, to have become the focus of new strategic concerns.

Inherent in any literary source analysis for reconstructing an historical event is a certain bias, that any account will relate a perspectival understanding of causality and significance. This is particularly true in the case of the available narratives of the Egyptian Revolt and its aftermath. Coming as they do from Greek historians, these accounts are naturally oriented toward Athenian involvement in the revolt and the impact the eventual Achaemenid triumph had on Greek interests. While some inferences may be drawn from these narratives that relate to the impact the revolt had on the internal affairs of the Persian empire, there is no real assurance that these inferences reflect the reality of mid-fifth century conditions in the western provinces. As a consequence, an effort must be made to utilize an additional source for the conditions in the Levantine holdings of the Persian empire distinct from both the Greek historians who provide the accounts of the Egyptian Revolt and its aftermath and the biblical narratives that are the subject of this analysis.

One of the continuing frustrations in dealing with the history of the Levant during the Persian period is the relative scarcity of historical sources outside of the biblical narratives. This condition can be ameliorated somewhat by the use of archaeological sources, though with such sources a different kind of interpretive problem is encountered. The evidence of material culture is subject to biasing on at least three levels. First, in the process of deposition some specific cultural activity can limit or preselect the kind of cultural remains encountered.[155] Second, the process of recovery greatly impacts the kind of material evidence recovered and frequently determines the distributional pattern of that evidence. For example, the tendency of archaeological research in the Levant to focus on urban sites has yielded a largely urbanized landscape for the Levant in the Persian period. If the same effort had instead been directed at more rural settings, the resulting picture would have been a rural landscape with quite a different configuration.[156]

Third, in the process of interpreting the data offered by the material culture of the Persian period, one necessarily employs selectivity in chosing what evidence to bring into consideration. Without a specific research design, it is rather simple to convince oneself that the unspoken assumptions that have guided the selection of some data and the exclusion of other data are "proven" by the resulting evidence. As a consequence, while the use of archaeological evidence provides the possibility of an alternative source for reconstructing the conditions of Achaemenid imperial rule in the Levant during the mid-fifth century, this cannot be done in a naive manner but requires a careful consideration of the method employed in utilizing this evidence.

With a comprehension of the events and impact of the Egyptian Revolt and its aftermath in hand as a result of a reexamination and reassessment of the Greek historical sources, and with some indication of the prevailing conditions of Achaemenid imperial rule in the Levant as a result of an examination of the archaeological evidence from the mid-fifth century, it is possible to turn to a consideration of the biblical narratives regarding the missions of Ezra and Nehemiah. Using selected passages, one can seek to relate the scope and particulars of these missions with imperial concerns in an effort to determine how the missions of these two figures reflected specific imperial goals, and how the Restoration community was transformed as the result of these two mis-

---

155 It should also be noted that depositional patterns are acted upon by natural processes that not only affect the varying preservation rates of certain substances but also in some circumstances transport artifactual materials away from the configuration they possessed at deposition.

156 An approximate sense of how urban-oriented archaeological research into the period has been can be seen in the survey of sites yielding Persian materials listed in Stern, *Material Culture,* 1-46.

sions. However, all of the evidence brought to bear on the interpretation of these passages may result in a misunderstanding of the meaning without a corresponding effort to place these activities and events within an explicitly imperial context.

In the discussion that appears in connection with the critique of the political reorganization hypothesis involving the lexical analysis of the various titles borne by the imperial officials in Yehud, one of the main points that was expressed was the necessity to interpret these titles not as they were reflected in a general usage in the biblical corpus but in accord with the technical meaning they possessed in their imperial usage. In an analogous sense, the events and activities that are recorded as part of the missions of Ezra and Nehemiah need to be interpeted not as the author of these materials wished them to be understood but as they relate to a probable imperial context. The biblical narratives present both Ezra and Nehemiah as imperial officials; and assuming there is some historical validity behind this representation, the actions and directives of these two figures may relate in some sense to the intentions and motivations behind their original commissions.

In seeking to understand the imperial context of the missions of Ezra and Nehemiah, it is essential that the distinctive cultural character of an empire be recognized. While it is possible for an individual ruler to amass the necessary military and political resources to impose governance over a spatially and ethnically diverse region, the reproduction of that rule by successors requires the utilization of those techniques and administrative structures normally associated with the term "empire."[157] Within the unique conditions that give rise to an empire, there is little reason to question the thesis that differentiated means emerge for organizing and reproducing the administrative, economic, strategic, and legal aspects of imperial governance. And in the analysis of such elements of the imperial system, the comparative studies of Shmuel Eisenstadt are of particular value in understanding the mechanisms which may be at work in the transformation of the Restoration community.[158] By utilizing such

---

[157] There is no generally accepted technical definition for the term "empire," and it is being used in this work in its widest sense. For a further discussion of this issue, see Maurice Duverger, "Le concept d'empire," 5-23 in *Le concept d'empire,* ed. M. Duverger, (Paris: Presses Universitaires de France, 1980).

[158] Central to this task is Eisenstadt's *The Political Systems of Empires* (New York: The Free Press of Glencoe, 1963) and his essay "Observations and Queries about Sociological Aspects of Imperialism in the Ancient World," 21-33 in *Power and Propaganda: A Symposium on Ancient Empires,* ed. Morgens Trolle Larsen, Mesopotamia 7. (Copenhagen: Akademisk Forlag, 1979).

comparative analyses of imperial systems, it is possible to perceive the means by which the Achaemenid empire might have sought to achieve its goals in the western territories in the midst of the unsettled conditions of the mid-fifth century.[159] With the provision of such an imperial context, the official dimensions of the missions of Ezra and Nehemiah and the means by which they may have contributed to the transformation of the community can receive due consideration.

With this synthesis of historical, archaeological, and biblical evidence, it should be possible to draw plausible conclusions on the meaning of the missions of Ezra and Nehemiah within their context of Achaemenid imperial administration in the Levant during the mid-fifth century BCE. Moreover, the processes that led to the transformation of the Restoration community as the result of these missions should become clearer.

159 Recently IsraelEphʿal has advocated a similar comparative analysis of the logistic techniques utilized by imperial military forces in the Levant; "On Warfare and Military Control in the Ancient Near Eastern Empires: A Research Outline," 86-106 in *History, Historiography, and Interpretation: Studies in Biblical and Cuneiform Languages*, eds. H. Tadmor and M. Weinfeld, (Jerusalem: Magnes Press, 1983).

3

The Literary Sources for the Egyptian Revolt

As discussed above, the reconstruction of Achaemenid imperial history in the mid-fifth century BCE is a necessary prelude to comprehending the context in which the missions of Ezra and Nehemiah were conducted. The dominant interest in this period, to judge from the available and, as will be argued, tendentious sources, was the Egyptian Revolt and its aftermath. It is most fortunate that a variety of Greek historians have left narratives touching on the revolt.[1] Without these narratives, contemporary scholarship would have no knowledge that such an event ever occurred. Being preserved in the works of several different authors, these narratives provide the impression of a variety of perspectives, though, as will be shown, this is not the case. By weighing the internal evidence in each of these narratives, it is possible to determine where they are mutually dependent, offering the possibility of reconstructing the particular history of the revolt.

There are additional difficulties in this situation as well. Perhaps the most serious problem is that all these narratives are the products of Greek historiographical tradition. As Arnaldo Momigliano has noted, the Greek historians believed that Persian royal tyranny was contrary to the logical political order of Athenian democracy, thus the univocally nega-

---

[1] A convenient concordance of these sources may be found in G. F. Hill, *Sources for Greek History Between the Persian and Peloponnesian Wars.* New edition by R. Meiggs and A. Andrewes. (Oxford: Clarendon Press, 1951), 343-44.

tive evaluation given to the Achaemenids.[2] In their understanding, the Achaemenid empire consisted simply of the extension of monarchical power over outlying territories:

> ...there was no effort to see what kept the empire together behind the administrative facade; and—most significantly—there was no attempt to understand how people lived under Persian rule.[3]

This tendency to underestimate Persian achievements is particularly true in the case of the narratives dealing with the Egyptian Revolt. Though ostensibly recounting an indigenous effort to throw off the yoke of Persian domination, these narratives provide little background to the revolt prior to Athenian involvement, and after the Athenian withdrawal from the conflict, they provide little in the way of information on the further conduct of the revolt.

A number of classical scholars have been drawn to the questions of Athenian motivation for involvement in the revolt and the ways in which the eventual Persian triumph affected Athenian imperial behavior prior to the Peloponnesian War. For example, shortly after World War II Paul Cloché published a major essay examining the foreign policy of Athens during the mid-fifth century, including the issue of Athenian diplomatic strategy in joining in the Egyptian Revolt.[4] Cloché returned to this theme a year later, though approaching the same issue on the basis of Athenian military activities during the mid-fifth century.[5] Several decades later, Pierre Salmon published a major study of Athenian policy toward Egypt in the sixth through fifth centuries, including the period of the revolt.[6] More recently, Russell Meiggs has incorporated a significant analysis of Athenian involvement in the Egyptian Revolt into his larger study of Athenian imperialism.[7] As important as each of these studies is for ascertaining the intent and degree of Athenian entanglement in the

---

[2] Arnaldo Momigliano, "Persian Empire and Greek Freedom," in *The Idea of Freedom: Essays in Honour of Isaiah Berlin,* ed. Alan Ryan (Oxford: University Press, 1979), 145.

[3] Momigliano, "Persian Empire and Greek Freedom," 150.

[4] Paul Cloché, "La Politique extérieure d'Athenes de 454-453 a 446-445 avant J.-C.," *Les Études Classiques* 14 (1946):3-32, 195-221.

[5] Paul Cloché, "L'activite militaire et politique d'Athenes en Grece de 457 a 454 et en Égypte de 459 a 454 avant J.-C.," *Revue Belgique* 25 (1946-47):39-86.

[6] Pierre Salmon, *La Politque égyptienne d'Athenes (VIe et Ve siècles avant J.-C.).* Academie Royale a Belgique. Classe des Lettres, Memoires, t. 57, fasc. 6. (Bruxelles: Palais des Academies, 1965).

[7] Russell Meiggs, *The Athenian Empire.* (Oxford: Clarendon Press, 1975), 92-151.

revolt, they are primarily concerned with the Athenian perspective on the event. There is little effort in any of these studies to assess the Achaemenid response to the revolt, nor what that response might reveal about Achaemenid concerns for the security of the contiguous territories.

This same specificity of focus is characteristic of the abundant shorter studies on the revolt in general or on selected aspects of the Athenian involvement.[8] Quite naturally, those studies concerned with the revolt as reflected in particular Greek historians also share this Athenian perspective.[9]

A different kind of specificity of focus is present in the few studies of the revolt from an Egyptian perspective. In these cases, the prevailing tendency of many Egyptologists to denigrate the period of Persian domination of Egypt is manifestly present.[10] The revolt is seen in terms of a nativistic resentment over the imposition of rule by foreigners, with little consideration of its broader implications for Achaemenid imperial policy either in Egypt or in the adjoining imperial holdings.

The reconstruction of the conditions in the western holdings of the Achaemenid empire during the mid-fifth century, however, is dependent on a broader understanding of the events surrounding the Egyptian Revolt. Such an analysis must also consider what historians of antiquity suggest was the import of the conflict on the region. The Athenian-oriented character of most of the previous historical analyses of the ancient accounts of the revolt does not provide this perspective. As a result, in

---

[8] As a brief sampling, see M. O. B. Caspari, "On the Egyptian Expedition of 459-4 B.C.," *CQ* 7 (1913):198-201; A. Momigliano, "La spedizione Ateniese in Egitto," *Aegyptus* 10 (1929):190-206; W. P. Wallace, "The Egyptian Expedition and the Chronology of the Decade 460-450 B.C.," *TAPA* 67 (1936):252-60; and Jan Libourel, "The Athenian Disaster in Egypt," *AJP* 92 (1971):605-15.

[9] See, for example, W. D. Westlake, "Thucydides and the Athenian Disaster in Egypt," *CP* 44 (1950):209-14 and J. M. Bigwood, "Ctesias' Account of the Revolt of Inarus," *Phoenix* 30 (1976):1-25.

[10] Specifically referred to here are F. Kienitz, *Die politische Geschichte Ägyptens vom 7. bis 4. Jahrhundert vor der Zeitwende.* (Berlin: Akademie-Verlag, 1953) and A. B. Lloyd, *Herodotus Book II. Introduction and Commentary.* 2 vols. Études préliminaires aux religions orientales dans l'Empire romain. Tome 43. (Leiden: E. J. Brill, 1975). Typical of the opinions of Egyptologists is John Wilson's four lines on the political history of the Persian period in Egypt: "Within a generation or two, the Persians invaded Egypt and took over the land without much effort. Cambyses was not content to place the land under an Egyptian deputy as the Assyrians had done. He had himself acknowledged by the Egyptian gods as their legitimate son, the pharaoh. There was no cohesion in the land of the Nile, and the rich land had become a dependency of other powers," *The Culture of Ancient Egypt*, 294.

what follows a new assessment of the relevant ancient accounts will be undertaken in an effort to determine what literary evidence may be utilized in reconstructing the Achaemenid side of the revolt.

In this new assessment, a somewhat different presentation will be utilized from the one that has characterized much of the previous literature on the Egyptian Revolt. As a first step, each ancient account will be evaluated on its own terms, in contrast to most other studies that attempt a synthesis of the various accounts in reconstructing the events.[11] Among the factors to be assessed are the individual historian's attitude toward the Achaemenid empire, their overall accuracy in dealing with Persian matters, and the historiographical context within which the narratives recounting the revolt appear.[12] The possibility that a particular historian has employed some preexistent source will also be evaluated.[13] With such information on each individual account of the revolt, it is possible to proceed with the second step of the analysis, a synthesis of the various accounts into a reconstruction of the revolt and its aftermath. Several epigraphic remains, both Greek and Egyptian, are also relevant to this process and will be employed in the synthesis. Throughout this analysis, any mention or inference regarding the Persian imperial response to the revolt will be examined for its significance in understanding the impact of the event on Achaemenid administration in the west.

The Greek Sources

Herodotus

As one of the great literary achievements of the Greek world, the *Histories* of Herodotus has stimulated a stream of studies on the work's

---

[11] It is quite possible that many Classical scholars who have written on the Egyptian Revolt have constructed their synthesis on the basis of a long and intimate acquaintance with the various ancient narratives. However, the criteria for the judgements employed in preferring one account over another are usually unarticulated and often appear arbitrary. For example, Wallace argued that Diodorus' dates for the revolt "are of little value," but to Wallace his dating of the apogee of Athenian naval power in the same period is taken as authoritative; "The Egyptian Expedition," 255, 258.

[12] As will be evident, many of the ancient accounts of the revolt are small portions of larger narratives. Hence, the historiographical context within which these accounts appear often directly relate to the question of what role these accounts play in the historian's overall work and how reliable are the accounts. See, for example, the following discussion of Herodotus.

[13] This is particularly critical for the later historians, such as Diodorus.

compositional unity or lack of it, and the veracity of its contents.[14] While many aspects of these issues are outside the scope of this study, it is essential to consider briefly the matter of the compositional character of the *Histories* and the degree to which Herodotus can be trusted on matters relating to the Persian Empire.

In basic structure, the *Histories* has two distinct parts. The first is made up of four books containing *logoi* dealing with observations on the customs and traditions of Lydia, Babylon, and Egypt. The second part deals with the war between the Persians and the Greeks during the reign of Xerxes (486-465).[15] This distinction in focus between the two parts of the *Histories* has led a number of writers to propose that the work possessed no deliberate overall scheme, but that Herodotus incorporated earlier ethnographic works into a recounting of the Persian campaigns against the Greeks. Challenging this assertion are the results of a number of studies on the unity of the *Histories*, which demonstrate the care with which the work was crafted and the role played by the various *logoi*.[16] As Henry Immerwahr has noted:

> The *Histories* begin and end with Greek relations with the East.... the subject of the work is the growth of the unified power of Asia under the Persians....the *Histories* deal not with Persian history per se, but with the unification of Asia, the attempted extension of empire beyond the borders of the continent, and the failure of this attempt.[17]

The seeming digressions into matters of ethnographic interest, such as the extensive discussion of Egypt in book 2 and part of book 3 of the *Histories*, serve to underline the achievement of the Persian king Cambyses in expanding Achaemenid might by the successful conquest of Egypt.[18] Also, the ethnographic interests of Herodotus may have brought

---

14 For example, see Hermann Bengtson, *Introduction to Ancient History*. Translated from the sixth edition by R. I. Frank and Frank D. Gilliard. (Berkeley, CA: University of California Press, 1970), 103-04.

15 Robert Drews, *The Greek Accounts of Eastern History*. (Washington, DC: Center for Hellenic Studies, 1973), 45-7.

16 For a recent survey of this question, see John Van Seters, *In Search of History: Historiography in the Ancient World and the Origins of Biblical History* (New Haven: Yale University Press, 1983), 15-7; see also the important discussion in Charles W. Fornara, *Herodotus: An Interpretative Essay* (Oxford: Clarendon Press, 1971), 1-23.

17 Henry R. Immerwahr, *Form and Thought in Herodotus*. American Philological Association Monographs No. 23. (Cleveland, OH: American Philological Association, 1966), 42.

18 Drews, *The Greek Accounts of Eastern History*, 56-63; see also Immerwahr, *Form and Thought in Herodotus*, 21-2 for the unified theme of *Histories* 2.1-3.38.

him to the realization that Persian expansion had altered the eastern world forever.[19]

Scholars have long debated the historical accuracy of Herodotus' knowledge of Persian affairs. In several recent studies, the authenticity of the satrapal lists in Herodotus, the Persian names, and even Herodotus' knowledge of family relationships between the various lines of the Persian upper class have been demonstrated.[20] Similarly, others have been able to demonstrate just how wrong Herodotus can be on other points regarding the Persians.[21] Herodotus' seeming insider knowledge of the Achaemenid world is often attributed to his having had access to an informant familiar with the Persian court. The usual candidate for this role is the nobleman Zopyrus, son of the Persian military commander Megabyzos. Herodotus himself records the desertion of Zopyrus to the Athenian side (3.160), and proponents of this thesis point to several places where Herodotus seems to have particularly detailed information about matters Zopyrus would have been in a position to know.[22] If the son of Megabyzos was in fact Herodotus' chief source for his account of Persian affairs, the importance of Herodotus' recounting of Achaemenid history would be considerably enhanced. However, there are strong reasons for rejecting this thesis, as D. M. Lewis has recently reiterated.[23]

Though the general issue of the accuracy of Herodotus' comments on the Achaemenid empire is of importance for any consideration of the *Histories* as a source for the events of the period, it is not the primary issue facing the evaluation of his brief comments on the Egyptian Revolt.

---

19 Fornara, *Herodotus*, 32-3.

20 George Cameron, "The Persian Satrapies and Related Matters," *JNES* 32 (1973):47-56; D. Hegyi, "Historical Authenticity of Herodotus in the Persian 'logoi'," *Acta Antiqua Academiae Scientiarum Hungaricae* 21 (1973):73-87. J. M. Cook's *The Persian Empire,* 15-19, exemplifies the most optimistic assessment of Herodotus' accuracy.

21 For example, O. Kimball Armayor, "Herodotus' Catalogues of the Persian Empire in the Light of the Monument and the Greek Literary Tradition," *Transactions of the American Philological Association* 108 (1978):1-9; see also Van Seters, *In Search of History,* 40-7.

22 For the classic argument for Zopyros as Herodotus' informant, see Joseph Wells, *Studies in Herodotus* (Oxford: Basil Blackwell, 1923), 95-111.

23 Lewis bases his argument on Herodotus' account of the revolt of Babylon, an event Megabyzos was deeply involved in. Among other serious factual errors, Herodotus has it taking place under Darius I, when in fact it was during the reign of Xerxes; "Persians in Herodotus," in *The Greek Historians, Literature, and History: Papers Presented to A. E. Raubitschek* (Stanford, CA: Anma Libri, Department of Classics, Stanford University, 1985), 105-06.

Rather, since most of these comments occur as digressions in the course of other narratives dealing with Egypt, it is of greater significance to assess Herodotus' authority on Egyptian matters. Here the prevailing view, based on Herodotus' own language of personal observation and involvement, is that sometime during the mid-fifth century Herodotus personally visited Egypt and collected his information.[24] Moreover, as will be seen from his comments in 3.12 of the *Histories* to be discussed below, Herodotus gives the impression that his visit came shortly after the suppression of the Egyptian Revolt.[25]

In contrast to this prevailing view, there have always been scholars who viewed with scepticism the extent of Herodotus' personal observations of Egypt. Over a century ago A. H. Sayce compiled some of the more glaring errors within the descriptions of Egypt in the *Histories* and noted that Herodotus validated the accuracy of these observations by claiming to speak from personal observation.[26] More recently, O. Kimball Armayor has thoroughly reviewed Herodotus' appeals to personal observation and noted these narratives reflect Greek perceptions of Egypt rather than actual Egyptian practices.[27] His final conclusion is that Herodotus' authority on any matter relating to Egypt requires careful rethinking.[28]

It is apparent that whatever Herodotus claims to know about Egypt, it cannot be simply accepted as authoritative. Indeed, some have suggested that anything Herodotus affirmed as coming from a source or personal observation is suspect since the appeal to exterior authority was a literary convention employed by the historian to bolster his own historiographic aims.[29] More to the point is the need to determine what role any particular account plays in his general presentation on Egyptian matters. It can be assumed that the more central a role the account plays, the more probable it is that some shaping of the account has occurred to

---

[24] For example, see A. D. Godley's comments in Herodotus, *Herodotus. Volume I: Books I and II.* Loeb Classical Library. (New York: G. P. Putnam's Sons, 1926), 8-9; and Drews, *The Greek Accounts of Eastern History,* 77-81. It should be noted that Herodotus never offers details of his presumed journey to Egypt, and in only one place, 2.29, makes a direct claim to personal travel in Egypt.

[25] Lloyd, *Herodotus Book II,* 61-2.

[26] A.H. Sayce, *The Ancient Empires of the East: Herodotos Books I-III* (London: Macmillan & Co., 1883), xxv-xxvii.

[27] O. Kimball Armayor, "Did Herodotus ever go to Egypt?" *JARCE* 15 (1978):69-71.

[28] Armayor, "Did Herodotus ever go to Egypt?," 70.

[29] See the discussion in Van Seters, *In Search of History,* 43-4, and the literature cited there.

support Herodotus' overall historical vision. As a corollary to this suggestion, the more peripheral a specific account is, the less probable it is that it has been altered to meet a larger historiographic aim.[30]

Given these general guidelines for evaluating Herodotus' statements, it should be noted that of all the Greek historians, he is the closest in date to the events of the Egyptian Revolt. Many have pointed out the absence in the *Histories* of any incidents beyond the years 431 BCE, suggesting that the work was completed in that year.[31] There is also reason to believe that one of the purposes behind the *Histories* was to show the inevitable tragedy associated with any form of imperial expansionism, a theme intended as a warning for the Athenian empire on the eve of the Peloponnesian War.[32] One may thus date the completion of the *Histories* to ca. 430 BCE and see in Herodotus' brief comments on the Egyptian Revolt of the mid-fifth century allusions to events of a few decades earlier.

The first account of the Egyptian Revolt in the *Histories* occurs in the course of Herodotus' recounting of Cambyses' final battle against the armies of an independent Egypt in 525 BCE (3.11). Herodotus then shifts his narrative with the opening, "I saw there a strange thing (*thoma de mega*) of which the people of the country had told me."[33] He goes on to recount that the bones of those who fought in the battle were still preserved on the field of conflict, the Egyptian remains in one place and the Persian remains in another. Herodotus notes the skulls of the Persians were weak while those of the Egyptians were solid, a difference he attributed to the Persian fondness for hats as opposed to the Egyptian preference for leaving the head uncovered. As if to affirm the truth of this observation to his readers, Herodotus adds, "such is the truth of the matter." This brings to the historian's mind another example of friable Persian skulls:

---

30 For a general assessment along similar lines, see the comments of Immerwahr, *Form and Thought in Herodotus*, 324-25.

31 For example, Drews, *The Greek Accounts of Eastern History*, 87-90 and Lloyd, *Herodotus Book II*, Volume 1, 63-66.

32 Fornara, *Herodotus*, 86-7.

33 Quoted from *Histories*, 3.12. The text and translation throughout this discussion is from Herodotus, *Herodotus. Volume 2: Books III and IV*. Loeb Classical Library. (New York: G. P. Putnam's Sons, 1921).

I saw too the skulls of those Persians at Papremis who were slain with Darius' son Achaemenes by Inaros the Libyan, and they were like the others.[34]

While the mixture of ethnological observation and implicit moral judgment that characterizes the main theme of this section has received some brief notice, the additional example of Persian skulls from Papremis has received little comment.[35] Papremis was understood by Herodotus to be located in the Delta of Egypt, probably in the western portion of that region.[36] Given the high humidity of the Delta region, it is hardly credible that Persian bodies would have been left uninterred for several decades, particularly when the Persians were eventually victorious.[37] Thus the historian's claim to personal observation is probably a convention to authenticate the information he is seeking to provide. The identification of Achaemenes as being in Egypt is consistent with other parts of the *Histories* where Achaemenes is said to have been a son of Darius and was sent by Xerxes to administer Egypt (7.7, 7.97). The record of his death here suggests that in the revolt of Inaros, Achaemenes as the main representative of the Persian court was slain. Given that these details are offered in the context of an aside by the historian in the course of a narrative dealing with Cambyses' conquest of Egypt, and despite the use of a conventional authentication technique, there is little reason to doubt the specific content of this aside.

The second account by Herodotus relating to the Egyptian Revolt also has the character of an aside. Again, in the course of a narrative on the fall of Egypt into Cambyses' hands, Herodotus recounts the treatment given to Psammenitus, king of Egypt and son of Amasis (3.14).[38] Though his son was put to death, Cambyses took pity on Psammenitus

---

34 The expression regarding Inaros is *Inaro to Libuos.*

35 For an insightful comment on the ethnographic discussion in relation to Herodotus' larger historiographic vision, see Immerwahr, *Form and Thought in Herodotus,* 242 n. 13.

36 See *Histories,* 2.71 where the hippopotomus is said to be sacred in Papremis, and 2.165 where Papremis is grouped with other western Delta cities. Several suggestions have been offered for a possible location, none receiving general consensus; see Herman de Meulenaere, "Papremis," in *Lexikon für Ägyptologie,* Wolfgang Helck and Wolfhart Westendorf, eds., Band IV (Wiesbaden: Otto Harrassowitz, 1982), 666-67. This point will be returned to in the reconstruction of the Egyptian Revolt.

37 For the high humidity of the Delta region, see Wilson, *The Culture of Ancient Egypt,* 15-7.

38 Herodotus begins by saying these events happened "on the tenth day" after the defeat of the Egyptian army.

and brought him into the court where he stayed until his death (3.15). With little in the way of explanation, Herodotus claims that had Psammenitus only minded his own business, he could have been governor over Egypt.[39] After all, the historian continues, it was the Persian custom to use local dynasties to rule imperial territories, the most notable example being the giving of their fathers' sovereign power (*patros arche*) to Thannyras, son of Inaros, and Pausiris, son of Amyrtaeus. To Herodotus, this is a particularly notable example since, "none ever did the Persians more harm than Inaros and Amyrtaeus."[40] Herodotus' notice of the impact of Inaros and Amyrtaeus on Achaemenid rule in Egypt is made to provide a contemporary example for his readers of a specific phenomenon, a past example of which he is recounting in his narrative. As such, this example plays a subsidiary role in supporting his main narrative (that Psammenitus could have been governor over Egypt); and in all likelihood the example of the treatment of the sons of Inaros and Amyrtaeus has not been shaped to fit this theme.

The third mention of the Egyptian Revolt occurs in a far less certain context than the previous instances. Following a protracted, and badly mistaken, account of Babylon under the Persians, Herodotus turns to tracing the lineage of one of the Persian noble families (3.160).[41] Zopyrus, instrumental in helping Darius' forces suppress a Babylonian revolt, was appointed by Darius as governor over Babylon.[42] Zopyrus was the father of Megabyzos, "who was general of an army in Egypt against the Athenians and their allies." Megabyzos, as the historian continues, was the father of Zopyrus, the one who deserted the Persians and now supported the Athenian cause. Herodotus seems to be trying to provide a connection between contemporaries of his readers (Zopyrus) and the past events he is narrating through the use of genealogical data. The lineage he draws here is brought into the flow of his discourse by the relation of its progenitor to a thoroughly questionable account of a Babylonian revolt against Darius. Still, his identification of Megabyzos as the commander of the army in Egypt that came against "the Athenians and their allies" has the sense of a digression, and probably was included because it brought to the audience's mind a known event.

---

[39] Herodotus says simply that he was caught plotting a revolt against Cambyses.

[40] *kaitoi Inaro ge kai Amurtaiou oudamoi ko Persas kaka pleo ergasanto* (3.15).

[41] For a highly critical summary of this narrative, see Lewis, "Persians in Herodotus," 105-06.

[42] For the centrality of Zopyrus, the father of Megabyzos, in this narrative, see the discussion of Immerwahr, *Form and Thought in Herodotus,* 105-6 n. 83.

The final notice in the *Histories* relating to the Egyptian Revolt appears in book 7. In the preceding section, Herodotus had launched into narrating the events that, in his historiographic vision, had led to the war with Persia. In discussing Xerxes' early reign, he notes that the Persian monarch first suppressed a revolt in Egypt that had broken out on his accession (7.5, 6). After regaining control over the country, Xerxes appointed Achaemenes, his brother, as governor over Egypt. The historian notes:

> This Achaemenes, being the viceroy (*epitropeuonta*) of Egypt, was at a later day slain by a Libyan, Inaros, son of Psammetichus (7.7).

This narrative is focused on a larger historiographic concern of Herodotus, namely the events leading up to the Persian effort to conquer Europe.[43] The additional details regarding Achaemenes, that he was viceroy over Egypt and was later slain by Inaros, function in a limited manner as a way of connecting the events surrounding Xerxes' planning to invade Europe with a later event familiar to Herodotus' audience. As such, there is little reason to suspect the authenticity of these details.

In sum, Herodotus offers a few significant points regarding the Egyptian Revolt of the mid-fifth century. It was led by two figures Inaros, a Libyan, and Amyrtaeus. In a battle at Papremis, the Persian governor (or possibly the satrap) Achaemenes, a brother of Xerxes and an uncle of Artaxerxes I, was killed. The Persians sent an army under the command of Megabyzos to suppress the revolt of Inaros, who in the meantime had been joined by "the Athenians and their allies." While the length of duration for the revolt is not given by Herodotus—nor does he supply any figures for the sizes of the military forces involved in the conflict—the historian does summarize the impact of the revolt on the Persians by noting that the two revolutionary leaders, Inaros and Amyrtaeus, did more damage to the Persians than any others. Since of all the surviving Greek sources, Herodotus was closer in date to the events of the mid-fifth century, his evaluation of the importance of the revolt must be taken seriously.

Thucydides

The Greek historian Thucydides intended to write a history of the Peloponnesian War, one of the most decisive events to affect Athenian fortunes in antiquity. In all probability the work was never completed,

---

[43] Immerwahr, *Form and Thought in Herodotus*, 127-28.

the author's death around 400 BCE bringing his narrative to a sudden end.[44] Nonetheless, Thucydides' reflections on the events that led to the outbreak of the war provide modern students of Greek history with an important window on the mid-fifth century BCE, particularly the events of the Egyptian Revolt.

Despite its incomplete nature, the overall work of Thucydides possesses a relatively clear and symmetrical structure. The structure is so overwhelming as to provide a definitive answer to several generations of scholars who sought to comprehend the *History* as a collection of fragments of various dates, loosely brought together in a narrative form.[45] Given the unified nature of the work as it has been preserved, it is fair to say that whether or not Thucydides ever completed the *History*, enough of the work has survived to provide a clear perception of the historian's artistry and historiographical framework.

The primary thematic concern of Thucydides was the recurrence of patterns and parallels from the past in the experience of the Greek peoples of his own day. That is, as an historian he sought to interpret the devastating events of the Peloponnesian War in light of Athens' previous experiences. Toward this end, the tragic effect of his narrative was emphasized by the use of speeches by primary protagonists, a device intended to create a sense of participation on the part of the reader.[46]

While such structuring and use of historical personages to give voice to the historian's perspectives have naturally engendered scepticism over the reliability of his narratives, there is not sufficient cause for a wholesale rejection of Thucydides as a source for the history of the mid-fifth century. His focus on the importance of individual events and decisions leads to a work of accuracy and authenticity. Thus, while the presentation of factual data has been shaped and molded by the historian's artistry, Thucydides should be allowed to retain his reputation as one of the most careful observers of antiquity.[47]

---

[44] For a detailed overview, see Henry Wade-Gery, "Thucydides," in *The Oxford Classical Dictionary*. Second edition. Eds., N. G. L. Hammond and H. H. Sullard (Oxford: Clarendon Press, 1970), 1067-69.

[45] Hunter R. Rawlings III, *The Structure of Thucydides' History* (Princeton: Princeton University Press, 1981), 250-54.

[46] Rawlings, *The Structure of Thucydides' History*, 259-65. On the general issue of the speeches in Thucydides, see M. I. Findley, *Ancient History: Evidence and Models* (New York: Viking, 1986), 12-3.

[47] Thucydides himself admitted to manipulating the speeches of protagonists to fit his purposes (1.22). For the general issue of the congruence of event and presentation

These general issues regarding Thucydides' approach and method in writing the *History* are crucial elements to understanding the contents of book 1 of his work. In what the historian seems to have regarded as a kind of prolegomenon to his narratives on the Peloponnesian War itself, Thucydides attempts to summarize Athenian history from the end of the Persian wars against Xerxes (ca. 479 BCE) until the outbreak of the hostilities that marked the inception of the Peloponnesian War (ca. 431 BCE).[48] This section, termed the "Pentekontaetia" for its coverage of a strategic half-century of Athenian experience, contains the accounts dealing with the Egyptian Revolt.

Two basic issues are involved in seeking to establish the value of these accounts in their narrative setting. The first question relates to the sources for Thucydides' narratives regarding this period: From what sources did he derive his knowledge of those events prior to his own time? The second question is somewhat more difficult to grasp, but is of crucial importance for understanding and assessing his accounts. The Egyptian Revolt accounts do not occur as a continuous narrative but are split up into three basic segments.[49] Is this literary dislocation the result of Thucydides' adherence to a strict chronological sequence in recounting his *History*, or are there structural or thematic considerations behind this dislocation? The resolution of this second question will provide a basic key to understanding the historian's perspective on the revolt and the chronology of the events themselves.

The question of the sources for the Pentekontaetia is, on the surface, relatively simple to resolve. In his opening comments on his historical method, Thucydides claims that whatever he did not personally know he gained from eyewitnesses whose credibility he had carefully evaluated (1.22). However, there is little probability that he gained most of the factual information on the Pentekontaetia from such eyewitnesses since he was at least a generation removed from many of the events he records.[50] For some aspects of Athenian history, the records of public inscriptions have been suggested as possible sources for his narratives, but where these can be consulted there are insurmountable problems in reconciling

in Thucydides, see Rawlings, *The Structure of Thucydides' History*, 264-72 and the literature cited there.

[48] See the comments of A. French, *The Athenian Half-Century 478-431 B C (Thucydides 1.89-118)* (Sydney: Sydney University Press, 1971), 1-2.

[49] They are 1.104, 1.109-110, and 1.112.

[50] See French, *The Athenian Half-Century*, 2-3.

the historian's accounts with the inscriptions.[51] The conclusion drawn by many scholars regarding the sources for the Pentekontaetia is that Thucydides largely combined oral tradition and a certain amount of extrapolation to fill out his account of the rise of Athenian power between these cataclysmic wars.

With specific reference to the accounts dealing with the Egyptian Revolt, several aspects have raised the suspicion that Thucydides was relying on a non-Athenian informant. For example, Thucydides fails to provide an overall summary of the losses incurred by the Delian League forces in Egypt, information apparently unknown to him.[52] The Soviet scholar R. A. Ghimadyev has taken this point further, arguing that Thucydides evidences a detailed knowledge of the Persian side of the conflict while only touching on the details of the Greek and Egyptian forces involved. Ghimadyev attributes this to the use of a Persian informant, and suggests the expatriate Zopyrus for the role.[53] This is the same Zopyrus mentioned earlier as a possible informant for Herodotus. It can be noted here that Thucydides' knowledge of the Persian side of the campaign is as limited as his knowledge of the Athenian side.[54] This will become apparent in the detailed discussion to follow.

While there are some unexpected elements in Thucydides' narratives of the Egyptian Revolt, these are perhaps best explained as the result of the historian's editorial process rather than indications of the sources for his information. This observation brings into the discussion the second issue relating to the Pentekontaetia, namely its literary and thematic character. It is generally agreed that part of Thucydides' purpose in recounting the events of this crucial half-century of Athenian experience

---

51 The classic example is the difficulty in reconciling Thucydides' accounts of the Delian League tribute payments with the actual Athenian tribute lists of the mid-fifth century. See French, *The Athenian Half-Century,* 79-86 for an extended discussion of this specific problem.

52 H. D. Westlake, "Thucydides and the Athenian Disaster in Egypt," *Classical Philology* 45 (1950):209-10.

53 R. A. Ghimadyev, "A Possible Persian Source for Thucydides' Description of the First Athenian Expedition to Egypt," *Vestnik Drevnej Istorii* 163 (1983):106-11 [Russian]. I am indebted to Dr. Stefan Pugh for his assistance in reading Ghimadyev's essay.

54 Ghimadyev also argues that Thucydides records an abbreviated version of the death of Inaros while Ctesias provides the fuller account. He claims the brevity of Thucydides' account is due to Zopyrus' efforts to conceal the role his family played in Inaros' execution. This attempt to harmonize the major variations in the ancient sources for the aftermath of the Egyptian Revolt is ill-conceived as will be detailed below.

is to trace the ascendancy of Athens from a city in ruins at the end of the Persian wars to a major imperial power by the last quarter of the fifth century.[55] The historian himself begins the narrative of the Pentekontaetia by saying "the way in which Athens reached her position of power was as follows" (1.89).[56] As a consequence, those elements Thucydides chose to recount in the Pentekontaetia were selected for their relevance in demonstrating Athenian imperial might.[57]

Beyond this selection process, Rawlings has been able to show how the structure and themes of the Pentekontaetia, indeed of the entire book 1 of the *History,* are arranged to present an identical pattern to book 6.1-93, which is an introduction to the Sicilian campaign of 415-13 BCE.[58] Specifically, the Pentekontaetia with its emphasis on Athenian expansionism and imperial optimism was intended to contrast with the indecision and internal dissension of the later Sicilian expedition. In the case of the Egyptian Revolt narratives, their inclusion in the Pentekontaetia emphasizes the efforts and energy the Athenians were willing to expend in attempting a far-reaching extension of their might. This contrasted strongly with the feeble attempts to invade Sicily in Thucydides' own time.[59]

This structural aspect to Thucydides' literary art provides the key to the ordering of the revolt narratives in the *History.* Many, following one possible interpretation of Thucydides' self-description of his method, have strenuously argued that the Pentekontaetia adheres to a strict chronological scheme.[60] In this view, the dislocation of the Egyptian Revolt narratives is in keeping with such strict chronological ordering, the narrative needing to be segmented in order to treat other events that occurred in the interval between the beginnings of Athenian involvement (1.104) and the suppression of the revolt by the Persians (1.109-110).[61]

---

55 French, *The Athenian Half-Century,* 2; G. L. Huxley, "Thucydides on the Growth of Athenian Power," *Proceedings of the Royal Irish Academy* 83c (1983):192-93.

56 Translation of A. French, *The Athenian Half-Century,* 17.

57 Hunter R. Rawlings III, "Thucydides on the Purpose of the Delian League," *Phoenix* 31 (1977):5.

58 Rawlings, *The Structure of Thucydides' History,* 62-4.

59 Rawlings, *The Structure of Thucydides' History,* 87-8.

60 For one of the most influential proponents of this view, see A. W. Gomme, *A Historical Commentary on Thucydides. Volume 1: Introduction and Commentary on Book 1.* (Oxford: Clarendon Press, 1945), 391-93. The statement by Thucydides in 1.97 criticizing Hellanikos' *History of Attica* by stating his chronology was "vague" has led Gomme and others to assume this implies the Pentakontaetia was ordered along more rigid chronological lines.

61 Gomme, *A Historical Commentary,* 320.

This understanding of the Pentekontaetia has been opposed by others on the basis of the clear thematic structuring of Thucydides' narratives. The dislocation of the narratives is not the result of some natural chronological scheme but rather is reflective of the emphases and implications that the historian wanted to communicate by the ordering of his presentation.[62] Consequently, in examining the narratives themselves, it is necessary to note French's cautionary observation on the Pentekontaetia as a whole:

> For us, the essay is the main historical source for the period 478-435 BC: we are forced to put it to a use for which it was never intended, and this must always be borne in mind when the essay is treated as a narrative of events.[63]

Thucydides first discusses the Egyptian Revolt in 1.104 of the *History*. This section follows an account of the surrender of the Helots who had revolted against Sparta in 464-463 BCE. Since Thucydides begins 1.103 with, "In the tenth year" (*dekato etei*), this would place the events of 1.103 in 455-454 BCE.[64] If, as has been previously discussed, Thucydides intended to follow a strict chronological presentation, the Egyptian Revolt would by implication have begun in 455-454 or shortly thereafter. Without going into the extensive literature on this point, it need only be noted that the argument has already been presented for understanding the internal ordering of the Pentekontaetia on grounds other than chronology.[65] Thus, in the opening of 1.104, Thucydides provided no chronological marker for the account of the Egyptian Revolt, and it is not necessary to understand that he meant the events to be assigned to the 450s.

The account begins simply:

> Inaros, son of Psammetichus, a Libyan and king of the Libyans adjacent to Egypt, set out from Mareia, the city over Pharos. He led most of Egypt in re-

---

62 See the general comments of French, *The Athenian Half-Century*, 3-4; Philip Deane, *Thucydides' Dates 465-431 B.C.* (Don Mill, Ontario: Longman Canada Ltd., 1972), 5-7; P. K. Walker, "The Purpose and Method of 'The Pentakontaetia' in Thucydides Book I," *Classical Quarterly* n.s. 7 (1957):27-9; and Ron K. Unz, "The Chronology of the Pentekontaetia," *Classical Quarterly* n. s. 36(1986):86.

63 French, *The Athenian Half-Century*, 4.

64 The Greek text of the *History* used in this section is that published in *Thucydides, Volume I: History of the Peloponnesian War Books I and II.* Loeb Classical Library. (New York: G. P. Putnam's Sons, 1919).

65 For a thorough discussion of the dating of the end of the Helot's revolt and the chronology of this section of the Pentakontaetia, see Deane, *Thucydides' Dates*, 22-30.

> volt against King Artaxerxes, and when he made himself ruler he called on the Athenians.[66]

Thucydides thus clearly identified the leader of the revolt and, like Herodotus, knows Inaros bore the title "king of the Libyans." It is important to note here that Thucydides presents a sequence of events: Inaros first initiated an uprising against the Persians and only after declaring himself ruler (*archon*) of Egypt did he seek Athenian aid. The significance of this order will be discussed at length below.

Having introduced the occasion of Athenian intervention in Egypt, Thucydides next turns to describe its extent. A fleet of 200 ships, both Athenian and Delian League vessels, was on an expedition to Cyprus.[67] Without indicating how the fleet was alerted to the Egyptian call for assistance, Thucydides recounts that they sailed "from the sea into the Nile, and were masters of the river and two-thirds of Memphis." Abruptly, the historian notes:

> They attacked the third part, called the White Fortress. Inside that place were Persians and Medes who took refuge there, and those Egyptians who had not joined in the revolt.

With this description of the direct Athenian military participation in the revolt against Achaemenid rule, the historian breaks off, having achieved his goal of highlighting Athenian willingness to commit a substantial force to an attack on Persian holdings.

To summarize this first account of the Egyptian Revolt, Thucydides introduces the Egyptian protagonist who led a popular nativistic revolt against Persian rule. After achieving a position of strength, Inaros called for Athenian assistance and a fleet of 200 Delian League vessels responded. The fleet entered the Nile and were able to move upstream as far as Memphis where a force of Persian loyalists held out in the White Fortress. The Greek forces made a direct assault on the stronghold.

In sections 105-108 of the *History,* Thucydides recounts several other military actions of the Athenians. In 1.105, a naval encounter between Athens and Aegina is recounted, the conflict being in part the result of earlier attacks on Peloponnesian territories by Athenian forces.[68] The date

---

[66] The English translation here and in the following discussions is the author's.

[67] The circumstances of this particular expedition to Cyprus are largely unknown; see French, *The Athenian Half-Century,* 49 n. 73; and Gomme, *A Historical Commentary,* 306.

[68] See Deane, *Thucydides' Dates,* 36 and 110 n. 17.

of this campaign is difficult to determine, but about 456 BCE seems to provide the best possibility.[69] Thucydides records that while Athens was battling Aegina, Corinth invaded the territory of Delian league member Megara, believing that Athens could not come to the assistance of its ally because "many of their forces were away in Aegina and in Egypt" (1.105.3). Assuming the date of 456 BCE is correct for the Aegina campaign, this section suggests enough troops were involved at that time in the operation to contribute to a perception of Athenian weakness by its rivals.

Thucydides resumes the accounts of the Egyptian Revolt in 1.109-110, the second portion of his treatment of Athenian involvement in the revolt. He notes the "Athenians and their allies" had remained in Egypt, presumably during the course of the events he has narrated between his initial discussion of the theme of the revolt in 1.104 and this opening.[70] He also notes that in this interval "the war took many forms," possibly a reference to military actions other than the siege of the White Fortress.[71]

According to Thucydides, the Athenians initially had the upper hand in the protracted siege. The Persian king sent a representative, Megabazus, to Laconia with a supply of gold in an effort to induce the Laconians into attacking the southern territories of the Delian League, thus giving the Athenians a second front closer to home, requiring a withdrawal of forces from Egypt. When this attempt failed, Megabyzos "the son of Zopyrus" was sent with a large army (*stratias polles*) to Egypt:

> They arrived by land, and defeated the Egyptians and their allies in battle and drove the Hellenes from Memphis and, in the end, blockaded them on the island of Prosopitis.

Thucydides' vagueness on the means by which the Persian army entered Egypt argues against Ghimadyev's assertion that the historian's account betrays an informant from the Persian side.[72] The particular

---

[69] See the extensive discussion in Deane, *Thucydides' Dates*, 35-40. A. French, *The Athenian Half-Century*, 50 n. 74 would seem to put the attack somewhat earlier, circa 459 BCE.

[70] For a similar interpretation, see Gomme, *A Historical Commentary*, 320; see also the comments of French, *The Athenian Half-Century*, 58 n. 99.

[71] French, *The Athenian Half-Century*, 58 n. 100 suggests this may also allude to a variety of results from the continuing siege of the White Fortress.

[72] Ghimadyev, "A Possible Persian Source," 108-09. If Thucydides' had received his account of the revolt from a Persian participant one would expect details on the size of the Persian force, the place where the force assembled before marching on Memphis, and the general location where the force entered Egypt.

choice of wording could be understood either as the way the Persian force entered Egypt, and thus implying that it marched through Palestine, or as the way the force attacked the army besieging Memphis. Perhaps Thucydides intended this reference as a contrast to the naval character of the Greek forces. The Persian army, in any event, would have assembled outside of the hostile territory of Egypt prior to arriving either by land or sea in the Delta in order to march on the revolutionary forces. The reference to the "Egyptians and their allies" is a probable label for the combined Egyptian and Greek forces, since there is no indication in the *History* that any other parties were involved in the conflict.[73] Thucydides takes particular note of the reversal suffered by the Greek forces, claiming they were driven out of Memphis and confined to the island of Prosopitis, located in the western Delta.[74]

Thucydides continues his account with one of the few chronological markers in his narrative of the revolt, mentioning that the Delian League forces were under siege at Prosopitis for one and a half years. The Persian army was unable to defeat the Delian forces until diverting the water flow of one of the channels that apparently formed the island in order to ground the Greek ships. Having taken away the Greek advantage of naval maneuverability, Megabyzos led the Persian ground forces over the exposed riverbed and conquered the island.[75]

The historian's narrative continues (1.110.1) by stating that:

> Thus the action of the Hellenes was fruitless after six years of war; and just a few out of the many, who went through Libya to Cyrene, escaped with their lives—most perished.

The fact that Thucydides provides temporal references only for those aspects of the revolt in which the Delian League forces were involved, serves to emphasize the Hellenocentric view of his narration. In this segment, the six year duration of conflict does not refer to the overall length of Inaros' revolt, but only to the period of Athenian involvement, which is apparent by the historian's wording. On the basis of several

---

[73] Contrary to Gomme, *A Historical Commentary*, 321 who suggests this refers to the Libyans. As will be discussed below, the identification of Inaros with the Libyans probably does not imply any foreign involvement in the revolt, and thus the "allies" would be an indirect reference to the Greek forces.

[74] The possible location and character of Prosopitis will be discussed in the reconstruction of the revolt.

[75] Thucydides here seems to contrast again the maritime character of the Delian League's forces with the land-based strength of the Persian forces.

datable events outside of Thucydides' naratives of the Egyptian Revolt, there is a general consensus that the defeat of the expedition occurred in 454 BCE.[76] Using Thucydides' chronological reckoning, the first involvement of Athens and its allies would have been in 460. The notice concerning how some were able to survive the disaster by escaping westward to Cyrene places Prosopitis in the western Delta.

Thucydides turns his attention briefly (1.110.2-3) to the fortunes of the two Egyptians who had initiated the uprising:

> The entirety of Egypt came under the King's rule, except Amyrtaeus, the king of the marshes. Both because of the expanse of the marshland and because the marsh dwellers are the best warriors among the Egyptians, they [the Persians] could not capture him. Inaros, the king of the Libyans who instigated the whole affair throughout Egypt, was taken by betrayal and impaled.

The historian's account reveals knowledge of the title, "king of the marshes," for Inaros' compatriot Amyrtaeus. The significance of this title will be discussed below. The escape of Amyrtaeus and his subsequent elusiveness implies that part of the Delta region continued to be unsettled.[77] Inaros, however, was delivered into the hands of the Persians by betrayal and was put to death. There is no indication in Thucydides' account of any time interval between Inaros' capture and his execution.

The narrative in the *History* shifts quite suddenly at this point (1.110.4-5) from the fates of the Egyptian revolutionary leaders to a new peril to the Greek naval forces:[78]

> From Athens and the other members of the confederacy, a relief fleet of fifty triremes sailed to Egypt and put in at the Mendesian mouth, not knowing what had happened. The infantry attacked them from the land and a Phoenician fleet from the sea, destroying most of the ships. Only a small number escaped. So ended the great Egyptian expedition of the Athenians and their allies.

The small size of the relief fleet as described by Thucydides contrasts sharply with the earlier fleet of two hundred ships. This difference has caused a number of historians of the period to offer several explanations

---

76 See Deane, *Thucydides' Dates*, 34 and the literature cited there. See also Meiggs, *The Athenian Empire*, 93-95.

77 Thucydides returns to Amyrtaeus at 1.112.

78 For example, French, *The Athenian Half-Century*, 60-61 n. 107, sees the discourse on the fates of Inaros and Amyrtaeus as an insert into Thucydides' narratives on the fate of those Athenians involved in the revolt.

of the narrative at this point. In that these explanations relate to reconciling Thucydides' narratives with those of other Greek historians, the matter of the differences in fleet size will be discussed in the course of reconstructing the events of the revolt. In terms of Thucydides' own narratives, the sending of the relief fleet demonstrates the continuing support of the revolt by the Delian League. The tragic end of the entire affair is reiterated by the historian's sobering conclusion to this section.[79]

Thucydides makes his final direct references to the Egyptian Revolt in *History* 1.112. Between his summary statement on the defeat of the allied forces in 1.110 and this segment, the historian reviews several inconclusive military efforts by the Athenian forces, including the failed effort to restore a deposed Thessalian monarch to his throne.[80] Though of an uncertain date, these events most likely occurred in the same year as the defeat of the allied forces in Egypt, namely, 454 BCE. At the opening of the segment containing a brief notice of the continuation of the revolt in Egypt, Thucydides includes a rare time reference, claiming "three years later a truce for five years was made between the Peloponnesians and the Athenians." The presumed date of this truce is three years after 454 BCE, or around 451.[81]

Following the notice of this diplomatic cessation of hostilities against the Peloponnesian states, Thucydides notes that an expedition was launched against Persian control of Cyprus. Led by Cimon, the force consisted of two hundred Delian League vessels.[82] The historian claims:

> Sixty of these vessels sailed to Egypt as requested by Amyrtaeus, the king of the marshes, while the rest laid siege to Kitium. Kimon died, and there was a famine, so they left Kitium, and sailing off Salamis in Cyprus, they battled the Phoenicians and Cilicians, on land and on sea. Victorious, they returned home, accompanied by the vessels that had been in Egypt.

With this turn from disappointment and frustration to victory, Thucydides moves on to other topics, never to resume the narration of events in Egypt.

---

[79] French, *The Athenian Half-Century,* 61 n. 108 notes how unusual this narrative closure is in the *History* and understands it as a deliberate effort to highlight the solemnity of the defeat in Egypt.

[80] See 1.111.

[81] For more detailed discussions on the dating of this truce, see Deane, *Thucydides' Dates,* 63-6 and French, *The Athenian Half-Century,* 63 n. 16.

[82] One should note the same number of ships were said to have embarked against Cyprus in 460 BCE (1.104).

The concerted Delian League action in Cyprus in 451 suggests a continuing Greek interest in disrupting Achaemenid control in the eastern Mediterranean basin even after the defeat in Egypt of 454 BCE. Amyrtaeus, the former co-conspirator with Inaros, is once again identified as the "king of the marshes" and is presumably leading the continuing unrest in the Delta region of Egypt.[83] Thucydides is true to form in failing to detail how the Delian fleet received Amyrtaeus' appeal for aid, but is quite precise in noting that sixty ships were sent in response. While his narrative is hardly clear as to the exact sequence of events following the decision to lift the attack against Kitium, it would appear that only the larger portion of the fleet engaged a combined Persian land and naval contingent off Salamis. After defeating the Persian forces, this portion of the fleet joined with the vessels that had been sent to Egypt and sailed for home port. True to his Hellenic bias, Thucydides provides no further information on the fortunes of Amyrtaeus, or how the Delian League vessels were employed in Egypt.

The overall episodic nature of Thucydides' treatment of Athenian involvement in the Egyptian Revolt serves to emphasize the historian's selective employment of the events of the revolt. His purpose is not to detail the events of the revolt in a connected narrative, but to present the revolt as a major effort by the Delian League acting in concert to drive Persian influence from the Mediterranean. The defeat of the allied forces, compounded by the loss of the relief squadron of fifty ships, provides a context for the Athenian decision to enter into the truce with the Peloponnesian states noted by Thucydides at the opening of 1.112. The losses suffered in the effort to insure the independence of Egypt left the Delian League too weak to attempt a direct military confrontation with Sparta and its allies.[84] Similarly, once the truce is mentioned, the historian simply notes renewed actions against Persian interests in the Mediterranean, both on Cyprus and in Egypt, to demonstrate the continuing threat the Delian League posed for Persian hegemony in the eastern Mediterranean.

For Thucydides, the Egyptian Revolt functions as both a paradigm for the authentic role of the Delian League under Athenian leadership and an illustration of the dire implications that follow a major military defeat. Acting jointly, the Delian League forces are portrayed as taking the struggle against Persia onto imperial territory, in keeping with the

---

[83] As he was at 1.110. The importance of this title, *en tois elesi basileos,* will be discussed further in the reconstruction of the Egyptian Revolt.

[84] Walker, "The Purpose and Method," 36.

historian's conception of the ideal of the league.[85] Yet, the tragedy for the historian lies in the fact that while pursuing such a noble cause both the league and Athens experienced a grave loss of naval capability, forcing a diplomatic agreement with its southern rival.

The disaster of the Egyptian expedition serves as a pivotal point in Athenian expansionism in Thucydides' view, marking the movement from military actions against both Sparta and Persia, to a concern with the struggle against Persia alone. In this light, it is significant that immediately following the safe return of the league fleet from the campaign in Cyprus in 451, Thucydides marks the passage of an indefinite time span in order to return to narrating Athenian efforts at expansion on the Greek mainland. In this case, it is a disastrous campaign against Boetia (1.113).[86] For Thucydides, despite the positive outcome to the expedition to Cyprus, Athenian strength and influence was still waning in the wake of the losses suffered in Egypt. In Thucydides' understanding, Athenian involvement in the Egyptian Revolt had forever altered the relations between Athens and the other Greek states, setting the stage for the subsequent disaster of the Peloponnesian War.

Ctesias

Another important source for the events of the Egyptian Revolt is contained in a section of the *Persica* by Ctesias. According to tradition, Ctesias served as a physician in the court of Artaxerxes II around the end of the fifth century and into the early years of the fourth century.[87] Following his return to his native Cnidos, Ctesias produced a series of works in the first quarter of the fourth century reflecting on his Persian experiences. The most ambitious of these productions was the *Persica,* a composition designed to trace Persian history from the Assyrians and the Medes up through the first years of Artaxerxes II (405-359 BCE).[88]

---

85 Rawlings, "Thucydides on the Purpose of the Delian League," 8.

86 Gomme, *A Historical Commentary*, 338-39.

87 For what can be reconstructed of Ctesias' life and career from various sources, see Felix Jacoby, "Ktesias," in *Paulys Real-Encyclopädie der Classischen Altertumswissenschaft,* Georg Wissowa and Wilhelm Kroll, eds.. Band 11, T. 2 (Stuttgart: J. B. Metzler, 1922), 2032-2034; and Truesdell S. Brown, "Suggestions for a Vita of Ctesias of Cnidus," *Historia* 27 (1978):1-19. The latter study by Brown is remarkably uncritical in its use of Ctesias' self-testimony considering the general character of Ctesias' work.

88 For the full list of Ctesias' literary activity, see Drews, *Greek Accounts of Eastern History,* 103-04.

One major purpose behind Ctesias' effort to cover the range of Persian history was to discredit Herodotus' previously circulated accounts of Persian affairs. Calling Herodotus a liar at several points, Ctesias made claim to a superior method in compiling his history, basing his narratives on matters he personally witnessed or had received from those who had witnessed them.[89] Regrettably, it is not possible to check the entirety of the *Persica* for other indications of Ctesias' historical method since the work is preserved solely as an epitome prepared by the reknowned Byzantine scholar Photius. While some have questioned the accuracy of Photius' summary of the *Persica,* there is adequate evidence to conclude that the epitome was prepared with care and provides an accurate, though selective, representation of Ctesias' work.[90]

Despite his claim to a superior historical method, Ctesias has not fared well at the hands of critics. In antiquity, it was widely reputed that he falsified his "facts" and thus was to be viewed with suspicion.[91] In more recent times, the verdict has rarely been kinder. In the course of a major summation of his work and historiographical method, Felix Jacoby concluded that Ctesias had invented much of his narrative in order to compile a "scandal history" (*Skandelgeschichte*).[92] Arnaldo Momigliano attempted to rehabilitate Ctesias somewhat by appealing to the historian's reliance on erroneous Greek traditions regarding the events in his *Persica,* though with mixed results.[93] On Ctesias' accounts of the Persian Wars, historians of the period have generally discounted his value as a

---

89 A description of Ctesias' overall historiographic approach was given by Photius, our primary source for the contents of the *Persica.* For a discussion of Photius' comments and their implications, see Drews, *Greek Accounts of Eastern History,* 104-05 and Joan M. Bigwood, "Ctesias as Historian of the Persian Wars," *Phoenix* 32 (1978):22-3.

90 Godefrey Goosens, "Le sommaire des Persica de Ctesias par Photius," *Revue Belge de Philologie et d'Histoire* 28 (1950): 513-21; and Bigwood, "Ctesias' Account of the Revolt of Inarus," 2-5.

91 See, for example, Plutarch's comments cited in Bigwood, "Ctesias' Account of the Revolt of Inaros," 1 n. 1.

92 Jacoby, "Ktesias," 2059-71.

93 Arnaldo Momigliano, "Tradizione e Invenzione in Ctesias," *Atene e Roma* n.s. 12 (1931):15-44, reprinted in *Quarto Contributo all storia Deglia Studi Classici e del Mondo Antico.* Storia e Letteratura 115. (Rome: Edizioni di Storia e Letteratura, 1969), 181-212. See also the comments of Drews, *Greek Accounts of Eastern History,* 197 n. 56. A similar evaluation has been made by Amelie Kuhrt, "Assyrian and Babylonian Traditions in Classical Athens: A Critical Synthesis" in *Mesopotamien und seine Nachbarn: Politische und kulturelle Wechselbeziehungen im Alten Vorderasien vom 4. bis 1. Jahrtausend,* Hans-Jorg Nissen and Johannes Renger, eds. [25th Recontre Assyriologique Internationale] Berliner Beiträge zum Vordern Orient Band 1. (Berlin: Dietrich Reimer Verlag, 1982), 544-45.

source for this pivotal conflict. One noted scholar, in describing Ctesias' account, concluded:

> Clearly the old aristocratic ideal of the pursuit of historical truth for its own sake, an ideal which was followed by Herodotus, Thucydides, and Xenophon in their different ways, had been discarded by Ktesias for the exciting possibilities of historical fiction.[94]

Moreover, in a very thorough evaluation of Ctesias' accounts of the Persian Wars, Joan Bigwood concluded:

> ...there is exceedingly little in this whole account of the Wars which could be right and nothing which suggests concern for the truth or careful investigation. Instead we have all the ingredients which one associates with Ctesias—reckless army statistics, misidentified characters, simplifications, astounding confusions, chronology which is muddled, some degree of anachronism, and a certain amount of bias.[95]

With specific reference to Ctesias' narratives regarding the Egyptian Revolt and its aftermath, it is indeed fortunate that they have been the subject of a detailed analysis by Professor Bigwood.[96] Though the following comments may slightly diverge at points from the conclusions she presents, Professor Bigwood's study remains an essential contribution to understanding Ctesias as a source for this event and its impact on Greek eastward expansionism.[97]

Ctesias begins his narration of the Egyptian Revolt on the heels of his account of Artaxerxes' successful conquest of Bactria.[98] He records

---

94 C. Hignett, *Xerxes' Invasion of Greece* (Oxford: Clarendon Press, 1963), 8-10. For a similar evaluation of Ctesias, see A. R. Burn, *Persia and the Greeks: The Defense of the West 546-478 B.C.* (New York: Minerva Press, 1968), 11-3.

95 Bigwood, "Ctesias as Historian of the Persian Wars," 36. In the light of the preceeding and clearly evidenced presentations for regarding Ctesias with scepticism, it would be superfluous here to critique in detail the naive and uncritical views of F.W. König, *Die Persika des Ktesias von Knidos.* Archiv für Orientforschung; Beiheft 18. (Graz: 1972). For the inadequacy of König's work, see Bigwood, "Ctesias as Historian of the Persian Wars," 1 n. 2; and Robert Drews, "Sargon, Cyrus, and Mesopotamian Folk History," *JNES* 33 (1974):391 n. 23.

96 Bigwood, "Ctesias' Account of the Revolt of Inarus."

97 For a similar positive evaluation, see Frye, *History of Ancient Iran,* 127 n. 154.

98 The standard text of Photius' epitome of Ctesias is that of Felix Jacoby, *Die Fragmente der griechischen Historiker: 3 Teil. Geschichte von Staedten ünd Volkern C. Autoren über einzelne Lander.* (Leiden: E. J. Brill, 1923-58), No. 688. This is the text used here. The account of the revolt and its aftermath covers sections 32-40. Regarding the conquest of Bactria, it was apparently under Achaemenid rule long before Artaxerxes

that Egypt revolted, led by Inaros, "a Lydian (*ludiou andros*)" and "another Egyptian" who had made preparations for the conflict. The Athenians sent forty ships to assist the revolt at the request of Inaros. According to Ctesias, Artaxerxes desired to personally lead the Persian forces being sent to suppress the revolt, but his advisors restrained him. In his place, he sent his brother Achemenides with 400,000 footsoldiers and a fleet of eighty ships. Inaros led the allied forces against this effort to quell the revolt and was victorious. In the course of the battle, Inaros had wounded Achemenides, who died from his wounds. The Greek naval force, led by the admiral Charitimides, was victorious over the Persian fleet, taking twenty vessels captive while sinking thirty others.

Artaxerxes responded by sending a new, larger force against the rebels, this time commanded by Megabyzos. This force consisted of another 300,000 footsoldiers who, when joined to the 200,000 troops remaining from Achemenides' army, made a total imperial force of 500,000 men. An additional naval force of 270 ships was sent, which, when added to the surviving thirty ships of Achemenides' fleet, gave a total of 300 ships for the new offensive. Ctesias also records that "a mighty battle occurred," with considerable losses among both armies, though the Egyptian forces incurred a higher number of casualties. Megabyzos managed to wound Inaros "in the thigh," causing him to try to escape the battle. The historian summarizes the outcome by simply stating that the Persians were completely victorious.

According to Ctesias, Inaros and "those Greeks who were not killed in combat along with Charitimides" escaped to a place called "Byblos," which is described as a "fortified city in Egypt."[99] With the exception of this city, all Egypt submitted to Megabyzos. Believing Byblos to be "impregnable (*analotos*)," Megabyzos entered into an agreement with Inaros and the soldiers with him, a group of more than 6,000. The agreement pledged that no harm would come to Inaros' forces, nor to the Greeks with him, if they would accompany Megabyzos on his return to Persia.

Megabyzos appointed Sarsamas to the post of satrap over Egypt and, taking Inaros and the Greeks with him, returned to the Persian court. There he found Artaxerxes extremely angry with Inaros on account of the death of Achemenides, his brother. Megabyzos related to

---

I, possibly as early as Darius I; Frye, *History of Ancient Iran*, 112. This is merely one example of Ctesias' freedom in dealing with the chronological order of events.

[99] The description of Charitimides' role at this point is somewhat vague. See Bigwood's comments in "Ctesias' Account of the Revolt of Inarus," 9 n. 31.

the king what had transpired and how he had captured Byblos by guaranteeing the rebels safe departure and promising no harm would come to Inaros and his army.

Ctesias goes on to claim that Amytis, the wife of Artaxerxes, was also outraged over the death of Achemenides and the fact that Inaros and the Greeks were not being punished. She demanded that they be punished, but both Artaxerxes and Megabyzos refused. She continued to plead her son's case to the king, and after five years had passed Artaxerxes gave in, turning Inaros and the Greeks over to Amytis.[100] The queen ordered Inaros impaled along with fifty of the Greeks and also demanded the Egyptian rebel's head be cut off.

According to Ctesias, Megabyzos was seized by a deep emotion over the incident, and went into mourning. He left the Persian court and returned to "Syria, to his estate (*surian ten eauton choran*)," where he had already transported the other Greeks in secret. Megabyzos revolted from the empire and was able to assemble a force of 50,000 men. The court sent Ousiris with 200,000 troops against Megabyzos, and a battle ensued. Megabyzos and Ousiris wounded each other; and when Ousiris fell to the ground severely wounded, Megabyzos insured that none of his forces would kill him. Many Persian troops fell in battle, and Megabyzos' two sons, Zopyrus and Artyphe, battled courageously as Megabyzos won a hard-fought victory. He sought to insure Ousiris' safety, and sent him back to Artaxerxes.

The Persian king responded by sending another expedition out against Megabyzos, this time led by Menostates, son of Artarius, the satrap of Babylon and brother of Artaxerxes. When Menotates and Megabyzos engaged in battle, the Persian forces fled. As in the earlier battle, Megabyzos wounded the Persian commander, though his wounds were not fatal. Menostates and his companions fled, and Megabyzos won a surprising victory. Artarius sent emissaries to Megabyzos and convinced him to negotiate with Artaxerxes to end the dispute. Megabyzos asked that he be allowed to stay in his territories, and his request was granted. Artaxerxes sent several representatives to Megabyzos and after assurances that he would not be harmed, Megabyzos returned to the Persian court where he received a full pardon from the Persian monarch. Ctesias' account goes on to describe other difficulties between Artaxerxes and Megabyzos, but these are presented as the result of circumstances

100 There is clearly some confusion here between Amytis, the wife of Artaxerxes, and Amestris, the mother of Artaxerxes and presumably, Achaemenides. See Bigwood, "Ctesias' Account of the Revolt of Inarus," 8 for a discussion of this point.

subsequent to the resolution of Megabyzos' revolt over the execution of Inaros and the fifty Greeks.

As is readily apparent, Ctesias' account of the Egyptian Revolt is at variance with the accounts of Herodotus and Thucydides. In her major survey of the historical value of Ctesias' account, J. M. Bigwood isolates the special problems of the participants' names and the sizes of the military forces involved. She offers important observations on the role of textual corruption in altering some of the names of the participants; but notes that in the case of Herodotus' "Achaemenes" and Ctesias' "Achaemenides" (in both historians the Persian official slain by Inaros), there is an unresolvable conflict.[101] In the case of military statistics, Ctesias' tendency to use conventional figures is particularly noticeable, as well as his ability to provide exact numbers for every military engagement recounted in the *Persica*.[102] For such details, it appears that one cannot claim the variations in Ctesias' narratives are indicative of access to a superior source of information on the revolt.

While the total narrative offered by Ctesias is of interest for its numerous deviations from the accounts of either Herodotus or Thucydides, for the purposes of the present study only a few critical portions require examination to determine the usefulness of Ctesias' version. These are the conditions under which Athenian forces entered the revolt, the manner in which the imperial forces under Megabyzos regained control over Egypt, and the circumstances of Megabyzos' revolt from the Achaemenid court.

The initial progress of the revolt as narrated in the surviving epitome of the *Persica* is sketchy at best, though whether due to the selectivity of Ctesias or Photius is uncertain.[103] Ctesias calls Inaros a "Lydian," in distinction to both Herodotus and Thucydides who knew him as a Libyan. Curiously, Ctesias knows another Egyptian was active with Inaros, but evidences no knowledge of his name. Ctesias attributes the revolt to Inaros' leadership, and both Thucydides and Ctesias have Inaros calling upon Athenian aid prior to any military action. The Athenian response as

---

101 Achaemenes is identified as the son of Darius, while Achaemenides is the brother of Artaxerxes and thus presumably the son of Xerxes; Bigwood, "Ctesias' Account of the Revolt of Inarus," 7-10.

102 Such specificity in every circumstance is suspicious; Bigwood, "Ctesias' Account of the Revolt of Inarus," 11.

103 Bigwood, "Ctesias' Account of the Revolt of Inarus," 17-8.

presented by Thucydides is far more dramatic than in Ctesias, with 200 vessels joining the effort versus Ctesias' forty vessels.[104]

Ctesias seems to understand that the Persian forces Inaros and the Athenians battled were sent from the Persian court in response to the revolt. By having the Persian forces sent by Artaxerxes, and by emphasizing that Artaxerxes himself wanted to lead the effort to suppress the revolt, Ctesias reduces the meaning of this international conflict to a dispute between individuals. This is further articulated by attributing the Persian commander Achemenides' death to a wound inflicted by Inaros. As will be seen below, this tendency is characteristic of Ctesias' historiography. In any event, it is highly probable that an open revolt against Persian control of Egypt would have encountered active resistance from garrisoned imperial forces. And, in all likelihood, at least a portion of these forces would have been stationed at Memphis, the administrative center of the satrapy since Cambyses' conquest of Egypt. Ctesias seems to have inserted an entire scenario in conflict with what might be expected under such circumstances.

Turning to the suppression of the revolt by the Persians, Ctesias knows it consisted of 300,000 troops. Following the breaking of the siege of Memphis, Ctesias has Megabyzos wound Inaros (another larger conflict reduced to individual terms), causing the Egyptian rebel and 6,000 surviving Greeks to escape to the fortified city of "Byblos." The historian records no siege of any duration and has Megabyzos negotiate a settlement because Byblos was thought to be impregnable. There is no known place in Egypt either from ancient or classical times called "Byblos," and one would be hard pressed to claim that such a place would drop from history if a major military force believed it to be impregnable.[105]

Regarding the fates of the leaders of the revolt, Thucydides has Amyrtaeus successfully continuing the revolt in the "marshland," while Inaros was captured and impaled by the Persians. Ctesias, though acknowledging "another Egyptian" was involved in instigating the revolt, has no interest in that individual's fate. Inaros, on the other hand, is spared only to become a pawn in another set of individual conflicts

[104] The degree of Athenian involvement in the revolt as indicated by the number of ships sent to assist Inaros has been the subject of considerable debate. This matter will be returned to in discussing the reconstruction of the revolt.

[105] See particularly the thorough discussion of this point, and other indications that Ctesias was rather careless with geographical references, in Bigwood, "Ctesias' Account of the Revolt of Inarus," 23-5.

involving the powerful Megabyzos, Artaxerxes, and the queenmother Amestris.

This apparently clear conflict in accounting for the death of Inaros between Thucydides and Ctesias has been the subject of a recent effort to harmonize these divergent narratives. R. A. Ghimadyev has argued that Thucydides' detailed knowledge of Persian military operations in his narrative of the Egyptian Revolt betrays a Persian informant. This assertion has been closely questioned in the course of the previous discussion of Thucydides' narratives. Ghimadyev goes on to postulate that Zopyrus, one of Megabyzos' sons, was the informant and sees Thucydides' account of Inaros's death as strangely abbreviated when compared to Ctesias. Ctesias, he argues, was an authority on court intrigues; and his account of Inaros' death at the hands of Amestris cannot be dismissed. Rather, since Zopyrus was related to Amestris, he deliberately withheld from Thucydides the role his relatives had in the death of the Egyptian rebel. Thus Ctesias' detailed and involved account of Inaros' ultimate demise is the correct one.[106]

Outside of any compelling need to seek a Persian informant for Thucydides' narratives, there is no reason to resort to Ghimadyev's defense of Ctesias. In addition, there are other flaws in his reasoning. The most telling critique is Ghimadyev's failure to recognize the role of individual conflict in Ctesias' *Persica.* Inaros fatally wounds Achaemenides, and Megabyzos wounds Inaros. Entering the court, Artaxerxes is angry with Inaros, not for instigating a major revolt, but because he wounded Achaemenides. Megabyzos puts his honor on the line to preserve Inaros, and Artaxerxes accedes to this, though the queenmother Amestris confronts both men over the need for vengeance against Inaros. This pattern of major conflicts in the sphere of international affairs being brought down in scale to the level of heroic contests or bitter arguments among members of the royal court is common in Ctesias, and at least in the latter case is a device used to expose the frailty of the Persians.[107] In short, even if Ctesias possessed access to gossip regarding the court intrigues of past Achaemenid monarchs, his narrative possesses nothing to lead one to conclude that, in fact, Inaros escaped the suppression of the revolt he instigated only to face execution five years later.

This brings into view the final aspect of Ctesias' narrative for analysis, the revolt of Megabyzos. As was discussed in chapter two, it is the assumption of the reality of this revolt that has led many to assume the

---

106 Ghimadyev, "A Possible Persian Source," 109-10.

107 Bigwood, "Ctesias' Account of the Revolt of Inarus," 19.

Levant was unsettled in the early years of the 440s BCE, triggering Nehemiah's mission to Jerusalem. As presented by Ctesias, Megabyzos' rebellion against Artaxerxes was the direct result of the impalement of Inaros after Megabyzos had given the rebel solemn assurances that no harm would come to him. Obviously, if Inaros had been captured in the course of the suppression of the revolt in Egypt and had been executed shortly afterwards there is no reason to accept the veracity of Ctesias' further narrative relating to Megabyzos and his break from Artaxerxes. Moreover, the character of the narratives of Megabyzos' revolt themselves demonstrate their artificiality and conformity to Ctesias' particular concerns, casting further doubt on their veracity.

In Ctesias' recounting of the events of Megabyzos' break from the Persian court, one finds the conflict is individualized, from Megabyzos versus the king to Megabyzos and the various commanders of the forces sent to quell his rebellion wounding each other. In addition, there are fantastic claims, such as Megabyzos having secretly transported 5,950 Greek troops to his estate before he revolted, or a large imperial expeditionary force fleeing in terror when Megabyzos and its commander locked horns in combat. There are repeating motifs, Megabyzos taking steps to insure no harm would come to Ousiris, just as he had promised Inaros no harm would come to him. And when there are clear historical allusions, such as making Aratxerxes' brother Artarius the satrap of Babylon, they are garbled. Akkadian texts from the Murashu archives mention an "Artaremu" who has a son "Manushtanu" (Ctesias' "Menostates") this same figure also served as the satrap of Babylon. However, Artaremu is functioning in the 420s, not the early 440s as Ctesias' narrative would imply.[108] In sum, the whole account of Megabyzos' revolt and reconciliation with Artaxerxes is riddled with suspect events and personalities. There is nothing in Ctesias' narratives of Megabyzos' revolt to lend credence to the account they present.

To conclude this assessment of the value of Ctesias' narrative for reconstructing the Egyptian Revolt, there is little reason to grant it any authority. What it possesses in human interest and heroic conflict, it lacks in substantive information. As J. M. Bigwood concludes, "This account of the Egyptian episode may afford us some amusement. But there is no major historical problem which it will help us resolve."[109]

---

108 A.L. Oppenheim, "The Babylonian Evidence of Achaemenian Rule in Mesopotamia," in *The Cambridge History of Iran. Volume 2: The Median and Achaemenian Periods*, ed. I. Gershevitch. (Cambridge: Cambridge University Press, 1985), 565.

109 Bigwood, "Ctesias' Account of the Revolt of Inarus," 21.

Diodorus Siculus

The final major account of the Egyptian Revolt by an ancient historian is found in the work of Diodorus Siculus. Writing in the second half of the first century BCE, Diodorus sought to write a universal world history and accordingly entitled the work the *bibliotheke istorike,* "Library of History." Seeking to connect all world events into a synchronistic framework, Diodorus structured his *bibliotheke* to reflect a chronological progression. Thus books 1-10 deal with descriptions of the ancient Near Eastern cultures and the early legends of the Greco-Roman world up to the Persian Wars. Books 11-20 cover the events from 480 to 302 BCE, while books 21-40, which are regrettably preserved only in fragmentary form, take the historian's accounts up to ca. 60 BCE.[110]

A continual question regarding the *bibliotheke* has been the nature of Diodorus' sources. The historian himself lays claim to various travels and in all likelihood visited Egypt at one point.[111] Despite this potential for firsthand reportage, Diodorus more often relies on other historians of antiquity, employing them in an arbitrary manner with little regard for their possible value.[112] For example, in book 1 when Diodorus discusses the history, religion and social customs of Egypt, he is apparently relying on Hecataeus of Abdera in the main, while incorporating other fourth- and third-century historians, all rearranged and tailored to fit his own concerns.[113] More to the point, in book 2 where he offers a discussion of Assyria and Media, Diodorus has made extensive use of Ctesias, though he has supplemented Ctesias' information with other narratives from other writers.[114]

For his recounting of the Egyptian Revolt in book 11, Ctesias is at least one of the sources Diodorus has consulted. Some of his information may also be derived from the now largely lost work of Ephorus, a Greek historian of the early fourth century BCE whose work underlies much of Diodorus' books 11-16.[115]

---

110 For a general overview of the *bibliotheke istorike,* see C. H. Oldfather's comments in the introduction to *Diodorus of Sicily, Vol. 1 Books 1 and 2.1-34.* Loeb Classical Library (London: William Heinemann Ltd., 1933), vii-xvi.

111 See the comments of Oldfather in *Diodorus of Sicily,* Vol. 1, xvi-xix.

112 Drews, *The Greek Accounts of Eastern History,* 131.

113 Anne Burton, *Diodorus Siculus Book 1: A Commentary.* Études preliminaires aux religions orientales dans l'empire romain. T. 29. (Leiden: E. J. Brill, 1972), 7-34.

114 J. M. Bigwood, "Diodorus and Ctesias," *Phoenix* 34 (1980):195-207.

115 G. L. Barber, "Ephorus" in *The Oxford Classical Dictionary.* Second Edition. ed. N. G. L. Hammond and H. H. Scullard (Oxford: Clarendon Press, 1970), 388.

The work of Ephorus was widely used in antiquity, and generally he was highly regarded, despite the knowledge in antiquity that his narratives were riddled with errors.[116] Where it is possible to isolate narratives in the *bibliotheke* that are dependent on Ephorus, it is apparent that Diodorus was no slavish copiest. Rather, he used considerable invention to adapt Ephorus to his moralizing purposes, and where Ephorus or the other major works available to him failed to provide a moral lesson, Diodorus turned to minor writers to fill out the narrative.[117] While it is not possible to determine a source for all of the information found in book 11, both Ctesias and Ephorus are the most likely, and there is little chance that Diodorus utilized otherwise unknown sources for his account.[118]

Diodorus begins his account of the Egyptian revolt with the accession of Artaxerxes to the throne:

> But when the inhabitants of Egypt learned of the death of Xerxes and of the general attempt upon the throne and the disorder in the Persian kingdom, they decided to strike for their liberty.[119]

After assembling an army, the insurgents threw out the Persians in charge of collecting Egyptian tribute and established "a man named Inaros" as king. He raised an army consisting of native Egyptians, and also hired foreign mercenaries until he possessed "a considerable army."

According to Diodorus, the next move by Inaros was to contact Athens and appeal for military assistance, offering them a "share of the kingdom:"

> And the Athenians, having decided that it was to their advantage to humble the Persians as far as they could and to attach the Egyptians closely to them-

---

116 Guido Schepens, "Historiographical Problems in Ephorus" in *Historiographia Antiqua: Commentationes Lovanienses in Honorem W. Peremans.* Symbolae Facultatis Litterarum et Philosophiae Lovaniensis. Series A Vol. 6 (Louvain: Leuven University Press, 1977), 96-7.

117 See C. I. Reid, "Ephorus Fragment 76 and Diodorus on the Cypriote War," *Phoenix* 28 (1974):142-3; and Robert Drews, "Diodorus and His Sources," *American Journal of Philology* 83 (1962):385-86.

118 J. M. Bigwood, "Ctesias' Account of the Revolt of Inarus," 5 makes the point that in places Ephorus has also made use of Ctesias, lending further complication to the question of Diodorus' reliability.

119 Book 11.71. The translation is that of C. H. Oldfather, published in *Diodorus of Sicily IV, Books IX-XII.40.* Loeb Classical Library (London: William Heinemann Ltd., 1946), 311. The Greek text as published in the Loeb series is the basis for all comment on Diodorus' phrasing in the present work.

selves against the unpredictable shiftings of Fortune, voted to send three hundred triremes to the aid of the Egyptians.

The Athenians enthusiastically began to prepare the force to join Inaros. On the other side, as soon as Artaxerxes heard of the full preparations the Egyptians were making to insure their independence, he decided he needed to muster a force greater than theirs if he was to suppress the revolt. He began to acquire soldiers from all parts of the empire and to build ships. With this conclusion, Diodorus breaks off his narration of the revolt to turn to other events in the western Mediterranean.

The narration of the revolt resumes at 11.74, where Diodorus offers a date of 462 BCE for the first Persian counterattack against Inaros. The historian records that Artaxerxes appointed Achaemenes, his uncle, to lead the forces. The combined army consisted of "more than three hundred thousand" troops. Without describing how long they marched, or what route they took, Diodorus claims the Persian forces entered Egypt and made camp "near the Nile." The Egyptian forces, supplemented with troops from Libya and Athens, were ready for the Persians. When the Athenians arrived with 200 ships, the battle order was drawn up and "a mighty struggle took place." The battle was initially in the Persians' favor, but when the Athenians began to take the offensive, the Persian forces fled. There was a great slaughter among the fleeing troops, and after losing much of their army, the Persians took refuge in the White Fortress. The Athenian forces then began to besiege the stronghold.

When Artaxerxes heard of his defeat, he sent emissaries to the Lacedaemons asking them to attack Athens in order to draw the Athenian forces out of Egypt. The Lacedaemons refused. Having failed on the diplomatic front, Artaxerxes prepared another expeditionary force, this time appointing Artabazus and Megabyzos, "men of outstanding merit," in charge of the effort.

In book 11.75, Diodorus continues his narration, noting that the second Persian force set out in 461 BCE. He records that Artabazus and Megabyzos left Persia with "more than three hundred thousand" men, resting their land-based forces when they arrived in Cilicia and Phoenicia. There they ordered "the Cyprians and Phoenicians and Cilicians" to provide naval vessels. Three hundred vessels were readied and outfitted with all the necessary armaments, while the land forces were drilled and trained. Almost the entire year was spent in these preparations. Diodorus concludes by stating that at the same time, the

Athenians still held the White Fortress "near Memphis" under siege but the Persian defenders continued to hold out.

Diodorus returns to the events of the revolt in book 11.77, dating the Persian counterattack to 460 BCE. With all their preparations completed, the land forces "advanced overland through Syria and Phoenicia, and with the fleet accompanying the army along the coast, they arrived at Memphis." The appearance of the expeditionary force broke the siege of the White Fortress. However, rather than follow up on this tactical advantage, the Persian forces "avoided any frontal encounters" and tried to bring the revolt to an end using "stratagems (*polemon*)." The Athenian navy was moored at the island of Prosopitis, so the Persians diverted the Nile from flowing around the island. This rendered the Athenian naval forces impotent and opened Prosopitis up for a land attack. The Egyptians, seeing the loss of Athenian naval maneuverability, deserted their Attic allies and surrendered to the Persians.

As the historian's narrative continues (11.77), the Athenians set their vessels on fire to prevent them from falling into Persian hands. They began to exhort each other to do nothing unworthy of their honor:

> ...with a display of deeds of valour surpassing in heroism the men who perished in Thermopylae in defense of Greece, they stood ready to fight it out with the enemy.

The Persian command, realizing they could not defeat such men without suffering terrible losses, "made a truce with the Athenians whereby they should with impunity depart from Egypt." The Athenians, who "saved their lives by their courage," made their way from Libya to Cyrene, eventually returning safely to Greece. With this, Diodorus closes his account of the revolt and provides a final closure (11.92.5) to the chapter as a whole.

While they are not directly linked by Diodorus to the events of the revolt, it is important to continue following the narratives of the *bibliotheke* that trace the subsequent affairs between the Greeks and the Persians because of their relevance to the issue of the impact of the revolt on Levantine affairs. In book 12, in a section Diodorus dates to the year 450 BCE (book 12.3), Diodorus opens by noting the Athenians had lost "all their ships" in the conflict in Egypt. "After a short time," the Athenians decide to militarily press the Persians again, "on behalf of the Greeks in Asia Minor." A fleet of 200 triremes was fitted for war and Cimon was placed in command. The objective was for Cimon to sail for

Cyprus where he was to engage the Persian forces located there. Diodorus claims that:

> At that time the generals of the Persian armaments were Artabazus and Megabyzos. Artabazus held the supreme command and was tarrying in Cyprus with three hundred triremes, and Megabyzos was encamped in Cilicia with the land forces, which numbered three hundred thousand men.

In the course of the campaign, the Athenian fleet quickly achieved dominance and conquered the cities of Citium and Marium "by siege." The Persians sent additional ships "from Cilicia and Phoenicia," and Cimon set out from Cyprus to meet them in battle in the open sea. The Athenians once again gained the upper hand, sinking "many" and capturing one hundred ships with their crews. The remainder of the Persian fleet escaped eastward, and Cimon pursued them "as far as Phoenicia." The survivors entered Cilicia in order to join Megabyzos and his land forces. The Athenians followed in after them, and after a battle the Athenian forces were victorious. Cimon and his men returned to their ships and sailed back to Cyprus. With this closure, Diodorus ends his narration of the year's events.

The account picks up again at 12.4, dated to 449 BCE. Diodorus recounts that Cimon "subdued the cities of Cyprus." Sensing the strategic importance of the Persian garrison at Salamis, Cimon decided it would make an ideal focus for the campaign. If he conquered Salamis, the capital of Cyprus, he would control the entire island. Moreover, since his fleet controlled the waters around Salamis, the Persians would be unable to break the siege. The Persian impotence in the face of a concerted military attack would "cause them to be despised," leading to total Athenian control of the eastern Mediterranean. Diodorus interjects, "and that is what actually happened." Cimon began the siege of Salamis, his men daily assailing the walls of the garrison.

Meanwhile, Artaxerxes learned of the defeat of the Persian forces on Cyprus (apparently a reference to the Athenian capture of Cypriot cities other than Salamis) and took counsel with his advisors. He concluded that it would be advantageous to arrive at a diplomatic solution to the friction between Persia and Athens over control of the Mediterranean. The solution was negotiated on the Athenian side by Callias, and involved Persian assurances to allow the Greek cities of Asia Minor "to live under laws of their own making," to prohibit Persian satraps from coming near the coast of Asia Minor, and to refrain from deploying Persian naval units beyond certain points in the Aegean. For their part, the Greeks promised to no longer send armies into regions under imperial control. Once the treaty was ratified, the Athenian forces withdrew from Cyprus, their leader Cimon having died of an illness while pressing the campaign. Diodorus concludes by claiming the Athenians "won a brilliant victory and concluded most noteworthy terms of peace."

The negotiations to which Diodorus refers, often termed the "Peace of Callias," marked a major change in the Athenian conflict with the Achaemenid empire. Diodorus understands the conditions that led to this diplomatic resolution as the result of a successful Athenian campaign against the Persian control of Cyprus.

The narratives of Diodorus regarding the Egyptian Revolt and succeeding events evidence certain tendencies that cast suspicion on their reliability as documentation of the period. One obvious aspect to his historiographic viewpoint is a strongly Athenian moralizing of the events. The Athenians enter the conflict to humble the Persians, and join in the task "with great enthusiasm (11.71.6)." In the first engagement between the supporters of the revolt and the Persian forces, the Persians had the upper hand until the Athenians went on the offensive (11.74.3). The Athenians, who Diodorus is quick to point out "won the victory by their own deeds of valour," are the only force that lays siege to the White Fortress, and the native Egyptian forces are not to be found (11.74.4). When the Egyptians see the second imperial army enter the arena and destroy the Athenian naval advantage, they surrender to the Persians (11.77.3). In contrast, the Athenians display "deeds of valour" that rival Greece's stand against Xerxes' effort to invade Europe a generation before (11.77.4). In short, Diodorus consistently portrays the events of the revolt with an eye toward glorifying the role of the Athenian forces. Their involvement in the Egyptian Revolt is presented as an heroic, yet ill-fated, blow against Persian tyranny.

A second tendency is the patterned use of numbers when Diodorus is ostensibly providing actual statistics of troop strength. The first imperial army sent against the revolt in Egypt numbered "more than three hundred thousand (11.74.1)." The second imperial army also numbered "more than three hundred thousand (11.75.1)." And later, when Megabyzos was encamped at Cilicia, he had with him "three hundred thousand (12.3.2)" troops. This use of "three hundred thousand" as a general number for a large force is not restricted in use to the narratives of the Egyptian Revolt but appears in a similar patterned use throughout the *bibliotheke*. For example, the Persian force readied for the invasion of

Greece under the command of Xerxes numbered "more than three hundred thousand (11.1.7)." Similarly, the Persian army commanded by Artaxerxes III (359-338) that attacked Egypt in order to bring it back into the empire numbered "three hundred thousand (16.40.6)."[120]

This same patterned use of numbers is evident in Diodorus' reports of naval strength. The Athenians sent "three hundred triremes" to assist the Egyptians (11.71.5), while the second imperial force sent to quell the revolt also had "three hundred triremes (11.75.2)." In the events succeeding the revolt, Diodorus claims the Persian fleet stationed on Cyprus also consisted of "three hundred triremes (12.3.1)." Again, this is a number that appears in other contexts throughout the *bibliotheke*.[121] In sum, Diodorus' military statistics are plainly arbitrary figures for a large force and demonstrate that he had no access to reliable documentation on the relative sizes of the forces involved in the conflict on either side.

The chronological framework utilized by Diodorus is no more reliable than the military statistics he supplied. The historian employed, in part, the *kronika* of Apollodorus of Athens, a work that attempted to arrange world events, both historical and legendary, from the fall of Troy to the year 144 BCE.[122] Even here, Diodorus has frequently compressed Apollodorus' time-spans or rearranged the sequence of events to fit his whims.[123] Moreover, in Diodorus' own chronology of the revolt there are internal contradictions. For example, at 11.77.1-5 he has the destruction of the Athenian fleet and the negotiated settlement of the revolt taking

---

120 Other examples abound: the Sybarians who faced the Crotonians numbered "three hundred thousand (10.23)" and the Carthaginian forces invading Sicily numbered "not less than three hundred thousand (11.20.2)." This clear tendency to use the number three hundred thousand as a stock figure for military strength also mitigates against Bigwood's contention that the numbers in Diodorus reflect a dependence on Ctesias; see "Ctesias' Account of the Revolt of Inarus," 6 n. 22. This does not affect Bigwood's other arguments for seeing Diodorus as utilizing Ctesias for this period.

121 For other examples, see Bigwood, "Ctesias' Account of the Revolt of Inarus," 11 n. 41.

122 John Francis Lockwood, "Apollodorus" in *The Oxford Classical Dictionary*. Second Edition. (New York: Oxford University Press, 1970), 83.

123 "The worthlessness of Diodoros as an independent authority for the chronology of the 5th century has often been demonstrated..." Gomme, *A Historical Commentary*, 53 n.3. Gomme provides a clear examination and assessment of Diodorus' chronological value in 51-54. Nor has this general opinion of Diodorus changed in the light of more recent research: "Diodorus' chronological blunders— arising from his ill-considered (and very lazy) attempt to fit the topical narratives of his sources into the annalistic framework of his own history— are...notorious..."; R. K. Unz, "The Chronology of the Pentekontaetia," 68 n.3.

place in the year 460 BCE. However, at 12.3 the loss of the Athenian fleet in Egypt is followed by an Athenian decision "after a short time" to prosecute the campaign against Persian forces on Cyprus, a decision dated to 450 BCE.[124] As a consequence, the chronological testimony of Diodorus can be accepted only after careful scrutiny.

Diodorus' narratives become more suspect when the influence of Ctesias can be traced in them. Diodorus has the first imperial expedition against the revolt sent straight from the court of Artaxerxes, apparently deriving this from Ctesias' description of Artaxerxes' sending Achaemenides to quell the revolt.[125] Diodorus recounts that the Athenians, trapped on the island of Prosopitis, turned themselves into a formidable adversary. Megabyzos and the Persians, on seeing the bravery of the Athenians, negotiated an agreement by which the Athenians received safe passage from Egypt (11.77.3-5). This certainly echoes Ctesias' account of the Greek retreat into "Byblos" where their impregnability caused Megabyzos to negotiate their surrender in exchange for their safe conduct to Persia.[126] Given the unreliability and sensationalism of Ctesias' account, the fact that Diodorus has partly relied upon it demonstrates Diodorus' lack of concern with his sources, casting further suspicion on his narrative.

In sum, Diodorus presents a mixed narrative of uncertain reliability. His moralizing tendencies, use of stock statistics, chronological inconsistencies, and reliance on Ctesias all raise serious questions as to the historical veracity of his narratives. There is no evidence that Diodorus, writing some four centuries after the events of the revolt, was either able to compile or disposed to author an account of the revolt with greater care than his predecessors.

The Egyptian Sources

Despite the attribution by the Greek historians of royal titles to both Inaros and Amyrtaeus, there are no direct Egyptian sources for the

---

124 Other contradictions are discussed by Lloyd, *Herodotus Book II. Volume 1 Introduction*, 39-40.

125 Bigwood, "Ctesias' Account of the Revolt of Inarus," 7 n. 25 sees this influence from Ctesias.

126 Bigwood has noted the close connection of a truce with the Greek forces in both Ctesias and Diodorus, but she did not draw attention to the similar circumstances under which both narratives understand the truce to have been made; "Ctesias' Account of the Revolt of Inarus," 6 n. 22. These two elements, the perception by the Persians of Greek military strength and the resulting promise of safe passage, are too similar in Ctesias and Diodorus to be coincidental.

revolt. P. G. Elgood has claimed that inscriptions of Amyrtaeus, accompanying repairs made to the temple of Amun of Hibis in the el-Kharga Oasis, point to control over all of Egypt by Inaros' associate.[127] The inscriptions Elgood referred to apparently do not exist, and his assertion may be the result of a misreading of the excavation publication.[128]

Though no direct references to the revolt appear in Egyptian texts, traditions of a much later date focus on Inaros, or at least the name Inaros, raising this individual to heroic proportions. One example is the partially published cycle of stories termed the *Cycle of Pedubastis.* Two of the narratives in this cycle, "Inaros and the Griffin" and "The Contest for the Breastplate of Inaros," focus on a figure named Inaros as a heroic personage.[129] In "The Contest for the Breastplate of Inaros," Inaros' son and another figure battle for possession of Inaros' prized armor, much like a scene in the *Iliad.*[130] There are clear indications that these legends did not achieve their final form until after the Persian period and this, when combined with the military prowess of the figure of Inaros, makes it likely that these stories grew up around the exploits of the revolutionary of the mid-fifth century.

---

127 P. G. Elgood, *Later Dynasties of Egypt* (Oxford: Basil Blackwell, 1951), 129.

128 No inscription of Amyrtaeus at Kharga is noted in Bertha Porter and Rosalind L. B. Moss, *Topographical Bibliography of Ancient Egyptian Hieroglyphic Texts, Reliefs, and Paintings. VII. Nubia, The Deserts, and Outside Egypt.* (Oxford: Clarendon Press, 1951), 277-90. In the final excavation report, H. E. Winlock disavowed the possibility of several minor repairs happening during the brief reign of another Amyrtaeus, an ephemeral ruler of the early Fifth century BCE; Winlock, *The Temple of Hibis in El Khargeh Oasis, Part I: The Excavations.* Publications of the Metropolitan Museum of Art, Egyptian Expedition, Volume XIII. (New York: Metropolitan Museum of Art, 1941), 20. In any event, no inscriptions of an "Amyrtaeus" were reported.

129 A description of the stories in this cycle, several of which are unpublished, as well as their extensive use of historical allusions is provided by Kitchen, *The Third Intermediate Period in Egypt,* 455-61.

130 Published with a German translation in Edda Bresciani, *Der Kampf un den Panzer des Inaros (Papyrus Kroll).* Mitteilungen aus der Papyrussammlung der osterreichischen Nationalbibliothek (Papyrus erzherzog Rainer), neue serie VIII. (Vienna: Georg Prachner, 1964). According to Bresciani, the text is written in a Demotic script of the Roman period (6). While one cannot be absolutely certain the figure of Inaros is rooted in the revolutionary of the mid-fifth century, the prominence of Inaros' son in this narrative seems in keeping with the high office granted to his son according to Herodotus. See Kitchen, *The Third Intermediate Period,* 458 for a general discussion of this point.

A second story cycle involving a figure named Inaros focuses on the deeds of Setne Khamwas.[131] An individual known in history as a son of Ramses II who also served as high priest at Memphis, Setne appears in these stories as a powerful magician. In his adventures he is often accompanied by his foster-brother Inaros, though it is doubtful that this is a confusion with the revolutionary of the same name from the Persian period.[132] At any rate, in these stories Inaros is portrayed as a passive figure, faithfully carrying out the esoteric instructions of his more prominent brother Setne. Thus, while the *Cycle of Pedubastis* seems to reflect the memory of an heroic stature for Inaros, the Khamwas cycle apparently has little to do with the revolutionary.

In a similar vein, Diodorus records a curious tradition that one of the three subsidiary pyramids to the south of the pyramid of Mycerinus at Giza was built by "Inaros," though the historian notes that several others are also credited with its construction (1.64.13).[133] Diodorus fails to specify which of the many figures bearing the name "Inaros" was the one credited with the pyramid.

None of these varied traditions contribute to the reconstruction of the Egyptian revolt with the exception of the *Cycle of Pedubastis,* which may provide a dim reflection of a protracted struggle for Egyptian independence. Inaros' effort to reinstate Egyptian self-determination against the superior imperial forces earned him a later memory of a great warrior and hero, an equal in a sense to the great military heros of early Greek legend.

Reconstruction of the Egyptian Revolt

As was discussed previously, a number of scholars have attempted to reconstruct the events of the Egyptian Revolt and its aftermath. Usually these reconstructions are based on efforts to achieve some synthesis or harmony of the variant narratives of the revolt found in the

---

[131] Preserved in Cairo Papyrus 30646, dated to the Ptolemaic era. See Battiscombe Gunn's comments in *Land of Enchanters: Egyptian Short Stories from the Earliest Times to the Present Day,* ed. Bernard Lewis (London: Harvill Press, 1948), 67-83. A convenient English translation may be found in Miriam Lichtheim, *Ancient Egyptian Literature: Volume III: The Late Period* (Berkeley: University of California Press, 1980), 125-38.

[132] There is no evidence that Ramses II had a son named Inaros; for additional discussion of the historical setting of these legends, see Kenneth A. Kitchen, *Pharaoh Triumphant: The Life and Times of Ramses II, King of Egypt* (Warminster: Aris & Phillips, 1982), 229-30.

[133] See also Burton, *Diodorus Siculus Book I: A Commentary,* 191 for a discussion of this tradition.

Greek historians just reviewed. However, as has also been shown, several of these narratives present completely divergent accounts of the revolt and its progress, compelling a synthetic approach to consist of little more than a process of picking and choosing among sometimes dubious sources. Moreover, most previous reconstructions seek to understand the revolt in terms of what it signified for Athenian domination of the Delian League both before and after the defeat of the league forces in Egypt. This is a legitimate concern of those seeking to comprehend the course of Aegean history, but offers limited insight into the internal dynamics of the Persian empire. To this end, yet another reconstruction is attempted here, but with more attention to the revolt within its Achaemenid imperial setting.

For the convenience of presenting a reconstruction of the course of the revolt, the event can be divided into four consecutive episodes. Each episode is marked by a significant shift in the course of the revolt. The first episode is the initiation of the revolt by the Egyptians without recourse to Athenian assistance. The second episode is marked by the intervention of Delian League forces and their joining the Egyptians in an effort to drive the Persians from Egypt. The imperial response in sending an expeditionary force against the revolutionaries and their allies constitutes the third episode. And finally, the aftermath of the revolt, particularly the disposition of the leaders of the rebellion, marks the close of the event.

First Episode: The Initiation of the Revolt

Of all the ancient literary sources, only Diodorus, who was the furthest removed in time from the event, presents a coherent picture of the revolt's inception. His claim that the revolt began when the death of Xerxes became commonly known in Egypt is plausible, though it is uncertain just how soon after 465 BCE this may have been. One document from the Persian garrison at Elephantine is dated to early in 464 BCE, "at the beginning of the reign of Artaxerxes," suggesting that the revolt could have begun as early as 464 when news of the transition in the crown would have first reached Egypt.[134] In all probability, either 464 or 463 BCE would have seen the initiation of Inarus' revolt. As an analogous situation, when Darius I died in 486 BCE, portions of Egypt revolted

134 Cowley, *Aramaic Papyri of the Fifth Century*, 15-17; S. H. Horn and L. H. Wood, "The Fifth-century Jewish Calendar at Elephantine," *JNES* 13 (1954):8-9; and Bezalel Porten, *Jews of Elephantine and Arameans of Syene: Fifty Aramaic Texts with Hebrew and English Translations* (Jerusalem: The Hebrew University, 1980), 6-7.

within the same year in a feeble attempt to gain independence, suggesting that once news of a change in monarchs had spread rapidly from the Iranian plateau to Egypt, the effort to seize the opportunity for national independence was soon to follow.[135]

Diodorus goes on to claim that the insurgents, "after expelling the Persians whose duty it was to collect the tribute from Egypt," declared Inaros king. Thucydides has a considerably different account, recording that Inaros, "a Libyan and king of the Libyans adjacent to Egypt, set out from Mareia" and led most of the country in revolt against the Persians. Ctesias also has Inaros leading the revolt, rather than being selected a king by a rebellious populace. The only solution to these divergent narratives is to examine the presentation of Inaros in the Greek accounts in order to determine his standing prior to the revolt.

Thucydides calls Inaros "king of the Libyans," and Herodotus, the writer closest in time to the revolt, calls him a "Libyan (3.11)," and implies that he possessed "sovereign power (3.15)," as well as noting that he was the "son of Psammetichus (7.7)." The name "Inaros" itself is Egyptian in origin, being the Hellenized form of the Egyptian *irt-ḥr-irw*, "May the eye of Horus be against them."[136]

Thucydides' reference to Inaros as "king of the Libyans" and Herodotus' knowledge that Inaros was a Libyan requires a thorough evaluation. In the history of Egypt, there are accounts as early as the reign of Ramses III (1182-1151 BCE) of tribes of Libyans moving from the western desert into the Delta region of Egypt and settling there.[137] Some

---

135 For this first Egyptian revolt, see Cook, *The Persian Empire,* 99. Bresciani, "La satrapia d'Egitto," 179-80 notes a number of inscriptions from Xerxes' second year (485 BCE), implying that news of Xerxes accession had travelled swiftly to Egypt and that the revolt was short-lived.

136 Following the grammatical analysis suggested by Marianne Guentch-Ogloueff, "Noms propres imprécatoires," *Bulletin d'Institut français d'archéologie Orientale* 40 (1941):117. Wilhelm Spiegelberg, "Der name *Inaros* in ägyptischen Texten," *Recueil de Travaux relatifs à la philologie et a l'archéologie égyptiennes et assyriennes* 28 (1906):197-201 interpreted the name as "The eye of Horus is against them," a rendering followed by Hermann Ranke, *Die aegyptischen Personennamen.* (Glückstadt: J. J. Augustin, 1935), Volume 1, 42 number 11, and Volume 2, 96. In the Pedubastis cycle the name is rendered *Irt-Hṛ-r-rw;* Bresciani, *Der Kampf um den Panzer des Inaros,* 18, Column 1, lines 5-6.

137 Gardiner, *Egypt of the Pharaohs,* 287; Jean Yoyotte, "Les Principautés du Delta au temps de l'anarchie Libyenne (études d'histoire politique)," *Mélanges Maspero: l'Orient Ancien.* Fasc. 4, Mémoires publiés par les membres de l'Institut francais d'Archéologie orientale, Caire. Tome 66. (Cairo: Institut français d'Archéologie orientale, 1961), 148.

time after 950 BCE, these Libyan groups had become powerful enough to lay claim to the Egyptian throne and members of these groups constituted the rulers of the Twenty-second Dynasty of Egypt, ruling Egypt until the mid-eighth century.[138] During the Twenty-second Dynasty, an hereditary line of rulers emerged among these "Libu" in the Delta region along the western edge. These rulers bore the title, "Great Chief of the Libu," and became increasingly important as semi-autonomous leaders of ethnically distinct warriors.[139] These "Great Chiefs" controlled the Western Delta of Egypt, and even into the period of Persian domination continued to play a significant role as district administrators in the Delta region.

The conclusion to be drawn from this evidence is that Inaros' identification as "king of the Libyans," possessing "sovereign power," is almost certainly a reference to his functioning as a "Great Chief of the Libu."[140] Such an hereditary chiefdom would also be consonant with the transferral of his office to his son, as recorded by Herodotus (3.15).

Herodotus' assertion that Inaros was the son of Psammetichus is more problematic to interpret. The most probable "Psammetichus" the historian has previously mentioned is Psammetichus III, pharaoh of Egypt when Cambyses conquered the land of the Nile. Psammetichus attempted to conspire against the Persian king and was put to death, presumably in 525 BCE.[141] If Inaros were born in 525, and the revolt began at its earliest possible date of 465 BCE (the accession of Artaxerxes I), then he would have been at least sixty years old when he led the Egyptians against their Persian overlords. Though not an impossibility, it does seem out of keeping with the general portrayal of Inaros as a vigorous and effective leader on the battlefield. Moreover, Inaros is never identified as "king of the Egyptians" prior to his successful revolt, a title he could rightly lay claim to if he was in fact the legitimate heir to Psammetichus' throne. In addition, none of the other Greek historians know of Inaros' parentage, a lineage one would rightly expect to have been widely circulated if it placed the revolutionary in the Egyptian

138 Kitchen, *The Third Intermediate Period,* 287-347; O'Connor, "New Kingdom and Third Intermediate Period," 277-78.

139 Lloyd, "The Late Period," 309-10; on their continuing service under Achaemenid rule, see Salmon, *La Politique égyptienne d'Athenes,* 93-4.

140 As noted by Donald B. Redford, "Notes on the History of Ancient Buto," *Bulletin of the Egyptological Seminar* 5 (1983):90 n. 171.

141 Herodotus 3.15. Herodotus also records that Psammetichus' son, unnamed but presumably the eldest and thus next in line for succession to the throne, was put to death when Cambyses conquered Egypt (3.14).

royal line. Consequently it seems more consistent with the evidence as it is preserved to adopt Donald Redford's observation that Herodotus is referring to a non-royal Psammetichus (Egyptian *Psamtek*), given the popularity of the name in the post-Saite (the Twenty-sixth) Dynasty era.[142]

Understanding Inaros' title "king of the Libyans" as a reference to his actual role as "Great Chief of the Libu" may also clarify the status of his corevolutionary Amyrtaeus. Though not mentioned by Herodotus, Amyrtaeus does figure prominently in the accounts of Thucydides, being twice called "the king of the marshes."[143] If this Greek title represents some Egyptian office, then a strong possibility for that office can be presented. In later Egyptian experience, an "Amyrtaeus" was able to defeat the Persians in 404 BCE, his rule constituting the brief Twenty-eighth Dynasty of the historian Manetho. In Egyptian, this king's name appeared as *Amun-ir-ds* or "Amun does effectively."[144] The Greek form of the name, Amyrtaeus, is thus rooted in an authentic Egyptian name. Since Amyrtaeus is called "king of the marshes" by Thucydides, and Herodotus claims he, like Inaros, possessed "sovereign power" that was granted to his son (3.15), then it would be reasonable to assume Amyrtaeus likewise held the post of an hereditary chiefdom.

In the Western Delta region in addition to the "Great Chief of the Libu" there is clear evidence of another hereditary post, that of the "Great Chief of the Meshwesh." The Meshwesh were a subgroup of Libyan people from the West who had gradually become assimilated into Egyptian society. Like the Libu with whom they were closely associated by native Egyptians, the Meshwesh instituted an hereditary leader over their communities, the "Great Chief."[145] By the era of Persian rule, the "Great Chief of the Meshwesh" had a long history as an integral part of Egyptian rule in the western Delta, having functioned as a regional

---

142 Redford, "Notes on the History of Ancient Buto," 90 n. 171. See also Salmon, *La Politique égyptienne d'Athenes*, 93 n. 4 for a similar rejection of Psammetichus III as Inaros' father.

143 In 1.110 and 1.112. Herodotus mentions an "Amyrtaeus" who is associated with the "marshlands" as part of a fabulous tale regarding the predecessor of Shabaka (Shebaco 716-701 BCE) in 2.140. Since Herodotus never associates this figure with any activity against the Persians and the context in which the name appears is so outrageous, it is conjecture to assume that this figure is the same as Inaros' corevolutionary.

144 Gauthier, *Le livre des rois d'Êgypte*, Volume 4, Mémoires publies par les membres de l'Institut français d'Archéologie orientale, Caire. Tome 20. (Cairo: Institut français d'Archéologie orientale, 1916), 157-60.

145 Yoyotte, "Les Principautés du Delta," 122-24; Kitchen, *The Third Intermediate Period*, 285-86.

administrator for the throne.[146] The possibility that Amyrtaeus was a "Great Chief of the Meshwesh" is strengthened by Thucydides' report that he kept the Persians out of the "marshes" in part "because the marsh dwellers are the best warriors among the Egyptians (1.110)." The Meshwesh along with the Libyans who resided in the Delta were significant sources of warriors in the Saite and later periods as outlined by Herodotus in his description of social classes in Egypt. Moreover, the marshlands of the Delta were the traditional regions of Egypt inhabited by the Meshwesh.[147]

The identification of both Inaros and Amyrtaeus as leaders of ethnic communities in the western Delta is crucial for understanding the nature of the Egyptian Revolt prior to Athenian intervention. Contrary to the assumptions of many, the revolt was not initiated by an outside interest or military force.[148] Rather, it was the internal dissatisfaction of regional administrators in Egypt that precipitated the effort to regain national independence. Moreover, the longstanding official positions held by both revolutionaries legitimized their claim to the reinstitution of the pharaonic office, making their leadership of the effort against the Persians a serious ideological challenge to Achaemenid claims to be the legitimate successors of the pharaohs.

After assembling loyal forces, the revolutionary army apparently moved down the Canopic branch of the Nile River, judging from the comments of Thucydides that the forces "set out from Mareia."[149] Apparently the satrap of Egypt, Achaemenes, recognizing the seriousness of Inaros' challenge to imperial rule, personally led an imperial force against the rebellion.[150] The two forces met at a site called 'Papremis,' where most of the ancient authorities agree that the revolt

---

146 Kitchen, *The Third Intermediate Period,* 395-96; Wilson, *The Culture of Ancient Egypt,* 292-93.

147 Herodotus 2.164-66; see also Lloyd, "the Late Period," 309-10.

148 For some of the range of opinions contrary to this conclusion, see Olmstead, *History of the Persian Empire,* 303 and Kienitz, *Die politische Geschichte Ägyptens,* 67, both of which see external Libyan forces as instrumental in the revolt; Cook, *The Persian Empire,* 127 has the Greeks fomenting the revolt.

149 Though not precisely locatable, Mareia was situated along the far western edge of the Egyptian Delta region. It was also a traditional urban stronghold of the Libu and Meshwesh; Lloyd, *Herodotus Book II,* Volume 2, 87-88 and 130.

150 See the discussion of the second episode of the revolt for a defense of this order of events.

scored a major victory. The only ancient historian at variance with this assessment is Thucydides who does not even mention the engagement.[151]

Papremis is impossible to locate conclusively, though most researchers agree it was located along the Canopic branch, the western-most branch of the Nile.[152] The death of the satrap, particularly Achaemenes a brother of Xerxes and the uncle of Artaxerxes, was a severe blow to imperial prestige in Egypt. While Egypt had revolted early in the reign of Xerxes I, on that occasion there was no reported loss of a high imperial official in the course of the revolt, nor were imperial armies defeated in a major battle. Clearly the second revolt from the empire posed a more serious challenge to Achaemenid pretensions to control over Egypt than any previous opposition since the conquest of Egypt in 525 BCE. Following the defeat at Papremis, the imperial forces retreated to Memphis, the satrapal capital, and there anticipated the attack by the revolutionary forces that was certain to come.

Second Episode: The Athenian Intervention

Thucydides implies by the vagueness of his narrative that it was only after the successful defeat of Achaemenes and his Persian forces at Papremis that Inaros called for Athenian intervention (1.104). This is further suggested by his later account of the Athenian arrival in Egypt, since on that occasion the Delian forces immediately join in the siege of Memphis where the Persian loyalists have presumably retreated after Papremis (1.104).[153] By contrast, both Ctesias and Diodorus directly state that the Athenians joined in the revolt of Inaros prior to Papremis, and it was the combined Delian and revolutionary forces that engaged the Persians, resulting in an allied victory and the death of the satrap Achaemenes. One is confronted with the task of deciding between these contradictory recountings of the timing of the Athenian intervention before being able to comprehend its significance for the empire.

---

[151] Thucydides' oversight at this point can be readily understood when one recognizes that his focus in the Pentecontaetia was on the growth of Athens as an imperial power prior to the Peloponnesian War, not the vicissitudes of the Achaemenid empire. If no Greeks were involved in the battle at Papremis, including it in his narrative would have served no purpose.

[152] See particularly the thorough discussion of Lloyd, *Herodotus Book II,* Volume 2, 270-72. More recently, J. D. Ray has attempted to resift the evidence to offer another possible identification; "Thoughts on Djeme and Papremis," *Göttinger Miszellen* 45 (1981):57-61.

[153] This is also the understanding of Meiggs, *The Athenian Empire,* 93 n. 4.

At first glance Herodotus' narratives, since they fail to mention Greek involvement in the revolt at all, seem peripheral to this dilemma. However, it is this very failure to mention Greek participation in the battle at Papremis that is decisive. Herodotus' overall historiographic aim was to show the valor of the Greeks in opposing the awesome force of the Persian invasion of Xerxes.[154] One would expect that had Greek forces been involved in the later victory at Papremis, which as has been seen is briefly mentioned by Herodotus, the historian would have sought a way to work this further evidence of Greek heroism into his narratives. The fact that he does not do so when discussing the battle is very telling support for the order of events in Thucydides.[155]

Moreover, both Ctesias and Diodorus have Artaxerxes I appointing Achaemenes as satrap over Egypt prior to his leading of the imperial expeditionary force against the revolt, an order of events that makes little sense. Since the reorganization of the empire under Darius I, Egypt would have had a satrap who acted as the central representative of imperial interests. It would be highly unusual for the Persian monarch to replace such a figure simply because of a military action within the territory he administered.[156] Either the satrap prior to Achaemenes was dead at the time of the revolt, or his replacement by Achaemenes signalled severe displeasure on the part of the Persian monarch. Neither option is alluded to by either Ctesias or Diodorus. However, Herodotus twice records that Xerxes, not Artaxerxes I, sent Achaemenes to Egypt as satrap many years before the revolt of Inaros(7.7, 7.97).[157] Thus the accounts by both Ctesias and Diodorus that Greek intervention in the revolt preceded the victory at Papremis are clearly confused and are to be discounted for a failure to reflect a coherent Achaemenid policy.

The death of Achaemenes in the course of a campaign into the Delta region to suppress Inaros' rebellion resulted in the remaining Persian forces and their Egyptian allies withdrawing into Memphis, the ancient

---

154 A. R. Burn, *Persia and the Greeks,* 3-4.

155 Libourel, "The Athenian Disaster in Egypt," 606.

156 For example, see the comments of Cook, *The Persian Empire,* 171; Frye, *History of Ancient Iran,* 115-16. The relationship between civil and military authority in the territories of the Achaemenid empire is often difficult to determine, but satrapal authority seems to supercede that of professional military commanders; Cook, "The Rise of the Achaemenids," 267-68.

157 Herodotus also has Achaemenes acting as commander of Egyptian naval forces during Xerxes' campaign against Greece (7.97). Regrettably, no epigraphic evidence has yet been discovered of Achaemenes term as satrap over Egypt, though there is no cause to doubt Herodotus' report.

capital of Egypt. At this point, according to Thucydides, Inaros called for Athenian assistance. Three major issues are raised by this action. First, there is the matter of Inaros' requiring any assistance to continue the rebellion. One would expect that following on the heels of the victory at Papremis, Inaros would have simply pursued the Persians on down the Nile valley until their surrender or destruction. Second, there is the related question of why the Athenians in particular were approached for assistance. And third, there is the need to identify the factors that led to the positive Athenian response to the Egyptian rebel's request.

As has already been alluded to, Thucydides has the Delian League forces immediately joining the revolutionary army in the siege of Memphis where the Persians are entrenched. Thucydides and Diodorus both record that the imperial forces were secure within a structure called the "White Fortress." Memphis as an urban center occupied a particularly strategic point along the Nile River, controlling entry into the valley that led up river into the narrow but fertile region known as Upper Egypt. From its earliest recorded history, the ceremonial and administrative center of Memphis was called the "White Wall," presumably a reference to a plaster perimeter wall enclosing this center of governmental power.[158] This was certainly the feature called the "White Fortress" by the Greeks. The city of Memphis itself spread out along the river banks both above and below the White Wall, though the precise boundaries still elude investigators.[159]

During the Persian domination of Egypt, Memphis served as the satrapal seat and the focus of imperial authority. As amply documented by epigraphic and papyrological evidence, a Persian military garrison was maintained at Memphis and the military authorities there acted as the central command for Persian forces stationed throughout Egypt.[160] Inaros may have understood that if his revolt was to succeed, the revolutionary forces had to control Memphis, both to deprive the remaining imperial forces of a central coordination point and to give his claim to rule over Egypt additional legitimacy by governing from the ancient cap-

---

158 Kees, *Ancient Egypt*, 238; Bresciani, "The Persian Occupation of Egypt," 518-19.

159 Memphis is currently being intensively explored by the Egyptian Exploration Fund. An informed summary of the results thus far may be found in Jill Kamil, "Ancient Memphis: Archaeologists Revive Interest in a Famous Egyptian Site," *Archaeology* 38 (1985):25-32.

160 Porten, *Archives from Elephantine*, 29 and 53-4. Emil G. Kraeling, *The Brooklyn Museum Aramaic Papyri: New Documents of the Fifth Century B. C. from the Jewish Colony of Elephantine* (New Haven: Yale University Press, 1953), 32 estimates the garrison contained a force of 10-12,000 troops, based on ration figures supplied by Herodotus.

ital. Thus, once the victory of Papremis was achieved, it is not surprising that Inaros forsook the chance to extend his control over the rest of the Delta in order to press the attack on Memphis.

While the size of the forces at Memphis is uncertain (Ctesias gives the dubious figure of 200,000 men), it is apparent that enough troops and supplies would be involved to present a significant challenge to any army. Possibly Inaros' troops lacked both the numerical strength and adequate equipment to undertake a frontal assault on the "White Fortress." More likely, Inaros decided to mount a combined land and river attack on the Persian stronghold, since Memphis was a major riverport and the Persians possessed a significant fleet that could be used to keep the Nile open for imperial reinforcements.[161] It seems doubtful that Inaros would have had naval vessels as part of his forces since there are no indications of such in any of the Greek accounts. On the other hand, the Greek victories at Salamis (479 BCE) and Eurymedon (ca. 466 BCE) over imperial naval forces had become legendary throughout the eastern Mediterranean. In sum, the request for Athenian assistance was made to obtain the naval forces necessary to control the Nile and to attack the imperial garrison from the river.

As has been noted in the previous discussions of the individual historical accounts dealing with the Egyptian Revolt, none of the Greek historians provide any description of how Inaros' appeal arrived in Athens, nor how the Delian forces were mustered for the expedition. Only Thucydides offers a consistent version of the appeal, implying that word of Inaros' request reached a Delian fleet sailing for Cyprus. While nothing is known of the expedition against Cyprus outside of this brief mention, it is consistent with the larger aims of Athenian policy toward Persia. The destruction of the Persian fleet at Eurymedon left the empire incapable of checking Athenian penetration into the eastern Mediterranean.[162]

Cyprus was under Persian control for much of the first half of the fifth century; and throughout Xerxes' efforts to conquer the Greek mainland, Cyprus played a pivotal role as a naval base for the Phoenician and Egyptian fleets in the imperial armadas.[163] For the Delian League to

161 Herodotus records a force of 200 Egyptian ships being part of Xerxes' armada during the invasion of Greece (7.89, 8.17).

162 Cook, *The Persian Empire*, 126; Olmstead, *History of the Persian Empire*, 268; Burns, "Persia and the Greeks," 334.

163 Burns, *Persia and the Greeks*, 83-4, 330 and 447; Cook, *The Persian Empire*, 95-6 and 105-6; Olmsted, *History of the Persian Empire*, 154-55, 246 and 293.

launch an expedition of 200 ships against Cyprus would represent a clear effort to open the eastern Mediterranean, specifically the Phoenician and Palestinian coastlands, to Athenian expansion.[164]

There is a question of chronology in interpreting this expedition as a challenge to Persian control of the eastern Mediterranean. While the date of the battle of Eurymedon is impossible to fix with certainty, it is usually placed in either 467 or 466 BCE. Assuming that Inaros' revolt began in 464 BCE (when news of Artaxerxes' accession had spread to Egypt) and the battle at Papremis some time subsequent to 464 BCE, then an interval of several years' time had intervened between the victory at Eurymedon and the expedition to Cyprus. The delay between the destruction of the Persian fleet and a Greek effort to take advantage of this setback could be interpreted as indicating a lack of Greek interest in the eastern Mediterranean. However, this interval becomes more comprehensible when the severe internal strains within the Delian League are considered. Apparently in the aftermath of Eurymedon, several league members believed the Achaemenid Empire no longer presented a sufficient threat to justify their continuing subservience to Athens. A series of revolts by individual cities, some under Persian instigation, as well as continuing political turmoil within the Athenian leadership prevented the Delian League from following up on the victory of Eurymedon.[165] Still, the basic goal of Athenian foreign policy with regard to the Achaemenid Empire was to expand Hellenic domination into the eastern Mediterranean, including the Levant.[166]

Having already committed a substantial naval force to the effort to capture Cyprus, the Athenian-controlled Delian League abruptly changed direction and responded to Inaros' call.[167] The strategy behind such a response is not difficult to reconstruct. Provided that Athenian control of the eastern Mediterranean was the larger aim for league operations after Eurymedon, Egypt presented a golden opportunity for these

---

164 See especially Meiggs, *The Athenian Empire*, 93-4; and M. I. Findley, "The Fifth-century Athenian Empire: A Balance Sheet," in *Imperialism in the Ancient World*, ed. P. D. A. Garnsey and C. R. Whittaker (Cambridge: Cambridge University Press, 1978), 105-6. For the strategic importance of holding Cyprus in order to control the eastern Mediterranean, see H. D. Purcell, *Cyprus* (New York: Frederick A. Praeger, Inc., 1968), 88.

165 Meiggs, *The Athenian Empire*, 82-91.

166 N. G. L. Hammond, *A History of Greece to 322 B.C.* Third edition. (Oxford: Clarendon Press, 1986), 292-93; also see the references in note 164.

167 It is the considered opinion of Meiggs that two hundred ships represented the largest fleet available at one time to the Delian League; *The Athenian Empire*, 77.

aspirations. With the success of the revolutionary forces at Papremis and the death of the satrap Achaemenes, the Persian forces in Egypt were in a rout, and the potential for an easy victory would have seemed strong. Once Inaros' rule was secure, the Athenians could anticipate the provision of a naval facility at one of the mouths of the Nile, giving the Greeks a strategic port within striking distance of the entire eastern Mediterranean.[168] In addition, there was always the possibility that Egypt might join the Delian League, contributing its considerable naval forces to the effort against the Achaemenid empire.

While none of the Greek historians provides any details of battles as the Delian forces entered the Nile and joined in the siege of the Persian forces at Memphis, there is a Greek inscription that suggests some military activity at this point. The text, in the form of an heroic poem, memorializes the victory of Greeks from Samos in a battle in the vicinity of Memphis.[169] The account claims the battle involved Phoenician vessels, fifteen of which were captured by the Samians. The text itself comes from an uncertain archaeological context, though the palaeography points to a mid-fifth century date. As a result, there is a general consensus that the account relates to some military action in the course of the Egyptian Revolt.[170] At what point this action occurred is impossible to determine, but it does lend credence to Thucydides' emphasis on the effort by the Delian forces to control the Nile River.[171]

The siege of Memphis lasted an indeterminate period of time, though as previously noted Diodorus implies that it was more than a year, during which time the empire made preparations for its counterattack. All the Greek historians seem to suggest that the Egyptian revolutionary forces and their Delian allies were unsuccessful in overcoming the Persian forces garrisoned at Memphis. It can be surmised that the inability of the revolutionary forces to break past Memphis and thus con-

---

168 There is no reason to accept Diodorus' statement that Inaros promised the Athenians a share in the kingdom in return for military assistance.

169 Russell Meiggs and David Lewis, eds., *A Selection of Greek Historical Inscriptions to the End of the Fifth Century B. C.*, corrected edition. (Oxford: Clarendon Press, 1980), no. 34, pages 76-77. The letter forms suggest a mid-fifth century date. For a more detailed discussion of the date of the inscription and a probable restoration, see Werner Peek, "Ein Seegefecht aus den Perserkriegen," *Klio* 32 (1939):289-306.

170 Bigwood, "Ctesias' Account of the Revolt of Inarus," 17 n. 59 is properly cautious, noting that this is not a necessary conclusion.

171 Thucydides 1.104.

trol the Nile to the south of the city allowed for supplies, and possibly additional troops, to replenish the White Fortress.[172]

Thucydides noted that the war "took many forms" while Memphis was under siege, an obscure reference that has been interpreted to refer to portions of the Delian League forces conducting sorties against other imperial holdings in the eastern Mediterranean.[173] The only positive evidence that has been adduced for support of this possibility is the casualty list for the Erechtheid tribe.[174] This memorial to tribal members commemorates those fallen in battles "in Cyprus, in Egypt, in Phoenicia, in Halae, in Aegina, in Megara." The last three campaigns are noted in the chronological order in which they appear in Thucydides' account of the Pentakontaetia, so the inference is usually drawn that the first three campaigns are also in chronological order.[175] In that no campaign in Phoenicia is known of outside of this mention, the assumption is made that such a campaign took place while Memphis was under siege and Athenian naval forces were in the eastern Mediterranean.

As attractive as this possibility may be, it is certainly not a necessary conclusion to Thucydides' comment on the war's "many forms." The dating of the casualty list is difficult to determine with precision, and there is no assurance that either Thucydides or the casualty list has maintained the proper chronological order for these battles. It should be noted that neither Thucydides, nor any of the other Greek historians, suggests actual hostilities on Cyprus prior to the Athenian intervention in Egypt. The most that can be concluded regarding the casualty list is that sometime in this larger contest between the Athenian empire and the Achaemenid empire for control of the eastern Mediterranean, some military action took place in territory or waters considered "Phoenicia," or in other words, along the Levantine coast. Since Thucydides' narrative of the revolt is tightly focussed on the activities of the Greeks while in Egypt, there is no warrant to seek additional meaning to his notice of a theater of activity outside the ongoing struggle in Egypt. Since the revolutionary forces and their Delian League allies had, in all probability, made their way to Memphis along the westernmost branch of the Nile,

---

[172] See Porten, *Archives from Elephantine,* 27 for a discussion of the loyalty of the imperial garrisons to the south of Memphis during the revolt.

[173] See Meiggs, *The Athenian Empire,* 102-3.

[174] Also called the "Nointel Marble" by some. Meiggs and Lewis, *A Selection of Greek Historical Inscriptions,* No. 33, pages 73-6. The paleography fits comfortably in the mid-fifth century.

[175] For example, Wallace, "The Egyptian Expedition and the Chronology of the Decade 460-450 B. C.," 254-55.

Thucydides' account of "many forms" may point toward expanded efforts to secure the Delta region in its entirety from Achaemenid influence and resistance to Inaros' rule.[176]

The protracted siege of the imperial garrison at Memphis brought the promise of a swift victory over the Persians to an abrupt halt. The addition of Delian League forces strengthened the hand of Inaros, but the inability of the combined forces to gain control over the ancient capital of Egypt frustrated his efforts to ratify his claim to sovereign rule, and stymied Athenian aspirations to dominate the Mediterranean. The stalemate also opened the possibility for a reassertion of control by the Achaemenid empire. With the Athenian forces tied up in a victoryless campaign in Egypt, problems closer to home, notably the rebellions of Aegina and Tanagra from the Delian League, distracted the Greeks from their ongoing struggle with the Persians.

Third Episode: The Imperial Counterattack

The first hint of the imperial concern over events in Egypt emerges in Thucydides' account of the initial Athenian involvement in the conflict. Once Memphis was put under siege, Artaxerxes I reportedly sent his emissary Megabazus to bribe the Spartans into attacking the southern flank of the Delian league.[177] Such an action served to emphasize that, for the empire, the real enemy was not Inaros but the more troubling intervention of Athens and its allies. The Persian offer was turned down, and the king began the process of mustering a great expeditionary force to crush the threat presented by the uprising. On this process, Thucydides is of little assistance, noting simply that the king sent a large army under the command of the satrap Megabyzos. Nor is Ctesias of any help here since he has Artaxerxes sending two massive expeditions in sequence. Only Diodorus, the furthest removed in time from these events, provides any details on the mobilization of the expeditionary force.

According to Diodorus, the force left the Persian heartland and marched towards the Mediterranean. His figure for the number of troops, 300,000, simply conforms to his formula for a large land force as discussed above. Diodorus notes that when these forces arrived "in

---

176 Gomme, *A Historical Commentary on Thucydides,* Vol. 1, 320 makes the same point, suggesting that there was more involved in the revolutionary effort than the simple siege of Memphis.

177 Thucydides 1.109. For some of the background on Persian relations with Sparta during this period, see David M. Lewis, *Sparta and Persia.* Cincinnati Classical Studies N.S. 1. (Leiden: E. J. Brill, 1977), 50-1.

Cilicia and Phoenicia," they rested and underwent extensive training for the campaign to follow.[178] This pattern of a massive land force marching out from Persia, moving across the Near Eastern landscape and staying at a point along the Mediterranean where the final preparations for an attack are made occurs in several other contexts in Diodorus. For example, when Xerxes I was preparing to launch his invasion of Greece (ca. 480 BCE), troops were gathered from all across the empire and marched from Susa to Sardis where they joined an imperial fleet and made ready their dramatic onslaught against the Greeks (11.2.3). And, when Artaxerxes II was preparing to retake Egypt (ca. 374 BCE) after a previously successful revolt, the imperial troops gathered at Acco for final preparations before their attack (15.41.3).

Given Diodorus' tendency to recast historical events into stereotypical formulas, the recurrence of a staging point along the Mediterranean coast prior to an imperial land attack is a matter of concern, though it could reflect the normal Achaemenid mode of military operations in the western holdings. It would be advantageous to establish a central staging area for a massive expeditionary force somewhere along the coast where port facilities would allow for the provisioning of an imperial fleet. The use of Acco for such a point in the first quarter of the fourth century could well have been preceded by the same city being the point of departure in the mid-fifth century, though such a conclusion is speculative until further data may be brought to bear on the issue.

Diodorus is quite specific in noting that the imperial forces moved along the coast toward Egypt with the imperial fleet of Phoenician and Cypriot ships sailing offshore (11.77.1). Again, such coordinated movement of land and naval forces is noted in Diodorus' narratives dealing with events over seventy-five years later when Artaxerxes II sought to retake Egypt (15.41.4). Rather than interpreting this similarity as the use of a patterned account by Diodorus, there is the strong possibility that similar strategic considerations prevailed in both of these situations, leading to the adoption of identical tactics. For the mid-fifth century, the Athenian interests in controlling the eastern Mediterranean represented a direct military threat to the imperial holdings in the Levant. Moreover, as will be discussed below, there was at least one point along the Levantine coast where Athens could claim an ally. A massive force, marching in a long column along a coastal route, could have been subject to a surprise attack by a Greek unit that had quietly landed along the coast. The use of

---

178 Diodorus 11.75.

the imperial fleet to guard the seaward flank effectively guaranteed that the expeditionary force would arrive in Egypt intact.

For the later fourth-century campaign to Egypt, the Persians faced a similar potential for an attack from the west. Egypt had hired Greek mercenaries and an Athenian general to assist in resisting the coming counterattack.[179] Cyprus, too, had gained partial independence from the empire and was engaged in extended diplomatic contacts with the Athenians.[180] From the Achaemenid perspective, for the first quarter of the fourth century, the eastern Mediterranean was again troubled by extended Greek military operations. The provision of ports on Cyprus would have given the still superior Greek naval forces ready access to the Levantine coast. Thus there was need for an offshore fleet to accompany the expeditionary column, to protect the seaward flank from an Athenian attack.

Diodorus' account of the fifth-century imperial force marching "through Syria and Phoenicia" does not clearly indicate the actual route taken, though it may be assumed that it was along the coastal highway, the "Way of the Sea." As the main thoroughfare from the Phoenician cities of Tyre and Sidon southward toward Egypt, the coastal highway had been for centuries the main route into Egypt for armies marching from points to the north and east.[181] Coming from the north, the imperial forces would have had to cross the Carmel range through one of a series of passes, at the northern mouths of which were the two ancient urban centers of Yokneam and Megiddo. The most direct route from the Plain of Acco, the entry point to the Carmel range whether the imperial army was coming from Acco itself or one of the Phoenician cities to the north, was through Yokneam. It would seem more troublesome for a large land force to swing southeastward and move through the Carmel range at Megiddo.

Assuming the army moved through at Yokneam, three routes led southward to the coastal highway, and what evidence exists suggests that all three were in use during the Persian period.[182] Of these three, the most direct route from the pass through the Carmel to the coastal high-

179 Olmstead, *History of the Persian Empire,* 397-99; Cook, *The Persian Empire,* 217.

180 Olmstead, *History of the Persian Empire,* 399-400; Cook, *The Persian Empire,* 216; Frye, *The History of Ancient Iran,* 130.

181 David A. Dorsey, "The Roads and Highways of Israel During the Iron Ages" (Ph.D. disseration, The Dropsie University, 1981), 175-87; Aharoni, *The Land of the Bible.* 2nd edition, 45-54.

182 Dorsey, "The Roads and Highways of Israel During the Iron Age," 199-200.

way has been called the "Gath-Padalla-Aruna-Jokneam Road" by David Dorsey. This route would have brought the expeditionary force out to the coastal highway at a point some twelve kilometers to the east of the Mediterranean seaport of Dor.[183] The other two routes out of the Carmel are both farther west and consequently closer to the coast and to the site of Dor.

The importance of this point to the narratives of Diodorus becomes clear once the distinctive political situation of Dor is assessed. On the tribute assessments of the Delian League for the year 454 BCE, a "Doros" appears.[184] While it cannot be said with certainty that this city is identical with the port of Dor just south of the Carmel range, there is no other known site in antiquity that affords as acceptable an identification.

The Levantine Dor was identified in the eleventh century BCE Egyptian tale of Wen-Amon as a city belonging to the Tjeker, one of the various groups among the Sea Peoples with a probable origin in the Aegean world.[185] Recent archaeological investigations at Dor have demonstrated the presence of extensive facilities in the Late Bronze Age, confirming the maritime character of the site.[186] Moreover, excavations at Dor have yielded clear evidence of Greek trade contacts in the mid-fifth century.[187] The fact that in the mid-fifth century Athens was seeking to

---

183 Dorsey, "The Roads and Highways of Israel During the Iron Age," 202-3.

184 Benjamin Meritt, H. T. Wade-Gery, and Malcolm McGregor, *The Athenian Tribute Lists, Volume 3* (Princeton: The American School of Classical Studies at Athens, 1950), 9. The period of the assessment ran from 454 to 451 BCE, but there is no indication either way on assessments for Doros after 454. The identification of "Doros" with the Levantine Dor is presented in Volume 1, 483.

185 Aharoni, *The Land of the Bible,* 2nd edition, 269; N. K. Sanders, *The Sea Peoples: Warriors of the Ancient Mediterranean, 1250-1150 B.C.* (London: Thames and Hudson, 1978), 158 and 170.

186 Avner Raban, "The Harbor of the Sea Peoples at Dor," *Biblical Archaeologist* 50 (1987):118-26. Raban cites evidence for the erection of major harbor facilities at Dor beginning in the Middle Bronze Age.

187 Ephraim Stern, "The Earliest Greek Settlement at Dor," *Eretz-Israel* 18 (1985):419-27 [Hebrew]. Stern reports on a deposit of Attic ware vessels and associates this deposit with a structure he identifies as a sanctuary. He goes on to assume the deposit was a *favissa,* and since the deposit contained only Attic materials, he concludes the sanctuary was founded by Greek colonists. There is no evidence offered by Stern to lead one to follow him in any of these conclusions. W. Kendrick Pritchett, "The Transfer of the Delian Treasury," *Historia* 18 (1969):17-21 argues that "Doros" was located in Caria along the southeastern coast of Asia Minor. He argues this point based on an identification by the Byzantine scholar Stephanos of "Doros" as a city in Caria. Part of Kendrick's argument in favor of this Carian Doros is his contention that as a placename, "Dor" was "of frequent occurrence." In fact, outside

extend membership in the Delian League to any city in the eastern Mediterranean with close ties to the Greek mainland makes it all the more probable that the "Doros" of the tribute assessments was the Levantine port of Dor.

By paying tribute to Athens, Dor was part of the Delian League and was supporting the Delian effort to aid Inaros in his rebellion against Achaemenid rule. The payment of tribute in 454 is a critical point in that, assuming Thucydides' chronology of events at this point is accepted, the rebellion was largely crushed by mid-454 BCE after an eighteen month siege of the Greek positions. This chronology would place the movement of the imperial expeditionary force through the Levant in 456 BCE, or just prior to the first recorded assessment of tribute from Dor.[188] The surviving tribute assessments reflect only the first years of administration of the Delian League treasury by Athens, and prior to 454 the treasury was located at the sacred complex of Delos. Considering that Dor was assessed in 454, it is likely that Dor had been paying tribute, and thus had been part of the Greek alliance opposing Persia, since the Greek victory at Eurymedon.

As a consequence of Dor's being part of the alliance opposing Achaemenid control of the eastern Mediterranean, it was absolutely necessary for the imperial expeditionary force marching along the coastal highway to be accompanied by the imperial fleet protecting its seaward flank. A relatively small force concentrated at the routes through the Carmel range could easily have impeded the progress of even a great land army seeking passage down to the coastal highway. Moreover, a convenient port along the Levantine coast, such as Dor, would have provided an ideal base from which the Greeks could have launched repeated attacks up and down the Levantine coast, sapping the imperial army of resources until it reached Egypt.

---

of Stephanos, the only Dor known in ancient sources is the Levantine Dor. Regarding Stephanos, he compiled his *Ethnica* in the fifth century C.E., the composition surviving only as an epitome. Consequently, any statement attributed to Stephanos is not without its own difficulties both in composition and in faithfulness of transmission. Most recently, Stern has reported on the Palestinian Dor's fortifications, noting that in the early fourth century BCE they "were still being constructed according to the Phoenician building tradition;" Ephraim Stern, "The Walls of Dor." *IEJ* 38 (1988):9. This further confirms the independant character of Dor, and the probability that in the mid-fifth century, it could have been allied with Athens.

188 See Meritt, Wade-Gery, and McGregor, *The Athenian Tribute Lists, Vol. 3,* 177-78; Meiggs, *The Athenian Empire,* 103.

None of the Greek historians describes the specific route by which the imperial army entered Egypt, nor do they indicate if the revolutionary forces and their Greek allies knew beforehand of the coming of Megabyzos and his men. All the historians concur, however, in having the imperial army move directly against the siege of Memphis, relieving the beleaguered garrison forces. The battle of Memphis was decisive, not only by breaking the siege, but by all accounts destroying most of Inaros' forces. The Delian League forces, apparently fighting together as a unit, were able to retreat to the Nilotic island of Prosopitis where, in an ironic reversal of fortune, they came under siege by the Persians.[189] Ctesias has an odd variant on this point, recording that the forces retreated into a fortified city named "Byblos." There is no record of such a city in Egypt in the Persian period, and it appears that Ctesias simply had no guide to what transpired following the reversal in the rebellion and has interjected a confused reference to the Phoenician port of the same name.[190]

Thucydides records that the imperial forces besieged Prosopitis for eighteen months; and Diodorus simply notes that the Persians adopted "a prudent course," avoiding any direct action with the trapped Greeks. Both historians have the imperial forces diverting the flow of the Nile around the island, causing the Athenian ships to be grounded. In Thucydides, once deprived of their ability to conduct land and river coordinated movements, the Athenians faced a massive land attack by the expeditionary force.[191] The Greeks were overwhelmed and most perished in this final encounter with the imperial forces. Diodorus' effort to aggrandize the bravery of the trapped Greeks has too many signs of catering to the historian's love of the Athenians and dependence on Ctesias to warrant credibility.

The major dilemma facing the wholesale acceptance of Thucydides' narrative of the end of the revolt is the implication that the Delian League lost all the ships and men sent six years earlier to assist Inaros. There are two points usually raised when objecting to the destruction of all 200 ships and their crews. First, in Thucydides' narration of the events

---

189 Herodotus mentions Prosopitis in 2.41 as a populous region located north of Memphis. An excellent summation of what can be derived from the ancient geographers regarding this region is provided by Lloyd, *Herodotus Book II, Commentary 1-98*, 186-87.

190 Bigwood, "Ctesias' Account of the Revolt of Inarus," 23-5 offers a detailed examination of this point.

191 A helpful summation of Achaemenid versus Greek military capability may be found in Paul Rahe, "The Military Situation in Western Asia on the Eve of Cunaxa," *AJP* 101 (1980):79-87.

following the defeat at Prosopitis, a "relief fleet" of fifty vessels was destroyed when it sailed into the Delta region, not knowing the Persian forces had triumphed. Second, Ctesias records that the initial forces sent to assist Inaros numbered only forty ships. Consequently, some have suggested that Ctesias' figures make more sense than Thucydides' since the relief fleet was so small. And, assuming the fleet size was around forty ships, the destruction of the Delian forces in Egypt, while a strategic setback, was not the total disaster portrayed by Thucydides.[192]

As attractive as this suggestion may be, there are compelling reasons for rejecting it. Jan Libourel has argued that the situation of the Athenian fleet blockaded on Prosopitis, combined with a somewhat expanded understanding of the Greek term *diadoxos* as "reinforcement," suggests that the "relief" fleet was actually intended as reinforcement for the entrapped Athenian forces. As such, the size was reflective of the maximum number of vessels that could be spared, and not of the number of vessels involved in hostilities in Egypt.[193] Russell Meiggs has taken the issue a step further by carefully analyzing the Athenian tribute lists for the period immediately after 454 BCE, the probable date for the final defeat of the Delian League at Prosopitis. According to Meiggs, for a number of years following 454, those league members on the outer limits of the confederation were markedly late in payment of tribute or, in some cases, had ceased to maintain membership in the league.[194] This diminished hold over its remotest allies is interpreted by Meiggs as the result of the Egyptian disaster and its accompanying loss of the naval forces necessary for maintaining cohesion within the Athenian empire.[195]

The crisis in Athenian control of the Delian League as attested in the tribute records parallels the dimensions of the defeat in Egypt recorded in Thucydides. There is no compelling reason to prefer Ctesias' account of the size of the forces originally committed by Athens to the Egyptian campaign, nor is Thucydides' account of the relief fleet necessarily connected to the number of Greek vessels trapped and destroyed on Prosopitis. The inescapable conclusion is that the Athenian loss in Egypt

---

192 As examples of this line of reasoning, see Wallace, "The Egyptian Expedition and the Chronology of the Decade 460-450 B.C.," 254 and 257-58; Westlake, "Thucydides and the Athenian Disaster in Egypt," 212.

193 Libourel, "The Athenian Disaster in Egypt," 611-13.

194 Russell Meiggs, "The Crisis of Athenian Imperialism," *Harvard Studies in Philology* 67 (1963): 4-9; also Meiggs, *The Athenian Empire*, 109-12.

195 "If this analysis of the evidence is on the right lines, the Egyptian disaster was followed by acute tension within the league" ; Meiggs, "The Crisis of Athenian Imperialism," 9.

was enormous in scale and opened the way for the resumption of Persian domination over the eastern Mediterranean.

Fourth Episode: The Aftermath of the Egyptian Disaster

The loss of 200 vessels and their crews in the disaster at Prosopitis was not the end of Athenian efforts to oppose Persian control of the eastern Mediterranean, nor was it the end of the imperial recognition of the Greek challenge. The consequences of the imperial triumph over the Egyptian and Delian League forces continued to impact the Achaemenid holdings in the west into the next decade.

Thucydides provides several details on the aftermath of the revolt not reported by any other source. One is the previously mentioned destruction of the "relief fleet" of fifty ships, sent from Athens in the same year as the resolution of the siege of Prosopitis. According to the historian, the fleet entered the Delta region unaware of the Achaemenid victory, only to meet defeat in a combined sea and land ambush. This additional loss of naval capability further weakened the ability of Athens to exert its will over the Delian League membership, imperiling the ability of the confederation to oppose Persian domination.[196]

Also according to Thucydides, with the victory of the Persians at Prosopitis, the revolt collapsed. Amyrtaeus, the co-leader of the revolt, was able to escape into the marshlands of the Delta where he continued the native opposition to Achaemenid rule of Egypt. Inaros, the main figure behind the revolt, was betrayed and handed over into the hands of the Persians and executed.

The resulting naval weakness of the Delian League's losses in Egypt led to a series of drastic political and diplomatic moves aimed at securing Athens the necessary time to regather its naval strength. Cimon, the famed commander of the Greek victory at Eurymedon who was ostracized from Athens some years earlier for opposition to the democratic forces of the city, was recalled from his banishment. Cimon was sent to Sparta to arrange a truce between Athens and its traditional antagonist to the south, and around 451 BCE he returned to Athens with a five year truce in hand.[197] From 454 to 451, the Athenians had taken steps to reassert their control over the Delian League, including the removal of the League treasury to Athens and the institution of new economic and polit-

---

196 Meiggs, *The Athenian Empire,* 104.

197 For the rationale behind Sparta's entry into this agreement, see Lewis, *Sparta and Persia,* 63.

ical controls over *poleis* that had disappeared from the tribute assessments of 454 BCE.[198] By 451 BCE, the League was returning to stability.

With the danger of an attack from the south removed by the truce with Sparta, and with the expanded financial resources of a stable confederacy, the Athenian leadership again sought to challenge Achaemenid control of the eastern Mediterranean. Thucydides records that in 451 BCE, Cimon was selected to lead a major expedition of 200 ships to once again try to oust the Persians from Cyprus. This not only pointed to the long-term strategic interests on the part of the Athenians in controlling Cyprus, but also signified a renewed determination to threaten the western holdings of the Achaemenid empire. Possibly during the initial attack on Cyprus, Amyrtaeus sent word of a need for Athenian naval support, and a squadron of sixty ships sailed to Egypt to assist him. Thucydides clearly intends for the reader to understand that from the setback at Prosopitis in 454 until this campaign in 451, Amyrtaeus had successfully evaded capture and had continued to oppose the empire. The reasons for his request, the actual role played by the Greek naval squadron, and the eventual outcome are all matters of no concern to Thucydides and remain unresolvable until other yet unknown sources are able to provide some light on these issues.

Thucydides' narrative of the campaign against the Persians on Cyprus is condensed, but relatively clear. The initial siege was laid against Kitium, but in the course of the campaign Cimon died suddenly. A famine also afflicted the island, limiting the availability of foodstuffs for the Delian League forces. Faced with a protracted and difficult campaign, the Greek forces broke off the campaign and began heading back toward Athens by sailing around Salamis on the eastern side of the island. A battle resulted with Phoenician forces on the sea and Cilician forces on land, with the Athenians gaining the upper hand. After joining the squadron that had been sent to Egypt, the Greeks returned to Athens.[199]

Diodorus' account of this campaign is far more detailed and patterned, though some of his information may be derived from earlier sources. Like Thucydides, Diodorus has a fleet of 200 ships (not his usual naval statistic of 300 vessels) under the command of Cimon sent to Cyprus. The historian notes that the Persians were apparently expecting an eventual attack, the admiral Artabazus holding supreme command

[198] Meiggs, *The Athenian Empire,* 112-15.

[199] The chronology for this campaign is difficult to reconstruct, but the argument for 451 BCE seems strongest: see Meiggs, *The Athenian Empire,* 124-26.

and staying off Cyprus with a fleet of 300 Persian vessels. Megabyzos commanded a land force of 300,000 located at Cilicia. Both Megabyzos and Artabazus appeared earlier as the commanders of the imperial expeditionary force that suppressed the Egyptian Revolt in 454 BCE, and it is likely that Diodorus has simply transferred the military data concerning that event to this Cyprian campaign.[200]

Diodorus goes on to claim that the Athenians were victorious in campaigns against the Cypriot cities of Kitium and Marium with Cimon leading the attack. The Persians counterattacked, and the Athenians defeated the imperial naval forces, chasing them into the land force's camp at Cilicia where the Greeks defeated the troops under Megabyzos' command (12.3). With the main imperial forces in disarray, Diodorus notes that Cimon returned the Greeks to Cyprus where the Persian garrison at Salamis was placed under siege. As Diodorus understands this sequence, these reversals of imperial fortune coupled with the imminent loss of Cyprus led Artaxerxes to negotiate a truce with the Delian League.

Diodorus' account is blatantly designed to glorify the supremacy of the Athenian military over the Persians: the same commanders who once humiliated the Greeks in Egypt now find themselves badly defeated by Cimon and his forces. At every turn in his narrative of the Cypriot campaign, Diodorus emphasizes that the new power in the eastern Mediterranean is the Athenians. In all this, Thucydides' narrative, with its considerably duller account of an expedition frustrated by the loss of leadership and famine, rings closer to reality. There is reason to believe that the battles off the coast of Cyprus at Salamis, and possibly along the coast of Cilicia, were major engagements in which the Athenians gained the upper hand.[201] This victory opened a new chapter in the relations between Athens and Persia.

Diodorus records that the victory of the Athenians against the imperial forces off Cyprus caused Artaxerxes I to consider entering into a truce with Athens. As with much of his narrative at this point, Diodorus emphasizes that the renewed Athenian military vigor brought Persia to its knees. Still, despite the suspicions raised by the glorification of Athenian military prowess in Diodorus, there may be something behind his report of a treaty between these two adversaries. From around 450 BCE on for several decades, there are no recorded Greek efforts against

---

200 The sizes of the forces (300 vessels and 300,000 footsoldiers) as well as the commanders of the forces are all identical.

201 Cook, *The Persian Empire*, 127-28; Olmstead, *History of the Persian Empire*, 309-10.

Persian interests in the eastern Mediterranean and no recorded Achaemenid efforts against the Greek cities of Asia Minor.[202]

No agreement between Athens and Persia is attested in any fifth-century source; and while noted by several Greek orators in the fourth century, other orators at the same time denounced the idea as fraudulent. Just as the existence of the treaty was debated in antiquity, so modern scholarship has wrestled with this issue. While some have embraced the existence of such an agreement as certain, others with equal conviction have rejected the possibility.[203] There can be no certainty on this point, but the contrast in Athenian actions in the eastern Mediterranean between the decade of 460-450 BCE and the years following 450 serves to support the existence of some sort of mutual recognition of each power's sphere of domination, whether this recognition was formalized in a treaty or not.

According to those sources that posit a formal treaty between Athens and Persia, the agreement was negotiated for Athens by Callias, one of Athens' wealthiest citizens.[204] Accordingly, it has come to be known as the "Peace of Callias." The precise terms of the Peace of Callias are difficult to reconstruct owing to the diversity of terms noted by the fourth-century orators, their selection and exposition being determined by their various polemical interests. In general, it appears that restrictions were placed on movements of naval and land forces of both parties. Athenian vessels were prohibited from sailing beyond the southern Asia Minor coast toward the imperial territories in the Levant and Egypt. Correspondingly, imperial naval forces were banned from entering the Aegean. Imperial land forces were to withdraw from the coastal areas of Asia Minor, though there is considerable confusion on this point. The East Greek cities of the coast were to remain autonomous but would continue to render tribute to the Achaemenid court. On the other hand, both the Athenians and the East Greek cities pledged not to move inland in action against the imperial holdings.[205] Thus, in what was essentially a formal recognition of the military stalemate that the Athenian victories off Cyprus had achieved, both Athens and Persia freed themselves to

---

202 Meiggs, *The Athenian Empire,* 129.

203 The major ancient and modern positions on the Peace of Callias are compactly set out in Appendix 8 of Meiggs, *The Athenian Empire,* 487-95.

204 A summary of what is known of Callias' career and influence may be found in Meiggs, *The Athenian Empire,* 145-46.

205 Discussions of the various terms of the Peace of Callias may be found in Meiggs, *The Athenian Empire,* 147-50; Olmstead, *History of the Persian Empire,* 310-11; Cook, *The Persian Empire,* 128; Frye, *History of Ancient Iran,* 128.

pursue the expansion of their respective empires in directions that did not bring them into conflict.

The existence of the Peace of Callias did not mean that the decades following 449 BCE were free of all tension in the eastern Mediterranean. Both powers kept a wary watch of each other's activities, never being lulled into a sense of security. Evidence for this mutual suspicion can be seen in Thucydides' accounts of the revolt of the island of Samos from the Delian League in 440 BCE. The Samian oligarchic party, initially suppressed by the Athenian democratic forces under the command of Pericles, was able to appeal to the Persian satrap at Sardis, Pissuthnes, for assistance in regaining control. By means of mercenaries supplied by Pissuthnes, the oligarchs retook the island and defied the Athenians to force them into submission.

Pericles responded by sending a large fleet to blockade the island and force it to surrender but a small squadron was sent farther southeast "toward Caria," the presumed southern boundary of Athenian naval operations under the Peace of Callias. The squadron was assigned the task of noting the movements of the Phoenician navy. Once other Delian League allies joined in the blockade of Samos, Pericles hurriedly led sixty additional vessels to Caria in response to a report that the Phoenician fleet was sailing toward Samos.[206] As Harold Mattingly has argued, Thucydides' use of "Phoenician" to refer to these naval forces can only mean Achaemenid imperial naval forces, and consequently it can be assumed that Pericles feared imperial intervention in the Samian rebellion.[207] Though Thucydides never indicates what came of this confrontation, it may be assumed that despite the existence of the Peace of Callias, there was still the potential of hostile actions by either side throughout the succeeding decades.

---

[206] Thucydides 1.116. For the Samian rebellion, see Meiggs, *The Athenian Empire*, 189-93; Lewis, *Sparta and Persia*, 59-62. Lewis' point that Pissuthnes was acting independent of the court in assisting the oligarchic party seems a strained conclusion designed to avoid any objections to the existence of the Peace of Callias. A satrap hiring and deploying a large force of mercenaries would certainly have come to the court's attention. Moreover, even in current times, it is not unusual for major powers to utilize the aspirations of factional elements in a society in order to wage a conflict that they are otherwise prohibited from entering. Pissuthnes could simply be perceived as representing Achaemenid interests in having anti-Athenian forces in control of Samos, but since a direct military role would be a violation of the Peace of Callias, he chose to support such a political change by sending mercenaries rather than imperial or satrapal forces.

[207] Harold Mattingly, "The Peace of Kallias," *Historia* 14 (1965):280.

This raises one final matter regarding the aftermath of the Egyptian disaster, namely Ctesias' report of the so-called revolt by Megabyzos, the satrap of Beyond the River, as the result of the execution of Inaros in the Achaemenid capital of Susa. As has been noted previously, there are considerable literary grounds for rejecting any authority to Ctesias' narrative of events from the retreat of the Delian League forces from Memphis on. It is essential to recognize that Ctesias' recounting of the revolt of Megabyzos is intertwined with his narratives of the termination of the Egyptian Revolt. It is not possible to dismiss Ctesias' account of the retreat of the Athenians and Inaros into the impregnable fortress "Byblos," where Megabyzos reportedly had to negotiate their safe passage in order to gain their surrender, and yet lend credibility to the narrative of Megabyzos' revolt over Inaros' later execution.[208] In short, Ctesias does not offer a supplemental narration to the condensed version of Thucydides: his account is at variance with that of all the other narratives.

According to Ctesias, following their surrender to Megabyzos in return for their safety, the Athenians and Inaros accompanied the Persian satrap to Susa. There, for five years or until around 449 BCE, their safety was assured. Once the Queen Amytis had prevailed on Artaxerxes I, Inaros and fifty Greeks were executed, and Megabyzos withdrew to his residence in "Syria" where his armed resistance to the empire began. There is not a shred of evidence independent of Ctesias to support any aspect of this account, and Thucydides' narrative flatly contradicts Ctesias on the end of the Greek effort in Egypt and the timing of Inaros' execution.[209] Moreover, Herodotus' brief recapitulation of the serious damage caused by Inaros' rebellion strongly suggests that if he was captured, Inaros would normally have been executed in Egypt in the presence of the Egyptian leadership as a demonstration of the empire's power.[210] In other, far less serious incidents of armed resistance to the Achaemenid empire, the usual Persian response was to make an example of the leadership of the rebellion to ensure that no future rebel would

---

[208] As does Meiggs, *The Athenian Empire,* who chastises Ctesias, claiming "much of his account is nonsense" (475), but accepts his account of the Megabyzos rebellion (145). It is striking that the same pattern of an individual who revolted, surrendered upon the promise that his life would be spared, was taken to Susa, and arbitrarily executed by the Persian king appears in Ctesias in his narrative of the revolt of Pissuthnes in c. 413 BCE (18, Ep. 83).

[209] Bigwood, "Ctesias' Account of the Revolt of Inarus," 15-6; Lloyd, *Herodotus Book II: Introduction,* 46 n. 187.

[210] Herodotus 3.15.

step forth.[211] In sum, outside of Ctesias' highly questionable narratives, there is not a single piece of evidence that can be produced to support the occurrence of a revolt by Megabyzos in the early 440s BCE.[212] Given the problems inherent in Ctesias' narrative itself, one must conclude that the Megabyzos revolt was not part of the aftermath of the Egyptian Revolt.

In summarizing the importance of the evidence from the available historical evidence, it is clear that the dramatic entry of Greek military power onto an imperial territory in support of an already serious indigenous revolt against the empire represented the most serious challenge to imperial control the Persians faced in the fifth century. A military success for Inaros and his Athenian allies would have represented the loss of Achaemenid control over the eastern Mediterranean and the probable loss of the western territories in the Levant and Asia Minor. As such, the decade of 460-450 BCE represented an extraordinary crisis in imperial control of the eastern Mediterranean sphere, a crisis that called forth extraordinary efforts to suppress the Egyptian Revolt and to keep Athenian naval power from gaining a military advantage over the empire. Nor was the perception of a threat completely removed by the Peace of Callias, since in 440 BCE there were still concerns over a possible clash between these two antagonists.

Consequently, for the period from 460 BCE on, it can be assumed that the Achaemenid empire was intensely involved in taking steps to consolidate its hold over those territories that were imperiled by the continuing Greek pressure in the eastern Mediterranean. Given the importance of the Levant both as a landbridge connecting Egypt with the rest of the empire and as a means of access to the eastern Mediterranean, it can be anticipated that the empire was concerned with security in the Levant. Such an assumption should be verifiable from some source of data on Achaemenid imperial administration in the Levant in this period.

---

211 For example, the revolt of Masistes, satrap of Bactria (Olmstead, *History of the Persian Empire,* 267); the revolt of Tennes, king of Sidon (Cook, *The Persian Empire,* 223).

212 The attempt by Olmstead, *History of the Persian Empire,* 312 to appeal to a cylinder seal in the Hermitage at Moscow as a depiction of Inaros' execution is flawed. There is no certain identification that the enemies being slain by a royal figure are Inaros and the Greeks, nor that the royal personnage is Artaxerxes I. Moreover, the commemoration of an historical event on a cylinder seal is out of keeping with the Achaemenid preference for depicting symbolic gestures of power; Henri Frankfort, *Cylindar Seals: A Documentary Essay on the Art and Religion of the Ancient Near East* (London: Macmillan and Co., 1939) 220-21.

Whatever transformations may have taken place internally with regard to the imperial administration of the Levantine territories, they would have been related to an overarching concern with gaining a stronger control over the region. Thus, if the missions of Ezra and Nehemiah are in some manner to be interpreted as the result of imperial disquiet in the face of the Egyptian Revolt and its aftermath, then their activities must be shown to have contributed toward some greater control and security in the region.

4

The Archaeology of the Imperial Response

The various interpretations of the imperial roles of Ezra and Nehemiah discussed earlier in Chapter Two suffered from a common inability to demonstrate effectively that the events of the Egyptian Revolt altered Achaemenid practices in administering the Levant in general, or Yehud in particular. As has been seen in the preceding analysis of the revolt, there is every reason to anticipate that Achaemenid rule in the Levantine territories would have been impacted by the events surrounding the revolt, without postulating a subsequent revolt by the territorial satrap against the Persian court (the "Megabyzos Revolt"). Having set such an historical context for the transformation of imperial rule, however, only enhances the possibility of such a transformation; it does not demonstrate that Achaemenid rule was in fact altered.

Despite the abundance of documentary sources outside of the biblical narratives regarding Achaemenid rule in the Near East, virtually none of this evidence is directly relevant to the Levantine region.[1] Within the biblical narratives themselves, neither the Egyptian Revolt nor other world events are ever mentioned; and the narratives only allude to imperial conditions in the period, preferring instead to interpret the

---

[1] Ackroyd, *Israel under Babylon and Persia,* 175-78; Hermann, *A History of Israel in Old Testament Times,* 298; Stern, *Material Culture,* xv.

missions in a theological framework.[2] Consequently, in the absence of literary and epigraphic sources, it is necessary to analyze the material remains of the period to determine if a transformation in the administration of the Restoration community did in fact take place.

The use of material cultural remains to reconstruct social and political systems has only become more commonplace in the last decade among the exponents of an explicitly anthropological archaeology, the so-called "New Archaeology".[3] Within this approach to archaeological research, scholars emphasize the necessary coherence of method and theory, since the theoretical assumptions of the investigator are determinant in the process of selecting and interpreting the artifactual data.[4] Consequently, before proceeding to analyze any aspect of the material culture of the Levant during the mid-fifth century, it is necessary to articulate the theoretical basis utilized in this analysis.

While much of the "New Archaeology" is concerned with generalizing paradigms of cultural developments, Near Eastern archaeology has been concerned with particularizing issues largely focused on reconstructing events in history.[5] The present study shares the particularizing interests of history, finding its focus on the impact of an historical event, the Egyptian Revolt, on the administration of the Levant as an imperial territory. At the same time, there is a generalizing aspect present in that the Achaemenid empire is conceived of as a specific adaptation of a certain social system possessing more universal characteristics. Phrased in a somewhat different manner, an empire represents a unique social adaptation to the need to control and govern a territory embracing diverse ethnic and cultural populations. As such, an empire's primary concern is with the reproduction of its control through a combination of interrelated mechanisms.[6] While coercive force is one means utilized for

---

[2] Ackroyd, *I and II Chronicles, Ezra, Nehemiah,* 239-40; Clines, *Ezra, Nehemiah, Esther,* 98-9 and 142-44; Williamson, *Ezra, Nehemiah,* xlv.

[3] An important survey can be found in Charles Redman, Edward Curtin, Nina Versaggi, and Jeffrey Wanser, "Social Archeology: The Future of the Past," 1-17 in *Social Archeology: Beyond Subsistence and Dating,* Charles Redman et al., eds. (New York: Academic Press, 1978).

[4] A recent restatement of this basic point has been made by Michael Shanks and Christopher Tilley, *Social Theory and Archaeology* (Albuquerque: University of New Mexico Press, 1988), 9-15 and 25-8.

[5] See particularly the comments of William G. Dever, "The Impact of the 'New Archaeology' on Syro-Palestinian Archaeology," *BASOR* 242 (1981):21.

[6] Shmuel Eisenstadt, *The Political Systems of Empires* (New York: Free Press of Glencoe, 1963), 16; and *A Sociological Approach to Comparative Civilizations: The*

the initial extension of imperial control over a subject territory, it becomes an ineffective means for maintaining continuing administrative dominance.[7] As a consequence, imperial systems must seek a mixture of coercive and voluntary mechanisms to insure the reproducibility of imperial rule of the subject territory.

There are a number of common mechanisms employed by imperial systems to achieve the full integration of a territory into the empire including the dissolution of self-sufficient economic structures, the incorporation of traditional territorial aristocracies into the imperial governing structure, and the development of new and efficient means of communication between the imperial center and the outlying imperial territories.[8] While these mechanisms are independent social developments, they are all contingent upon the empire's ability to force its will upon the subject territory. Without the ability to actualize such far-reaching changes within a subject territory, an imperial system was incapable of transforming a recently conquered territory into a fully integrated part of the system.

A primary means for insuring compliance with the empire's goals was a system of local garrisons representing the coercive power of the imperial system's superior military resources. The garrisoning of imperial forces scattered throughout the subject territory insured the acquiescence of the territory to the empire's efforts at social transformation and integration into the larger imperial system.[9] As a technique of imperial administration, the use of garrisons within imperial territories was widespread in the first millennium BCE, having been employed by the Assyrian and Babylonian empires.[10] Within the Athenian empire, the use of garrisons was accompanied by far-reaching changes in the social and political fabric of the subject cities, including formal oaths of loyalty to the Athenian people, the appointment of Athenian representatives as regulators of the subject city's ports, and various economic reforms to bring the practices of the subject city's marketplace into conformity with

---

Development and Directions of a Research Program (Jerusalem: Department of Sociology and Social Anthropology, Hebrew University, 1986) 3-4.

[7] Michael Mann, *The Sources of Social Power. Volume 1: A History of Power from the Beginning to A. D. 1760* (Cambridge: University Press, 1986) 174-75.

[8] Eisenstadt, *The Political Systems of Empires*, 33-4.

[9] Mann, *The Sources of Social Power. Volume 1*, 176.

[10] For the use of garrisons in Assyrian practice, see the comments of Brinkman, "Babylonia under the Assyrian Empire, 745-627 B. C.," 235. On Babylonian garrisons, see Saggs, *The Greatness That Was Babylon*, 148.

Athenian desires.[11] In sum, by the mid-fifth century the use of garrisons in a subject territory was only part of a larger imperial effort to control and integrate that territory into the imperial system.

For the Achaemenid empire, the evidence is suggestive of a similar pattern in the employment of garrisons, though the available sources are not as precise on this point as could be desired. Of the ancient writers, Xenophon's *Cyropaedia* and *Oeconomicus* present the most complete portrayal, suggesting that once a territory had been coerced into the empire, a complete system of garrisons was established, some in outlying regions while others were located in strategic urban centers.[12] Inferring further from this point, Pierre Briant has argued that such garrisons functioned as the basic revenue collection units across the empire and that their presence was an integral part of the full administrative system being established in any particular territory.[13] There is little direct evidence either to support or call into question Briant's thesis, though there can be no doubt that the formation of Achaemenid imperial garrisons within a territory was, at a minimum, only part of a series of administrative moves intended to break down a subject territory's independence and to bring it to a point of dependence upon the resources and structures of the imperial system.[14]

Given this theoretical and historical background, if it could be shown that an intensified presence of imperial garrisons appeared as a contemporaneous phenomenon in the Levant, then it could be anticipated that their appearance was part of a larger effort to integrate the Levant more fully into the Achaemenid imperial system. Moreover, if the time of such an intensification in the garrisoning of imperial military forces could be fixed in the mid-fifth century while the Egyptian revolt was presenting a severe challenge to imperial control of the eastern

---

11 On Athenian practices, see the specific responses to the revolt of Erythrae, ca. 450 BCE in Meiggs, *The Athenian Empire,* 112-15 and Naphtali Lewis, *The Fifth Century B. C.* Greek Historical Documents. (Toronto: A. M. Hakkert, 1971) 7-8. On a more general note, see Meiggs, *The Athenian Empire,* 206-7.

12 For a synopsis of the evidence from Xenophon along with some of the difficulties with this evidence, see Christopher Tuplin, "Persian Garrisons in Xenophon and Other Sources," *Achaemenid History* 3 (1988):67-70.

13 Pierre Briant, "Contrainte militaire, Dépendance rurale et Exploitation des territoires en Asie achéménide," *Index* 8 (1978/79):48-98.

14 For a discussion of Briant's thesis in relation to the available data, see Tuplin, "Persian Garrisons in Xenophon and Other Sources," 69 and Christopher Tuplin, "The Administration of the Achaemenid Empire," 121 in *Coinage and Administration in the Athenian and Persian Empires,* I. Carradice, ed. BAR International Series 343. (Oxford: British Archaeological Reports, 1987).

Mediterranean, then it could be assumed that the intensified militarization of the Levant at the same point in time was part of the Achaemenid response to the Athenian threat to its western holdings. Thus, the material remains of imperial garrisons in the Levant, namely fortresses built specifically to maintain imperial interests, are the primary archaeological features for investigations. Such remains hold the potential of providing an archaeological witness to one integral aspect of the transformation of imperial administration in the Levant in the mid-fifth century BCE.

There is a significant methodological problem to be resolved in any effort to pursue this line of inquiry, however, and that is the difficulty in dating the material remains of Achaemenid fortresses with enough precision first, to demonstrate their contemporaneity to each other and second, to place their foundation in the decade of 460-50 BCE when the outcome of the Egyptian Revolt was still unresolved. The primary means for making such chronological determinations of material remains from the fifth century is the analysis of recovered ceramics. However, native Palestinian ceramic traditions of the fifth century for most classes of vessels are marked by substantial continuity with earlier forms, extending back into the sixth century.[15] While occasional finds of imported Attic wares allow for some chronological markers in the development of common forms, in general there are relatively few vessel types possessing enough variation in form over the fifth century to allow for a precise chronological location in the decade at issue. On the other hand, the well-refined chronology for Attic wares does allow for greater chronological precision among certain specific types when such imported ceramic wares are present.

Given the restricted utility of Palestinian ceramic typology for the mid-fifth century, it is apparent that other means must also be employed to provide the kind of chronological precision required. One option is to attempt to determine an architectural typology for those fortress structures that can be shown by other means to fit the chronological parameters of the Egyptian revolt. If such a typology can also be shown to be distinctive for the mid-fifth century, then an important analytical tool has been created for assessing the possible intensification of the garrisoning of imperial forces in the Levant.

---

[15] The main study of Persian period ceramics in Palestine is Paul W. Lapp, "The Pottery of Palestine in the Persian Period," 179-97 in *Archäologie und altes Testament*, Arnulf Kuschke and Ernst Kutsch, eds. (Tübingen: T. C. B. Mohr, 1970). See also the comments of Walter E. Rast, *Taanach I: Studies in the Iron Age Pottery*. ASOR Excavation Reports, 1. (Cambridge, MA: American Schools of Oriental Research, 1978), 47.

As will be seen below, there are a number of fortresses in the Levant that for various reasons have been assigned to the mid-fifth century BCE. However, very few of these sites have been excavated, and of those that have been excavated, few have benefitted from stratigraphically correct procedures in excavation. Still fewer in number are those sites that have yielded sufficient imported ceramics or other chronologically sensitive data to allow for a precise chronological determination. However, three sites do seem to fit these requirements, namely an unnamed fortress along the Palestinian coast north of Ashdod, a site called Ḥorvat Mesora (one of series of fortresses recently excavated in the Negev), and a fortress located at the site of Tell es-Saʿidiyeh on the eastern side of the Jordan River Valley. Since each of these locations presents a unique combination of archaeological and architectural data, each site will initially be treated separately before bringing their combined data to bear on refining a specific definition for a mid-fifth-century Achaemenid garrison.

In 1969, Joseph Porath directed a salvage excavation along a ridge some 2 kms north of the ancient site of Ashdod along the Mediterranean coast. In the 1974 publication of this excavation, Porath identified the structure he found as a fortress of the Persian period.[16] The structure itself was precisely square, its exterior measurements being 29.8 meters by 29.8 meters, and consisted of a series of rooms built along all four sides around a central courtyard. The courtyard was 16 by 16 meters square.[17] There were sixteen rooms around the courtyard of varying length but all featured a uniform width of 4 meters.

Within the structure a variety of ceramic materials was recovered, along with iron and bronze weaponry. Of the local ceramics, few were of types with a limited chronological range. For example, a typical lamp with a flat base, wide flange, and sharply pinched lip was recovered, which Porath dated broadly to the sixth through fourth centuries.[18] Porath did note a large bowl with flat base and lug handles as a variant of a well-attested type and claims this particular form was limited to the fifth through fourth centuries BCE.[19] However, it appears that this type of

---

16 The descriptions of the site and the results of the excavations appear in Joseph Porath, "A Fortress of the Persian Period Above Ashdod," *ʿAtiqot* [Hebrew Series] 7 (1974):43-55. See also the English summary in Stern, *Material Culture,* 19.

17 A diagram of this fortress appears in Figure 1, and was taken from Porath, "Fortress," 44.

18 Porath, "Fortress," 47; also Figure 5:6.

19 Porath, "Fortress," 46; also Figure 4:3.

bowl has both a wider geographical and chronological distribution than indicated by Porath, ranging from the late seventh century to the fourth century BCE.[20] In sum, there was little in the local ceramic finds to limit the foundation of the structure to any point more specific than the Persian period.

More telling was the recovery of several fragments of Attic black-glazed wares, along with some Cypriot imported wares. The Attic materials were analyzed with the assistance of Saul Weinberg, and included a typical mid-fifth century lekythos as well as the rim and handle of a skhyphos, also of the mid-fifth century.[21] The Cypriot wares consisted of several painted bowls, identified with similar wares recovered from strata of the fifth through fourth centuries BCE.[22] On the basis of this ceramic data, Porath dated the foundation of the fortress to the mid-fifth century and its abandonment to the difficulties the Persians encountered in controlling the Levantine coast in the first quarter of the fourth century BCE.[23]

A second fortress for consideration in establishing a typology of design for such structures in the mid-fifth century was excavated at Ḥorvat Mesora, though its identification as a mid-fifth century installation took several efforts in excavation. Though initially identified and surveyed in 1958, Ḥorvat Mesora was not actually excavated until 1975 when Rudolph Cohen led a salvage effort at the site.[24] The site is situated on a hill adjacent to the Naḥal Besor, and guards a portion of the central Negev road system of antiquity.[25]

In the initial excavations, the visible ruins were analyzed and revealed a perfectly square structure, almost precisely 21 by 21 meters in exterior dimension. Nine casemate rooms surrounded a central courtyard, the courtyard measuring 11 by 11 meters.[26] The rooms had a uniform width of about 2.5 meters and varied in length. Two of the rooms were excavated in this initial effort, and Cohen reported finding a "layer

---

20 Stern, *Material Culture*, 97.

21 Porath, "Fortress," 47; also Figure 5:7-12. Professor Weinberg's contribution is acknowledged in 47 note 23.

22 Porath, "Fortress," 47-8.

23 Porath, "Fortress," 49.

24 Rudolph Cohen, "The Iron Age Fortresses in the Central Negev," *BASOR* 236 (1980):70; Rudolph Cohen, "Ḥ. Mesora," *IEJ* 27 (1977):170-71.

25 Cohen, "The Iron Age Fortresses," 77.

26 These measurements follow those given in Rudolph Cohen, "Ḥorvat Mesora," *IEJ* 36 (1986):113, the most recent excavation of the site. Some of the earlier data contain variant figures for the structure's measurements.

of ashes" covering the floors of the rooms, in which a ceramic type he called "Negev" pottery was present.[27]

On the basis of the Negev pottery and several chronological ties between Negev ceramic types and the wheel-made wares of the tenth century BCE found at other sites in the central Negev, Cohen dated Ḥorvat Mesora to the tenth century. He also saw the fortress as part of a larger system of defenses guarding the southern border of the Solomonic kingdom.[28]

The site of Ḥorvat Mesora was revisited in 1985 for a second round of excavation, again under the direction of Rudolph Cohen. In this effort, four rooms surrounding the courtyard were excavated with considerably different results. All four rooms yielded ceramics of the fifth-fourth century BCE, the earliest forms dating from the mid-fifth century, according to Cohen. The remains of clay ovens situated on the fortress floors within the rooms also indicated that there was only a single phase of occupation in the fortress, with no reuse of the structure. This new evidence demonstrated that the fortress had actually been founded and occupied beginning in the mid-fifth century, and accordingly Cohen published a retraction of his earlier dating of the site.[29] He also used the data from Ḥorvat Mesora to reinterpret several other installations as forts of the Persian period, and has claimed that these constitute a southern boundary of Yehud in that period.[30]

The final site to be examined, Tell es-Saʿidiyeh, is located in the central Jordan Valley and was excavated by a joint expedition in the mid-1960s under the direction of James Pritchard. Though the field research of the site was never completed, an architectural feature called the "square building" was fully excavated and a final report on the results of the excavation has appeared.[31]

---

27 Cohen, "The Iron Age Fortresses," 70; Cohen, "Ḥ. Mesora," 170. In a later publication, Cohen implied that no Negev pottery was actually recovered from the fortress: Rudolph Cohen, "Solomon's Negev Defense Line Contained Three Fewer Fortresses," *Biblical Archaeology Review* 12 (1986):40-42.

28 Cohen, "The Iron Age Fortresses," 77-78; Rudolph Cohen, "The Fortresses King Solomon Built to Protect His Southern Border," *Biblical Archaeology Review* 11/3 (1985):69-70.

29 Cohen, "Ḥorvat Mesora," 113; Cohen, "Solomon's Negev Defense Line," 42.

30 Cohen, "Solomon's Negev Defense Line," 43-5.

31 James B. Pritchard, *Tell es-Saʿidiyeh: Excavations on the Tell, 1964-1966*. University Museum Monograph 60. (Philadelphia: The University Museum, University of Pennsylvania, 1985). A discussion of the disruption in the excavations caused by natural disasters and the 1967 war can be found on xv-xvi, and a discussion of the excavation of the "square building" on 60.

The square building, so named because of its exact 22 by 22 meter exterior dimensions (the north-south line was 21.95 meters in length and the east-west line was 22.05 meters), was made of mudbrick with timber reinforcements around several doorways. In plan, the building consisted of ten rooms of unequal length surrounding a paved courtyard approximately 9.5 by 7.8 meters in dimension. The rooms were placed on all four sides of the courtyard, and some evidence of roofing was found in the debris on the floors of the rooms. The courtyard itself possessed a covered channel that drained water from the courtyard to a point outside the exterior walls of the structure.[32]

There was no reported stratigraphic evidence of phases of use in the square building, although the existence of two spaces in the southern corner of the structure, both lacking entries, led the excavator to conclude alterations were made to the structure's original design to support the erection of a tower over the southern corner.[33] No time interval was postulated between the original foundation of the building and these subsequent alterations to the structure's basic plan.

That the building had two chronologically distinct phases of occupation is clear from the distribution of artifactual materials found within the structure. The excavator, however, did not offer this conclusion. Most rooms contained little or no remains of habitation, suggesting to the excavator that the structure had been abandoned.[34] However, room 103, which was a corridor leading from the exterior entry of the building to the north toward the interior rooms, yielded numerous charred beams and clay roofing tiles, along with loom weights and a cosmetic palette.[35] Room 104, immediately to the north of room 103, also yielded evidence of burning as well as roofing tiles and an important incense burner bearing an Aramaic inscription. Only rooms 103 and 104 showed evidence of burning and a concentration of roofing remains. This factor, when combined with the concentration of loom weights and other domestic articles in room 103, indicate that following the abandonment of the structure, these two rooms alone were reoccupied for a time until fire destroyed them.[36]

---

32 All details of the square building are derived from the data presented in the final report; Pritchard, *Tell es-Saᶜidiyeh*, 60-66.

33 See the discussion of Rooms 109 and 110 in Pritchard, *Tell es-Saᶜidiyeh*, 64.

34 Pritchard, *Tell es-Saᶜidiyeh*, 64-5.

35 See the discussion of room 103 in Pritchard, *Tell es-Sa idiyeh*, 62.

36 The excavator notes that architectural features and not soil layers were used to determine the various strata of the site; *Tell es-Saᶜidiyeh*, xvi. The lack of stratigraphic profiles for any of the interior features of the building further demonstrates the non-

Though not recognized by the excavator, this alternative reconstruction is crucial for determining the date of the structure. The relative poverty of artifactual materials found in the structure led the excavator to date the building on the basis of one carbon-14 sample taken from the ashy debris of room 104, as interpreted in the context of samples from the floor immediately beneath the square building.[37] He then concluded that the building "belongs to the Persian period," and was part of an occupational phase dated from 420 to 180 BCE.[38] However, the carbon sample from the burn debris in room 104 would simply provide a date for the secondary reoccupation of the structure and not for the period of construction and primary use. In order to determine that date, it is necessary to examine some of the other finds from the building outside of rooms 103 and 104.

Within the courtyard paving (designated room 101), a partial lamp was recovered (S1186/P665). The lamp is of the closed lamp type with a wide mouth in the center for holding the fuel. This type first appears in the Levant during the fifth century BCE and continues into the early decades of the Hellenistic period.[39] The particular form found in the courtyard is an early stage in the development of the closed lamp type and is paralleled by a similar closed lamp from the "Residency" at Lachish, recovered in the original excavations of 1932-38.[40] The final publication report of these excavations dated the "Residency" to the mid-fifth century on the basis of several indicators, including sherds of imported Attic pottery.[41] This dating scheme has recently been confirmed by the renewed excavations at Lachish under the direction of David Usshishkin.[42] Consequently, the lamp from the courtyard of the square building at Tell es-Saʿidiyeh suggests a mid-fifth century date for the structure.

---

stratigraphical nature of the excavations. Were such profiles available, it might be possible to test the alternative reconstruction of the structure's history presented here.

[37] Pritchard, *Tell es-Saʿidiyeh*, 65-66, 79-80.

[38] Pritchard, *Tell es-Saʿidiyeh*, 79-80.

[39] Lamp S1186/P665 is published in Figure 18 No. 20, not No. 4 as indicated in the text and the table to Figure 18. For a general description of the type, see Stern, *Material Culture*, 129.

[40] Olga Tufnell, *Lachish III: The Iron Age* (London: Oxford University Press, 1953), Plate 82 No. 137; see also the discussion on 286.

[41] Tufnell, *Lachish III*, 133-35.

[42] David Ussishkin, "The Destruction of Lachish by Sennacherib and the Dating of the Royal Judean Storage Jars," *Tel Aviv* 4 (1977):38-9.

A mid-fifth century date for the square building is also suggested by a bronze fibula recovered in room 107 of the building.[43] The fibula is of a simple triangular bow form that finds distribution in the Levant primarily during the fifth century.[44] None of the other artifactual remains found in the areas outside of rooms 103 and 104 are of a specific enough type to allow a chronological determination to be made. While the lamp and the fibula are meager remains for so large a building, they are consistent in suggesting a mid-fifth century date for the primary occupation of the structure. Consequently, the interpretation of the structure's history most consistent with the material remains suggests that the building was constructed in the mid-fifth century BCE. Subsequent to its construction, a tower was erected over the southern corner of the building, perhaps to provide a better vantage point over the routes that ran south of this location. This primary use ended with a general abandonment of the structure, possibly within a few decades of its having been built. After the abandonment, and by the first quarter of the fourth century, only rooms 103 and 104 were reoccupied. The nature of this reoccupation is obscure, but these spaces may have been used as a textile workshop, based on the large number of loom weights found in the rooms as well as the absence of typical domestic ceramics of the period, such as storage jars. This second phase of use ended with a fire that destroyed both rooms.

The general architectural form of the square building, combined with the unusual distribution of materials within the structure, led the excavator to conclude that the square building was a Persian period fortress. Pritchard also drew attention to the great similarity in architectural design between the square building and several of the Negev fortresses such as Ḥorvat Mesora, although he rejected the possibility of an immediate parallel, based on the erroneous tenth-century BCE date assigned to several of these Negev fortresses.[45]

Other excavated fortresses in the Levant can be added to this group once the results of their excavation are fully published. One example is the fortress at Naḥal Yattir, near Beersheba, where excavations in 1986-87 revealed a stone structure measuring 21.5 by 21.5 meters, featuring a central courtyard surrounded by rooms on all four sides. The ceramics

43 Fibula S1160/Br72 appears in Figure 18 No. 25, not No. 9 as listed in the description of the finds from room 107 on 63.

44 David Stronach, "The Development of the Fibula in the Near East," *Iraq* 21 (1959):194-95; Judy Birmingham, "The Development of the Fibula in Cyprus and the Levant," *PEQ* 95 (1963):108-9.

45 Pritchard, *Tell es-Saᶜidiyeh,* 65.

recovered from the structure led the excavators to date it to the mid-fifth century and to classify it as part of the Negev fortress group represented by Ḥorvat Mesora.[46] An additional example appears in the preliminary reports of the excavations at Tell Seraᶜ. The reports noted the discovery of a rectangular fortress of the Persian period similar in form to the one excavated by Porath north of Ashdod and the square building at Tell es-Saᶜidiyeh. Early reports of the excavations assigned all Persian period remains to one phase of occupation, stratum V, dated from the mid-fifth to the fourth centuries on the basis of imported Attic wares.[47]

The basic features of the excavated examples of Persian garrisons are summarized in Table 1, and the excavated groundplans are shown in Figure 1. As was noted by Ephraim Stern, all of these structures share an affinity with the Assyrian open-court architectural form.[48] However, Stern classifies these particular structures under the general heading of "domestic architecture," and fails to deal directly with their character as imperial, that is, public architecture. As imperial structures, one could anticipate a certain amount of shared design characteristics between these various fortresses. Despite variations in exterior wall thicknesses, exterior measurements, and courtyard measurements, the percentage of the courtyard's area in relation to the total area of the structure is similar at all three fortresses (Table 1). In terms of the three representative fortresses in Table 1, the mean percentage of the total area devoted to the courtyard is 24.6%. The consistency in this relationship between the courtyard and the structure as a whole, combined with the centrality of the courtyard to the architectural design of these structures, suggests that the courtyard was an integral element in the function of these structures. As such, the relationship of the courtyard to the structure as a whole is a

---

[46] Steven Derfler, "The Persian Fortress of Naḥal Yattir and Its Relationship to the Regional Center of Tel Beersheva," Paper delivered at the American Schools of Oriental Research Annual Meetings, Boston, December 5, 1987. Also personal communication, Steven Derfler to the author, August 24, 1988. I am indebted to Prof. Derfler for his willingness to share this information. See also the preliminary report of the first season at the site, Steven Derfler, "Naḥal Yattir," *IEJ* 37 (1987):195-7.

[47] See the discussion in Stern, *Material Culture,* 26-7; also E. D. Oren, "Esh-Shariᶜa, Tell (Tel Seraᶜ)," 1059-69 in *Encyclopedia of Archaeological Excavations in the Holy Land, Volume 4,* Michael Avi-Yonah and Ephraim Stern, eds. (Englewood Cliffs, NJ: Prentice-Hall, Inc, 1978); and Eliezer Oren, "Ziglag—A Biblical City on the Edge of the Negev," *Biblical Archaeologist* 45 (1982):158.

[48] Stern, *Material Culture,* 54-5; Stern in part follows the analysis of Ruth Amiran and I. Dunayevsky, "The Assyrian Open-court Building and Its Palestinian Derivatives," *BASOR* 149 (1958):25-32.

key factor in developing a typology of such structures from the mid-fifth century.

Table 1.—Comparative Features of Excavated Fortresses

Site	*Ext. Meas.*	*Ext. Wall*	*Courtyard*	*Rms*	*Ave. Rm. Area*	*%**
N. Ashdod	29.8 X 29.8	1.4-2 m	16 X 16	16	23.13m^2	28.8
H. Mesora	21 X 21	.8 m	11.4 X 11.4	9	17.08m^2	29.5
T. es-Saʿidiyeh	22 X 22	1.25	9.5 X 8	10	24.67m^2	15.7

**The percentage figure represents the percentage of the total area of the fortress occupied by the courtyard.*

The importance of the central court to the function of these structures was recently reaffirmed in the work of Israel Finkelstein, although Cohen's initial misdating of Ḥorvat Mesora caused Finkelstein to make several erroneous assumptions. Building on the work of Cohen and others on the fortresses of the Negev region, Finkelstein questioned the assumption of a military or strategic role to these sites on the basis of their geographical distribution and architectural layout.[49]

As a point of departure, Finkelstein assumed all so-called fortresses reported by modern surveys of the Negev were part of the same cultural phenomena, despite their dissimilarity in architectural form.[50] Taking this cluster of structures together, he contended they could not function as fortresses because of their remoteness from any reconstructable road system for the Negev.[51] He also pointed out the range in width of the

49 Finkelstein's original Hebrew essay, "The Iron Age Fortresses of the Negev—Sedentarization of Desert Nomads," appeared in *Eretz-Israel* 18 (1985):366-79. An English translation with some slight revisions appeared as "The Iron Age Fortresses of the Negev Highlands—Sedentarization of the Nomads," in *Tel Aviv* 11 (1984):189-209. Since, despite the publication dates, the English version was written subsequent to the Hebrew version, the following references will be to the English form of the essay.

50 See Finkelstein, "The Iron Age Fortresses of the Negev Highlands," 193-4 where he denies such formal analysis has validity since "there is no real uniformity even within these groupings." This is simply a critique on the previous means of defining the types of forms, not on the validity of using the formal characteristics of such structures to provide data pertinent to their original function. For the usual typology of the Negev structures, see Yohanan Aharoni, "Forerunners of the Limes: Iron Age Fortesses in the Negev," *IEJ* 17 (1967):1-17.

51 "The Iron Age Fortresses of the Negev Highlands," 190-92.

outer walls of these structures, arguing that the average of .5 to .8 meters in width was hardly sufficient for a defensive function.[52] He then assumed that the structures identified as fortresses were contemporaneous with other nearby domestic structures, and that the preferable way to determine the "functional character" of these sites was by analyzing the "ratio between the open courtyard area of a site and its built-up area." Finkelstein contended that the relationship between habitation area and courtyard was reflective of the subsistence pattern of the original inhabitants without offering any support for this assertion.[53] Working with estimates of relative population density at these sites, Finkelstein calculated an estimate for the amount of courtyard area per inhabitant, arguing that sites with a larger amount of courtyard area per inhabitant were reflective of a pastoral subsistence pattern.[54] His final conclusion was that the Negev "fortresses" actually represented habitation areas and signified the transition of pastoral nomadic groups to sedentary agriculturalists during the early Iron Age in the Levant.

This analysis by Finkelstein is fraught with problems, not the least of which is his insistence on analyzing all the "fortress" structures as part of the same cultural phenomenon. In this regard he was partly misled by the dating of several of the square forms of these structures to the early Iron Age by the principal investigators. This was certainly true in his handling of the data from Ḥorvat Mesora, in which he followed Cohen's earlier dating of the site to the early Iron Age.[55]

Of more significance is Finkelstein's isolation of the central courtyard as an integral element in the design and function of these structures. Finkelstein's analysis would benefit from more controls, most notably a comparison with clear ethnographic analogies from contemporary examples of cultures following a nomadic pastoralism subsistence pattern. Neither does he offer any evidence from the artifactual materials recovered in association with these structures to buttress his claim that they are reflective of such a subsistence pattern. However, his assumption that a high ratio of courtyard area per person is indicative of nomadic pastoralism seems plausible on the surface, although far more evidence than Finkelstein presents is needed before such an assumption can be considered a working hypothesis.

---

52 "The Iron Age Fortresses of the Negev Highlands," 193.

53 "The Iron Age Fortresses of the Negev Highlands," 193-94.

54 "The Iron Age Fortresses of the Negev Highlands," 194-95.

55 See his references in "The Iron Age Fortresses of the Negev Highlands," 204 n. 12.

Less secure is Finkelstein's assertion that those sites possessing a lower ratio of courtyard area per inhabitant reflect a sedentary agrarian subsistence pattern.[56] Again, the failure to provide either analogous ethnographic comparisons or assemblages of materials in association with these structures that are indicative of seasonal agrarian activities is a serious deficiency in Finkelstein's argumentation. In fact, he offers no justification for making such an assumption.

If one analyses his data from a slightly different set of hypotheses, a different conclusion emerges. The sites within his database presenting the lowest amount of courtyard per inhabitant (under five square meters per person), are almost uniformly square in form and have eight to nine casemate rooms surrounding the courtyard on all four sides.[57] This suggests that contrary to Finkelstein's initial assumption, the typology of architectural design for these structures is significant and needs to be included in any analysis of the plausible chronology and function of these Negev sites.

Despite its shortcomings, Finkelstein's study emphasizes that the courtyard of these structures is not an isolated feature but an integral element in the overall conception of these sites. Moreover, the courtyard will play the same function in those structures that are reflective of the same subsistence patterning, despite differences in size or location. This sameness of function can be revealed by a mathematical analysis of the courtyard area. Where Finkelstein's analysis is not helpful is in his mixing together various architectural forms under the assumption that the architectural plan is not significant.

It is common sense to assume that a structure's architectural form must, in some measure, reflect its anticipated function. Structures possessing similar exterior shapes and interior spaces are plausibly designed for the same function within a particular culture. There is the issue of size, however, and the possible chronological or functional significance of size differentials. For those structures possessing a central courtyard design, the courtyard would presumably play the same role in the function of the structure as a whole. If that is the case, then sites having similar exterior forms and interior plans will also share a similar relationship to the courtyard area, in spite of size differences.

---

56 "The Iron Age Fortresses of the Negev Highlands," 197.

57 See the chart on "The Iron Age Fortresses of the Negev Highlands," 191. The sites are "Near Haroʿa" (4.1 square meters per person), Ritma (4.6), Mesora (4.2), and Laʿana (4.7). Only Laʿana is not square in form, but is oval.

While Finkelstein attempted to express this relationship in terms of the ratio of courtyard area per inhabitant, it is more direct to compare sites on the basis of the percentage of the structure's total area dedicated to the courtyard. This avoids the speculative character of assuming a certain population size calculated on the basis of the site's total area (a ratio that in itself is contingent on the subsistence pattern of the population). It also provides a useful tool for comparing fortress plans over a broad range of Levantine history, as will be seen below.

To return to the excavated examples of fortresses from the mid-fifth century, three basic characteristics define their form. First and foremost, the fortresses of the mid-fifth century are square, and in each of the excavated examples, the shape is laid out with considerable precision. This implies that their squared form is a deliberate design characteristic. Second, they consist of a central courtyard with casemate rooms surrounding the open area on all four sides. Third, the courtyard constitutes roughly one-quarter of the total area of the structure. While there is some variation in this relationship, in general the courtyard can be said never to occupy more than one-third of the total structure's area, the example of the fortress at Ḥorvat Mesora being the largest of the excavated group (29.5%).[58] These three factors can be considered the most diagnostic of a mid-fifth century fortress, at least as defined by the excavated examples treated thus far.

The utility of this proposed typology for fortresses of the mid-fifth century is perhaps best seen when assessing other examples of excavated Levantine fortresses from the first millennium BCE. Table 2 presents examples of free-standing fortresses, the excavation or survey of which has provided a reasonably clear chronological setting. In that each site has some special circumstances associated with it, a brief discussion of each is in order.

---

[58] The statistical mean is 24.6% for this population, with a standard deviation of 6.4%. This would suggest that the percentage of the fortress area occupied by the courtyard could range from 18.2%-31%. These figures are presented as an observation on the excavated examples and can only provide an estimated range given the limited population involved. However, the regularity within the sample population suggests the variation in percentage will follow a standard distribution, placing 68.26% of all examples within this range. On the utility of this form of statistical description for establishing a typology and the problems inherent in the limited populations analyzed by archaeologists see Stephen Shennan, *Quantifying Archaeology* (Edinburgh: Edinburgh University Press, 1988), 102-08.

Table 2.—Excavated Fortresses of the First Millennium BCE Having Courtyards

Site, Date	Form	Rooms	Percentage*
Beer Hafir, 10th cent.	rectang.	4 sides	44.2
T. Nagila, 8th cent.	rectang.	4 sides	63.1
Qumran, 8th cent.	rectang.	3 sides	37.6
Meṣad Hašavyahu, 7th cent.	rectang.	4 sides	45.6
Hazor [Str. III], 7th cent.	rectang.	4 sides	19.2
Megiddo [Str. II], 7th cent.	rectang.	3 sides	20
Beth Zur, 2nd cent.	rectang.	3 sides	25

**The percentage figure represents the percentage of the total area of the fortress occupied by the courtyard.*

The table begins with the site of Beer Ḥafir, located southwest of Ramat Maṭred, a plateau near the modern settlement of ʿAvdat. The site was first reported by Nelson Glueck, who classified the remains as Nabatean.[59] The ruins were reexamined by a survey team under the direction of Yohanan Aharoni and were found to possess three distinct phases of occupation.[60] According to the recovered ceramics, the earliest phase was a tenth-century structure, nearly square in form, consisting of casemate rooms surrounding an open courtyard on all four sides.[61] The exterior dimensions of the structure were 19 meters by 20 meters, and the courtyard measured approximately 12 meters by 14 meters. These dimensions reflect the fact that over 44% of the total structure's area was taken up by the courtyard.

---

59 Nelson Glueck, "The Third Season of Explorations in the Negeb," *BASOR* 138 (1955):21.

60 Y. Aharoni, M. Evenari, L. Shanan and N. H. Tadmor, "The Ancient Desert Agriculture of the Negev V. An Israelite Agricultural Settlement at Ramat Maṭred," *IEJ* 10 (1960):107-09.

61 See the drawing in Aharoni et al, "The Ancient Desert Agriculture of the Negev," 108 Figure 17.

The next example is a vast surface ruin at Tel Nagila. This structure forms an irregular rectangle consisting of a central courtyard surrounded on all four sides by a number of casemate rooms. The number and sizes of the rooms could not be determined from the few probes made at the site. The exterior dimensions were 104 meters by 91 meters, and the courtyard measured some 84 meters by 71 meters. The ceramics from probe trenches set along the walls indicated the site was founded in the eighth century BCE.[62] Given the approximate dimensions of the site, the courtyard occupied over 60% of the total structure's area.

Also from the eighth century BCE is the Judean fortress at Qumran, the meager remains of which were located beneath the more substantial remains of the Essene community. As reported by the excavator, the Qumran fortress consisted of a rectangular structure with casemate rooms along at least one side of a central courtyard.[63] Excluding the structure built around a cistern that was attached to the western end of the fortress, the exterior dimensions were approximately 46.5 meters by 35 meters. The courtyard measured approximately 35 meters by 17.5 meters. Given these dimensions, the courtyard occupied more than 37% of the total area of the structure.

Toward the end of the Judean monarchy in the seventh century BCE, the fortress complex at Meṣad Hashavyahu was founded. Excavated by Joseph Naveh in 1960, the recovered plan of the fortress presented a unique "L" shape formed by two rectangular structures, the end of one butting into the side of the other.[64] The portion of the fortress containing the main gateway was formed by a large central courtyard with casemate rooms surrounding it on all four sides.[65] While Naveh did not report any evidence to suggest that the fortress was built in stages, both portions of the structure appear to have been planned independent of each other. For example, the primary interior dividing walls of the portion containing the courtyard are circa .5 meters thick, while the interior dividing walls of the other portion of the fortress are 1 to 1.5 meters thick.

---

62 A full account of the Tel Nagila fortress may be found in S. Bulow and R. A. Mitchell, "An Iron Age II Fortress on Tel Nagila," *IEJ* 11 (1961):101-10.

63 Roland de Vaux, *Archaeology and the Dead Sea Scrolls*. Schweich Lectures, 1959. revised edition. (London: British Academy, 1973), 1-3 and plate III. There is a good possibility that rooms were arranged along the northern and southern sides of the courtyard, though the fragmentary nature of the Iron 2 remains at Qumran make it impossible to determine this with certainty.

64 Joseph Naveh, "The Excavations at Meṣad Hashavyahu: Preliminary Report," *IEJ* 12 (1962):89-90.

65 See Naveh, "The Excavations at Meṣad Hashavyahu," 91 Figure 2.

The possibility that the original form of the fortress was like most Israelite strongholds, a central courtyard surrounded by casemate walls, and was only subsequently expanded by the addition of the extensive storage areas in the rear part of the structure, merits further investigation. Apart from such a reexamination of the site, it cannot be assumed that the "L" shape was original. For the purposes of this comparison, only the front portion of the fortress will be utilized. As a rectangular shape, the front portion of Meṣad Hashavyahu was approximately 78 meters by 54 meters. The central courtyard was 60 meters by 32 meters in dimension, and was surrounded on all four sides by casemate rooms. Given these dimensions, the courtyard occupied over 45% of the total area of the fortress.

It is usually presumed that these examples represent native Israelite traditions in fortress design, and the ceramics that have been discovered at each of the sites includes large quantities of native Palestinian forms. The same cannot be said of the last three examples on Table 2. Though located at the important urban center of Hazor, the citadel of stratum III was completely separated from the rest of the occupation areas of this phase and had no relationship to any of the city fortifications.[66] In form, the citadel was rectangular in shape with exterior dimensions of 30 meters by 26 meters. The interior consisted of a central courtyard with casemate rooms surrounding all four sides, the courtyard measuring 12.5 meters by 12 meters. While there was some ambiguity in the date of the citadel, ceramic materials of a presumed Assyrian provenance, coupled with several small object finds, led the excavators to date the citadel to the seventh century BCE and identify it as an Assyrian garrison.[67] With the dimensions given in the excavation publication, the courtyard occupied little more than 19% of the total area of the structure.

In many ways, the fortress at Megiddo in stratum II nicely parallels the example from Hazor. The excavators reported that in stratum II there were no city fortifications other than the fortress, and that it sat isolated on the eastern edge of the tell.[68] The fortress was a large rectangle in form

---

[66] Yigael Yadin et al, *Hazor I: An Account of the First Season of Excavations, 1955* (Jerusalem: Magnes Press, 1958), 45-6 and Plate CLXXVII.

[67] Yadin et al, *Hazor I*, 53-4. See also the comments by Yohanan Aharoni, *The Archaeology of the Land of Israel*, ed. Miriam Aharoni, trans. Anson Rainey (Philadelphia: Westminster Press, 1982), 252-3.

[68] For the complete discussion of the citadel of stratum II, see Robert S. Lamon and Geoffrey M. Shipton, *Megiddo I: Seasons of 1925-34, Strata I-V*. Oriental Institute Publications, 42. (Chicago: University of Chicago Press, 1939), 83. A helpful discussion of the stratigraphic problems associated with this citadel may be found in Graham I.

with a central courtyard and casemate rooms around three of the sides of the courtyard. Since the entire eastern wall of the fortress was lost due to erosion, there is the possibility that it, like the Hazor example, had casemate rooms on all four sides of the courtyard. In dimension, the fortress was quite massive, the exterior being some 75 meters by 50 meters. The central courtyard was approximately 30 meters by 25 meters. Using these data, the courtyard of the Megiddo fortress can be computed to have occupied about 20% of the structure's total area.

The final example on Table 2 is the citadel at Beth-Zur in the southern Judean territory. The citadel itself was excavated in 1931 by O. R. Sellers who delineated three distinct phases. While most subsequent analyses of the citadel have retained the tripartite phasing scheme, various dates have been assigned to these different phases.[69] The site was revisited in 1957; and while the citadel itself was not reexcavated, the clarification of the site's occupation history has greatly assisted in the determination of dates for the various stages of the citadel.

To summarize briefly, phase I marked the foundation of the citadel, and only scanty remains were encountered, making it impossible to reconstruct the plan of the structure.[70] In light of the very limited evidence for any activity at the site during the Persian period as a whole, and in the absence of any settlement at this time, phase I of the citadel most likely post-dates the Persian period. Presumably, the foundation of the citadel at Beth-Zur took place under the Ptolemies, or perhaps even later.[71]

Of more assistance to a comparative study is phase II of the citadel. Extensive architectural remains were recovered, and historical references combined with the ceramic evidence suggest a date in the Hasmonean period, the structure being destroyed in 163/2 BCE. As reconstructed on

---

Davies, *Megiddo.* Cities of the Biblical World. (Grand Rapids: William B. Eerdmans, 1986), 100-01.

[69] The initial results of the 1931 campaign were published in O. R. Sellers, *The Citadel of Beth-Zur* (Philadelphia: Westminster Press, 1933). An important retrospective assessment of the interpretations that appeared in that report along with a description of subsequent alternative dating schemes appears in O. R. Sellers, "Echoes of the Campaign," 1-3 in *The 1957 Excavation at Beth-Zur.* Paul Lapp, ed. AASOR 38. (Cambridge, MA: American Schools of Oriental Research, 1968).

[70] See William Foxwell Albright, *The Archaeology of Palestine,* rev. ed. (Harmondsworth: Penguin Books, 1954), 152 and Stern, *Material Culture,* 36.

[71] See the comments of Robert W. Funk, "The History of Beth-Zur with Reference to its Defenses," 15-16 in *The 1957 Excavation at Beth-Zur.* The discussion of this point in Stern, *Material Culture,* 36-8 misrepresents the results of the 1957 excavations and their importance for dating phase I of the citadel.

the basis of the 1931 excavation, the citadel was rectangular in form, some 40 meters by 32.5 meters in exterior dimension. The interior consisted of a central courtyard surrounded by casemate rooms on three sides.[72] These figures suggest that around 25% of the structure's total area was used for the courtyard.

These comparisons provide three essential aspects to fortress design in the first millennium. First, the central courtyard is not limited to periods of eastern Mesopotamian cultural influence in Palestine but is a common feature in most free-standing fortresses.

The second feature follows on the first observation, namely that while the use of a central courtyard in such fortifications is common, there are essential differences in the relationship of the courtyard to the structure's overall design. For the native Israelite designs, the courtyard is the major spatial feature of the structure. Once imperial traditions begin to influence fortress design, the role of the courtyard apparently changes, and in fortress design the courtyard itself requires considerably less space in order to fulfill its intended role. Starting with the Assyrian domination of the former territory of the kingdom of Israel in the seventh century, the percentage of the total area of the structure allocated to the courtyard is considerably reduced. In this regard, the 24% mean of the structure's total area occupied by the courtyard noted among the excavated examples of mid-fifth century fortresses reflects this trend. This change may be related to a shift in the kinds of forces deployed in such fortresses, perhaps chariotry being superseded by heavy cavalry forces, but this can only be speculated without additional data. At any rate, the function of the courtyard in fortresses from the intervention of the Assyrian empire on apparently remains constant and reflects the broad cultural continuity that emerges in the Levant as the ancient empires attempted to break down regional cultural patterns.[73]

The third and final aspect this comparison highlights is the rarity of square forms for fortresses in any period of the first millennium.[74] Not

---

72 The measurments for the Beth-Zur citadel, phase II, are derived from the reconstruction published by Carl Watzinger, *Denkmaler palästinas: eine Einführung in die archäologie des Heiligen Landes,* Volume 2. (Leipzig: J. C. Hinrichs, 1935), tafel 3, abb. 20. On the accuracy of this rendering, see Funk, "The History of Beth-Zur," 15.

73 This point has been recently reemphasized by Fergus Millar, "The Problem of Hellenistic Syria," 129-33 in *Hellenism in the East: The Interaction of Greek and Non-Greek Civilizations from Syria to Central Asia After Alexander,* Amelie Kuhrt and Susan Sherwin-White, editors. (Berkeley: University of California Press, 1987).

74 In Aharoni, "Forerunners of the Limes," 5-7, some seven fortresses are classified as "Square Forts without Towers." Of these seven, only one (at the intersection of

only are such square forms atypical for fortresses, but the precision with which the excavated examples of mid-fifth century fortresses are executed betrays careful planning and skilled construction. Considering the extensive resources available to the Achaemenid empire, such engineering capabilities are not surprising.

As a result of this comparison, it is apparent that a precisely executed square fortress whose courtyard utilizes about one-quarter of the total area of the structure is a phenomenon with a very limited chronological range in Palestine. Indeed, it is only evident in the three sites that were discussed earlier, all of which were founded in the mid-fifth century. Consequently, this proposed typology, while no substitute for actual excavation, can help establish a probable date for an unexcavated site or an excavated one yielding ambiguous results. As noted above, the importance of such a typology is compounded by the difficulties faced in trying to utilize native Palestinian ceramic forms to fix the foundation date for a fortress within the Persian period.

The proposed typology of mid-fifth century Persian fortresses provides an important tool for reconstructing the distribution of these structures throughout the Levant. In most cases, such sites have only been surveyed with meager ceramic collections accompanying the survey. As will be seen, the similarities among those sites that fit the proposed typology are striking and strongly argue in favor of a mid-fifth century date. Moreover, the similarities are suggestive of centralized planning and execution, exactly the kind of shared relationship one would anticipate if such fortresses were being founded by an imperial administration over a relatively short time-span.

Since surveys of the various regions of the Levant have not been made in a systematic manner, the following analysis can only at best be

---

Naḥal Haluqim, Naḥal Besor and Naḥal Boqer) is truely square, measuring some 20 meters by 20 meters. Aharoni did not excavate or collect sherds from the site; thus no date for it has been offered. The other locations are only vaguely square in form and should be classified as rectangular. In Cohen, "The Iron Age Fortresses in the Central Negev," 70-2, four fortresses are classified as square. Three of these have subsequently been redated to the mid-fifth century and the remaining one, Naḥal Raviv, is only roughly square (19 meters by 22 meters). While it has not been excavated, it would appear to be an Israelite fortress, based on the fact that the courtyard occupies 55% of the structure's total area. Several other square fortresses of various dates have been noted in the preliminary reports of the Negev salvage excavations directed by Cohen; but without plans or clear descriptions of the recovered ceramics, it is not possible to evaluate them; see, for example, Rudolph Cohen, "Ḥorvat Tov," *IEJ* 36 (1986):111-2.

an overview of the distribution of such fortresses. There are undoubtedly other sites missed by the various survey efforts or, in some cases, so altered by later occupational phases that their original architectural plan has been masked. For most of the sites discussed in what follows, the original plan is clear. In a few cases, it is necessary to disentangle the original plan from the surviving ruins in order to form a basis for their analysis. Where this has been done, a full discussion of the rationale for such a process will be included in the description of the site.

The analysis will begin with the Negev where a number of square structures have been surveyed and identified as fortresses. As was noted in the earlier description of Ḥorvat Mesora, once Cohen realized the mid-fifth century date of that fortress, he redated several others on the basis of their shared architectural plan with Mesora.[75] These sites are Ḥorvat Ritma and Meṣad Naḥal Haroᶜa.

The site of Ḥorvat Ritma is located slightly north and west of the modern settlement of Sede Boqer, sitting on the top of a ridge of the Haluqim mountain range. From its setting, it commands an unobstructed view over the valley below that is a junction for several ancient routes.[76] The site was first surveyed in 1934 by Nelson Glueck, who reported that numerous "Roman-Byzantine" ceramics were present.[77] After several intervening surveys, Ḥorvat Ritma was excavated in 1969-72 and a final excavation report appeared in 1977.[78]

---

75 Cohen, "Solomon's Negev Defense Line Contained Three Fewer Fortresses," 42-3.

76 For the physical setting of Ḥorvat Ritma, see Zeev Meshel, "Ḥorvat Ritma—An Iron Age Fortress in the Negev Highlands," *Tel Aviv* 4 (1977):110, and Cohen, "The Iron Age Fortresses in the Central Negev," 70-1.

77 Nelson Glueck, *Explorations in Eastern Palestine, II.* AASOR 15. (New Haven: American Schools of Oriental Research, 1935), 117.

78 Cohen, "The Iron Age Fortresses in the Central Negev," 70-1. The full report is that of Meshel, "Ḥorvat Ritma."

Table 3.—Mid-fifth Century Fortresses in the Negev

Site	Ext. Meas.	Court Meas.	Percentage*
H. Ritma	21 X 21	12.8 X 11.5	33
Meṣad Naḥal Haroʿa	20 X 20	12 X 12	31
Naḥal Yattir	21.5 X 21.5	15 X 15	48.7

**The percentage figure represents the percentage of the total area of the fortress occupied by the courtyard.*

As indicated by an extensive survey, the site contains several components including domestic structures and a square building sitting on the highest point of the site. The square building was reported as 21 meters by 21 meters in exterior measure, the outer wall being preserved at approximately .8 meters in thickness (see Table 3). In plan, the building possessed a central courtyard some 12.8 meters by 11.5 meters in size, surrounded on all four sides by eight casemate rooms.[79] Several rooms were excavated and Roman period sherds were recovered, although a few Iron 1 ceramics were also reported. The excavators concluded that this artifactual material was the result of a secondary occupation of the building, and that its similar design to other Iron 1 fortresses in the Negev made it probable that this fortress was founded during the tenth century BCE.[80]

Once Cohen had corrected his dating of Ḥorvat Mesora, he argued, on the basis of the "nearly identical" plan of Ḥorvat Ritma, that this latter fortress must also be of a mid-fifth century date.[81] In the initial excavations of Ritma, scattered remains were recovered from the Persian period (Period II), indicating that portions of the site had been occupied at that time. In his analysis of these ceramics, Meshel concluded that Period II extended from the mid-fifth century to the mid-fourth century BCE.[82] Therefore, if the fortress at Ritma was founded during the Persian period, its founding can be placed anywhere within this range.

---

79 The physical description of the building is derived from Meshel, "Ḥorvat Ritma," 116 and 117, Figure 4.

80 Meshel, "Ḥorvat Ritma," 116; also Cohen, "The Iron Age Fortresses in the Central Negev," 71.

81 Cohen, "Solomon's Negev Defense Line Contained Three Fewer Fortresses," 42.

82 Meshel, "Ḥorvat Ritma," 129.

As summarized in Table 3, the basic plan of the fortress at Ritma strongly parallels the plan of Ḥorvat Mesora. Moreover, the 33% amount of the total structure's space dedicated to the courtyard, though a bit high, still fits within the typology of the excavated mid-fifth century fortresses. The same figure does not fit any of the Iron 1 structures. Accordingly, there can be little doubt that the fortress at Ḥorvat Ritma was founded when the Persian occupation began in the mid-fifth century. The absence of Persian period ceramics in the fortress itself is troubling, but it should be recalled that only a few rooms of the structure were excavated. In addition, Meshel noted that the later Roman reoccupation of the building either completely cleared the structure out or engaged in extensive renovation of the interior of the structure.[83] It is also helpful to recall the relative poverty of materials in the fortress at Tell es-Saᶜidiyeh.

As for the second site redated by Cohen, Meṣad Naḥal Haroᶜa, the evidence for a mid-fifth century dating is far clearer. Situated on a ridge facing Atar Haroᶜa, the site was first surveyed by Cohen in the mid-1960s.[84] The groundplan of the fortress was considered to be identical with that of Ḥorvat Mesora, namely a square form, 20 meters by 20 meters, with a central courtyard. The courtyard was surrounded on all four sides by a total of nine casemate rooms (see the diagram in Figure 2). In that its plan was so similar to Ḥorvat Mesora, Cohen dated the structure at Meṣad Naḥal Haroᶜa to the tenth century BCE. However, once the excavations at Mesora had demonstrated the mid-fifth century founding of that fortress, Cohen recognized the need for further excavation at Haroᶜa.

In the spring of 1985, several of the rooms surrounding the courtyard were cleared. On the floors of the rooms were recovered ceramics of the mid-fifth through fourth centuries.[85] Cohen reported that there was unequivocal evidence of a single phase of occupation at the site, stretching over this range. Thus by virtue of its architectural design and by

---

83 On the incompatibility of the courtyard relationship to the structure for Iron 1, see Finkelstein, "The Iron Age Fortresses of the Negev Highlands," 191 where Ritma is one of the sites with the lowest ratio of courtyard area per person. See also our note 57. On the disturbance to the site by the Roman reoccupation, see Meshel, "Ḥorvat Ritma," 129.

84 Cohen, "The Iron Age Fortresses of the Central Negev," 72.

85 Cohen, "Solomon's Negev Defense Line Contained Three Fewer Fortresses," 42 and Rudolph Cohen, "Meṣad Naḥal Haroᶜa," *IEJ* 36 (1986): 112-13. There is some discrepancy in the exact extent of the excavations. In the former article Cohen claims eight rooms were cleared, while in the latter he claims only six were cleared.

selected excavation, the fortress at Meṣad Naḥal Haroʿa was founded in the mid-fifth century.

To these examples can be added the previously mentioned fortress at Naḥal Yattir, excavated in 1986-87 (see Figure 2). While the percentage of the total area occupied by the courtyard is higher than other mid-fifth century examples (48.7%), the excavations demonstrated that the surviving southern wall of the courtyard was the result of a secondary alteration to the original plan, the original wall lying more to the north. This would imply that at the founding of the fortress, the courtyard would have been considerably smaller, thus occupying a smaller percentage of the total area of the structure. The ceramics from the site are consistently mid-fifth century local forms, further pointing to the foundation of the fortress in the mid-fifth century.[86]

In attempting to reconstruct the distribution of mid-fifth century fortresses in the Negev, the site of Arad may also be added, though there is little direct evidence of the fortress structure itself. The excavations of the site, undertaken in the early 1960s, encountered few structural remains of the Persian period (Stratum V), although a number of Aramaic ostraca were found. One of these ostraca, No. 12, makes reference to the "*degel* of Abdnanay," *degel* being the usual Imperial Aramaic term for a large military unit.[87] The excavator, Yohanan Aharoni, interpreted this as an indication that a fortress had stood on the upper city of Arad during the Persian occupation and argued that the later Hellenistic tower, whose foundations reached down to the bedrock, had been erected over the area of the Persian fortress.[88] The Hellenistic tower was square in form, some 20 meters by 20 meters, and it is tempting to hypothesize a fortress similar to the other Negev examples preceding the tower.[89] In terms of the date for the founding of this structure, the Aramaic ostraca were from the terminus of stratum V and dated predominantly from the first half of the fourth century BCE, though none were recovered from a stratified context.[90] The Persian period ceramics from stratum V included imported Attic wares, leading the excavator to place the beginnings of the Persian

---

86 Personal communication from Steven Derfler to the author, August 26, 1988.

87 See the discussion and references by Joseph Naveh in Yohanan Aharoni, *Arad Inscriptions.* Anson Rainey, ed. and rev. Judean Desert Studies. (Jerusalem: Israel Exploration Society, 1981), 158.

88 Yohanan Aharoni, "Excavations at Tel Arad: Preliminary Report on the Second Season, 1963," *IEJ* 17 (1967): 243 and Aharoni, *Arad Inscriptions,* 8.

89 See the diagram in Aharoni, *Arad Inscriptions,* 6-7.

90 Naveh's dating in Aharoni, *Arad Inscriptions,* 153.

period at Arad in the mid-fifth century.[91] While there can be no certainty that the fortress at Arad was founded at the beginning of Persian occupation at the site, there is every indication that the fortress was the primary reason for the Persian presence. No Persian settlement was encountered at Arad, so it is not speculative to assume the fortress was also founded in the mid-fifth century.

To summarize this evidence of Persian fortresses in the Negev, there is clear evidence of a mid-fifth century intensification of a military presence. Moreover, the regularity in design points to a centralized effort; and since several of the fortresses are removed from any settlements of the Persian period, their placement was dictated by strategic concerns other than the protection of specific population centers.

In addition to the fortresses of the Negev, similar structures have been noted throughout the region of the Judean hill country.[92] However, due to the more intensive occupation of this region from the mid-fifth century on, the number of such sites preserved in an unaltered state is considerably less than in the Negev. Moreover, the archaeological interest that has concentrated on earlier phases of culture in the Judean hill country has largely ignored the Persian period. Consequently, there have been few efforts to excavate Persian period sites of any kind, and only one survey of a wide enough scope to incorporate Persian sites in its report. As a result, it is not possible to utilize excavated data from several sites to confirm the mid-fifth century dating for these structures as was the case with some of the Negev sites.

One site in the Judean hill country that has been excavated is Khirbet Abu et-Twain. Located on the highest point of an isolated hill, the site is opposite the Valley of Elah.[93] From its setting, it is possible to gain a clear view of the Shephelah to the west, as well as the southern slopes of the Judean hill country to the north.

Following a survey of the site, excavations were conducted on selected portions of the ruins in 1974 and 1975, a full report on these excavations appearing in 1981.[94] The excavations yielded a square

---

[91] Yohanan Aharoni and Ruth Amiran, "Excavations at Tel Arad: Preliminary Report on the First Season, 1962," *IEJ* 14 (1964): 133 and 144.

[92] For the purposes of this discussion, the geographical boundaries of the Judean hillcountry are those utilized by Aharoni, *The Land of the Bible,* 27-8 and 71-2.

[93] The description of the site location is from Amihai Mazar, "Iron Age Fortresses in the Judean Hills," *Palestine Exploration Quarterly* 114 (1982):89.

[94] Amihai Mazar, "The Excavations at Khirbet Abu et-Twein and the System of Iron Age Fortresses in Judah," *Eretz-Israel* 15 (1981):229-49 [Hebrew]. A corrected English version of this essay appeared in 1982 as Mazar, "Iron Age Fortresses." Since

building of approximately 31 meters by 29.5 meters, the walls varying somewhat due to the difficult terrain on which the structure was erected.[95] The corners of the building were reinforced, and the exterior walls were approximately .9 meter wide and built of fieldstones. The interior to the structure consisted of ten rooms arrayed around all four sides of the central courtyard. The rooms varied in width from 3.5 to 7 meters, and in several cases were bisected by rows of squared pillars. The courtyard was 12 meters by 13.5 meters in dimension and was apparently paved with stone, although only a small area of the courtyard was actually excavated.[96]

The rubble from collapsed walls and roofing material was encountered throughout the building, and since there were no signs of intentional destruction, the excavator, Amihai Mazar, concluded that the building was abandoned and allowed to deteriorate over time.[97] Additional evidence for the abandonment of the structure is the scarcity of artifactual materials within the few rooms that were cleared.[98]

This scarcity of materials associated with the structure creates a dilemma in terms of interpreting these materials. The limited excavations of the building were conducted with no effort at stratigraphic observation. Thus the published ceramic data reflect a mixture of materials, some from the floors of the building but the majority from the rubble of the collapsed walls.[99]

According to the analysis of the ceramic evidence, Mazar grouped these materials into three distinct chronological categories. The majority of the ceramics came from the eighth to seventh centuries BCE, although some characteristic forms of that period were missing from the assemblage.[100] Some ceramic evidence of types thought to appear from the late seventh century through the fifth century was present, while some scat-

---

the English version appeared subsequent to the Hebrew version, all citations that follow are to the English version unless otherwise indicated.

[95] Mazar, "Iron Age Fortresses," 89.

[96] Mazar, "Iron Age Fortresses," 92.

[97] Mazar, "Iron Age Fortresses," 105.

[98] Mazar, "Iron Age Fortresses," 95 and 105.

[99] "The pottery sherds were collected from the fallen debris inside the rooms, while the floors were almost empty of any finds...," Mazar, "Iron Age Fortresses," 99. The term "almost" is puzzling here: the published reports do not differentiate between materials from the wall collapse and those found on the floors. Indeed, there is no indication other than this that any materials were recovered that could be directly tied to the occupation of the structure.

[100] Among those forms missing from the assemblage are the hole-mouth jars and black juglets common to the Iron 2 period; Mazar, "Iron Age Fortresses," 101.

tered sherds represented types that "cannot be earlier" than the Persian period.[101]

In considering the date for the square building, Mazar pointed out that there seemed to be only one phase of occupation, and no evidence was encountered that suggested the building was erected over a previously inhabited area. He concluded from this that the chronological span of the ceramic evidence represented the period in which the building was being utilized. Mazar thus placed the founding of the building in the Iron 2 period and assumed that the building was continuously occupied until the "later phase" of the Persian period, when it was abandoned.[102]

Mazar's reasoning at this point must be seriously challenged, as well as his ultimate chronological conclusions. To begin with, it is fallacious to use ceramic evidence that cannot be directly tied to the occupation of a structure as an indication of the date of that structure. Most of the ceramics recovered at Khirbet Abu et-Twain came from wall collapse and can only establish a *terminus post quem* for the construction of the structure. In other words, the presence of Iron 2 ceramics in the wall collapse suggests that the structure could not have been built earlier than the Iron 2 period and, indeed, was most likely erected after the period.

If the structure was not founded in the Iron 2 period, it remains necessary to propose a reasonable explanation for how the Iron 2 ceramics came to be present in the wall collapse cleared from the structure. Surveys of the immediate vicinity undertaken by the excavation team revealed an Iron 2 occupation at the base of the hill on which the structure stands.[103] It would not be unusual for building materials, including loosened soils and squared fieldstones, to be removed from such occupation areas and utilized in a major nearby construction. The fact that the excavation of the building did not produce a single piece of ceramic evidence from the Iron 2 period that could be unequivocally related to the structure's occupation makes it doubtful that the structure could date to that period. Indeed, as Mazar grudgingly admits, it would be more correct methodologically to date the structure on the basis of the latest materials recovered in this mixed debris.[104] These are the Persian period ceramics noted above.

101 Mazar, "Iron Age Fortresses," 101.

102 Mazar, "Iron Age Fortresses," 105.

103 Mazar, "Iron Age Fortresses," 105.

104 "Though one may claim that only the latest sherds (i.e. those of the Persian period) should be considered in dating the building, we believe the quantities of Iron Age pottery must be taken into account;" Mazar, "Iron Age Fortresses," 104-5. This is

Given the importance of the Persian period ceramic evidence for dating the structure at Khirbet Abu et-Twain, it is disappointing that no imported wares were recovered in the excavations that might assist in providing a more precise chronological determination. Of the Palestinian forms that were present, most were of types with a range extending throughout the period, from the late sixth to mid-fourth centuries.[105] For example, several sherds of bowls and craters reflect forms common from the late seventh to the fourth centuries.[106] Several large storage jar sherds also reflect types common from the seventh to the fourth centuries.[107] In short, the ceramics from the site are unable to provide more than a generic date in the Persian period.

Since the ceramics from the site are unable to provide a clear chronological setting for the building, it is necessary to evaluate the architectural form of the building. It is nearly square and consists of a central courtyard surrounded by casemate rooms on all four sides. When the percentage of the total structure's area allocated to the courtyard is calculated, the resulting figure is slightly better than 17%. All these factors are in accord with the typology of mid-fifth century fortresses. Mazar interpereted the structure as a fortress, based mainly on its overall design characteristics and its location away from any urban settlement.[108]

In his discussion of architectural parallels to the structure, Mazar cited both Ḥorvat Ritma and Ḥorvat Mesora. Based on Cohen's earlier misdating of Mesora, he considered both to belong to the tenth century BCE.[109] Given the mid-fifth century date of Mesora and Ritma, the closest parallels to Abu et-Twain, and the consonance between the design of Abu et-Twain and the typology of mid-fifth century fortresses, it can be concluded that Khirbet Abu et-Twain was founded in the mid-fifth century. The ceramic evidence, reflecting types spanning the entire range of the Persian period, does not contradict this conclusion.

In his publications of the materials from Khirbet Abu et-Twain, Mazar attempted to place the fortress within a network of Iron Age fortresses established to defend the kingdom of Judah. In the course of

---

simply an argument from the quantity of ceramics recovered, a dubious point considering that only a portion of the structure was excavated and none of the ceramic evidence can be associated with the occupation of the building.

105 See Mazar's summary comments in "Iron Age Fortresses," 104.

106 See "Iron Age Fortresses," Figure 13 nos. 14 and 20 and the discussion of parallels in 108, footnote 8.

107 See "Iron Age Fortresses," 104.

108 Mazar, "Iron Age Fortresses," 97.

109 Mazar, "Iron Age Fortresses," 97.

this effort, Mazar briefly discussed several other sites that shared similar design characteristics and geographical placement with Abu et-Twain.

The first such site Mazar noted was "Deir Baghl," situated on a ridge to the east of the Wadi Fukin.[110] The site was initially discovered and surveyed during the 1967-68 archaeological survey of the occupied West Bank territories.[111] At that time, a general groundplan was prepared and an initial collection of surface ceramics made. The plan revealed a roughly square shape, approximately 30 meters by 30 meters.[112] There is apparently some distortion to this form to the south due to the configuration of the summit on which it was placed (see Figure 3). In addition, the remains of a large tower were encountered on the southwest side of the structure.

In overall layout the structure consisted of a central courtyard, some 19 meters by 18 meters in size, with casemate rooms surrounding all four sides. The rooms possessed a standard width of approximately 3.5 meters and varied in length. The exterior walls of the structure were more than a meter in thickness, leading the survey team to classify the structure as a fortress.[113]

The ceramics recovered by the survey spanned a wide range, from Iron 2 through the Ottoman (1516-1917 CE) periods. While the survey reported a predominance of Iron 2 ceramics, it needs to be stressed that these collections were made of surface finds and do not represent excavated materials. No ceramics characteristic of the Persian period were reported.[114]

In his discussion, Mazar noted that in its location, overall dimensions and plan, the fortress at Deir Baghl had strong parallels to the fortess at Abu et-Twain. On this basis, he asserted that Deir Baghl was part of an effort to establish a group of fortresses to defend the western region of

---

110 Mazar, "Iron Age Fortresses," 105.

111 The results of this survey appeared as Moshe Kochavi, ed., *Judaea, Samaria and the Golan: Archaeological Survey 1967-1968.* (Jerusalem: The Archaelogical Survey of Israel, 1972) [Hebrew].

112 In the description of the ruins, the 30 meters by 30 meters dimensions are given. However, the accompanying scale drawing would lead one to assume the sides of the fortress were closer to 32 meters in length; Kochavi, *Judaea, Samaria and the Golan,* 41. Since there is the possibility of some distortion in the reproduction of the drawing, the discussion of the site and the data in Table 4 is taken from the written description.

113 See the discussion in Kochavi, *Judaea, Samaria and the Golan,* 41.

114 Kochavi, *Judaea, Samaria and the Golan,* 41. Despite repeated efforts in the summer of 1986 to reexamine the sherds collected during the original survey, it was not possible to locate them.

the kingdom of Judah in the Iron 2 period.[115] When a full assessment of Deir Baghl's architectural form is made, however it appears to have been founded in the mid-fifth century like Kh. Abu et-Twain.

While not precisely square, Deir Baghl's variation from the ideal form appears to be the result of topographic factors. Moreover, the central courtyard with casemate rooms on all four sides reflects a design that parallels that of the mid-fifth century excavated fortresses. When the percentage of the structure's total area devoted to the courtyard is calculated, the resulting figure of 38% is very close to the range of other mid-fifth century examples (see Table 4).[116] It can be concluded that the Deir Baghl fortress was founded in the mid-fifth century on the basis of this typological analysis.

Mazar also drew additional architectural parallels between Abu et-Twain and a fortress located at Khirbet el-Qaṭṭ.[117] Khirbet el-Qaṭṭ was also discovered during the 1967-68 archaeological survey and is situated along the western side of the main road between Jerusalem and Hebron, approximately 2 kilometers north of Beth-Zur.[118] The survey was able to trace the outlines of a square building approximately 30 meters by 30 meters in dimension. A central court occupied the interior space of the structure, and was surrounded to the north, east and west by a single row of casemate rooms. To the south, the courtyard was edged by a double row of casemate rooms (see the plan in Figure 3). In the northwest corner of the structure was a 9 meters by 9 meters tower that appeared to be a secondary modification to the original groundplan. The survey collected ceramic materials from the structure and reported only a few Iron 2 sherds, the majority of the ceramic materials being Persian and Roman 1 and 2 in date.[119]

In his comparison of Abu et-Twain with el-Qaṭṭ, Mazar noted that the geographical setting, the overall fortress plan and construction techniques were shared elements between these two sites. These factors were similar enough for him to conclude that both sites were part of the same defensive strategy.[120]

---

115 Mazar, "Iron Age Fortresses," 105-6.

116 The percentage figure, though slightly more than a third of the structure's total area, may actually be smaller if no distortion of the published plan has taken place. If the exterior dimensions of the fortress are as large as indicated in the plan, then the resulting percentage of the courtyard would be 34.4%.

117 Mazar, "Iron Age Fortresses," 106-7.

118 Kochavi, *Judaea, Samaria and the Golan,* 50.

119 Kochavi, *Judaea, Samaria and the Golan,* 50.

120 Mazar, "Iron Age Fortresses," 109 note 17.

While Mazar's general observations on the similarity of the design are substantially correct, el-Qaṭṭ presents some distinctive features. Like Abu et-Twain and the Negev fortresses, el-Qaṭṭ is basically square in form with a central courtyard. The courtyard occupies approximately 33.7% of the total area of the structure, a figure that accords well with the typology of mid-fifth century fortresses (see Table 4). As reconstructed by the survey, the courtyard of el-Qaṭṭ had a wall running across one portion of the area near the main entrance to the fortress. If this wall was part of the original building plan, it would considerably reduce the size of the courtyard. However, it appears that the original survey team found only traces of the wall *in situ*, and considering the extensive alteration to the plan of the fortress in the Roman period, it is probable that this wall is a secondary modification to the structure's design.[121]

Table 4.—Mid-fifth Century Fortresses in the Judean Hill Country

Site	Ext. Meas.	Court Meas.	Percentage*
Abu et-Twain	31 X 29.5	13.5 X 12	17.7
Deir Baghl	30 X 30	19 X 18	38
el-Qaṭṭ	30 X 30	19 X 16	33.7

**The percentage figure represents the percentage of the total area of the fortress occupied by the courtyard.*

The double row of rooms along the southern edge of the courtyard are also distinctive, finding no parallel among the other fortresses of the mid-fifth century. However, in all other respects the fortress at el-Qaṭṭ parallels the architectural characteristics of mid-fifth century fortresses; and the presence of Persian period ceramics at the site, though without a clear relationship to the founding of the fortress, may be taken as favoring this dating.[122]

121 A visit to the site in June of 1986 for the purpose of checking this aspect of the structure as well as other factors determined that no surface remains of el-Qaṭṭ are discernible. In the original 1967 survey, part of the fortress was incorporated into a vineyard, and since that time the cultivation of the entire height of the ridge has obscured any remaining architectural features.

122 Efforts by the author and representatives of the Archaeological Survey of Israel to locate the original ceramic materials from the 1967 survey were unsuccessful. What little ceramic material was observable during the visit to the site was too badly weathered to allow any more specific typological determination other than "Persian."

These three examples of mid-fifth century fortresses are the most fully documented representatives of the characteristic form of such installations for the Judean hill country. However, there are other sites where there exists a strong probability of additional mid-fifth century fortresses, though without excavation the evidence is lacking to arrive at a firm conclusion. The following discussion of two specific locations may be taken as representative of such sites.

The site of Khirbet Kabar, like so many others in the Judean hill country, was discovered in the course of the 1967-68 survey. Located on a ridge southwest of Bethlehem, Kabar is in a position to dominate the main roadway from Jerusalem to Hebron that even today wraps around the base of the ridge. The site is a settlement of about 4 dunams, and at the highest point of the settlement the survey located a sprawling fortress complex. The complex had several architectural phases, the earliest being a wall approximately 30 meters long running beneath a later Roman period wall.[123] During a visit to the site in June of 1986, it appeared that the remains of another wall of the same construction ran perpendicular from the end of this wall. Though only traces remained, it appeared to be about 30 meters in length as well. It may well be that the first phase of fortification at Kabar was a square plan fortress measuring 30 meters by 30 meters, and that subsequent construction at the site has destroyed most of this early fortress.

The sherd materials collected at the site ranged from the Persian period to the Byzantine. In the area around the early wall the survey recovered a large quantity of Persian period ceramics and concluded that this earliest fortress at the site was founded in the Persian period.[124] Only the excavation of the site will reveal the original plan of the initial fortress at Kabar and the date of its founding; but considering the affinity of the mid-fifth century for 30 meters by 30 meters square forms, there is a strong possibility that this fortress comes from that era.

A second possible fortress of a mid-fifth century date is located at Khirbet ez-Zawiyye in the far southeastern corner of the Judean hill country. The site was situated on a high ridge to the south of the main

---

[123] Kochavi, *Judaea, Samaria and the Golan*, 40.

[124] Kochavi, *Judaea, Samaria and the Golan*, 41 mentions sherds from the Persian, Roman and Byzantine periods being recovered. During the author's evaluation of the site in June of 1986, several Hellenistic period sherds were observed, including a handle bearing a "Yehud-ṭet" seal impression that was turned over to the Israel Department of Antiquities.

route from Halhul to Seir.[125] The 1967-68 survey determined that a fortress was placed on the north slope of the ridge, facing to the north. From the rudimentary remains, it was possible to discern a 20 meters by 20 meters square form with a trapezoidal-shaped chamber spanning the northern end of the fortress.[126] The remains were too fragmentary to determine the size of the central court, if indeed there was one, though only Persian period ceramics were recovered from the structure.[127] There are many uncertainties regarding this particular fortress, and without excavation it is impossible to arrive at a firm conclusion as to its date. However, the 20 meters by 20 meters square form is similar to the mid-fifth century fortresses of the Negev, and the fact that only Persian period ceramics were recovered from this fortress at Khirbet ez-Zawiyye suggests that a mid-fifth century date for its founding is likely.

As was the case in the Negev, there is clear evidence of an intensified military presence in the Judean hill country in the mid-fifth century. These fortresses present a common pattern in distribution, appearing as isolated structures on elevated landforms in proximity of major roadways. This pattern suggests that the fortresses of the Judean hill country were not placed to protect specific population centers, but rather to control movement along the arterial routes of the region.

As has been seen in both the Negev and the Judean hill country, there are a number of sites that represent fortresses founded in the mid-fifth century. Not surprisingly, similar fortresses have been reported in the Samarian (or Ephraimite) hill country, though none have been excavated to date.[128] There are two sites in particular that appear from the groundplans recovered by survey efforts to be of a mid-fifth century form.

The first site is located at el-Qulᶜah (S), a surface ruin located on the southern promontory of Mount Ebal, overlooking the modern city of

---

125 Kochavi, *Judaea, Samaria and the Golan*, 51-2. It was identified as a fortress on the basis of its geographical setting and the thickness of its exterior walls (ca. 1.5 meters).

126 An examination of the site in June, 1986 revealed that since the original survey, the ridge on which the fortress sits has been extensively cultivated. Only a few wall sections could be located, and these gave only a bare outline of the fortress's form.

127 Kochavi, *Judaea, Samaria and the Golan*, 52. In July, 1986 the author was able to locate a box of ceramic materials reportedly collected from Kh. ez-Zawiyye during the original survey, although there was some uncertainty on this point. The three Persian period sherds present among these materials were of mid-fifth to mid-fourth century types. This is inadequate evidence on which to date the installation.

128 The definition of the Samarian hill country used in this study is that proposed by Aharoni, *The Land of the Bible*, 26-7.

Nablus. First reported in the 1967-68 survey, the ruin consists of a square building with exterior walls some 1.2 meters thick (see Figure 4).[129] The structure measures 28 meters by 28 meters and consists of a central courtyard surrounded by casemate rooms on all four sides. The courtyard measures 16.5 meters by 15.5 meters and is basically square in form though some alteration to this design may have taken place in subsequent periods of use.[130] When the percentage of the total area of the structure devoted to the courtyard is calculated, the result is 32.6%, a figure that accords with the typology of the mid-fifth century fortresses (see Table 5). While the survey reported finding only Byzantine period ceramic materials at the site, the overall architectural form and space configuration points strongly in the direction of the proposed typology for fortresses founded in the mid-fifth century BCE.[131]

Table 5.—Mid-fifth Century Fortresses in the Ephraimite Hill Country

Site		Ext. Meas.	Court Meas.	Percentage*
el-Qulʿah	(S)	28 X 28	16.5 X 15.5	32.6
Zakariyah	(N)	41 X 40.5	25 X 18	27.1

**The percentage figure represents the percentage of the total area of the fortress occupied by the courtyard.*

The second site is that of Khirbet Zakariya, located on the summit of a high ridge northwest of the modern city of Ramallah. Like the previous site, this ruin was discovered in the course of the 1967-68 survey, and a general plan of the ruin appeared in the report of the survey.[132] From the plan, it is evident that the structure grew in stages, a portion of the com-

129 Kochavi, *Judaea, Samaria and the Golan,* 165.

130 In the northwest corner of the courtyard is a chamber that disturbs the regularity of the internal design of the structure. In all probability, this chamber represents a secondary adaptation of the building's plan.

131 The architectural form does not fit a Byzantine date, as can be seen by comparing the form of el-Qulʿah with the fortress of Rujm Abu Hashabe; Kochavi, 181. The later site while square (12 meters by 12 meters) lacks a central courtyard and has outer walls that are nearly 2 meters in width. Other Byzantine fortresses in the region similarly lack a true central courtyard; see, for example Khirbet er-Rasm in the Judean hill country; Kochavi, 46.

132 Kochavi, *Judaea, Samaria and the Golan,* 177. Mazar, "Iron Age Fortresses," 106 cites Kh. Zakariya as a potential parallel to Kh. Abu et-Twain.

plex to the east near an elaborate gateway consisting of walls that uniformly butt against the western portions of the complex (see Figure 4). Assuming then that the western portion of the fortress represents the original design, the structure consisted of a square form, approximately 41 meters by 40.5 meters. The interior is arranged around a central courtyard with single rows of casemate rooms to the north and west and double-rows of rooms to the south and east.

The courtyard measures approximately 25 meters by 18 meters, and the percentage of the total area of the building utilized by the courtyard is slightly more than 27% (see Table 5). The original survey reported finding ceramic materials from the Iron 2 and Roman periods, though the architectural form of the structure has its affinities only with the mid-fifth century. Consequently, Kh. Zakariya can be regarded as a further representative of the mid-fifth century fortresses in the Levant.

Along the Coastal plain, the fortress north of Ashdod has already been noted as one of the excavated examples of this form that can be clearly dated. It is, not surprisingly, only one of several possible fortresses from the same period along the Coastal plain. An example of one possibility is Tell el-Ḥesi. The renewed American excavations at the site have demonstrated that the Persian period occupation (stratum 5) had a number of phases over the course of the period. The first of these phases (stratum 5d) was related to the existence of a military installation at the site, a feature first reported by Sir Flinders Petrie, the initial investigator at the site, on the basis of scattered evidence of heavy fortification walls around the summit of the city.[133] Petrie also recovered a large amount of Attic imported wares in the Persian stratum, including a red-figured lekythos that appears for a limited time in the mid-fifth century.[134] The additional excavations by Frederick Bliss concurred with Petrie's analysis of the mid-fifth century date for this military activity.

Over the last decade, a consortium of North American institutions has been stratigraphicaly re-excavating el-Ḥesi, a process that has offered considerable refinements to the sequence that Petrie proposed. These investigations have led to the conclusion that following a very meager

133 A helpful summary of the recovery of Persian period materials as the result of the repeated excavations at Tell el-Ḥesi can be found in Stern, *Material Culture,* 20-1. For a summation of the results regarding all periods of the site, see Ruth Amiran and J. Worrell, "Hesi, Tel." In *Encyclopedia of Archaeological Excavations in the Holy Land. Volume* 2 (Englewood Cliffs, NJ: Prentice-Hall, 1976), 514-20.

134 For a discussion of the Attic imported wares from Tell el-Ḥesi within their larger context, see C. Clairmont, "Greek Pottery from the Near East," *Berytus* 11 (1954/55):85-139. See also Stern, *Material Culture,* 20.

occupation at the site in the late sixth century, a major change takes place with the founding of stratum 5d. This phase of Persian period occupation is characterized by several large public structures, apparently related to an expanded military presence. Among other indications of such a presence are weaponry and body armor found in trash pits of the period.[135] The recovery of additional imported Attic wares in association with this phase has clearly fixed the military activity at el-Ḥesi to the mid-fifth century, just as Petrie's results from earlier excavations had implied. Thus, while no clearly recognizable fortress remains have been recovered at Tell el-Ḥesi, there is a strong probability that a mid-fifth century fortress was present.

Taking all of the examples of mid-fifth century fortresses together, there is a clear pattern in the location of these installations. They are almost always away from population centers and are placed on high elevations overlooking major roadway systems. This distribution suggests that their strategic importance was related to keeping the arterial roadways secure from attack. Moreover, in the few cases where these fortresses have been excavated, there appears to be a pattern of abandonment shortly after their initial founding, as was seen at Tell es-Saʿidiyeh, the fortress north of Ashdod, Ḥorvat Ritma and Khirbet Abu et-Twain. This factor is a strong argument in favor of these fortresses representing a strategic response to a specific condition that, once no longer a threat to the empire, allowed for the disbandment of the fortress system.

The importance of these observations is that they call into question the dominant interpretation of these structures as an effort to secure the border of the province of Yehud. Ephraim Stern has been the chief proponent of this interpretation, arguing that the fortresses in the Judean hill country especially constitute "a clear line of border fortresses" separating Yehud from the Edomites in the south.[136] The impossibility of this inter-

135 D. Glenn Rose and Lawrence E. Toombs, "Four Seasons of Excavation at Tell el-Ḥesi: A Preliminary Report," in *Preliminary Excavation Reports: Bab Edh-Dhra , Sardis, Meiron, Tell el-Ḥesi, Carthage (Punic),* ed. David Noel Freedman. Annual of the American Schools of Oriental Research 43. (Cambridge, MA: American Schools of Oriental Research, 1978), 121-2; Lawrence E. Toombs, "Tell el-Ḥesi, 1981," *PEQ* 115 (1983):33-4; and a recent summary of the stratigraphy in R. Doermann and V. Fargo, "Tell el-Ḥesi, 1983," *PEQ* 117 (1985):10.

136 Ephraim Stern, "Yehud: The Vision and the Reality." *Cathedra* 4 (1977):20; see also Stern, *Material Culture,* 250; and Ephraim Stern, "The Persian Empire and the Political and Social History of Palestine in the Persian Period." In *The Cambridge*

pretation can be readily seen when considering the location of Khirbet ez-Zawiyye, one of the sites Stern uses to argue his case. The fortress is located on the northern side of the ridge it sits on, and faces to the north toward Yehud. Any Edomite force that might come upon the fortress would command the higher elevation to the south and could easily overwhelm what forces may have been deployed in the fortress.[137] Consequently, Stern's interpretation of this installation as a border fortress makes little sense, nor is it possible to reconstruct the boundaries of Yehud from the distribution of these fortresses.

The claim that these fortresses functioned as a way of defending the borders of Yehud also fails to deal with the widespread nature of this military intensification. The fortresses of the mid-fifth century are not restricted to any region thought to constitute the postexilic province of Yehud but are prevalent throughout the Levant. As such, they represent an imperial response to a regional condition, not a localized concern.

Given the founding of these structures in the mid-fifth century and the apparent abandonment of some of them within a few decades of their construction, the most reasonable interpretation of the mid-fifth century fortresses is that they represent an imperial response to the strategic challenges presented by the Egyptian Revolt.

The intrusion of Athenian forces into the populist revolt of Inaros threatened the security of the Achaemenid holdings along the eastern Mediterranean. The imperial response of first, mounting a massive effort to quell the rebellion in Egypt and to defeat the Greek forces and then, taking steps to insure the continued security of the western holdings, involved the movement and deployment of military forces. This intensification of military activity throughout the Levant is attested to by the founding of a number of new fortresses to protect the primary and subsidiary routes that knit this region together under imperial control.[138] It was not the Peace of Callias that brought an end to the threat in the western holdings of the empire, but more likely it was the terrible toll of the Peloponnesian War (431-404 BCE) that destroyed any ability on the part of the Delian League to mount a campaign against Achaemenid interests in the Levant. With such infighting among the Greek city-states, there

History of Judaism. Volume 1: Introduction, The Persian Period, ed. W. D. Davies and L. Finkelstein. (Cambridge: Cambridge University Press, 1984), 86.

[137] See Stern, "The Persian Empire," 86, and the description of the site's setting in Kochavi, *Judaea, Samaria and the Golan,* 51.

[138] For an overview of the importance of effective road systems for the Achaemenid empire, see Cook, *The Persian Empire,* 107-10.

was no longer the need to maintain an extensive network of garrisons. This chronological framework accords nicely with the pattern of abandonment seen in the excavated Levantine fortresses.

While the present study has focussed on the remains of such structures as a way of demonstrating a fundamental change in imperial administration in the Levant, these are not the only archaeological elements that can be used to demonstrate such a change. In a recent study of the distribution of a figural form of pottery known as a "Bes jug," it was demonstrated that one particular type of this pottery was manufactured in southern Palestine in the mid-fifth century and was distributed as far north as Deve Huyuk in Anatolia. Since examples of this type were recoverd from a military cemetery at Deve Huyuk and from a stratum 5d deposit at Tell el-Ḥesi, the authors of the report concluded the distribution of this vessel pointed to imperial troops being stationed throughout southern Palestine, and eventually being redeployed to Anatolia.[139] The occasion of their redeployment was the cessation of the Egyptian Revolt. With an expanded knowledge of the ceramic repertoire of the Persian period, it may be possible in the future to trace similar movements on the basis of ceramic evidence.

The enlargement of military activity in the Levant in the mid-fifth century is only a signal of deeper changes taking place within the administration of the western imperial holdings. These fortresses, built upon standardized plans, were staffed with imperial forces drawn from all over the empire. As such, they were garrisons, pockets of concentrated force established by the imperial system to maintain the empire's interests within the Levant. As was noted earlier, there is some evidence to suggest that the appearance of these garrisons was directly related to the collection of revenues and the maintenance of the administrative machinery over the territory.

That such was the case in the Levant is far from clear. The enigmatic evidence presented in the Aramaic ostraca from Arad and Beersheba, both largely dated to the fourth century BCE, has been interpreted as representing tax receipts from the local landowners intended for the imperial government. Though of a later date, they presumably reflect the standard procedures for Achaemenid garrisons of an earlier period. However, the ostraca cannot be identified with certainty as tax receipts; and until examples are recovered that present more unequivocal evi-

---

139 Jeffrey A. Blakely and Fred L. Horton, Jr., "South Palestinian Bes Vessels of the Persian Period." *Levant* 18 (1986):111-19.

dence, the appearance of these garrisons cannot be conclusively linked to changes in the means of revenue collection.

The intensification of imperial garrisons does indicate the seriousness with which the Achaemenid empire viewed the Egyptian Revolt as a challenge to its control over the Levant. This intensification also demonstrates an increased imperial interest in the importance of the Levant and a commitment to maintain control over the territory. While an increased military presence is effective as a temporary mechanism to achieve this end, it is only part of the means exercised by imperial systems to enhance the integration of a subject territory into the larger empire. Given the intensification of military activity in the mid-fifth century as establishing a context for the employment of additional mechanisms to secure control over the Levant, it is still necessary to assess what specific mechanisms may have been employed, and how these impacted the Levant.

5

IMPERIAL ADMINISTRATION AND THE MISSION OF EZRA AND NEHEMIAH

In light of the archaeological indications of an expanded imperial interest in the Levant stimulated by strategic concerns raised during the Egyptian Revolt, it is clear that the empire undertook certain steps to enhance the integration of the Levantine territories into the imperial system. It is in the midst of this development that the biblical narratives of Ezra-Nehemiah place the missions of two imperial officials, Ezra and Nehemiah, whose wide-ranging activities result in the transformation of the postexilic community.

If a correlation can be made between the larger imperial concerns over the security of the western territories and the specific activities of Ezra and Nehemiah, then one may conclude that their missions did not represent a special disposition toward the postexilic community on the part of the Achaemenid court. Rather, their missions would represent a localized manifestation of a policy being conducted within the larger region of the western territories.

This conclusion possesses implications for reconstructing the administrative structure of the postexilic community in the mid-fifth century and for providing the social context within which the narratives of Ezra-Nehemiah were formed. Consequently, in order to determine if a correlation can be made between the imperial concerns of the mid-fifth century and the missions of Ezra and Nehemiah, it is necessary to analyze the biblical presentation of the activities of these two reformers.

The Mission of Nehemiah

As was noted earlier, the narratives of Ezra-Nehemiah present a far more comprehensive portrayal of Nehemiah's actions in his role as "governor" of the community than of Ezra as an imperial "scribe." It seems unlikely that this focus on Nehemiah is due to the employment of a more detailed source on his tenure as an official (the "Nehemiah Memoir"). Nor does it seem that the greater detail on Nehemiah's autocratic behavior is intended to elevate the figure of Ezra by contrast, as has been argued by Otto Plöger.[1]

As a number of recent writers have demonstrated, the emphasis on Nehemiah's actions serves a structural purpose in the composition as a whole. This purpose is to focus attention on the formation of a holy community through the process of separating the community from the peoples around it, physically by rebuilding the walls of Jerusalem and religiously by the reinforcement of cultic regulations such as the observance of the Sabbath.[2] The fuller portrayal of his official duties makes it preferable to begin the process of analyzing the missions of the mid-fifth century reformers' with Nehemiah.

Whatever the circumstances of Nehemiah's concern over the condition of Jerusalem, it is in the specific requests and charge that he receives from the Achaemenid court that his official role is introduced. As recounted in Nehemiah 2, after providing Artaxerxes I with the reasons for his sorrow, Nehemiah is invited to make a request of the court. He asks to be sent to "Judah, to the city of my fathers' graves" in order to rebuild the city (2:5).[3] After this proposal meets with the king's favor, Nehemiah requests a court authorization for free passage (2:7) and authorization to obtain timber from the "king's park" for three specific

---

[1] Otto Plöger, "Reden und Gebete im deuteronomistischen und chronistischen Geschichtswerk." In *Festschrift für Gunther Dehn*, ed. Wilhelm Schneemelcher (Neukirchen: Neukirchener Verlag des Erziehungsvereins, 1957), 35-49.

[2] For example, see Eskenazi, *In an Age of Prose*, 80-81; and Brevard S. Childs, *Introduction to the Old Testament as Scripture* (Philadelphia: Fortress, 1979), 632-34.

[3] While the dialogue between Artaxerxes and Nehemiah is the reconstruction of the author of Ezra-Nehemiah, it is presumably based on some factual grounds concerning the perimeters of Nehemiah's mission. There is an interesting pattern to the use of "Judah" in Nehemiah, finding use in chapters 1 and 2, echoed in 4:10, and then not utilized as a toponym for the region until the end of the book (13:15-7, 24). While the phenomonon deserves further study, it appears to be a deliberate literary device by the author. The circumlocution in discussing the rebuilding of Jerusalem ("city of my fathers' graves") may be an effort to alert the reader to the earlier abortive effort to rebuild the city walls without imperial sanction (Ezra 4:7-23).

construction tasks (2:8).[4] The wood is necessary "to make beams for the citadel of the Temple, for the walls of the city, and for the house I will occupy (2:8)." The first two projects are directly related to strategic concerns, and deserve a closer scrutiny.

The "citadel of the Temple (*habbîrāh ʾăšer labayit*)" is not only mentioned here in chapter 2, but is alluded to again in Nehemiah 7:2 where a "Hananiah the commander of the citadel" is given shared authority over the city of Jerusalem proper.[5] The Hebrew term used here, *bîrāh*, appears only in postexilic literature and always has the sense of a fortress or citadel.[6] In Imperial Aramaic, the administrative language of the Achaemenid empire, the cognate form has the same restricted usage to denote a military installation.[7] For example, in several of the Aramaic documents of the fifth century from Egypt, now in the collections of the Brooklyn Museum, the garrisons at Elephantine and Syene are both termed a *byrh*.[8]

The Hebrew and Aramaic forms are customarily understood to be loanwords, being derived from the Akkadian term *birtū*. The Akkadian term from Neo-babylonian times on is used exclusively to refer to a military installation.[9] In sum, Nehemiah's request relates to the use of timber

---

[4] The expression *happarĕdēs ʾăšer lammelek* has been varyingly rendered as the "forest," "estate," or "park" of the king. The term *prds* is a Persian loanword, as has been noted by a number of commentators. See, for example, Batten, *Ezra-Nehemiah*, 197; Rudolph, *Esra und Nehemia*, 108; Ackroyd, *I & II Chronicles, Ezra, Nehemiah*, 270-71; Clines, *Ezra-Nehemiah*, 143; and Fensham, *The Books of Ezra and Nehemiah*, 162-63. For a discussion of the various options that have been proposed for a location, see Williamson, *Ezra, Nehemiah*, 181.

[5] Hananiah is called the *sar* of the citadel, a term with wide semantic application in Hebrew. However, considering the military context of *bîrāh* and the common use of *śar* to designate a military commander in late Biblical Hebrew, its meaning here as "commander" seems clear. For examples of its military use in postexilic literature, see Nehemiah 2:9; 1 Chronicles 13:1; 26:26; 27:3; 2 Chronicles 32:6 and 33:14.

[6] For examples, see Nehemiah 1:1; Esther 1:2, 5; 3:15; 9:6; and Daniel 8:2, all in reference to the Persian capital at Susa. For a recent evaluation of the fortified nature of Susa under the Achaemenid kings, see Roman Ghirshman, "Susa." In *The International Standard Bible Encyclopedia*. Volume 4, ed. Geoffrey Bromiley (Grand Rapids: Wm. B.Eerdmans, 1988), 667-69; and Jean Parrot, "L'Architecture militaire et palatiale des Achéménides à Suse." In *150 Jahre, Deutsches Archäologisches Institut 1829-1979*. (Mainz: Philipp von Zabern, 1981), 79-94.

[7] Jean and Hoftijzer, *Dictionnaire*, 35.

[8] See Kraeling, *The Brooklyn Museum Aramaic Papyri*, Nos. 2, 4, and 8, where the term is used with either Elephantine or Syene.

[9] See the comments of Benjamin Mazar, "The Tobiads," *IEJ* 7 (1957):140. See also I. J. Gelb et. al., *The Assyrian Dictionary of the Oriental Institute of the University of Chicago*,

supplies for the construction of a fortress or citadel to be located adjacent to the Temple to the north of the most concentrated portion of the city. Presumably manned by imperial troops, this citadel not only would serve to protect a vulnerable portion of the city, but also would place a concentration of imperial force just outside the city where it would be noticed by the inhabitants of Jerusalem. The fact that Nehemiah sought to build such a citadel in 445 BCE, a time when the deployment of imperial garrisons was taking place throughout the Levant as demonstrated by the archaeological record, suggests Nehemiah's task was simply part of a larger imperial policy.

Regarding the authorization to rebuild the walls of Jerusalem, this is a central theme for the redactor of Ezra-Nehemiah. There is considerable symbolism employed, the walls creating an enclosure, a physical separation of the "holy city (Nehemiah 11:1)" from the profanation without.[10] This theological interest has somewhat obscured the considerable strategic and political importance in refortifying Jerusalem, an event for which there is archaeological confirmation.[11]

The presence of urban fortifications allowed a city to consider itself independent of the empire, capable of determining its own destiny. Such independent thinking was naturally fraught with the potential for rebellion. The importance of such urban fortifications was not lost on the Achaemenid empire. For example, when Babylon staged a brief, abortive revolt against the Persians in 521 BCE, Darius I ordered the destruction of the inner citadel walls in order to render the city's main stronghold impotent. Babylon revolted again in 484 BCE; and once Xerxes had managed to suppress the uprising, the entire city wall system was destroyed.[12] The accusations by Nehemiah's opponents that in rebuilding Jerusalem's walls the Restoration community was planning to rebel (Nehemiah 6:67) had some plausibility within this ideological context.

There is other evidence to suggest that in the Levant, urban fortification systems were rarely encouraged by the imperial officials. As far as can be determined, Samaria never had an urban wall system in the

---

Volume 2—"B". (Gluckstadt: J. J. Augustin, 1965), 261 and Meyers, "The Persian Period and the Judean Restoration," 516.

[10] See the comments of Eskenazi, *In an Age of Prose*, 113-14.

[11] A fine recent summary of the archaeological and biblical materials may be found in H. G. M. Williamson, "Nehemiah's Walls Revisited," *PEQ* 116 (1984):81-8.

[12] M. Meuleau, "Mesopotamia Under Persian Rule." In *The Greeks and the Persians from the Sixth to the Fourth Centuries*, ed. H. Bengtson. Delacorte World History, 5. (New York: Delacorte Press, 1968), 357-58, 360-61.

Persian period, despite its certain status as a provincial capital.[13] Similarly, urban wall systems of the mid-fifth century appear only at Lachish and Tell en-Naṣbeh, though in the case of the latter site the dating is only approximate.[14] The rarity of such urban fortification systems in the mid-fifth century should serve to highlight the unusual nature of Nehemiah's request and the imperial court's willingness to permit the refortification of Jerusalem.

The author of Ezra-Nehemiah has highlighted Nehemiah's imperial authorization as a reversal in the court's attitude towards Jerusalem by including the account in Ezra 4:7-23 of an earlier attempt to rebuild the city fortifications. This attempt, made without authorization, was reported to the court by a number of district officials in Samaria.[15] Artaxerxes I responded by ordering the work to be stopped swiftly, and the Samarian authorities used imperial military forces to insure the royal wishes were obeyed.[16] This incident functions in the narrative of Ezra-

---

13 See particularly Kenyon, *Royal Cities of the Old Testament*, 132-4; and the summary in Stern, *Material Culture*, 29-30.

14 See Stern, *Material Culture*, 50-1 where most of the urban wall systems of the Persian period are mid-fourth century in date. Dor may be a possible exception for this trend, but as has been argued in chapter 3, Dor may not have been allied with the Achaemenid empire in the fifth century; see Stern, "The Walls of Dor," 8.

15 The events of Ezra 4:7-23 make sense only when placed within the context of the transition of power from the assassination of Xerxes to the point when Artaxerxes I was secure on the Achaemenid throne, around the year 464 BCE. In the vacuum of effective central control, various local leaders might attempt to exert autonomy. On the political situation upon Artaxerxes's accession, see Frye, *History of Ancient Iran*, 127. Though some have seen the reference to a movement of population in 4:12 as denoting Ezra's coming to Jerusalem, this is doubtful if the full context of Ezra's mission is considered. Moreover, the constant movement of imperial troops through the Levant during the period of the Egyptian Revolt would make it virtually impossible for a local group to attempt a task of such gravity as rebuilding a city wall system without the explicit authorization of the imperial court. Consequently, a period prior to the Egyptian victory at Papremis would make more sense for such an effort to have been attempted. For a convenient summary of the various views on this matter that have been advocated, see Williamson, *Ezra, Nehemiah*, 61-4.

16 The narrative states that the refortification effort was halted by the Samarian authorities arriving in Jerusalem with "force and power." The Aramaic expression, *ʾedrāʿ wĕḥāyil* has a certain military connotation, *ḥāyil* being the usual Imperial Aramaic term for an imperial garrison. The Hebrew cognate for *ʾedrāʿ* is *zĕrōʿ*, a term that appears in late biblical Hebrew with the meaning of a military force (see Daniel 11:15, 22, 31). In the Greek version of 1 Esdras 2:30, the construction of the wall was stopped "with cavalry and a multitude in battle array," suggesting that an ancient exegetical tradition also understood the phraseology in military terms; see further, Clines, *Ezra, Nehemiah, Esther*, 82.

Nehemiah to reinforce the uniqueness of the authorization that Nehemiah received from Artaxerxes I to rebuild Jerusalem's walls.

This shift in the imperial court's attitude toward the refortifying of Jerusalem signals some dramatic change in the political and strategic conditions in the region. If, as seems most probable, the unauthorized effort to rebuild the city walls took place shortly after Artaxerxes' accession in 465 BCE, then it is possible this effort would have predated the point at which the Egyptian Revolt became a serious challenge to Achaemenid control of the Levant, that being the Egyptian victory at Papremis. The succeeding events' connected with the revolt, most notably being the intervention of the Delian League and continued Greek naval operations in the eastern Mediterranean into the decade of the 440's, certainly would have presented a need for a change in the imperial court's attitude toward the refortification of Jerusalem.

However, if these strategic concerns were the only issues impacting the imperial decision, then the lack of urban fortifications at other sites throughout the Levant would make little sense. If conditions in the western territories called for fortifications at Jerusalem, then it would seem that similar fortifications should have been erected at Samaria and other urban centers.

The biblical narratives indicate that Nehemiah was occupied with a number of tasks in addition to the author's primary concern with his efforts in rebuilding the city walls. Taken together with the strategic elements involved in building the citadel of the Temple and rebuilding the city wall system, these activities suggest that Nehemiah's mission was not intended simply to meet the requirements of military exigencies but were intended to achieve a broader goal.

In Nehemiah 5:1-19, for example, the populace complains about various conditions that are creating an undue economic hardship on them while they are seeking to rebuild the walls. The problem for some was a famine that was driving up the prices of grain (5:2-3), while others complained about the burden of mortgaging their fields to pay "the king's tax upon our fields and our vineyards" (5:4). While many commentators have interpreted these complaints as coming from differing conditions, there are ample reasons to see them as related to the burdens imposed on the populace of Yehud by the significant changes being undertaken by the expanded intervention of the imperial administration.[17]

---

[17] See the thorough discussion in Williamson, *Ezra, Nehemiah*, 235-42, though Williamson is certainly mistaken in claiming that Nehemiah was cancelling all debts.

While many have assumed that the imperial taxes were to be paid in silver only, there is no evidence to suggest that this was, in fact, the practice of the Achaemenid empire.[18] Economic receipts and accounts from across the empire lead to the inevitable conclusion that payments of obligations to the imperial system were usually made in terms of volumes of grain.[19] Thus, temporary shortfalls in the availability of grain, as would be the case in a famine, would not only have the effect of driving prices upward, but would make the payment of imperial taxes by the subject populace more difficult. In Nehemiah 5:4, some members of the Restoration community complain that they have had to mortgage their lands in order to pay a specific obligation, the "King's tax" (*middat hamelek*). The Hebrew term used here, *middāh,* is a loanword from the Akkadian *mandattu,* the same term used for the primary revenue collected from imperial territories within the Assyrian empire.[20] The term also appears in an Aramaic form, *mndh,* in a mid-fifth century BCE document from Saqqara in Egypt, where the reference is to a tax collected specifically to support an imperial garrison.[21] This is in accord with the fourth century Greek historian and general Xenophon who reported that within the Achaemenid empire, subject territories were obligated to maintain the imperial garrisons in their region.[22]

The degree to which imperial territories were obligated to support garrisons in their regions in the mid-fifth century is unclear. The Saqqara document suggests a specific tax for the support of such installations was levied in the western territories in the mid-fifth century. However, there is additional evidence from the material remains of garrisons in the Levant that they were deeply involved in the process of collecting and transporting grains. For example, at Tell el-Ḥesi the mid-fifth century stratum of the city was marked by numerous storage pits for grains.[23]

On the connection of the complaints with the building of the walls, see Batten, *Ezra and Nehemiah,* 237.

[18] H. Kippenberg, *Religion und Klassenbildung im antiken Judäa.* Studien zur Umwelt des Neuen Testaments 14. (Göttingen: Vandenhoeck und Ruprecht, 1978), 49-53.

[19] See particularly the comments of Tuplin, "The Administration of the Achaemenid Empire," 141-42.

[20] See the comments of Myers, *Ezra.Nehemiah,* 128.

[21] Text No. 24, line 11 in J. B. Segal, *Aramaic Texts from North Saqqara with Some Fragments in Phoenician.* Excavations at N. Saqqara: Documentary Series 4. (London: Egypt Exploration Society, 1983), 39-40. The expression in this text is *mndt ḥylʾ*, "tax of the garrison."

[22] Xenophon, *Cyropaedia,* 7.5.69.

[23] See the summary in Stern, *Material Culture,* 20-21.

Similarly, at Tell Jemmeh an extensive complex for grain storage was encountered and assigned by the excavator, Flinders Petrie, to the efforts by the Achaemenid empire to supply a large force preparing for the invasion of Egypt during the Egyptian Revolt.[24] While these granaries may not point directly to the institution of a new levy to support the increased military activity in the Levant in the mid-fifth century, they raise the issue of how these imperial installations were maintained. It would seem simplest for the local populace to be required to provide a portion of the considerable supplies needed to maintain the garrisons.

These factors relating to the means of levying and collecting imperial taxes lead to the following interpretation of the situation in Nehemiah 5. Some natural occurrence, possibly a drought, had led to a shortfall in the grain harvest. This failure in agricultural productivity led to extreme market pressures on the prices of grain since this commodity was necessary not only for individual nutrition but in order to pay the imperial taxes.[25] The burden of these taxes had grown with the intensification of the empire's military presence in the region during the mid-fifth century. The populace, finding itself under economic duress, appealed to Nehemiah as the provincial governor to intervene and bring some relief.

Nehemiah's response was not to exempt the population from the burden of these imperial obligations in consideration of the circumstances but to alleviate the short-term impact of this economic crisis by forcing lenders, including himself (5:10), to forgo the demand of interest payments and pledges.[26] This demand is made in a specific communal context, the convening of a "great assembly," that is a meeting of the *qāhāl* (5:7). Here the *qāhāl* takes up an economic issue that is affecting the entire province; and by virtue of Nehemiah's request in his role as governor, the *qāhāl* accedes to this solution. With the immediate crisis eased, Nehemiah was able to refocus the community's efforts on completing the walls of Jerusalem.

---

24 See Stern, *Material Culture*, 22-24.

25 See especially the evidence offered by Tuplin, "The Administration of the Achaemenid Empire," 141 of commodities, specifically grains, as part of the imperial stores.

26 While there is some uncertainty as to the wording, Nehemiah 5:11-12 seems to call for two steps. The first, the return of productive agrarian property to the debtors, property that had been seized in pledge against non-payment of loans (5:3,4). The second step involves the remission of interest on these debts (the *mʾt* of 5:11), but retaining the principal as a debt obligation. See the comments of Clines, *Ezra, Nehemiah, Esther*, 169-70 for a detailed presentation of this interpretation.

In addition to these economic reforms, Nehemiah undertook several actions that were related to the administration of Jerusalem as an urban center. For example, as was noted above, in Nehemiah 7:2 the reformer places the city in the hands of his brother Hanani and "Hananiah the commander of the fortress."[27] While there is no specification in the narrative as to exact nature of this authority, this account coming right after the placement of the gates in the walls (Nehemiah 7:1) would suggest these official responsibilities related to the security of the city itself and the control of access to the city.[28] As will be seen below, this action is an important piece of evidence in interpreting the larger mission of Nehemiah.

An additional action usually credited to Nehemiah is the enforced repopulation of Jerusalem. Once the refortification of the city was complete, the narratives note that the city was "wide and large," though there were few who actually dwelt within the walls (Nehemiah 7:4). The repopulation of the city is recorded in Nehemiah 11:1-2 where the leadership of the community is said to reside in Jerusalem, while the people in the outlying settlements cast lots to select ten percent of the population for resettlement within Jerusalem, "the holy city." For many commentators, despite the failure of Nehemiah 11:1-2 to directly mention Nehemiah, he was the force behind the repopulation effort since the lack of population in Nehemiah 7:4, ascribed to the "Nehemiah Memoir," is aptly resolved by the repopulation account.[29]

Since there is an enforced movement of population into Jerusalem (based on the assumption that Nehemiah as the provincial governor is behind the effort), many commentators go on to compare this action to the Greek practice of *synoikismos*, or enforced population of an urban center.[30] In this comparison, Nehemiah's actions represent a new relation-

---

[27] Several commentators have made the suggestion that the *waw* here acts as a specifier; thus the clause should be translated, "my brother Hanani, namely Hananiah the commander of the fortress;" so Clines, *Ezra, Nehemiah, Esther*, 178. Williamson, *Ezra, Nehemiah*, 266 offers some cogent reasons why this reading does not agree with the larger context of the passage, though it still must be reckoned a possibility.

[28] The text is ambiguous at this point, though verses 3 and following could be understood as the specification of the charge given to these officials.

[29] For a positive assessment of these verses in chapter 11 being part of the "Nehemiah Memoir," see Rudolph, *Esra und Nehemia*, 181; Clines, *Ezra, Nehemiah, Esther*, 211-12; and Williamson, *Ezra, Nehemiah*, 344-45.

[30] Rudolph, *Esra und Nehemia*, 181; Clines, *Ezra, Nehemiah, Esther*, 211.

ship between an urban center and the surrounding countryside, marking the emergence of Jerusalem as a provincial capital.[31]

There are a number of interpretive problems associated with this reading of the repopulation effort. To begin with, the Greek employment of *synoikismos* as a political mechanism was restricted to situations where various diverse settlements were fused into a true *polis* or self-governing political entity.[32] While the refortification of Jerusalem and any effort to increase its population would naturally have resulted in a new prominence for the city, no place in the narratives of Ezra-Nehemiah suggests that this move is made to create a new self-governing entity. Indeed, one must question whether a mechanism employed in a region of strong city-state traditions would have applicability in another region under imperial domination.

More to the point, there are substantial reasons to question Nehemiah's connection with this repopulation effort. Several commentators have pointed out that Nehemiah 11 has a number of stylistic differences from those portions of the narratives of Ezra-Nehmiah that most scholars have regarded as part of the "Nehemiah Memoir."[33] In her innovative literary reading of these narratives, Eskenazi has pointed out that Jerusalem is termed the "holy city" both at the opening and closing (11:2 and 11:18) of the repopulation effort, marking the transformation of the city into a sacral realm. In addition, the community has just pledged to insure the tithe is delivered to the "house of God (10:37-39)," and now a tenth of the population enters the "holy city." She notes that Nehemiah 11:3 praises those who "willingly" joined in the repopulation effort, and argues that the author intended this effort to be seen as the community's effort to establish the sacral realm, and not an enforced policy of Nehemiah's.[34]

Eskenazi's reading of this repopulation effort is persuasive, and consequently there is no need to see this as an official action by Nehemiah in his capacity as the provincial governor. The focus of the narrative on the action of the community as a whole in reestablishing the "holy city" makes it apparent that this narrative is the contribution of the author of Ezra-Nehemiah.

---

31 Alt, "Die Rolle Samarias," 336-37.

32 Victor Ehrenberg, *The Greek State*. Second edition. (London: Methuen and Co., 1969), 24-25.

33 See especially the discussion in Williamson, *Ezra, Nehemiah*, 345-46.

34 Eskenazi, *In an Age of Prose*, 111-15.

While there is little reason to conclude that some form of *synoikismos* precipitated a change in the relationship between Jerusalem as an urban center and the surrounding region, the narratives of Ezra-Nehemiah indicate some change in fact had taken place. The opposition of the imperial leadership in Samaria once Nehemiah began his mission in Jerusalem (Nehemiah 3:33-4:3 [Eng. 4:1-9]) signaled the initiation of a new relationship between these urban centers. Several portions of the "Nehemiah Memoir" focus on the continuing struggle between Sanballat, the governor of Samaria accompanied by several allies, and Nehemiah.[35] However, these same narratives never specify the reasons for this opposition.

As Ackroyd has pointed out, the role played by the allies of Sanballat is minimal: it is Sanballat as an imperial official in Samaria who serves as the focal point of opposition in Nehemiah chapters 2, 4, and the first part of 6.[36] The opposition of Tobiah in Nehemiah 6:10-19 seems to be predicated on some different grounds, and accordingly Sanballat is present but in a secondary role.[37] The degree of literary shaping of this opposition in the narratives precludes any derivation from the narratives themselves of the grounds for Sanballat's opposition. However, it is certain that the presence of such opposition points in the direction of a changed relationship between Samaria and Yehud as the result of Nehemiah's mission, a change that can perhaps be explained once the totality of Nehemiah's reforms are evaluated.

The last activities connected with Nehemiah's mission are noted in Nehemiah 13 and are placed within the reformer's "second" governorship. In Nehemiah 13:67, a first person narrative recounts the reformer's journey to the imperial court in 433 BCE and his later return to Jerusalem. Upon his return, he finds a series of conditions that he must address, including Tobiah's having set up residency within the "house of God" (13:79), the failure of the community to provide for the Levites serving in the "house of God" (13:10-14), the profanation of the Sabbath by individuals working on the Sabbath and Tyrian traders entering the city to hawk their wares (13:15-22), and intermarriage between "Yehudians"

---

35 On the place of these narratives in the "Nehemiah Memior," see Kellermann, *Nehemia*, 17-23. There is a prevailing structure to these accounts, a successful action being followed by opposition from without; Williamson, *Ezra, Nehemiah*, 216-17. This structured character is suggestive of the literary nature of the "Nehemiah Memoir."

36 Ackroyd, "Archaeology, Politics and Religion: The Persian Period," 14.

37 Williamson, *Ezra, Nehemiah*, 257-58; Ackroyd, "Archaeology, Politics and Religion: The Persian Period," 145.

(*yěhūdîm*) and foreigners (13:23-29). These conditions are, in reverse order, precisely the obligations that the community took a solemn oath to uphold in Nehemiah 10:1-40.[38] Yet most critics deny that Nehemiah 10 was part of the "Nehemiah Memoir" while maintaining that Nehemiah 13 was from the hand of the reformer himself, creating a serious problem as to the temporal relationship between the oath and these conditions.

The literary complexity of the reformer's actions in chapter 13 is further highlighted by the phrase "on that day" in 13:1 and 12:44. These markers relate the materials back to the covenant ceremony of Nehemiah 9. And, as the narratives now stand, it is in response to that ceremony that the community undertakes its oath in chapter 10.[39] Clearly the author of these materials has so arranged and linked the contents and structure of these narratives that it is impossible to act as though the supposed Nehemiah Memoir materials of 13:4-31 can be treated apart from the oath of chapter 10.[40] While the covenant ceremony of chapter 9 does not need to be related to the oath of chapter 10, the author clearly intended the readers of Ezra-Nehemiah to see a connection by the employment of temporal markers.

The oath of chapter 10 is introduced by a problematical clause in verse 1 [Eng. 9:38]: "because of all this (*ûběcol-zōt*)." The clause relates back to some condition or conditions that have stimulated the oath, and critics have struggled with its original setting. Again, there is no certain way to reconstruct what this clause relates to, and only the contents of the oath itself can be used to propose the particular concerns being addressed.[41]

The narrative opens with a listing of the primary members of the community who were signatories to the agreement.[42] This is followed by a summation of all the elements of the community who were joining the signatories in making the oath, namely "all who had separated from the peoples of the lands" (Nehemiah 10:29 [Eng. 10:28]), possibly a reference

---

[38] See, for example, the chart in Williamson, *Ezra, Nehemiah*, 331.

[39] See the comments in Williamson, *Ezra, Nehemiah*, 380-81. On the assignment of these materials to an origin outside of the Nehemiah Memoir, see Rudolph, *Esra und Nehemia*, 172-76, 201-3; and Kellermann, *Nehemia*, 41-48.

[40] This is also the argument of Eskenazi, *In an Age of Prose*, 101-2 and 151 though her position that there is a tension between the community's actions and Nehemiah's efforts to take credit for these actions is more difficult to maintain.

[41] For a sampling of opinions, see Rudolph, *Esra und Nehemia*, 172-73; Myers, *Ezra.Nehemiah*, 173-75; Clines, *Ezra, Nehemiah, Esther*, 200-01; and Williamson, *Ezra, Nehemiah*, 325.

[42] For a helpful discussion of this form, see Clines, *Ezra, Nehemiah, Esther*, 201.

back to Ezra 10:11.[43] Then the group covenants to follow "God's law which was given by the hand of Moses." The first issue addressed in this process is the oath to refrain from intermarriage with the "peoples of the lands" (10:31 [Eng. 10:30]), followed immediately with the pledge not to buy their goods on the Sabbath or other holy days. These are followed by pledges to supply various offerings and contributions to the "house of God" for the service of the cult.[44]

Whatever its proper chronological setting, the narrative of Nehemiah 10 ties together two central themes that are reaffirmed in Nehemiah 13:4-31, namely the unacceptability of intermarriage outside of the community and concern for the sacral nature of the "house of God," understood both as the Temple proper and as the community joined around the Temple. Of these two concerns, the priority of the narratives is the issue of intermarriage, which begins the oath of chapter 10 and finds its reaffirmation at the close of Ezra-Nehemiah in Nehemiah 13:23-31. The possibility that these concerns are related to a changing social fabric in the Restoration community has been raised by Kippenberg. He ties the conditions of this oath into the economic problems and reforms of Nehemiah 5 and sees the whole of Nehemiah's mission as the forging of a coalition of imperial interests, peasant concerns, and the Temple community.[45] The purpose for forming such a coalition was to oppose the urban-centered aristocracy that tended to look westward toward the Hellenic world.[46] There are a number of problems with this understanding of these narratives, not the least of which is the portrayal of Jerusalem as a depopulated urban center until the mission of Nehemiah (Nehemiah 7:4). Without a strong urban center, one wonders where the aristocracy would have received their alleged urban orientation. Moreover, one cannot find in the narratives themselves any simple division between the aristocracy and a peasant class.

The close connection in these narratives between the issue of intermarriage and the care for the "house of God" points in a somewhat different direction, that of a new definition of the community (the ban on intermarriage) receiving a theological validation as part of a larger con-

---

43 Only in Ezra are those outside of the *qāhāl* called the "peoples of the lands (*ʿamê hāʾărāṣôt*);" 9:11, 10:2, 11. In Nehemiah 9, the problem is defined as intermarriage with "foreigners (*bĕnê nēkār*);" 9:2.

44 A useful summary of these offerings and their background in the Pentateuchal legislation may be found in Myers, *Ezra.Nehemiah*, 178-80.

45 Kippenberg, *Religion und Klassenbildung*, 73.

46 Kippenberg, *Religion und Klassenbildung*, 76-7.

cern for the sanctity of the community in Jerusalem. The reforms of Nehemiah may well have addressed matters pertaining to provisions for the Temple cult, but in their present setting, the narratives of Nehemiah chapters 10 and 13 dealing with the "house of God" have an expanded meaning extending beyond the Temple and including the entire Jerusalemite population.[47] Thus, the care for the "house of God" (i.e. the community) not only includes the maintenance of the Temple cult itself but also involves the proper observance of the sanctity of appointed times and the sanctity of the physical constitution of the community.[48]

It remains to summarize what the biblical narratives present as constituting the primary facets of Nehemiah's mission. First, there was a strategic dimension, most dramatically represented by the refortification of Jerusalem by the restoration of the city wall system, but also including the establishment of an imperial garrison to the north of the city. Second, there were a series of economic reforms directed at lessening the impact of the increased imperial activity in the region. Finally, there was some form of reiterated opposition to intermarriage, circumscribing the community within a set of ethnic boundaries.

These activities by Nehemiah have received varying interpretations at the hands of critics. As was noted in the previous discussions of explanations that have been offered for the imperial court's motivation in sending Nehemiah, the usual understanding advanced for his mission was to reward the Restoration community for its loyalty to the empire, or as an inducement to greater loyalty by the show of imperial favor. However, the economic distress indicated in Nehemiah 5, the active opposition from imperial officials in the surrounding territories, and the internal dissension caused by some of Nehemiah's actions (particularly as recounted in Nehemiah 13:25) would suggest that his program of reform was a curious path to induce loyalty.

Several critics have been sensitive to the inconsistencies between Nehemiah's actions and the larger imperial concern to ensure the loyalty of the Restoration community, and have accordingly sought to explain Nehemiah's mission by appealing to the model of the actions of Greek tyrants. In the most influential synthesis, Morton Smith argues that in the aftermath of the Egyptian Revolt, the revolt of Megabyzos, and the continuing expansion from the south by Edomite groups the empire desired

[47] See especially the comments of Clines, *Ezra, Nehemiah, Esther*, 242-45; and Eskenazi, *In an Age of Prose*, 124-25.

[48] Eskenazi, *In an Age of Prose*, 101-4.

a fortified, loyal center in Jerusalem.[49] Nehemiah was sent to Yehud only to rebuild the walls of Jerusalem; but as a member of a sectarian group that held to the prophetic ideal of the exclusive worship of Yahweh (the "Yahweh-alone party" in Smith's terms), Nehemiah undertook to garner popular support in an effort to suppress assimilationist tendencies among other parts of the community. As such, the economic reforms of Nehemiah 5 were an effort to appeal to the masses and to set them against the assimilationist aristocracy. Following his brief time at the imperial court, he returned to embark on an even more drastic campaign of religious reform, recorded in Nehemiah 13.[50]

For Smith, Nehemiah's religious reforms were not an intrinsic part of the imperial commission he received, but a series of independent actions undertaken by the reformer in an effort to promote a sectarian religious program. These actions were an effort to capitalize on the political tensions and "social instability" created by a newly emergent aristocracy quick to take advantage of increasing population by seeking to control foreign trade and the available monetary surplus. By gaining popular support for his religious program through efforts to remove the economic advantages employed by the aristocracy, Nehemiah assured the ultimate triumph of an exclusionistic understanding of earlier Israelite religious traditions. As such, Nehemiah's program possessed a number of parallels to the actions of a series of tyrants in the Aegean world, recorded in the Greek historiographic tradition.[51]

For Smith, the parallels to Nehemiah's program consist of such moves as public building projects aimed at giving a broad cross-section of the populace work, the use of alleged threats from outside powers to create greater solidarity within the community, the remitting of debts and the use of "lavish hospitality" as a way of showing public interest, and the employment of *synoikismos* to build a constituency within an urban center. Each of these various mechanisms had its employment within a particular program of an individual tyrant in the Aegean world.[52]

Smith's basic model has been specified somewhat by Edwin Yamauchi who has drawn a series of parallels between Nehemiah's reforms and the actions of the sixth century Athenian reformer Solon.

---

[49] Morton Smith, *Palestinian Parties and Politics that Shaped the Old Testament* (New York; Columbia University Press, 1971), 127-28.

[50] Smith, *Palestinian Parties*, 128-29.

[51] Smith, *Palestinian Parties*, 138-39.

[52] Smith, *Palestinian Parties*, 141-44.

Like Smith, Yamauchi begins with the postulation of economic tensions within the Restoration community arising out of the growth of burdensome debt to the local aristocracy.[53] Consequently the reforms of Nehemiah 5 are not the direct result of the imperial refortification program but were "problems that had long been simmering."[54] The measures of Nehemiah 5 were directed not at limiting the impact of new imperial demands on the local populace but at the achievement of more long-term stability by banning the use of interest on indebtedness to the advantage of the wealthy. Like Smith, Yamauchi sees this effort not as part of Nehemiah's imperial task, but as an independent response to social inequality. However, Yamauchi appears to differ from Smith in that he sees Nehemiah's response as motivated from genuine concern over social injustice rather than an effort to gain a following for an otherwise unpopular religious program.[55] All of these elements in Nehemiah's reforms have their corollary in Solon's reforms that similarly sought to acheive social stability in the face of economic tensions.

There are a series of problems with both Smith's and Yamauchi's positions, beginning with their reconstruction of the economic situation in Yehud in the mid-fifth century. Both perceive the emergence of a new class of aristocracy as the result of the increasing utilization of coinage (necessary for payment of the imperial taxes) and the growth of foreign trade. Yet, as was discussed above, there is no real evidence for coinage being required for the payment of imperial taxes and every reason to believe that payment was in the form of units of grain. Moreover, there is no archaeological evidence for the widespread use of coinage in Yehud in the mid-fifth century.[56] On the growth of foreign trade, while there is some evidence for such expansion, it is not clear who controlled this exchange and how resources gained by trade were returned to the

---

53 Edwin Yamauchi, "Two Reformers Compared: Solon of Athens and Nehemiah of Jerusalem," 270-76 in *The Bible World: Essays in Honor of Cyrus H. Gordon*, eds. Gary Rendsburg, Ruth Adler, Milton Arfa, and Nathan H. Winter. (New York: Ktav Publising House, 1980).

54 Yamauchi, "Two Reformers Compared," 285.

55 Yamauchi, "Two Reformers Compared," 290-91.

56 See especially the remarks of Stern, *Material Culture*, 218, 220, and 223. In summarizing this evidence, Stern has also commented that, "we may assume that the use of coins was common only from the end of the fifth century, and mainly during the fourth century;" Stern, "The Archaeology of Persian Palestine," 110 in *The Cambridge History of Judaism. Volume One: Introduction: The Persian Period*, eds.W. D. Davies and L. Finkelstein (Cambridge: Cambridge University Press, 1984).

region.[57] In short, the conditions that both Smith and Yamauchi presuppose as the grounds for the economic developments that led to some need for adjustment by Nehemiah are untenable.

As for Smith's marshalling of parallels between the programs of various tyrants and the reforms of Nehemiah, there is a fundamental weakness in his line of argument. While individual tyrants may have utilized a specific mechanism parallel to a reform of Nehemiah, none of the tyrants Smith noted employed the full range of reforms that characterized Nehemiah's mission. One may thus question the applicability of the broad characterization of Nehemiah as a "tyrant" on the basis of actions that have only isolated parallels to particular tyrants. In this sense, Yamauchi's effort to parallel the reforms of Solon with those of Nehemiah represents a more coherent approach.

A fundamental problem with the approach of both Smith and Yamauchi involves their perception of Nehemiah's actions as independent of his imperial commission. This denies the relationship between the complaints of Nehemiah 5 and the refortification of Jerusalem. It also denys the relationship between Ezra's and Nehemiah's opposition to intermarriage, both reformers acting as imperial officials.[58] This consistency in policy between the two reformers would suggest that the opposition to intermarriage was related in some way to their respective imperial missions, and was not simply an independent policy growing out of sectarian interests.

In trying to arrive at a clear understanding of the relationship between Nehemiah's actions and the goals of imperial administration, it is useful to begin by recognizing that the reformer's program involved strategic, economic, and social changes. The breadth of Nehemiah's reforms points to a new change in the administrative relationship between the imperial court and the province of Yehud.[59] This is further indicated

---

[57] Provisionally, see Stern, *Material Culture*, 236 who thinks the "chief carriers" of this trade were Phoenician.

[58] Smith argues that Ezra, like Nehemiah, was a member of the "Yahweh-alone" party that represented the majority of the Exilic population. Ezra's mission ended in disgrace when he assisted in the rebuilding of the city fortifications without imperial sanction (Ezra 4:7-23), and he was recalled to the imperial court; *Palestinian Parties*, 122-24.

[59] Eisenstadt has noted that relations between the center of an empire and peripheral territories are transformed by the reorganization of economic, social, and political factors; "Observations and Queries about Sociological Aspects of Imperialism in the Ancient World," 30-31 in *Power and Propaganda: A Symposium on Ancient Empires*, ed. Morgens Trolle Larsen. Mesopotamia 7. (Copenhagen: Akademisk Forlag, 1979).

by the uniqueness of the imperial commission to refortify Jerusalem, a commission that went contrary to earlier imperial attitudes toward the city (Ezra 4:17-22).

The new relationship between the imperial court and the district of Yehud is further indicated by two telling elements in the biblical narratives. The first is the commission to rebuild the walls of Jerusalem, itself an extraordinary move when set against the archaeological background of the mid-fifth century in the Levant. As has been repeatedly pointed out, there were very few urban centers with wall systems within the Achaemenid empire. Thus it is not enough to postulate, as does Morton Smith, that continued Edomite expansion from the south led to the imperial desire for a wall around Jerusalem. Rather, the city wall system points to a new status for Jerusalem as an urban center within the imperial system, a change also indicated by the establishment of the imperial garrison to the north of the city.

The second indication of a change is found within the nature of the opposition from Sanballat and his allies. Whatever the source for these narratives, in their present form these narratives demonstrate a continuous effort to diminish the value of the effort and to threaten Nehemiah with imperial sanctions by alleging that he is going too far with the refortification effort. For example, the walls are being constructed of inferior materials (Nehemiah 3:33-34 [Eng. 4:12]), and a report has gone out that Nehemiah is plotting a rebellion, a report that Sanballat feels must be passed along to the imperial court (Nehemiah 6:67). Both efforts to discredit the actions of Nehemiah suggest that the opposite perspectives were closer to the truth, namely that having a wall system marked Jerusalem as enjoying some status denied to Samaria and that Nehemiah enjoyed a special relationship to the imperial court that could only be threatened by a direct charge of rebellion against the Achaemenid king.

In this sense, Briant's thesis that the presence of a garrison also signified a center for the collection of imperial revenues has some merit. The combination of a new imperial garrison in Jerusalem and a refortified city would strongly suggest that Jerusalem was now to serve as a collection and storage center for imperial revenues, a function that would also mark a new relationship between the city and the surrounding region as well as a new relationship between the city and the imperial system. The district of Yehud was now to attain a new importance in the imperial system as the empire sought to gain a stronger grip on the Levant to prevent the continued intrusion of Hellenic influence into the eastern Mediterranean.

As was noted in the discussion of the economic reforms of Nehemiah 5, these reforms were not aimed at achieving some larger economic equality between peasant and aristocracy as much as they were an effort to minimize the increased taxation burden that was the result of the new function of the district within the imperial system. The chain of garrisons throughout the Judean hill country in the mid-fifth century required that new local revenues be raised in order to maintain them. The strains these new revenue requirements placed on the populace were magnified by famine and the requirement for pledges against default for loans to pay the imperial revenues. Nehemiah did not address the major cause of the economic stresses within the district, but only ameliorated the conditions that were intensifying the distress.

The actions reflected in the narratives regarding Nehemiah's mission are not a reward for past loyalty, nor the provision of special favors upon Jerusalem simply to ensure that the community continues in its obedience to the empire. Rather, the actions of Nehemiah are reflective of an effort on the part of the Achaemenid empire to tighten its control over the district in the face of continued Greek pressure along the Mediterranean coast. While there were undoubtedly some benefits for Jerusalem to function as an imperial administrative center, these were of secondary concern to the goal of Nehemiah's mission.

A further indication of this interpretation of Nehemiah's mission is found in the account of his appointment of the commander of the garrison to be "over Jerusalem" (Nehemiah 7:2). While the specifics of this appointment are lacking in the narrative, the general social setting is well known from contemporaneous Greek practices.[60] For example, when a city-state revolted from the Delian League in the mid-fifth century and the revolt was suppressed by Athens, in the process of the Athenian effort to regain control over the *polis*, the garrison commander (*phourarchos*) was appointed to control the city-state's council as well as insure that no new conspiracies against Athenian control could be launched.[61] Similar military and political roles were frequently interchanged in the responsibilities of Achaemenid imperial officials in the subject territories.[62] Thus, this appointment of the garrison commander

---

60 Clines, *Ezra, Nehemiah, Esther*, 178 sees him a "governor over the city," while Williamson, *Ezra, Nehemiah*, 270 would see him as simply supervising the security of the city. Neither author draws upon parallels from outside the narrative itself.

61 Meiggs, *The Athenian Empire*, 212-13.

62 See particularly the discussion and references in H. S. Smith and A. Kuhrt, "A Letter to a Foreign General," *JEA* 68 (1982): 207.

to be over the city is another indication that Nehemiah's mission was aimed at enhancing imperial control over Jerusalem and Yehud.

Thus far in this discussion, Nehemiah's opposition to intermarriage has not been brought into the analysis. However, as will be seen below, the redefinition of a community in terms of its ethnic character was a mechanism employed by imperial systems to insure control over a subject territory. Since this issue receives a somewhat fuller articulation in the biblical narratives dealing with the mission of Ezra, a further analysis of its importance as a means of imperial control will be reserved until Ezra's actions have been assessed.

The Mission of Ezra

The narratives of Ezra-Nehemiah introduce the figure of Ezra in Ezra 7, beginning the account of his reforms with a unique genealogical recounting of his priestly lineage.[63] After this introduction to the man Ezra, the narrative abruptly shifts to a focus on the people, specifically those who were involved in the Temple (Ezra 7:7). This interjection is quite deliberate, reinforcing the author's overall concern with the community as the "house of God."[64] Following this focus on the community, the narrative returns to Ezra, noting that he came to Jerusalem in "the seventh year of the king (Ezra 7:8)," a formula equivalent to the year 458 BCE if the king in question was Artaxerxes I. Assuming the Egyptian victory at Papremis took place around the year 460 BCE, Ezra's arrival in Jerusalem would have come as the imperial court was assembling a great expeditionary force to counteract the Greek intrusion into the Egyptian Revolt.

The account continues on to its highpoint in Ezra 7:10 where Ezra is said to be a person who had "set his heart to study the torah of the LORD, to do it, and to teach his statutes and ordinances in Israel."[65] This introduces the main thrust of the commission of Artaxerxes I to Ezra, namely the largely legal character of his mission.

With Ezra 7:11-26 the reader is introduced to Ezra's role in the community by means of what is presented as an official letter from

---

63 For a very insightful analysis of the role of this portion of the narrative, see Eskenazi, *In an Age of Prose*, 62-63.

64 See Eskenazi, *In an Age of Prose*, 64-65.

65 See the comments in Eskenazi, *In an Age of Prose*, 65. The reference here to Ezra's desire to teach "in Israel" rather than in Yehud points to the peculiar understanding of the narratives of Yehud as alone constituting the "true" Israel. Williamson, *Ezra, Nehemiah*, 92-3 has demonstrated how closely related this pericope is to various parts of the Nehemiah Memoir.

Artaxerxes I to Ezra. There has been considerable scholarly debate over the authenticity of this document, and as was noted earlier, very little in the way of consensus has emerged.[66] Most critics would agree that the letter contains a number of technical terms and expressions that betray an intimate familiarity with the Jerusalem cult.[67] As was noted in the earlier discussion of the use of official documents in Ezra-Nehemiah, there are some form critical grounds for regarding this edict as significantly different from the less-suspect documents in Ezra chapters 1-6. However, it is possible to find in contemporaneous imperial materials some of the same concerns for the cultic affairs in subject territories, the provision of sacrificial and financial support from the imperial court to a cult, and the specific exemption of cultic officials from imperial taxation.[68] There is no simple way to resolve the matter of the letter's authenticity, but it would appear that those elements impinging on the cultic side of Ezra's commission have more of a potential for alteration and modification to fit the author's larger concern over the status of the "house of God."[69] While it is not improbable that some aspect of Ezra's mission involved the distribution of funds from the imperial court to the Temple, there is no certain way to distinguish in the commission as it now stands what this distribution entailed.

The commission as recorded in Ezra 7:12 opens with the usual identification of the king, and then addresses "Ezra the priest, the scribe of the law of the God of heaven." This combination of titles is a bit unusual, and in part led Hans Schaeder to propose that "the scribe of the law of the God of heaven" was an imperial title designating an official in charge of Jewish affairs within the empire.[70]

---

66 For a representative sampling of opinions and discussion of the literature, see Rudolph, *Esra und Nehemia*, 73-77; Myers, *Ezra.Nehemiah*, 57-63; Clines, *Ezra, Nehemiah, Esther*, 10-16; and Williamson, *Ezra, Nehemiah*, 97-105.

67 For example, the distinction between priests and Levites (vs. 13), the distinctions among the various forms of offerings presented at the Temple (vs.17), and the listing of the various levels of temple personnel (vs. 24).

68 See especially the presentation of Williamson, *Ezra, Nehemiah*, 104-5.

69 Indeed, this would seem to be the main point the author wishes the reader to comprehend about the commission, given the praise offered to God for causing the king "to beautify the house of the LORD in Jerusalem" (vs. 27).

70 See Hans Heinrich Schaeder, *Esra der Schreiber*. Beiträge zur historichen Theologie, 5. (Tübingen: J. C. B. Mohr, 1930), 48-57. On Ezra's identification as a priest within the Aaronide line, several points should be made. First, nowhere in the narratives does Ezra act as a priest, that is offer sacrifices or act as the chief administrative officer over the Temple. Second, the lineage given him in Ezra 7:15 is the contribution of the author, as most critics would concur (see Williamson, *Ezra, Nehemiah*,

Several subsequent authors following Schaeder's lead have been able to amass a variety of titles of similar form relating to scribes holding civil or religious positions in the second and first millennium BCE.[71] The difficulty is in finding a parallel during any point in the existence of the Achaemenid empire for an individual who served as the official in charge of imperial interests for any religious or nationalistic group.

The absense of such a position in the fairly well-known imperial structure of the Achaemenid empire, combined with the relatively minor role the community in Yehud would have played in the larger sphere of imperial interests, were the basic points in Mowinckel's strong argument against Schaeder's thesis.[72] Williamson has attempted to moderate Schaeder's view by suggesting that the title marks an official office, but one which Ezra received only as a consequence of his imperial commission to go to Jerusalem. For Williamson, it is the "degree of authority" that the commission confers on Ezra that makes the official character of the title plausible.[73] A resolution of this issue cannot be readily made since, whatever the "degree of authority" one finds reflected in the narratives, the accounts of Ezra's mission are highly selective. Thus, one simply is not provided with a clear portrayal of the full role Ezra was to play in the imperial system.

Given the inability to determine on the basis of the commission's opening what official standing Ezra possessed, it is essential to assess carefully the narrative of the commission for whatever evidence it may offer of the scope of the reformer's authority. The primary statement in the commission itself of Ezra's task appears in 7:14 where Ezra is said to be sent "to make inquiry concerning Yehud and Jerusalem with the law

---

91-2 and the literature cited there). This raises the possibility that the reference to "the priest" here in 7:12 is an insertion of the author to elevate the status of Ezra in the community.

[71] See especially Myers, *Ezra.Nehemiah*, 57-58, 60-61.

[72] Mowinckel, *Studien zu dem Buche Ezra-Nehemiah, Volume 3*, 117-24. See also the very negative evaluation of Robert North, "Civil Authority in Ezra." In *Studi in onore di Edoaro Volterra, Volume 6*. (Milan: A. Giuffre, 1971), 389-90. On what can be adduced regarding the role of scribes in the administration of the empire, both in the imperial court itself and in the outlying satrapal and provincial centers, see Tuplin, "The Administration of the Achaemenid Empire," 116-19. In no instance are any of these functionaries performing a role that resembles the office Ezra is presumed to have held in Schaeder's hypothesis.

[73] Williamson, *Ezra, Nehemiah*, 100. Williamson's point would have more weight if he could produce an example of an official document being addressed to an appointee bearing an opening title that relates to the position the person is being given.

of your god that is in your hand." While the larger context of Ezra 7-10 makes it probable that this law was understood by the author of Ezra-Nehemiah to be the completed Pentateuch, such an inference cannot be superimposed on the narrative here.[74] Kellermann has argued that this law is more or less the equivalent of Deuteronomy, a conclusion he arrives at by accepting as the only authentic reflection of Ezra's role the commission of Ezra 7:12-26.[75] However, Kellermann's position can be criticized on several grounds, not the least of which is the lack of a clear indication in the commission of any particular element that could be correlated with some part of the Pentateuchal legislation.

The identity of "the law of your god" is evasive primarily because the author of the narratives has utilized a wide range of terms in a synonymous fashion. By utilizing such terminological variation, the author seeks to reinforce the conception that the community must be governed by the Torah of the Pentateuch.[76] Thus it is fruitless to speculate on the possible contents of this legal corpus that Ezra is to utilize as a standard.[77] Since the identification of the "law of your god" is so problematical, it becomes nearly impossible to ascertain what form of "inquiry" Ezra was commissioned to make. This, like the sphere of his authority, can only be derived from the limited perspective afforded by the narratives.

The second aspect of Ezra's mission is detailed in 7:15 where he is instructed to transport and distribute monetary gifts and temple vessels to the "god of Israel who is in Jerusalem." This charge receives further refinement by the specification of the kinds of offerings the monies are to be used to support (vss. 17-18). An intrusion appears within the flow of these instructions, namely verses 21-24 that contain instructions to the "treasurers" of the satrapy to release goods and monies to Ezra for use in

---

[74] See Williamson, *Ezra, Nehemiah*, xxxvii-xxxix, 100; and the comments of Morton Smith, "Ezra," in *Ex Orbe Religionum: Studia Geo Widengren, Pars Prior*. Studies in the History of Religions, 21. (Leiden: E. J. Brill, 1972), 142.

[75] Ulrich Kellermann, "Erwägungen zum Esragesetz," *ZAW* 80 (1968):373-85.

[76] Eskenazi, *In an Age of Prose*, 75 n. 93; Rolf Rendtorff, "Esra und das 'Gesetz,'" *ZAW* 96 (1984):165-84.

[77] Williamson, *Ezra, Nehemiah*, xxxix contends that while it included "parts...of D and P" the "law of your god" was not equivalent to the full Pentateuchal sources of the same character. However, Williamson seems to limit Ezra's role to the cultic sphere, something that is unwarranted by the narratives themselves.

the Temple, as well as notice of the various temple officials who are exempted from taxation (vs. 24).[78]

The third aspect of Ezra's mission is found in Ezra 7:25-26 where the reformer is ordered to act "according to the wisdom of your god that is in your hand," a probable reiteration of the "law of your god that is in your hand" of 7:14. Ezra is commanded to appoint "magistrates and judges" to uphold the "law of your god and the law of the king," that the condition may come about that "all the people" of the satrapy would be judged, that all "would know the laws of your god," and that those who do not know the laws would be taught them.[79] This charge is followed by a penalty clause, that those who do not obey "the law of your god and the law of the king" would receive punishment, including execution.

It is likely that Ezra's commission to make "inquiry" concerning Yehud and Jerusalem is connected with this activity and that the inquiry related to the status of legal administration within Yehud and Jerusalem. The appointment of various legal officials is suggestive of the imperial imposition of a new legal order, represented by the law of God that Ezra has with him ("in your hand" can be interpreted as being equivalent to "in your power/authority").[80] Presumably, since the time of Achaemenid rule over the Levant, a judicial system of some form was in place. The sending of an official by the imperial court to appoint new personnel makes sense only if there has been some general defection from the imperial system (for which there is no evidence) or if a new legal order was being established within the region and the imperial system was committed to its complete and rigorous enforcement through the replacement of existing officials by new personnel. The correlation in Ezra 7:26 of the "law of your god" and the "law of the king" demon-

---

[78] On this intrusion, see the comments of Myers, *Ezra.Nehemiah*, 62-63; Clines, *Ezra, Nehemiah, Esther*, 104-5; and Williamson, *Ezra, Nehemiah*, 98.

[79] The grammar and syntax of 7:25-26 is difficult. As a number of commentators have pointed out, the phrase "all who know the laws of your god" has an unclear relationship to what precedes it; Rudolph, *Esra und Nehemia*, 74; Clines, *Ezra, Nehemiah, Esther*, 105; and Williamson, *Ezra, Nehemiah*, 103-5.

[80] For an example of an inseparable preposition plus *yd* having the sense of "authority," see letter No. 4, line 1 in Driver, *Aramaic Documents*, 24-25, where a garrison commander and the troops "under his command (*zy lydh*)" are mentioned. In this understanding, it is not necessary to propose an elaborate scheme in which Ezra, as a representative of the Babylonian exilic community, came to Jerusalem with a completed Pentateuch in order to impose the exilic community's will on an uninterested Palestinian populace.

strates further the close ties between Ezra's "inquiry" and the imperial order.

In reviewing the commission of Ezra, there is the possibility that the "law of your god" is, in some measure, related to social and familial customs. If this is the case, then such a body of materials may have included, or been composed by, portions of the Pentateuchal legislation though probably not identical with these materials as they appear in their canonical forms. Assuming the phrase "in your hand" relates to a sphere of authority rather than a physical form of these laws, Ezra's commission extends only to the aspects of the "law of your god" that are under Ezra's domain, a sphere of authority left undefined within the present narratives. Thus, while Schaeder's thesis has attracted many followers, there is no evidence in support of the concept of Ezra as an official in charge of Jewish affairs.

While the appointment of "judges and magistrates" to enforce a new legal order would seem to be of considerable significance, the narratives of Ezra-Nehemiah do not record how Ezra accomplished this part of his mandate. This lacuna has disturbed a number of commentators who fail to realize the degree to which the author of the narratives has selectively presented the materials in order to reinforce a few select ideologies.[81] In the case of Ezra, it is on the issue of intermarriage that the author has focused the narrative.

Following the uneventful journey to Jerusalem, the distribution of the imperial funds, and the circulation of the king's orders to the provincial treasurers (chapter 8), Ezra is called upon to deal with a dilemma that becomes the central focus of the narratives that follow, namely the problem of intermarriage. Various "officials" approach Ezra and claim that the "people of Israel" and members of the priests and the Levites "have not separated themselves from the peoples of the lands with their abominations," and then specify who these "peoples" are, "the Canaanites, the Hittites, the Perizzites, the Jebusites, the Ammonites, the Moabites, the Egyptians, and the Amorites" (Ezra 9:1). The charge is further refined to note that the daughters of these peoples have been taken by members of the community "to be wives for themselves and their sons." The end result is that "the holy seed has become mixed with the peoples of the lands," and that the leadership of the community "has been foremost in this faithlessness" (Ezra 9:2).

---

81 "...the only evidences we have of Ezra's work amount to nothing like fulfillment of his commission;" Clines, *Ezra, Nehemiah, Esther*, 106.

As many commentators have noted, within this narrative are a variety of expressions reflecting the breadth of interaction with the earlier written traditions of Israel. The ban on intermarriage closely resembles the narratives of Deuteronomy 7:14, where the giving and receiving of daughters in marriage is prohibited with the "seven nations," namely the "Hittites, the Girgashites, the Amorites, the Canaanites, the Perizzites, the Hivites, and the Jebusites (Deuteronomy 7:1)."[82] The modification of this list to drop some of these peoples and to add others is most likely due to an effort to incorporate the legislation of Deuteronomy 23:3-8 in some fashion.[83] Finally, the expression that the "holy seed" has become "mixed" with the "peoples of the lands" represents a kind of innovative exegesis of earlier biblical traditions. The Holiness Code of Leviticus 19 forbids the intermixture of unlike materials or species, but says nothing about the intermarriage of the Israelite community with those outside. Where intermixture is referred to with regard to the people of Israel as in Psalm 106:35, the context is one of religious syncretism and not ethnic intermarriage.[84] In sum, what is presented in the charge against intermarriage in Ezra 9:12 is an extension and elaboration of earlier biblical traditions, and a movement from the prohibition against specific peoples to the more generic "peoples of the lands."

More characteristic of the narratives of Ezra-Nehemiah is the association of intermarriage with a terminology expressive of the most negative connotations for Israelite traditions. The "peoples of the lands" are characterized as practicing "their abominations (*tôʿăbōtêhem*)" and those engaging in intermarriage acting in "faithlessness (*riʾšōnāh*)." At work here is the employment of a terminology aimed at creating a web in which the issue of intermarriage is inextricably connected with an extreme rejection of faithful practice.

The theological sophistication behind the exegesis utilized by those who raised the issue of intermarriage in Ezra 9:12 and the manner of insuring the indelibly negative religious attitude toward the practice betray the hand of the author in the narratives of Ezra 9. Commentators have struggled to explain Ezra's seemingly surprised reaction on hearing

---

[82] For a sampling of discussion, see Rudolph, *Esra und Nehemia*, 86-87; Myers, *Ezra.Nehemiah*, 76; Clines, *Ezra, Nehemiah, Esther*, 119; and Williamson, *Ezra, Nehemiah*, 130-31.

[83] See especially Myers, *Ezra.Nehemiah*, 76; and Williamson, *Ezra, Nehemiah*, 131.

[84] The hiphil form of *ʿrb* that is used here is fairly rare in the biblical corpus, Psalm 106:35 being one of the few places where the same form occurs. On the ideational connections with the Holiness Code, see Myers, *Ezra.Nehemiah*, 77-78; and Williamson, *Ezra, Nehemiah*, 131-32.

the news that the intermarriage was pervasive in the community (Ezra 9:3-4), or how the issue had not come to his attention in the four months he had already spent in Jerusalem since his arrival.[85] These are non-issues since it is not the officials of Yehud who are giving expression to the concern over intermarriage but the author of the book.

This understanding of the manner in which intermarriage is theologized by the author of Ezra-Nehemiah is important in attempting to reconstruct the relationship between Ezra's mission and the issue of intermarriage within the Restoration community. As the narratives continue to trace Ezra's wrestling with the issue, two very different emphases are discernible. In the dominant one, the practice of intermarriage is a theological error of the most grievous kind. However within the same narratives, there are suggestions of a communal threat posed by intermarriage that is not directly related to the religious faith of the community. It is this less evident emphasis that seems to be the source for the theologized understanding of the issue of intermarriage.

For example, following his public demonstration of mourning over the presence of intermarriage in the community (Ezra 9:3-5), Ezra makes a public prayer in which he states that the "iniquities" of the community have risen higher than their heads and the "guilt" has mounted up to heaven, both epithets relating to the practice of intermarriage (9:6). Later, the community has forsaken the commandments of God by intermarrying (9:10) and the practice is the community's "great guilt" (9:13). This prayer is replete with the theological understanding of the issue of intermarriage and is the work of the author of the narratives.

However, once the community response is made to Ezra's prayer, several non-theologized elements appear in the narratives. In Ezra 10:1-5, the community leadership decides to make a covenant to divorce the foreign wives: and Ezra "forced (*wayyašbaᶜ*) the leaders of the priests, the Levites, and all Israel" to make an oath to carry through on the plan (Ezra 10:5).[86] The community then sent a proclamation to "Judah and Jerusalem" calling on all the "exiles" to assemble at Jerusalem (Ezra 10:7). Anyone failing to attend the convocation within three days faced severe penalties: "by the instruction of the officials and the elders, all his prop-

[85] For example, see Myers, *Ezra.Nehemiah*, 76; and Williamson, *Ezra, Nehemiah*, 132-33.

[86] It is intriguing that Nehemiah is reported as having extracted an oath to insure that economic reforms will take place, the same verb form being used in Nehemiah 5:12. Eskenazi, *In an Age of Prose*, 69 makes a weak argument that Ezra's willingness to let the community determine its course lessens the weight of his involvement here.

erty is forfeited, and he is excluded from the assembly of the exiles (Ezra 10:8)."

These penalties for failure to attend a gathering that ostensibly will deal with a practice that has theological implications are strange within their narrative context. The proclamation simply asks the "exiles" to convene in Jerusalem, but as recounted in the text provides no rationale for the assembly. The penalties are fairly extreme, yet according to the narrative apply to those who only fail to attend the convocation. More to the point, there are no prescribed penalites for those who fail to agree to divorce their "foreign wives." Moreover, the judicial powers of the community that underlie the penalties are suggestive of a communal economic structure. Failure to attend the convocation results first in the loss of one's property (*rěkûš*), probably applying to the category of movable property.[87] The community here presumes a kind of communal domain over any individual's assets. This deprivation of assets is followed by removal from the "assembly of the exile," the primary social grouping of the Restoration community. In sum, there is nothing particularly sacral about the penalties for not attending the convocation.

Once the assembly is convened, Ezra addresses them in the same terminology noted earlier. The practice of intermarriage has increased the "guilt" of the community and is a transgression against God (Ezra 10:10). The people concur with Ezra's assessment but plead for more time to resolve the matter, so officials are appointed to examine the various cases and make their decisions (Ezra 10:12-17). The narratives dealing with Ezra conclude with a listing of those who had married "foreign women" but had separated from them.

It remains to try to comprehend how Ezra's activity relates to possible imperial concerns regarding Yehud. As was noted in the discussion of Ezra's commission, his role in establishing a new imperial legal apparatus is suggestive of a transformation in the imperial administration of law within the province. One of the hallmarks of the Achaemenid imperial system was its flexibility in the face of established local customs. Rather than superimposing a rigid set of imperial laws over a subject territory, the imperial system sought to work within the legal structures already in place.[88] This process required a class of imperial functionaries possessing legal expertise, a group that appears in various documents as the "royal judges" who were charged with the application of the imperial

[87] See the discussion of the term in Driver, *Aramaic Documents*, 61.

[88] See particularly the comments of Tuplin, "The Administration of the Achaemenid Empire," 112.

law within more localized settings.[89] However, this leaves unresolved the nature and reasons behind the transformation of the legal administration in the mid-fifth century. Given the concerns of the Achaemenid empire at this time arising out of the Athenian participation in the Egyptian Revolt, it remains to assess how the transformation of the provincial legal system under Ezra would have advanced security in the region.

In attempting to understand Ezra's role many commentators have referred to the mission of the Egyptian priest Udjahorresnet, who was charged with various tasks for the Achaemenid administration in Egypt by Darius I (522-486). Related to Udjahorresnet's role was the codification of Egyptian law around the same time.[90] These activities took place shortly after the various uprisings throughout the empire that had occupied Darius' first year on the throne. After the conquest of Cambyses in 525 BCE, Egypt had not been stabilized and subsequently revolted in 522-21 when Darius ascended the throne.[91] It was shortly after this that Darius ordered the codification of traditional Egyptian laws and sent Udjahorresnet to reestablish a scribal institution at Sais.[92] The transformation of the Egyptian legal system and the provision of imperial funding to reestablish scribal institutions point to the importance of both law and record-keeping in the establishment of imperial control over a subject territory. These actions by the imperial court were not demonstrations of kindness, but the initiation of mechanisms of control.

In imperial systems, juridical developments are utilized to establish and maintain the relationships between various groups within a subject territory and the imperial center.[93] Wholesale reforms of the legal system are required when developments in the relationship between the imperial center and the subject territory are so extensive as to require new structures. The legal formulation usually precedes the actualization of a new structure, delineating the rules that will govern the new relationship. In our own century, the desire of western imperial societies for a new economic relationship to West African territories that had been oc-

---

89 See especially Frye, *The History of Ancient Iran*, 118-18; and Tuplin, "The Administration of the Achaemenid Empire," 119-20.

90 For example, see Myers, *Ezra,Nehemiah*, 60; Clines, *Ezra, Nehemiah, Esther*, 105; and Williamson, *Ezra, Nehemiah*, 104-5. See also the general discussion of Udjahorresnet's mission in chapter one of this work.

91 Cook, *The Persian Empire*, 60.

92 Blenkinsopp, "The Mission of Udjahorresnet," 412-13.

93 Eisenstadt, *The Political Systems of Empires*, 306-7.

cupied led to a broad revision of traditional tribal laws.[94] Perhaps most instructive in this modern example is that one of the primary areas requiring new legal definitions dealt with the transfer of land rights and tribal surplus through marriage.[95]

Ezra's commission to appoint new personnel for the administration of law in Yehud marked some fundamental change in the relationship between the imperial court and the province. The threatening conditions in the eastern Mediterranean following on the intervention of the Delian League into the Egyptian Revolt led to the desire for greater control over the Levantine region. While this change probably extended over a variety of matters, the narratives allow access only to the issue of intermarriage within the community, an issue that also occupied at least some of the focus of Nehemiah. Consequently, some consideration needs to be given to the relationship between the regulation of intermarriage and imperial security.

Social Reorganization and Imperial Administration

In the earlier discussion of the transformation of the Restoration community, the point was made that it is only within the period of the mid-fifth century that a new understanding of the constitution of the community emerges, that is, a concept that stresses the ethnicity of the community over all other distinctions.[96] The introduction of this concept has usually been associated with the reforms of Ezra or Nehemiah, depending on how one understood their chronological relationship.

There can be little question that the primary emphasis in the biblical narratives regarding the reforms of Ezra and Nehemiah is the issue of intermarriage. However, apart from what appears to be a later theological conceptualization of this practice as a transgression against God, no indication is provided in the narratives as to why two imperial officials would be so concerned over the practice. However, by seeking to analyze the way imperial systems interacted with social groups within subject territories, it is possible to reconstruct a way in which the

---

94 See the study of Francis Snyder, *Capitalism and Legal Change: An African Transformation*. Studies on Law and Social Control. (New York: Academic Press, 1981).

95 Snyder, *Capitalism and Legal Change*, 200.

96 The term "ethnic" is used here, as throughout this work, as denoting a population group perceived of possessing a common denominator. In most cases in Achaemenid imperial texts, this commonality is the geographic region or country of origin. Once a group has been removed from its geographic origin, it is difficult to determine precisely whether such perceived commonality also included religious, linguistic, or racial factors.

prohibition against intermarriage contributed to a larger imperial purpose.

To begin such an analysis, the impact of a change in marriage customs needs to be briefly considered. One dimension of marriage is as a means of transferring property and social status from one group to another. By circumscribing the options available in marriage through the prohibition of marriage outside of the group, all property, kinship-related rights and status remain within a closed community.

Among the administrative requirements of an imperial system is the need to integrate various groups within a subject territory into the imperial structure. This could be done by utilizing pre-existent group denominators such as kinship, cult or trade, or it could be accomplished by groups that transcended existing denominators.[97] Often such groups possessed an economic role within the imperial system, insuring the group perception that their self-interest was bound up in the well-being of the empire.

This requirement for group identity was more pressing when an imperial system was engaged in the use of deportation and resettlement as a means of political control over a subject region. The deportees, being tied to the new territories where they were being settled, had a certain legal status only while remaining on the land they were assigned to. As was noted in the discussion of imperial mechanisms in chapter one, the Achaemenid empire on occasion practiced the wholesale deportation of communities as a means of administrative control. Moreover, there is ample evidence to suggest that such communities were assigned to communal lands as a corporate entity. For example, there are cuneiform texts from the time of Cambyses relating to various communities of Egyptians living in various Mesopotamian cities. Their lands are treated as being under the jurisdiction of local assemblies (*puḫur*) of Egyptians. These entities resolved issues of land allotment and matters relating to the satisfaction of imperial corvee levies.[98]

While there are a number of clearly attested instances of such deportations and resettlements, the precise conditions that governed the status of the dependent populations is less than certain. Briant has collected a variety of data to suggest that the Persians, like their Assyrian and Neo-Babylonian predecessors, utilized the mechanism of dependent popula-

---

[97] Eisenstadt, *The Political Systems of Empires*, 79-80.

[98] M. Dandamayev, "Aliens and the Community in Babylonia in the 6th-5th Centuries B. C.," in *Les Communates rurales*. Deuxieme partie—Antiquitié (Paris: Dessain et Tolra, 1983), 143-45.

tions to maximize the agrarian potential of sparsely settled regions.[99] D. M. Lewis has similarly offered evidence of various groups being transplanted as dependent populations.[100] One of the more interesting examples of such activity is found in Herodotus, who records that a community of Paeonians were deported by Darius I from their homeland in Thrace to the inland portions of Asia Minor where they continued to live as an identifiable enclave fifteen years later (*Histories* 5.15; 5.98). This may well suggest that communities of such land-tied dependent groups were kept separate as an intentional practice of the imperial administration.[101]

Returning to the biblical narratives, one may see in the penalties of Ezra 10:8 a possible reference to the concept of a land-tied dependent group. The form of communal domain over the property of members of the community expressed in the first penalty clause is suggestive of a structure wherein the community as a whole has rights and privileges that are held only as a group, not as individuals. A transgression against the better interests of the group, in this case a failure to respond to the assembly to put an end to the practice of intermarriage, could result in the deprivation of property that is, in effect, the group's. Similarly, banishment from the group as a penalty would deny the possibility of regaining access to the rights and privileges enjoyed by the group as a unit.

There is clear evidence from Mesopotamia that the Achaemenid court practiced a form of imperial domain, treating land gained by conquest as imperial territory and disposing of it to courtiers and various officials.[102] It would be in keeping with this view of territorial rights to assume that the Levantine holdings of the empire were also regarded as imperial domain. Thus any group of returning exiles, such as the Neirabians of Syria or the various groups of Judean exiles who returned to Yehud, were not reclaiming a right to land tenure based on past land allotment systems but were being allowed to reside in a homeland by the graciousness of the empire.

---

99 Pierre Briant, "Appareils d'état et Developement des forces productives au Moyen-orient ancien: Le Cas de l'Empire achéménide," *La Pensée* (Fev., 1981):475-89.

100 Lewis, *Sparta and Persia*, 6-7.

101 This is how Lewis, *Sparta and Persia*, 7 interprets the account. Herodotus simply notes that they resided in "villages of their own." In the various cuneiform texts relating to communities of Egyptians, Dandamayev has noted that they "lived in considerable number in distinct settlements forming a separate cultural-ethnic group;" Dandamayev, "Aliens and the Community in Babylonia," 144.

102 M. Dandamayev, "The Domain-lands of Achaemenes in Babylonia," *Altorientalische Forschungen* 1 (1974):123-27.

Such systems of allocating territories to dependent populations will work as long as the imperial system is capable of maintaining some clarity as to who is allowed access to a particular region and who is not. Intermarriage among various groups would tend to smudge the demarcation between the groups. In situations where there was no perception of a strategic value to keeping these distinctions sharply defined, one might anticipate a certain relaxation on the part of the imperial authorities towards ongoing processes of assimilation. On the other hand, when a territory is imperilled and it becomes essential to administrative control to have a clear sense of who is allowed to function in a region and who is not, one could anticipate imperial efforts to control the mechanisms of assimilation.

This scenario accords well with the efforts by Ezra and Nehemiah to prohibit intermarriage. There are hints in the text that the community possesses land-tenure only at the will of the empire. For example, in the troublesome speech of Nehemiah 9, the speaker claims that the community is enslaved, and that all the rich produce of the land goes to the kings that God has appointed to be over the community: "and the land which you gave to our fathers, to eat its fruit and good produce, behold—we are slaves because of it (Nehemiah 9:36)." This sounds very much like a land-tied dependent community.

Assuming then that the community is dependent on the empire for its right of access to the land, then one can understand the serious threat to the community as a whole that intermarriage might represent. Particularly at a time of extreme sensitivity to the degree of control the empire had over the various populations, one could comprehend the sending of an imperial official to redefine, among other actions, exactly who belonged to the group and who did not. In this sense, the *qāhāl* of Ezra-Nehemiah would function as an administrative collective, and failure to be part of the *qāhāl* would mean one could be banished from the province.[103]

In this light, the concerns expressed by Ezra and Nehemiah over the practice of intermarriage within the community would be in keeping

---

103 Gerald Blidstein, "*ʾAtimia*: A Greek Parallel to Ezra X 8 and to Post-biblical Exclusion from the Community," *VT* 24 (1974):357-60 cites the exclusion from the community practiced in Athens under the technical term *ʾatimia* as an example of the same group process. However, Blidstein does not offer a clear sense of the conditions under which the practice was employed, and concedes that by the fifth century the use of this penalty was quite rare. There is the possibility that *ʾatimia* does represent a useful analogue to the exclusion from the *qāhāl* in Ezra 10, but further work in assessing the practice is needed.

with the effort of the imperial court to enhance the degree of control over the Levantine region. Ezra's legal reforms and Nehemiah's anger over the continuing presence of intermarriage would represent a perception of the danger such activity presented to the continuation of the *qāhāl* in Yehud.

6

SUMMARY AND CONCLUSIONS

The biblical narratives relating the missions of Ezra and Nehemiah as Achaemenid imperial officials present little direct evidence pertaining to the historical setting of these missions and the motivations that lay behind their actions as reformers of the postexilic community. In part, this situation is a reflection of the author's skillful adaptation of the materials contained in these narratives, since that individual has managed to submerge the social and historical factors that gave rise to the missions in order to emphasize a distinctly theological interpretation of the transformation of the postexilic community.

That the community was transformed in the mid-fifth century is clear from two basic points of evidence that emerge for the first time in the narratives of Ezra-Nehemiah. The first of these points is an innovative interpretation of pre-existent traditions: the intermarriage of community members with those outside of the community is prohibited. The second point is a new emphasis on the communal nature of the people with a new terminology utilized to express that nature. Both the ban on intermarriage and the emphasis on the "assembly (*qāhāl*)" of the people are associated with the reforms of Ezra and Nehemiah. Since both figures are presented as acting within the community as imperial officials, the question of the relationship of their reforms to the Achaemenid empire's administration of Yehud becomes a primary issue in understanding these narratives.

A survey of the suggestions that have been offered by scholars to explain this relationship demonstrated that these suggestions fail on a variety of issues. One of the critical problems is a failure to articulate clearly the political concerns of the Achaemenid empire in the Levant during the mid-fifth century. Without a focused understanding of the larger context of the mid-fifth century, the imperial motivations behind the commissioning of Ezra and Nehemiah are unrecoverable. A further problem is the failure to demonstrate how the reforms of Ezra and Nehemiah were directly connected to any larger imperial concerns.

In that the biblical narratives provide so little evidence with which to reconstruct the motivations behind the missions of Ezra and Nehemiah, it is necessary to attempt a new synthesis of the available data to explore the relationship between the content of the missions and their imperial setting. This effort is clarified by seeking to comprehend the basic institutional needs of the Achaemenid imperial system. In recognizing that an imperial system represents a unique social and institutional adaptation to the control of territories with diverse environments and ethnic groups, it is possible to isolate the factors that would lead an imperial system to attempt a transformation of a particular community. Moreover, it is possible to anticipate the mechanisms that might be employed in such an effort.

A thorough reassessment of the Greek historiographic tradition regarding the Egyptian Revolt of the mid-fifth century revealed the gravity of this challenge to Achaemenid rule. While serious enough as a localized nationalistic rebellion against the Persians, the intervention of Delian League forces on the side of the Egyptians dramatically changed the nature of the conflict. No longer was the suppression of the Egyptian Revolt simply an effort by the Persians to regain control over a restless, distant imperial holding. After the intervention of the Greek forces, it was a struggle for control of the eastern Mediterranean, including the Levantine coast. Despite the final defeat of the Delian League forces and the death of the rebel Inaros, there remained considerable tension in the eastern Mediterranean into the last few decades of the fifth century.

The reassessment of Greek sources also demonstrated that the Egyptian Revolt itself was the decisive event affecting the western holdings of the Achaemenid empire in the mid-fifth century. Only one Greek source, Ctesias, has an account of a subsequent revolt by Megabyzos, the satrap of Beyond the River. For a variety of literary and historical reasons, nothing in the narratives lends any credibility to Ctesias' account. This conclusion goes directly against an assumption made by many biblical scholars that "clear evidence" exists for the Revolt of Megabyzos.[1] Consequently, whatever steps the empire took to insure continued control over the Levant were the result of the Egyptian rebellion against their Achaemenid overlords and the subsequent Greek involvement in the conflict.

Given the military nature of the challenge to Achaemenid control of the eastern Mediterranean, the effort to find archaeological indication of a change in the administration of the western territories should focus on strategic issues. The clearest evidence that some extensive efforts were enacted to alter the character of the Achaemenid presence in the Levant is the widely dispersed remains of a distinctive form of fortress, unique to the mid-fifth century. The proliferation of these fortresses throughout all the regions of the Levant seems probable, based on clearly recognizable examples on both sides of the Jordan River, along the coastal plain, and throughout the hill country of Palestine. Presumably these fortresses were manned by imperial garrisons representing the coercive power of the empire. The appearance of these garrisons in the mid-fifth century is the indelible fingerprint of the hand of the Achaemenid empire tightening its grip on local affairs in the Levant.

It is within this context that the missions of Ezra and Nehemiah take place. Nehemiah in particular is concerned with issues of direct strategic importance, the most notable being the refortification of Jerusalem. At a time when very few urban sites in the Levant possessed a city wall system, Nehemiah was charged by the imperial court to rebuild Jerusalem's walls in order to provide an inland defensive center. His activities, however, were not limited to refortifying the city, but also addressed issues of economic reform and, most particularly, the question of mixed marriages within the Restoration community. The combination of strategic, economic, and social reforms attributed to Nehemiah's governorship is not simply a reflection of his alignment with one "party" or another within the Restoration community but conforms to the pattern of a transformation of the relationship between an imperial center and an outlying territory.

With Ezra, the emphasis of the narratives relating his mission is on legal reform, the kind of legal reform that preceded efforts to restructure and integrate other imperial territories into the Achaemenid imperial

---

1 The expression is from Ackroyd, *Israel in the Exilic and Post-Exilic Periods*, 334. For similar expressions of the certainty of a revolt by Megabyzos, see Noth, *The History of Israel*, 318; Bright, *A History of Israel*, 375; and Herrmann, *A History of Israel in Old Testament Times*, 308.

system. The concentration of the biblical narratives on Ezra's opposition to mixed marriages and the emphasis on the need for the "assembly" to refrain from such marital situations demonstrate that his primary legal role was to clarify the membership of the community for the empire. Moreover, the narratives also point to the harsh economic consequences inflicted by the "assembly" on those who failed to conform to this new legal definition. By insisting on an ethnically circumscribed community, Ezra was enhancing the empire's ability to determine who was part of a new collectivity that enjoyed certain privileges from the hand of the empire.

As a consequence of this understanding of the context for the missions of Ezra and Nehemiah, it is clear that these missions were not, as has often been argued, the result of the empire rewarding the Restoration community for loyalty in the face of regional revolts. Rather, their missions were an effort on the part of the Achaemenid empire to create a web of economic and social relationships that would tie the community more completely into the imperial system. Part of this process involved the clarification of the population under imperial control by legislating some means of defining that community. Rather than being a reward, the missions of Ezra and Nehemiah were an effort to compel loyalty to the imperial system by tying the community's self-interest to the goals of the empire.

In this regard, the prohibition against mixed marriages that characterized the missions of both Ezra and Nehemiah stands as a further example of the long-standing imperial need to displace populations and define them in ethnic terms, a practice that began under the Assyrian empire and continued with slight modification into Achaemenid practice. Both reformers were sent to the Restoration community in the mid-fifth century precisely because of the need to insure continued control over the community in the face of the challenges resulting from the Egyptian Revolt. Whether by design or not, the prohibition of intermarriage also played on long-standing Israelite concerns over the potential for idolatry in intermarriage. However, in other strands of opposition to intermarriage, it is not the community as a whole that is imperiled by the practice, as is the case in Ezra-Nehemiah.[2]

---

[2] For example, both Deuteronomy 7:3-4 and Exodus 34:16 tie intermarriage into idolatrous practice but make no reference to this as a threat to the community as a whole. In Malachi 2:11, the marriage to "the daughter of a foreign god" is linked to the profanation of the sanctuary. While this is followed by the call for Yahweh to "cut off from the tents of Jacob" anyone engaging in this activity (2:12), this is clearly

It is this enhanced control and domination of the community that resulted in the anti-Persian sentiments scattered throughout the narratives of Ezra-Nehemiah. The author of the biblical narratives, writing perhaps a generation after the reforms, senses that the community has been radically transformed as the result of the actions of these two imperial officials, yet holds the empire responsible for the sense of powerlessness that pervades the community. Thus, while clearly recognizing the theological benefits from both reformers by having God act on Artaxerxes to bring about their missions (Ezra 7:27; Nehemiah 2:8), the author also sees the imperial context as a source of the community's troubles. Ezra notes that the community has suffered "great shame" from being dominated by various "kings of the lands," a condition that prevails "at this day (Ezra 9:7)." Ezra's first-person appeal goes on to note that "we are slaves (Ezra 9:9)," underlining the community's contemporary status under the Achaemenids. Similarly, Nehemiah notes that he has not collected taxes due him, as did the "former governors" who laid heavy economic obligations on the people (Nehemiah 5:14-18).

This powerlessness was the result of a tightened imperial grip on the Levant, a tightening brought to Yehud by the same two reformers who had insured the survival of the inheritors of Israel's faith. Thus the perception of the Achaemenid monarchy within the narratives is ambivalent, recognizing the reality of the community's dependency on the continued graciousness of the imperial court, but sensing the costs of this dependency.

The redefinition of membership in the community may also signify a major transformation in the socio-economic structure of the Restoration community. J. P. Weinberg has advocated a model of a "civic-temple" community where a collectivity apart from the provincial population, made up primarily of returned exiles, assisted in supporting the temple cultus. In return for their support, the imperial authorities allowed them to gain economic and social dominance within the community.[3] In

---

distinct from the prohibitions of Ezra-Nehemiah. For example, while Malachi 2:16 claims Yahweh hates divorce, that is precisely the stipulation the community is to enforce in Ezra 10:11. In Zechariah 5:7-8, a woman seated in an ephah may serve to signify intermarriage, but the nature of her relationship to the prophet's community is not indicated; see Meyers and Meyers, *Haggai, Zechariah 1-8*, 301-02.

[3] See Weinberg's "Probleme der Sozialökonomischen Struktur Judaas vom 6. Jahrhundert v. u. z. bis zum 1. Jahrhundert u. z." *Jahrbuch für Wirtschaftsgeschichte* 1973/1: 237-51. Some additional refinements are offered in his essay "Die agrarverhaltnisse in der Bürger-Tempel-Gemeinde der Achämenidenzeit." In *Wirtschaft und Gesellschaft im Alten Vorderasien*, eds. J. Harmatta and G. Komoroczy,

Weinberg's reconstruction, by the mid-fifth century most of the inhabitants of Yehud had aligned with this group, and the opposition to intermarriage became a hallmark of the priestly influences within the group. Weinberg's evidence for the existence of such a collectivity is very weak, but several writers have supported the basic outline of his proposal.[4]

For the adherents of this proposal, the mission of Nehemiah marks the culmination of the process of identifying the provincial population with a temple-centered community, thus initiating the prominence that the Second Temple enjoyed in later Hellenistic and Roman Judaism. There are a great many problems with the theoretical grounds for Weinberg's thesis, as well as in his use of the biblical data; but in some senses the present study affords a parallel effort to comprehend the economic and social changes that marked the mid-fifth century. Where Weinberg has stressed the importance of the Temple as an organizing principle, our perspective has emphasized the role of imperial concerns in reconstructing the scope of Nehemiah's mission. It may be that some synthesis between the two positions will emerge in the light of further research on the period and the nature of social structures under imperial rule.

One primary implication of the present study is the locus of the developments that marked the formative phase of postexilic religion. The missions of Ezra and Nehemiah appear to have transformed the fabric of the Restoration community by forcing a new self-understanding on the community, rooted in the need to maintain a clear identity for the purposes of imperial administration. However, it is the writer of the biblical narratives who, with skill and imagination, has tied these political concerns to a profoundly theological understanding of the community and its role in the world. The writer also has moved the figures of the reformers from mere imperial collaborators to individuals of considerable importance to the writer's own day. For example, by seeking to identify Ezra's reforms with the contents of a completed Pentateuch, the author opened the way for Ezra to be enshrined in later tradition as the paradigm of the teacher of Torah to the community. With regard to the community's self-identity, by rendering the opposition to intermarriage

473-86. Nachdruck aus den Acta Antiqua Academiae Scientarum Hungaricae Tom. 22/1-4. (Budapest: Akademiai Kiado, 1976).

[4] See, for example, Bernd Funck, "Zur Bürger-Tempel-Gemeinde im nachexilischen Juda," *Klio* 59 (1977):491-96; and Heinz Kressig, "Eine beachtenswerte Theorie zur Organisation altvorderorientalischer Tempelgemeinden im Achämenidenreich," *Klio* 66 (1984):35-9.

into a theological framework the narratives of Ezra-Nehemiah provided subsequent generations with the means for self-preservation in a setting where assimilation and the loss of identity would have been disastrous.

FIGURES

Fig. 1: Excavated Mid-fifth Century Fortresses

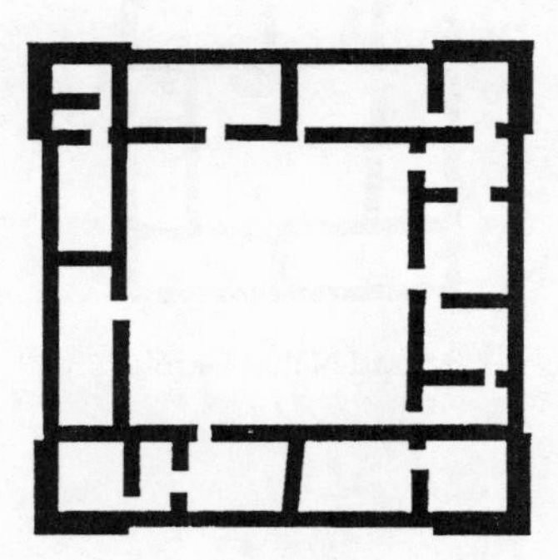

North of Ashdod

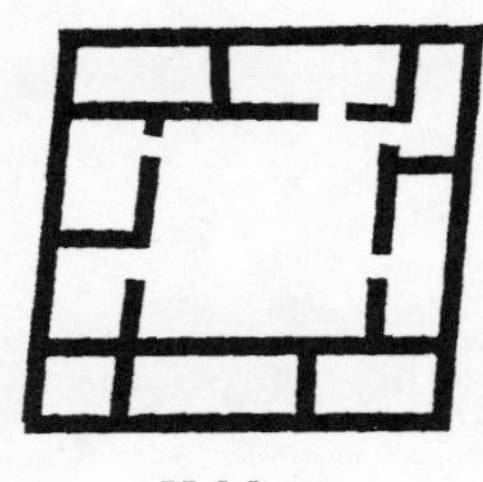

Ḥ. Mesora

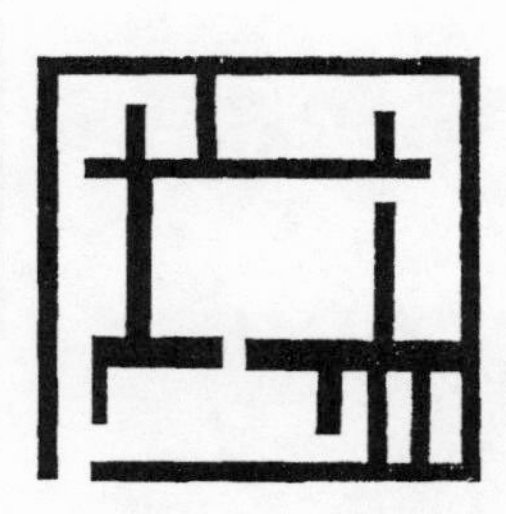

Tell es-Saʿidiyah

Fig. 2: Negev Fortresses

Ḥ. Ritma

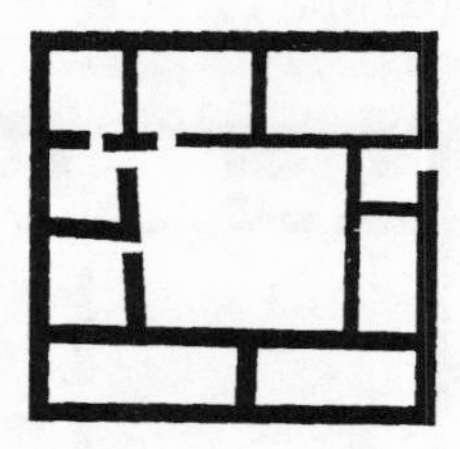

Meṣad Naḥal Haroʿa

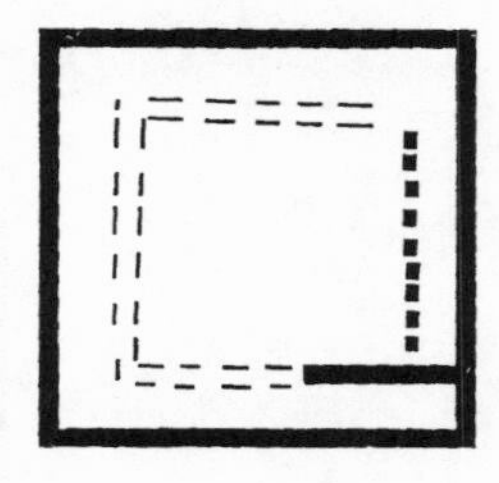

Naḥal Yattir

Fig. 3: Judean Hillcountry Fortresses

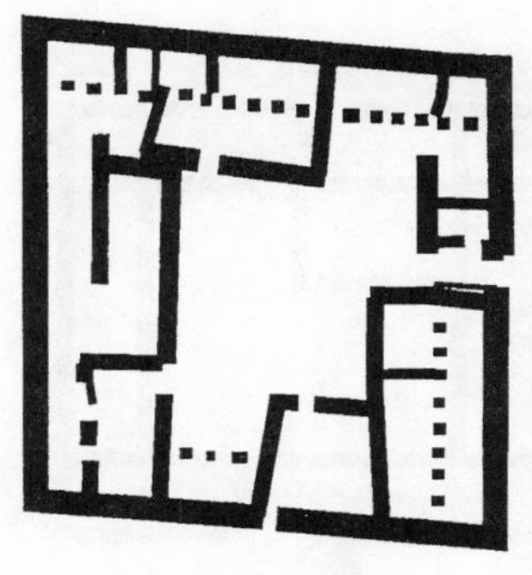

Kh. Abu et-Twain

Deir Baghl

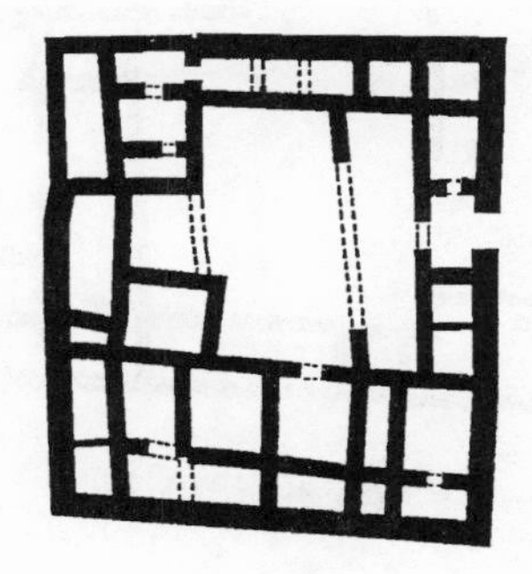

Kh. el-Qaṭṭ

Fig. 4: Ephraimite Hillcountry Fortresses

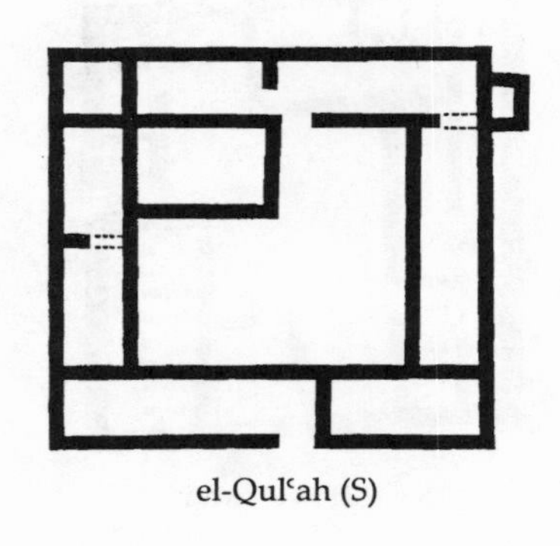

el-Qulʿah (S)

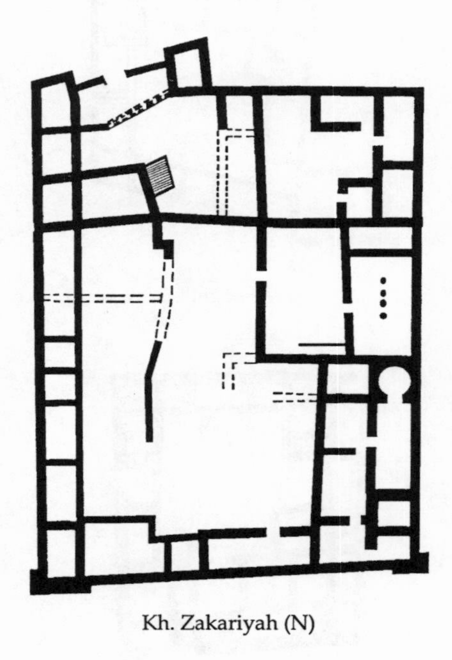

Kh. Zakariyah (N)

BIBLIOGRAPHY

Ackroyd, Peter. *I & II Chronicles, Ezra, Nehemiah.* Torch Bible Commentaries. London: SCM Press, 1973.

———. "Archaeology, Politics and Religion: The Persian Period," *The Iliff Review* 39 (1982): 5-24.

———. *Exile and restoration: A Study of Hebrew Thought in the Sixth Century B. C.* Old Testament Library. Philadelphia: Westminster Press, 1968.

———. "God and People in the Chronicler's Presentation of Ezra." In *La Notion biblique de Dieu,* ed. J. Coppens, 145-62. Bibliotheca Ephemeridum Theologicarum Lovaniensium 41. Leuven: Leuven University Press, 1976.

———. "The History of Israel in the Exilic and Post- exilic Periods." In *Tradition and Interpretation: Essays by Members of the Society for Old Testament Study,* ed. G. W. Anderson, 320-50. Oxford: Clarendon Press, 1979.

———. *Israel Under Babylon and Persia.* The New Clarendon Bible: Old Testament, 4. New York: Oxford University Press, 1970.

Adams, Robert. "The Emerging Place of Trade in Civilization Studies." In *Ancient Civilization and Trade,* eds. J. A. Sabloff and C. C. Lamberg- Karlovsky, 451-65. Albuquerque: University of New Mexico Press, 1975.

———. *Land Behind Baghdad: A History of Settlement on the Diyala Plains.* Chicago: University of Chicago Press, 1965.

Aharoni, Yohanan. *Arad Inscriptions,* ed. and rev. Anson Rainey. Judean Desert Studies. Jerusalem: Israel Exploration Society, 1981.

———. *The Archaeology of the Land of Israel.* ed. Miriam Aharoni, trans. Anson Rainey. Philadelphia: Westminster Press, 1982.

———."Excavations at Tel Arad: Preliminary Report on the Second Season, 1963." *Israel Exploration Journal* 17 (1967):233-49.

———. "Forerunners of the Limes: Iron Age Fortresses in the Negev." *Israel Exploration Journal* 17 (1967):1-17.

———. *The Land of the Bible: A Historical Geography.* trans. A. F. Rainey. Philadelphia: Westminster Press, 1967.

———. *The Land of the Bible: A Historical Geography.* revised and enlarged edition. trans. and ed. by A. F. Rainey. Philadelphia: Westminster Press, 1979.

Aharoni, Yohanan and Ruth Amiran. "Excavations at Tel Arad: Preliminary Report on the First Season, 1962." *Israel Exploration Journal* 14 (1964):131-47.

Aharoni, Yohanan, M. Evenari, L. Shanan, and N. Tadmor, "The Ancient Desert Agriculture of the Negev. V. An Israelite Agricultural Settlement at Ramat Maṭred." *Israel Exploration Journal* 10 (1960): 97-111.

Ahituv, Shemuel. "Economic Factors in the Egyptian Conquest of Canaan." *Israel Exploration Journal* 28 (1978):93-105.

Albright, William Foxwell. *The Archaeology of Palestine.* revised edition. Harmonsworth: Penguin Books, 1954.

Alt, Albrecht. "Die Rolle Samarias bei der Entstehung des Judentums." In *Kleine Schriften zur Geschichte des Volkes Israel.* Zweiter Band, 316-37. Munich: C. H. Beck, 1953.

———. "Zur Geschichte der Grenze zwischen Judaa und Samaria." *Palästinajahrbuch des Deutschen evangelischen Institut für Altertumswissenschaft* 31 (1935):94-111.

Amiran, Ruth and I. Dunayevsky. "The Assyrian Open-court Building and Its Palestinian Derivatives." *Bulletin of the American Schools of Oriental Research* 149 (1958):25-32.

Amiran, Ruth and J. Worrell. "Ḥesi, Tel." In *Encyclopedia of Archaeological Excavations in the Holy Land, Volume* 2, 514-20. Englewood Cliffs, NJ: Prentice-Hall, 1976.

Andrewes, A. "Thucydides and the Persians." *Historia* 10 (1961):1-18.

Argentati, A. "La spedizione in Egitto (459-454?) nel quadro della politica estera Ateniese." *Acme* 6 (1953):379-404.

Armayor, O. Kimball. "Did Herodotus Ever Go to Egypt?" *Journal of the American Research Center in Egypt* 15 (1978):59-73.

———. "Herodotus' Catalogues of the Persian Empire in the Light of the Monuments and the Greek Literary Tradition." *Transactions of the American Philological Association* 108 (1978):1-9.

Austin, M. and Vidal-Naquet, P.. *Economic and Social History of Ancient Greece: An Introduction.* Trans. and rev. by M. Austin. Berkeley: University of California Press, 1977.

Avigad, Nahman. *Bullae and Seals from a Post-exilic Judean Archive.* Qedem 4. Jerusalem: The Institute of Archaeology of the Hebrew University, 1976.

———. "The Epitaph of a Royal Steward from Siloam Village." *Israel Exploration Journal* 3 (1953): 137-52.

Barag, D. Review of *Winery, Defenses and Soundings at Gibeon* by James B. Pritchard. *Journal of Near Eastern Studies* 26 (1967):142-43.

Barber, G. L. "Ephorus." In *The Oxford Classical Dictionary.* Second edition. Eds. N. G. L. Hammond and H. H. Scullard, 388. Oxford: Clarendon Press, 1970.

Baron, Salo W. *History and Jewish Historians: Essays and Addresses.* Comps. Arthur Hertzberg and Lan A. Feldman. Philadelphia: Jewish Publication Society of America, 1964.

Bartlett, J. R. "From Edomites to Nabataeans: A Study in Continuity." *Palestine Exploration Quarterly* 111 (1979):53-66.

———. "The Moabites and Edomites." In *Peoples of Old Testament Times,* ed. D. J. Wiseman, 229-58. Oxford: Clarendon Press, 1973.

———. "The Rise and Fall of the Kingdom of Edom." *Palestine Exploration Quarterly* 104 (1972):26-37.

Batten, L. *The Books of Ezra and Nehemiah.* International Critical Commentary. Edinburgh: T & T Clark, 1913.

Bengtson, Hermann. *Introduction to Ancient History.* trans. R. I. Frank and Frank D. Gillard. Berkeley: University of California Press, 1970.

Bennett, Crystal-M. "Excavations at Buseirah (Biblical Bozrah)." In *Midian, Moab and Edom: The History and Archaeology of Late Bronze and Iron Age Jordan and Northwest Arabia,* eds. John F. A. Sawyer and David J. A. Clines, 9-17. JSOT Supplementary Series 24. Sheffield: JSOT Press, 1983.

Berger, Paul-Richard. *Die neubabylonischen Königsinschriften des ausgehenden babylonischen Reiches (626-539 a. Chr.).* Altes Orient und Altes Testament Band 4/1. Neukirchen-Vluyun: Butzon and Bercker Kevelaer, 1973.

Bigwood, Joan M. "Ctesias' Account of the Revolt of Inarus." *Phoenix* 30 (1976):1-25.

———. "Ctesias as Historian of the Persian Wars." *Phoenix* 32 (1978):19-41.

———. "Diodorus and Ctesias. *Phoenix* 34 (1980): 195-207.

Birmingham, Judy. "The Development of the Fibula in Cyprus and the Levant." *Palestine Exploration Quarterly* 95 (1963):80-112.

Blakely, Jeffrey A., and Fred L. Horton, Jr. "South Palestinian Bes Vessels of the Persian Period." *Levant* 18 (1986):111-19.

Blenkinsopp, Joseph. "The Mission of Udjahorresnet and Those of Ezra and Nehemiah." *Journal of Biblical Literature* 106 (1987):409-21.

Blidstein, Gerald J. "'*Atimia:* A Greek Parallel to Ezra X 8 and to Post-biblical Exclusion from the Community." *Vetus Testamentum* 24 (1974):357-60.

Bossman, David. "Ezra's Marriage Reform: Israel Redefined." *Biblical Theology Bulletin* 9 (1979):32-8.

Bourriot, F. "L'empire achéménide et les Rapports entre Grecs et Perses dans la litterature grecque du Ve siècle." *L'information Historique* 43 (1981):21-30.

Bresciani, Edda. *Der Kampf um den Panzer des Inaros (Papyrus Kroll).* Mitteilungen aus der Papyrus-sammlung der österreichischen Nationalbibliothek (Papyrus erzherzog Rainer), n.s. 8. Vienna: Georg Prachner, 1964.

———. "The Persian Occupation of Egypt." In *The Cambridge History of Iran. Volume 2: The Median and Achaemenian Periods,* ed. Ilya Gershevitch, 502-28. Cambridge: Cambridge University Press, 1985.

———. "La satrapia d'egitto." *Studi Classici e Orientali* 7 (1958):132-88.

Briant, Pierre. "Appareils d'état et Developement des forces productives au Moyen-orient ancien: Le Cas de L'Empire achéménide." *La Pensée* (Fev., 1981):475-89.

———. "Contrainte militarie, Dépendance rurale et Exploitation des territoires en Asie achéménide." *Index* 8 (1978/79):175-225.

———. "La Perse avant l'Empire (un état de la question)." *Iranica Antiqua* 19 (1984):71-118.

Bright, John. *A History of Israel.* Third edition. Philadelphia: Westminster Press, 1981.

Brinkman, J. A. "Babylonia under the Assyrian Empire, 745-627 B. C." In *Power and Propaganda: A Symposium on Ancient Empires,* ed. Mogens Trolle Larsen, 223-50. Mesopotamia 7. Copenhagen: Akademisk Forlag, 1979.

———. *Prelude to Empire: Babylonian Society and Politics, 747-626 B. C.* Occasional Publications of the Babylonian Fund, 7. Philadelphia: University Museum, 1984.

Brockington, L. H. *Ezra, Nehemiah and Esther.* The Century Bible, New Series. Greenwood, SC: Attic Press, 1969.

Brown, Truesdell S. "Suggestions for a Vita of Ctesias of Cnidus." *Historia* 27 (1978):1-19.

Bryce, Trevor R, "A Ruling Dynasty in Lycia." *Klio* 64 (1982):329-37.

Buhn, S. and R. A. Mitchel, "An Iron Age II Fortress on Tel Nagila." *Israel Exploration Journal* 11 (1961):101-110.

Bull, Robert J., Joseph A. Callaway, Edward F. Campbell, James F. Ross, and G. Ernest Wright. "The Fifth Campaign at Balaṭah (Shechem)." *Bulletin of the American Schools of Oriental Research* 180 (1965): 7-41.

Burn, Andrew Robert. *Persia and the Greeks: The Defense of the West, 546-478 B. C.* New York: Minerva Press, 1962.

———. "Persia and the Greeks." In *The Cambridge History of Iran. Volume 2: The Median and Achaemenian Periods,* ed. Ilya Gershevitch, 292-391. Cambridge: Cambridge University Press, 1985.

Burton, Anne. *Diodorus Siculus Book 1: A Commentary.* Études préliminaires aux religions orientales dans l'empire Romain, T. 29. Leiden: E. J. Brill, 1972.

Cameron, George C. "Cyrus the 'Father' and Babylonia." In *Acta Iranica. Prèmiere serie commemoration Cyrus,* 45-8. Leiden: E. J. Brill, 1974.

———. "Darius and Xerxes in Babylonia." *American Journal of the Semitic Languages* 58 (1941):314-25.

———. "The Persian Satrapies and Related Matters." *Journal of Near Eastern Studies* 32 (1973):47-56.

Cargill, Jack. "The Nabonidus Chronicles and the Fall of Lydia." *American Journal of Ancient History* 2 (1977):97-116.

Caspari, M. "On the Egyptian Expedition of 459-4 B. C." *Classical Quarterly* 7 (1913):198-201.

Casson, Lionel. *Ancient Trade and Society.* Detroit: Wayne State University Press, 1984.

Cazelles, Henri. "La Mission d'Esdras." *Vetus Testamentum* 4 (1954):113-40.

Chassinat, Emile. "Textes provenant du Serapeum de Memphis (suite)." *Recueil de Travaux Relatifs à la philologie et a l'archéologie Égyptiennes et Assyriennes* 22 (1900):163-80.

Childs, Brevard S. *Introduction to the Old Testament as Scripture.* Philadelphia: Fortress Press, 1979.

Clairmont, C. "Greek Pottery from the Near East." *Berytus* 11 (1954/55):85-139.

Clines, David J. A. *Ezra, Nehemiah, Esther.* New Century Bible Commentary. Grand Rapids: Wm. B. Eerdmans, 1984.

———. "Nehemiah 10 as an Example of Early Jewish Biblical Exegesis." *Journal for the Study of the Old Testament* 21 (1981):111-17.

Cloché, Paul. "L'activitie militaire et politique d'Athenes en Grece de 457 a 454 avant J.-C." *Revue belge de Philologie et d'Histoire* 25 (1946-47): 39-86.

———. "La Politique extérieure d'Athenes de 454-453 a 446-445 avant J.-C." *Les Études Classiques* 14 (1946):3-32, 195-221.

Cogan, Morton. *Imperialism and Religion: Assyria Judah and Israel in the Eighth and Seventh Centuries B. C. E.* SBL Monograph Series, 11. Missoula, MT: Scholars Press, 1974.

Cohen, Rudolph. "The Fortresses King Solomon Built to Protect his Southern Border." *Biblical Archaeology Review* 11 (1985):57-70.

———. "Ḥ. Mesora." *Israel Exploration Journal* 27 (1977):170-71.

———. "Ḥorvat Mesora." *Israel Exploration Journal* 36 (1986):113.

———. "Ḥorvat Tov." *Israel Exploration Journal* 36 (1986):111-12.

———. "The Iron Age Fortresses in the Central Negev." *Bulletin of the American Schools of Oriental Research* 236 (1980):61-79.

———. "Solomon's Negev Defense Line Contained Three Fewer Fortresses." *Biblical Archaeology Review* 12 (1986):40-45.

Cohen, Shaye J. D. "From the Bible to the Talmud: The Prohibition of Intermarriage." *Hebrew Annual Review* 7 (1983):23-39.

Cook, J. M. *The Persian Empire.* New York: Shocken Books, 1983.

———. "The Rise of the Achaemenids and Establishment of their Empire." In *The Cambridge History of Iran. Volume 2: The Median and Achaemenian Periods,* ed. I. Gershevitch, 200-91. Cambridge: Cambridge University Press, 1985.

Cowley, A. *Aramaic Papyri of the Fifth Century B. C.* Oxford: Clarendon Press, 1923.

Cross, Frank M, Jr. "Alphabets and Pots: Reflections on Typological Method in the Dating of Human Artifacts." *Maarav* 3 (1982):121-36.

———. "Aspects of Samaritan and Jewish History in Late Persian and Hellenistic Times." *Harvard Theological Review* 59 (1966):201-11.

———. "A Reconstruction of the Judean Restoration." *Journal of Biblical Literature* 94 (1975):4-18.

Ctesias. *La Perse, L'Inde: les sommaires de Photius,* ed. P. Henry. Collection le Begne 7, ser. no. 84. Bruxelles: Office de publicité, 1947.

Dalley, Stephanie. "Foreign Chariotry and Calvary in the Armies of Tiglath-Pileser III and Sargon II." *Iraq* 47 (1985):31-48.

Dandamayev, M. "Aliens and the Community in Babylonia in the 6th-5th Centuries B. C." In *Les Communautes rurales.* Deuxieme partie—Antiquité, 133-45. Recueils de la société Jean Bodin 41. Paris: Dessain et Tolra, 1983.

———. "The Domain-Lands of Achaemenes in Babylonia." *Altorientalische Forschungen* 1 (1974):123-27.

———. "Free Hired Labor in Babylonia During the Sixth Through Fourth Centuries B. C." In *Labor in the Ancient Near East,* ed. Marvin A. Powell, 271-79. American Oriental Series 68. New Haven: American Oriental Society, 1987.

———. "Die Lehnsbeziehungen in Babylonien unter den ersten Achämeniden." In *Festschrift für Wilhelm Eilers: Ein Dokument der intenationalen Forschung zum 27 September 1966,* ed. Gernst Wiessner, 37-42. Wiesbaden: Otto Harrassowitz, 1967.

———. "The Neo-babylonian Elders." In *Societies and Languages of the Ancient Near East: Studies in Honour of I. M. Diakonoff,* ed. J. N. Postgate, 38-41. Warminster: Aris & Phillips, 1982.

———. *Persien unter der ersten Achämeniden.* trans. Heinz-Dieter Pohl. Beiträge zur Iranistik Bd. 8. Wiesbaden: Otto Harrassowitz, 1976.

Davies, Graham I. *Megiddo.* Cities of the Biblical World. Grand Rapids: Wm. B. Eerdmans, 1986.

Deane, Philip. *Thucydides' Dates 465-431 B. C.* Don Mills, Ont.: Longman Canada, 1972.

Demsky, Aaron. "*Pelekh* in Nehemiah 3." *Israel Exploration Journal* 33 (1983):242-44.

Derfler, Steven. "Naḥal Yattir." *Israel Exploration Journal* 37 (1987):195-7.

———. "The Persian Fortress of Naḥal Yattir and Its Relationship to the Regional Center of Tel Beersheva." Paper delivered at the Annual Meeting of the American Schools of Oriental Research, December 5, 1987.

Dever, William G. "The Impact of the 'New Archaeology' on Syro-palestinian Archaeology." *Bulletin of the American Schools of Oriental Research* 242 (1981): 15-29.

Dhorme, P. "Les tablettes babyloniennes de Neirab." *Revue d'assyriologie et d'archéologie Orientale* 25 (1928):53-82.

Diakonoff, I. M. "Slaves, Helots and Serfs in Early Antiquity." In *Wirtschaft und Gesellschaft im Alten Vorderasien,* eds. J. Harmatta and G. Komoroczy, 45-78. Nachdruck aus den Acta Antiqua Academiae Scientarum Hungaricae 22. Budapest: Akademiai Kiado, 1976.

Diodorus. *Diodorus of Sicily.* with an English translation by C. H. Oldfather. Loeb Classical Library. 12 volumes. Cambridge, MA: Harvard University Press, 1933-67.

Doermann, Ralph W. and Fargo, Valerie. "Tell el-Ḥesi, 1983." *Palestine Exploration Quarterly* 117 (1985):1-24.

Donner, Herbert. "The Separate States of Israel and Judah." In *Israelite and Judean History,* eds. John H. Hayes and J. Maxwell Miller, 381-434. Philadelphia: Westminster Press, 1977.

Dornemann, Rudolph H. *The Archaeology of the Transjordan in the Bronze and Iron Ages.* Milwaukee: Milwaukee Public Museum, 1983.

Dorsey, David A. "The Roads and Highways of Israel During the Iron Age." Ph. D. dissertation, The Dropsie University, 1981.

Drews, Robert. "Diodorus and His Sources." *American Journal of Philology* 83 (1962):383-92.

———. *The Greek Accounts of Eastern History.* Cambridge: Harvard University Press, 1973.

———. "Sargon, Cyrus and Mesopotamian Folk History." *Journal of Near Eastern Studies* 33 (1974):387-93.

Driver, G. R. *Aramaic Documents of the Fifth Century B. C.* Abridged and revised edition. Oxford: Clarendon Press, 1957.

Dubberstein, Waldo H. "Comparative Prices in Later Babylonia (625-400 B. C.)." *American Journal of the Semitic Languages* 56 (1938):20-43.

Dumbrell, W. J. "Malachi and the Ezra-Nehemiah Reforms." *Reformed Theological Review* 35 (1976):42-52.

Dunand, Maurice. "La Defense du Front méditerranéen de l'Empire achéménide." In *The Role of the Phoenicians in the Interaction of Mediterranean Civilizations,* ed. William A. Ward, 43-51. Beirut: American University of Beirut, 1967.

———. "Byblos, Sidon, Jerusalem: Monuments apparentes des temps Achéménides." *Supplements to Vetus Testamentum* 17 (1969):64-70.

Duverger, M. "Le Concept d'empire." In *Le Concept d'empire,* ed. M. Duverger, 5-23. Paris: Presses Universitaires de France, 1980.

Ehrenberg, Victor. *The Greek State.* Second Edition. London: Methuen and Co., 1969.

Eisenstadt, S. N. "Observations and Queries about Sociological Aspects of Imperialism in the Ancient World." In *Power and Propaganda: A Symposium on Ancient Empires,* ed. Morgens Trolle Larsen, 7-46. Mesopotamia 7. Copenhagen: Akademisk Forlag, 1979.

———. *The Political Systems of Empires.* New York: The Free Press of Glencoe, 1963.

———. *A Sociological Approach to Comparative Civilizations: The Development and Directions of a Research Program.* Jerusalem: Department of Sociology and Social Anthropology, The Hebrew University, 1986.

Eissfeldt, Otto. *The Old Testament: An Introduction.* trans. Peter R. Ackroyd. New York: Harper & Row, 1965.

Elgood, P. G. *Later Dynasties of Egypt.* Oxford: Basil Blackwell, 1951.

Emerton, J. A. Review of *Nehemia: Quellen, Überlieferung und Geschichte* by U. Kellermann. *Journal of Theological Studies* n.s. 23 (1972):171-85.

Ephʿal, Israel. "On the Political and Social Organization of the Jews in Babylonian Exile." In *XXI. Deutscher Orientalistentag. Vorträge,* ed. Fritz Steppat, 106-12. Zeitschrift der Deutschen mörgenlandischen Gesellschaft Supp. V. Wiesbaden: Franz Steiner, 1983.

———. "On Warfare and Military Control in the Ancient Near Eastern Empires: A Research Outline." In *History, Historiography and Interpretation: Studies in Biblical and Cuneiform Literatures,* eds. H. Tadmor and M. Weinfeld, 88-106. Jerusalem: The Magnes Press, 1983.

———. "The Western Minorities in Babylonia in the 6th-5th Centuries B. C.: Maintenance and Cohesion." *Orientalia* n.s. 47 (1978):74-90.

Eskenazi, Tamara Cohn. "In An Age of Prose: A Literary Approach to Ezra-Nehemiah." Ph.D. dissertation. Iliff School of Theology, 1986.

———. *In an Age of Prose: A Literary Approach to Ezra-Nehemiah.* SBL Monograph Series. Atlanta: Scholars Press, 1988.

Ewald, Heinrich. *The History of Israel. Volume V: The History of Ezra and of the Hagiocracy in Israel to the Time of Christ.* trans. J. Estlin Carpenter. Second edition. London: Longman, Green and Co., 1880.

Fales, F. M. "Remarks on the Neirab Texts." *Oriens Antiquus* 12 (1973):131-42.

Faulkner, R. O. *A Concise Dictionary of Middle Egyptian.* Oxford: The Griffith Institute, 1962.

Fensham, F. C. *The Books of Ezra and Nehemiah.* New International Commentary on the Old Testament. Grand Rapids: Wm. B. Eerdmans, 1982.

———. "*Medina* in Ezra and Nehemiah." *Vetus Testamentum* 25 (1975):795-97.

———. "Some Theological and Religious Aspects in Ezra and Nehemiah." *Journal of Northwest Semitic Languages* 11 (1983):59-68.

Finkelstein, Israel. "The Iron Age 'Fortresses' of the Negev—Sedentarization of Desert Nomads." *Eretz- Israel* 18 (1985):366-79 [Hebrew].

———. "The Iron Age Fortresses of the Negev Highlands: Sedentarization of the Nomads." *Tel Aviv* 11 (1984):189-209.

Finley, M. I. "The Fifth-century Athenian Empire: A Balance-sheet." In *Imperialism in the Ancient World,* eds. P. D. A. Garnsey and C. R. Whittaker, 103-26. Cambridge: Cambridge University Press, 1978.

Fitzmyer, J. A. "The Aramaic Letter of the King Adon to the Egyptian Pharaoh." *Biblica* 46 (1965):41-55.

———. *A Wandering Aramean: Collected Aramaic Essays.* SBL Monograph Series, 25. Chico, CA: Scholars Press, 1979.

Fornara, Charles W. *Herodotus: An Interpretative Essay.* Oxford: Clarendon Press, 1971.

Forrer, Emil. *Die Provinzeinteilung des assyrischen Reiches.* Leipzig: J. C. Hinrichs, 1920.

Frame, Grant. "Neo-babylonian and Achaemenid Economic Texts from the Sippar Collection of the British Museum." *Journal of the American Oriental Society* 104 (1984):745-52.

Frankenstein, Susan. "The Phoenicians in the Far West: A Function of Neo-Assyrian Imperialism." In *Power and Propaganda: A Symposium on Ancient Empires,* ed. Mogens Trolle Larsen, 263-94. Mesopotamia 7. Copenhagen: Akademisk Forlag, 1979.

Frankfort, Henri. *Cylindar Seals: A Documentary Essay on the Art and Religion of the Ancient Near East.* London: Macmillan and Co., 1939.

Freedy, K. S. and D. B. Redford. "The Dates in Ezekiel in Relation to Biblical, Babylonian and Egyptian Sources." *Journal of the American Oriental Society* 90 (1970):462-85.

Frei, Peter and Klaus Koch. *Reichsidee und Reichsorganisation im Perserreich.* Orbis Biblicus et Orientalis 55. Göttingen: Vandenhoeck & Ruprecht, 1984.

French, A. *The Athenian Half-century 478-431 B. C. (Thucydides 1 89-118).* Sydney: Sydney University Press, 1971.

Frye, Richard N. *The History of Ancient Iran.* Handbuch der Altertumswissenschaft, dritte Abteilung, siebenter Teil. Munich: C. H. Beck, 1984.

Funck, Bernd. "Zur Bürger-Tempel-Gemeinde im nachexilischen Juda." *Klio* 59 (1977): 491-96.

Funk, Robert W. "The History of Beth-zur with Reference to Its Defenses." In *The 1957 Excavation at Beth-Zur.* ed. Paul Lapp, 4-17. Annual of the American Schools of Oriental Research 38. Cambridge, MA: American Schools of Oriental Research, 1968.

Gadd, C. J. "Inscribed Prisms of Sargon II from Nimrud." *Iraq* 16 (1954):173-201.

Galling, Kurt. *Die Bücher der Chronik, Esra, Nehemia.* Die Alte Testament Deutsch, Teilband 12. Göttingen: Vandenhoeck & Ruprecht, 1954.

———. "Assyrische und persische Präfekten in Geser." *Palästinajahrbuch des Deutschen evangelischen Instituts für Altertumswissenschaft* 31 (1935): 75-93.

———. *Syrien in der politik der Achaemeniden bis zum aufstand des Megabyzos 448 v. Chr.* Der Alte Orient 36 3/4. Leipzig: J. C. Hinrichs, 1937.

———. *Studien zur Geschichte Israels im persischen Zeitalter.* Tübingen: J. C. B. Mohr, 1964.

Gardiner, Alan. *Egypt of the Pharaohs: An Introduction.* London: Oxford University Press, 1964.

Garelli, Paul. "Les empires mésopotamiens." In *Le concept d'Empire,* ed. Maurice Duverger, 25-47. Paris: Presses Universitaires de France, 1980.

———. "Importance et Role des Arameens dans l'Administration de l'Empire assyrien." In *Mesopotamien und seine Nachbarn: Politische und Kulturale Wechselbeziehungen im Alten Vorderasien vom 4. bis 1. Jahrtausend v. Chr.,* eds. Hans-Jorg Nissen and Johannes Renger, 437-47. 25th Recontre Assyriologique Internationale, Berliner Beiträge zum Vorderen Orient 1. Berlin: Dietrich Reimer Verlag, 1982.

Garelli, Paul and V. Nikiprowetzky. *Le Proche-orient asiatique: les Empires mésopotamiens, Israel.* Paris: Presses Universitaires de France, 1974.

Gauthier, Henri. *Le Livre de Rois d'égypte,* Volume 4. Mémoires publiés par les Membres de L'Institut francais d'Archéologie orientale du Caire; Tome 20. Cairo: L'Institut francais d'Archéologie orientale, 1916.

Gershevitch, Ilya, ed. *The Cambridge History of Iran. Volume 2: The Median and Achaemenian Periods.* Cambridge: Cambridge University Press, 1985.

Ghimadyev, R. A. "A Possible Persian Source for Thucydides' Description of the First Athenian Expedition to Egypt." *Vestnik Drevnes Istorii* 163 (1983):106-11 [Russian].

Girshman, Roman. "Susa." In *The International Standard Bible Encyclopedia.* Volume 4, ed. Geoffrey Bromiley, 667-69. Grand Rapids: Wm. B. Eerdmans, 1988.

Glazier-McDonald, Beth. "Intermarriage, Divorce, and the *bat-ʾēl nēkār.*" *Journal of Biblical Literature* 106 (1987):603-11.

Glueck, Nelson. *Explorations in Eastern Palestine, II.* Annual of the American Schools of Oriental Research, 15. New Haven: American Schools of Oriental Research, 1935.

———. "The Third Season of Explorations in the Negeb." *Bulletin of the American Schools of Oriental Research* 138 (1955):7-29.

Gomme, A. W. *A Historical Commentary on Thucydides. Volume 1: Introduction and Commentary on Book I.* Oxford: Clarendon Press, 1945.

Goosens, Godefrey. "Le sommaire des Persica de Ctesias par Photius." *Revue Belge de Philologie et d'Histoire* 28 (1950):513-21.

Graetz, Heinrich. *History of the Jews. Volume 1: From the Earliest Period to the Death of Simon the Maccabee (135 B. C. E.).* trans. of 1870 German edition, Bella Lowy. Philadelphia: Jewish Publication Society of America, 1891.

Graham, J. N. "Vinedressers and Plowmen: 2 Kings 25:12 and Jeremiah 52:16." *Biblical Archaeologist* 47 (1984):55-8.

Grayson, A. K. *Assyrian and Babylonian Chronicles*. Texts from Cuneiform Sources, 5. New York: J. J. Augustin, 1975.

Greenfield, Jonas C. "Babylonian-Aramaic Relationship." In *Mesopotamien und seine Nachbarn: Politische und Kulturelle Wechselbeziehungen im Alten Vorderasien vom 4. bis 1. Jahrtausend v. Chr.* eds. Hans-Jorg Nissen and Johannes Renger, 471-82. 25th Recontre Assyriologique Internationale. Berliner Beiträge zum vorderen Orient Band 1. Berlin: Dietrich Reimer Verlag, 1982.

Guentch-Ogloueff, Marianne. "Noms propres imprécatoires." *Bulletin d'Institut francais d'archéologie Orientale* 40 (1941):117-33.

Gunn, Battiscombe. "The Story of Khamwise." In *Land of Enchanters: Egyptian Short Stories from the Earliest Times to the Present Day*, ed. Bernard Lewis, 67-83. London: Harvill Press, 1948.

Gunneweg, A. H. J. "*ʿm hʾrṣ*—A Semantic Revolution." *Zeitschrift für die alttestamentliche Wissenschaft* 95 (1983):437-40.

Gyles, Mary Francis. *Pharaonic Policies and Administration, 663 to 323 B. C.* James Sprunt Studies 41. Chapel Hill: University of North Carolina Press, 1959.

Hallo, William W. and William Kelly Simpson. *The Ancient Near East: A History*. New York: Harcourt Brace Jovanovich, 1971.

Hallock, R. T. "The Evidence of the Persepolis Tablets." In *The Cambridge History of Iran. Volume 2: The Median and Achaemenian Periods*, ed. Ilya Gershevitch, 588-609. Cambridge: Cambridge University Press, 1985.

Hammond, N. G. L. *A History of Greece to 322 B. C.* Third edition. Oxford: Clarendon Press, 1986.

Harmatta, J. "The Rise of the Old Persian Empire—Cyrus the Great." *Acta Antiqua Academiae Scientarium Hungaricae* 19 (1971):3-15.

Hayes, John H. "The History of the Study of Israelite and Judean History." In *Israelite and Judean History*, eds. John H. Hayes and J. Maxwell Miller, 1-69. Philadelphia: Westminster Press, 1977.

Hegyi, D. "Athen und die Achämeniden in der Zweiten Halfte des 5. Jahrhunderts v. u. z." *Oikumene* 4 (1983):53-9.

———. "Historical Authenticity of Herodotus in the Persian 'Logoi'." *Acta Antiqua Academie Scientiarum Hungaricae* 21 (1973):73-87.

Heichelheim, Fritz M. "Ezra's Palestine and Periclean Athens." *Zeitschrift für Religions— und Geistesgeschichte* 3 (1951):251-53.

Herodotus. *Herodotus. Volume 2: Books III and IV*, Loeb Classical Library. New York: G. P. Putnam's Sons, 1921.

Herr, Larry G. *The Scripts of Ancient Northwest Semitic Seals*. Harvard Semitic Monograph Series, 18. Missoula, MT: Scholars Press, 1978.

Herrenschmidt, Clarisse. "L'Empire perse achéménide." In *Le Concept d'Empire*, ed. Maurice Duverger, 69-102. Paris: Presses Universitaires de France, 1980.

Herrman, Siegfried. *A History of Israel in Old Testament Times*. rev. and enlarged ed., trans. John Bowden. Philadelphia: Fortress Press, 1981.

Herzfeld, Ernst. *The Persian Empire: Studies in Geography and Ethnography of the Ancient Near East*, ed. Gerold Walser. Wiesbaden: Franz Steiner, 1968.

Hignett, C. *Xerxes' Invasion of Greece*. Oxford: Clarendon Press, 1963.

Hill, G. F. *Sources for Greek History between the Persian and Peloponnesian Wars.* A new edition by R. Meiggs. Oxford: Clarendon Press, 1951.

Horn, S. H. and L. H. Wood. "The Fifth-century Jewish Calendar at Elephantine." *Journal of Near Eastern Studies* 13 (1954):1-20.

Huxley, G. L. "Thucydides on the Growth of Athenian Power." *Proceedings of the Royal Irish Academy* 83c (1983):191-204.

Immerwahr, Henry R. *Form and Thought in Herodotus.* American Phililogical Association, Philological Monographs, 23. Cleveland: American Philological Association, 1966.

In der Smitten, Wilhelm Th. "Der *Tirschata* in Esra-Nehemiah." *Vetus Testamentum* 21 (1971): 618-20.

Jacoby, Fritz. "Ketsias." In *Pauly Real-Encyclopädie der Classischen Altertumswissenschaft,* ed. Georg Wissowa and Wilhelm Kroll, Band 11, T. 2, 2032-73. Stuttgart: J. B. Metzler, 1922.

Jagersma, H. *A History of Israel in the Old Testament Period.* London: SCM Press, 1982.

Jakobson, V. A. "The Social Structure of the Neo-Assyrian Empire." In *Ancient Mesopotamia: Socio-economic History,* ed. I. M. Diakonoff, 277-95. Moscow: Nauka Publishing House, 1969.

Jankowska, N. B. "Some Problems of the Economy of the Assyrian Empire." In *Ancient Mesopotamia: Socio-economic History,* ed. I. M. Diakonoff, 253-76. Moscow: Nauka Publishing House, 1969.

Japhet, Sara. "People and Land in the Restoration Period." In *Das Land Israel in biblischer Zeit,* ed. G. Strecker, 103-25. Göttinger theologische Arbeiten, 25. Göttingen: Vandenhoeck & Ruprecht, 1983.

———. "Sheshbazzar and Zerubabel Against the Background of the Historical and Religious Tendencies of Ezra-Nehemiah." *Zeitschrift für die alttestamentliche Wissenschaft* 95 (1983):218-29.

———. "The Supposed Common Authorship of Chronicles and Ezra-Nehemiah Investigated Anew." *Vetus Testamentum* 18 (1968):330-71.

Jean, C. F. and J. Hoftijzer. *Dictionnaire des Inscriptions sémitiques de l'Ouest.* Leiden: E. J. Brill, 1965.

Jenner, K. D. "The Old Testament and Its Appreciation of Cyrus." *Persica* 10 (1982):283-84.

Kamil, Jill. "Ancient Memphis: Archaeologists Revive Interest in a Famous Egyptian Site." *Archaeology* 38 (1985):25-32.

Keel, Othmar. "Ancient Seals and the Bible." *Journal of the American Oriental Society* 106 (1986):307-11.

Kellermann, Ulrich. "Erwägungen zum Esragesetz." *Zeitschrift für die alttestamentliche Wissenschaft* 80 (1968):373-85.

———. *Nehemiah: Quellen Überlieferung und Geschichte.* Beiheft zur Zeitschrift für die Alttestamentliche Wissenschaft, 102. Berlin: Alfred Töpelmann, 1967.

Kelso, James L. "Bethel." In *Encyclopedia of Archaeological Excavations in the Holy Land, Volume 1,* ed. Michael Avi-Yonah, 190-93. Englewood Cliffs, NJ: Prentice-Hall, 1975.

———. *The Excavation of Bethel (1934-1960)*. Annual of the American Schools of Oriental Research 39. Cambridge, MA: American Schools of Oriental Research, 1968.

Kemp, B. J. "Imperialism and Empire in New Kingdom Egypt." In *Imperialism in the Ancient World*, eds. P. D. A. Garnsey and C. R. Whittaker, 7-57. Cambridge: Cambridge University Press, 1978.

Kent, Roland G. *Old Persian: Grammar, Texts, Lexicon*. American Oriental Society Series 33. New Haven: American Oriental Society, 1950.

Kenyon, Kathleen M. *Jerusalem: Excavating 3000 Years of History*. New Aspects of Archaeology. London: Thames and Hudson, 1967.

———. *Royal Cities of the Old Testament*. New York: Schocken Books, 1971.

Kienitz, Friedrich K. *Die politische Geschicte Ägyptens vom 7. bis zum 4. Jahrhundert vor der Zeitwende* Berlin: Akademie-verlag, 1953.

Kippenberg, H. *Religion und Klassenbildung im antiken Judäa*. Studien zur Umwelt des Neuen Testaments 14. Göttingen: Vandenhoeck und Ruprecht, 1978.

Kitchen, Kenneth A. "Inaros." In *Lexikon der Ägyptologie, Band 3*, eds. Wolfgang Helck and Wolfhart Westendorf, 152. Wiesbaden: Otto Harrassowitz, 1980.

———. *Pharaoh Triumphant: The Life and Times of Ramesses II, King of Egypt*. Warminster: Aris & Phillips, 1982.

———. *The Third Intermediate Period in Egypt (1100-650 B. C.)*. Warminster: Aris & Phillips, 1973.

Klima, M. J. "Beiträge zur Struktur der neubabylonischen Gesellschaft." In *Compte Rendu de l'Onzième Rencontre Assyriologique Internationale*, 11-21. Leiden: Nederlands Instituut voor hut Nabije Oosten, 1964.

Koch, K. "Ezra and the Origins of Judaism." *Journal of Semitic Studies* 19 (1974):173-97.

Kochavi, Moshe, ed. *Judaea, Samaria and the Golan: Archaeological Survey 1967-1968*. Jerusalem: The Survey of Israel, 1972.

Komoroczy, G. "Landed Property in Ancient Mesopotamia and the Theory of the SoCalled Asiatic Mode of Production." *Oikumene* 2 (1978):9-26.

König, Friedrich Wilhelm. *Die Persika des Ktesias von Knidos*. Archiv für Orientforschung, Beiheft 18. Graz: In Selbstverlage des Herausgebers, 1972.

Kraeling, Emil G. *The Brooklyn Museum Aramaic Papyri: New Documents of the Fifth Century B. C. from the Jewish Colony at Elephantine*. New Haven: Yale University Press, 1953.

Kreissig, Heinz. "Eine beachtenswerte Theorie zur Organisation altvorderorientalischer Templegemeinden im Achämenidenreich." *Klio* 66 (1984):35-9.

———. *Die Sozialökonomische situation in Juda zur Achämenidenzeit*. Schriften zur Geschichte und Kultur des Alten Orients 7. Berlin: Akademie Verlag, 1973.

Kuhrt, Amelie. "Assyrian and Babylonian Traditions in Classical Athens: A Critical Synthesis." In *Mesopotamien und seine Nachbarn: Politische und Kulturelle Wechselbeziehungen im Alten Vorderasien vom 4. bis 1. Jahrtausend v. Chr.*, eds. Hans-Jorg Nissen and Johannes Renger, 539-53. 25th Recontre Assyriologique Internationale, Berliner Beiträge zum Vorderen Orient 1. Berlin: Dietrich Reimer, 1982.

———. "The Cyrus Cylinder and Achaemenid Imperial Policy." *Journal for the Study of the Old Testament* 25 (1983):83-97.

Lamon, Robert S. and Geoffrey M. Shipton. *Megiddo I: Seasons of 1925-34, Strata I-V.* Oriental Institute Publications 42. Chicago: University of Chicago Press, 1939.

Lance, H. Darrell. "The Royal Stamps and the Kingdom of Judah." *Harvard Theological Review* 64 (1971):315-32.

Landsberger, Benno and Th. Bauer. "Zu neuveröffentlichten Geschichtsquellen der Zeit von Asarhaddon bis Nabonid." *Zeitschrift für Assyriologie* 27 (1926):61-98.

Lapp, Nancy. "Appendix 7: Some Black— and Red—Figured Attic Ware." In *Shechem: The Biography of a Biblical City,* by George Ernest Wright, 238-41. New York: McGraw-Hill Book Co., 1965.

———. "The Stratum V Pottery from Balaṭah (Shechem)." *Bulletin of the American Schools of Oriental Research* 257 (1985):19-43.

———. *The Third Campaign at Tell el-Ful: The Excavations of 1964.* Annual of the American Schools of Oriental Research, 45. Cambridge, MA: American Schools of Oriental Research, 1981.

Lapp, Paul W. "The Pottery of Palestine in the Persian Period." In *Archäologie und Altes Testament,* eds. Arnulf Kuschke and Ernst Kutsch, 179-97. Tübingen: J. C. B. Mohr, 1970.

———. Review of *Winery, Defenses, and Soundings at Gibeon* by James B. Pritchard. *American Journal of Archaeology* 72 (1968):391-93.

———. "Tell el-Ful." *Biblical Archaeologist* 28 (1965):2-10.

Lewis, D. M. "Persians in Herodotus." In *The Greek Historians, Literature and History: Papers Presented to A. E. Raubitschek,* 101-17. Stanford, CA: Anma Libri, Dept. of Classics, Stanford University, 1985.

———. *Sparta and Persia.* Cincinnati Classical Studies n.s. 1. Leiden: E. J. Brill, 1977.

Lewis, Naphtali. *The Fifth Century B. C.* Greek Historical Documents. Toronto: A. M. Hakkert, 1971.

Liagre Böhl, F. M. Th. "Die babylonischen Prätendenten zur Zeit des Xerxes." *Bibliotheca Orientalis* 19 (1962): 110-14.

Libourel, Jan M. "The Athenian Disaster in Egypt." *American Journal of Philology* 92 (1971):605-15.

Lichtheim, Miriam. *Ancient Egyptian Literature. Volume 3: The Late Period.* Berkeley: University of California Press, 1980.

Lloyd, Alan B. *Herodotus Book II: Introduction and Commentary.* Études préliminaires aux religions orientales dans l'Empire Romain, 43. Leiden: E. J. Brill, 1975.

———. "The Inscription of Udjahorresnet, a Collaborator's Testament." *Journal of Egyptian Archaeology* 68 (1982):166-80.

———. "The Late Period, 664-323 BC." In *Ancient Egypt: A Social History,* ed. B. G. Trigger, 279-48. Cambridge: Cambridge University Press, 1983.

Luckenbill, Daniel David. *Ancient Records of Assyria and Babylonia. Volume II: Historical Records of Assyria.* Chicago: University of Chicago Press, 1927.

Macdonald, John. "The Discovery of Samaritan Religion." *Religion: Journal of Religion and Religions* 2 (1972):141-53.

McConville, J. G. "Ezra-Nehemiah and the Fulfillment of Prophecy." *Vetus Testamentum* 36 (1986):205-24.

Malamat, Abraham. "Josiah's Bid for Armageddon: The Background of the Judean-Egyptian Encounter in 609 B. C." *Journal of the Ancient Near Eastern Society of Columbia University* 5 (1973):267-79.

———. "The Last Kings of Judah and the Fall of Jerusalem." *Israel Exploration Journal* 18 (1968): 137-56.

———. "The Last Wars of the Kingdom of Judah." *Journal of Near Eastern Studies* 9 (1950):218-27.

———. "The Twilight of Judah: In the Egyptian-Babylonian Maelstrom." *Supplements to Vetus Testamentum* 28 (1974):123-45.

Mallowan, Max. "Cyrus the Great (558-529 B. C.)." In *The Cambridge History of Iran. Volume 2: The Median and Achaemenian Periods,* ed. Ilya Gershevitch, 392-419. Cambridge: Cambridge University Press, 1985.

Mann, Michael. *The Sources of Social Power. Volume 1: A History of Power from the Beginning to A. D. 1760.* Cambridge: Cambridge University Press, 1986.

Margalith, Othniel. "The Political Role of Ezra as Persian Governor." *Zeitschrift für die alttestamentliche Wissenschaft* 98 (1986):110-12.

Mattingly, Harold. "The Peace of Kallias." *Historia* 14 (1965):273-81.

Mazar, Amihai. "The Excavations at Khirbet Abu et-Twein and the System of Iron Age Fortresses in Judah." *Eretz-Israel* 15 (1981):229-49 [Hebrew].

———. "Iron Age Fortresses in the Judean Hills." *Palestine Exploration Quarterly* 114 (1982):87-109.

Mazar, Benjamin. "The Tobiads." *Israel Exploration Journal* 7 (1957):137-45; 227-38.

McCown, Chester Charlton. *Tell en-Naṣbeh. Volume 1: Archaeological and Historical Results.* Berkeley: Palestine Institute of Pacific School of Religion, 1947.

McCullough, William Stewart. *The History and Literature of the Palestinian Jews from Cyrus to Herod, 550 BC to 4 BC.* Toronto: University of Toronto Press, 1975.

McEvenue, Sean E. "The Political Structure in Judah from Cyrus to Nehemiah." *Catholic Biblical Quarterly* 43 (1981):353-64.

Meiggs, Russell. *The Athenian Empire.* Oxford: Clarendon Press, 1972.

———. "The Crisis of Athenian Imperialism." *Harvard Studies in Philology* 67 (1963):1-36.

Meiggs, Russell and David Lewis, eds. *A Selection of Greek Historical Inscriptions to the End of the Fifth Century B. C.* corrected edition. Oxford: Clarendon Press, 1980.

Meritt, Benjamin H. T. Wade-Gery and Malcolm McGregor. *The Athenian Tribute Lists. Volumes I-IV*. Princeton: American School of Classical Studies at Athens, 1939-53.

Meshel, Zeev. "Ḥorvat Ritma—An Iron Age Fortress in the Negev Highlands." *Tel Aviv* 4 (1977):110-35.

de Meulenaere, Herman J. "Amyrtaios." In *Lexikon der Ägyptologie. Band I,* eds. Wolfgang Helck and Eberhard Otto, 252-3. Wiesbaden: Otto Harrassowitz, 1973.

———. "Papremis." In *Lexikon der Ägyptologie. Band IV,* eds. Wolfgang Helck and Wolfhart Westendorf, 666-7. Wiesbaden: Otto Harrassowitz, 1982.

Meyers, Eric M. "The Persian Period and the Judean Restoration: From Zerubbabel to Nehemiah." In *Ancient Israelite Religion: Essays in Honor of Frank Moore Cross,* eds. P. D. Hanson, D. McBride, and P. D. Miller, 509-21. Philadelphia: Fortress Press, 1987.

———. "The Shelomith Seal and the Judean Restoration: Some Additional Considerations." *Eretz-Israel* 18 (1985):35*-8*.

Meyers, Carol L. and Eric M. Meyers. *Haggai, Zechariah 1—8*. The Anchor Bible 25B. Garden City: Doubleday & Co., 1987.

Millar, Fergus. "The Problem of Hellenistic Syria." In *Hellenism and the East: The Interaction of Greek and Non-Greek Civilizations from Syria to Central Asia after Alexander*, eds. Amelie Kuhrt and Susan Sherwin-White, 110-33. Berkeley: University of California Press, 1987.

Millard, Alan R. "The Scythian Problem." In *Orbis Aegyptiorum Speculum: Glimpses of Ancient Egypt, Studies in Honour of H. W. Fairman*, eds. John Ruffle, G. A. Gaballa, and Kenneth A. Kitchen, 119-22. Warminster: Aris & Phillips, 1979.

Miller, J. Maxwell. "Archaeological Survey of Central Moab." *Bulletin of the American Schools of Oriental Research* 234 (1979):43-52.

Miller, J. Maxwell, and John H. Hayes. *A History of Ancient Israel and Judah*. Philadelphia: Westminster Press, 1986.

Momigliano, Arnaldo. "Persian Empire and Greek Freedom." In *The Idea of Freedom: Essays in Honour of Isaiah Berlin*, ed. Alan Ryan, 139-51. Oxford: Oxford University Press, 1979.

———. "Tradizione e Invenzione in Ctesias." *Atene e Roma* n.s. 12 (1931):15-44. Reprinted in *Quarto Contributo alla Storia degli Studi Classici e del Mondo Antico*, 181-212. Storia e Letteratura 115. Rome: Edizioni di Storia e Letteratura, 1969.

Moorey, P. R. S. *Cemeteries of the First Millennium B. C. at Deve Huyuk, Near Carchemish, Salvaged by T. E. Lawrence and C. L. Wooley in 1915*. BAR International Series 87. Oxford: British Archaeological Reports, 1980.

Morgenstern, Julian. "A Chapter in the History of the High-priesthood—Concluded." *American Journal of Semitic Languages* 55 (1938):360-77.

———. "The Dates of Ezra and Nehemiah." *Journal of Semitic Studies* 7 (1962):1-11.

———. "Further Light from the Book of Isaiah upon the Catastrophe of 485 B. C." *Hebrew Union College Annual* 37 (1966):1-28.

———. "Isaiah 61." *Hebrew Union College Annual* 40-41 (1969-70):109-21.

———. "Jerusalem—485 B. C." *Hebrew Union College Annual* 27 (1956):101-79.

———. "Jerusalem—485 B. C., cont." *Hebrew Union College Annual* 28 (1957):15-47.

———. "Jerusalem—485 B. C. (concluded)." *Hebrew Union College Annual* 31 (1960):1-29.

———. "The Oppressor of Isa. 51:13—Who Was He?" *Journal of Biblical Literature* 81 (1969):25-34.

———. "Psalm 48." *Hebrew Union College Annual* 16 (1941):1-95.

———. "Two Prophecies from 520-516 B. C." *Hebrew Union College Annual* 22 (1949):365-427.

Mowinckel, Sigmund. *Studien zu dem Buche Ezra- Nehemiah*, I-III. Skrifter utgitt au det Norske Videnskaps-Akademi I. Oslo II. Hist.-Filos. Klasse, Nu Serie, 3, 5 and 7. Oslo: Universitetsforlaget, 1964-65.

Myers, J. L. "Persia, Greece and Israel." *Palestine Exploration Quarterly* 85 (1953):8-22.

Myers, Jacob. *Ezra.Nehemiah.* The Anchor Bible 14. Garden City: Doubleday & Co., 1965.

———. *The World of the Restoration.* Englewood Cliffs, NJ: Prentice-Hall, 1968.

Naveh, Joseph. "The Excavations at Meṣad Hashavyahu." *Israel Exploration Journal* 12 (1962):89-113.

North, Robert. "Civil Authority in Ezra." In *Studi in onore di Edoardo Volterra, Volume 6,* 377- 404. Milan: A. Giuffre, 1971.

Noth, Martin. *The History of Israel.* rev. ed. New York: Harper & Row, 1960.

O'Connor, David. "New Kingdom and Third Intermediate Period, 1552-664 B. C." In *Ancient Egypt: A Social History,* ed. B. G. Trigger, 183-278. Cambridge: Cambridge University Press, 1983.

Oded, Bustenay. "Judah and the Exile." In *Israelite and Judaean History,* eds. John H. Hayes and J. Maxwell Miller, 435-88. Philadelphia: Westminster Press, 1977.

———. *Mass Deportations and Deportees in the Neo-Assyrian Empire.* Wiesbaden: Ludwig Reichert, 1979.

———. "Mass Deportation in the Neo-Assyrian Empire— Aims and Objectives." *Shnaton* 3 (1978-9):159-73 [Hebrew].

———. "Mass Deportations in the Neo-Assyrian Empire—Facts and Figures." *Eretz-Israel* 14 (1978):62-68 [Hebrew].

———. "Observations on Methods of Assyrian Rule in Transjordania After the Palestinian Campaign of Tiglath-Pileser III." *Journal of Near Eastern Studies* 29 (1970):177-86.

———. "The Phoenician Cities and the Assyrian Empire in the Time of Tiglath-Pileser III." *Zeitschrift des Deutsches Palestins Veriens* 90 (1974):38-49.

———. "The Relations Between the City-states of Phoenicia and Assyria in the Reigns of Esarhaddon and Ashurbanipal." In *Studies in the History of the Jewish People and the Land of Israel. Volume* 3, ed. B. Oded, 31-42. Haifa: University of Haifa, 1974 [Hebrew].

Oelsner, Joachim. "Zwischen Xerxes und Alexander: babylonische Rechtsurkunden und Wirtschaftstexte aus der späten Achämenidenzeit." *Welt des Orients* 8 (1976):310-18.

Olmstead, A. T. *History of Palestine and Syria to the Macedonian Conquest.* New York: Charles Scribner's Sons, 1931.

———. *History of the Persian Empire.* Chicago: University of Chicago Press, 1948.

———. "Tattenai, Governor of 'Across the River'." *Journal of Near Eastern Studies* 3 (1944):46.

Oppenheim, A. L. "The Babylonian Evidence of Achaemenian Rule in Mesopotamia." In *The Cambridge History of Iran. Volume 2: The Median and Achaemenian Periods,* ed. Ilya Gershevitch, 529-87. Cambridge: Cambridge University Press, 1985.

———. "Neo-Assyrian and Neo-Babylonian Empires." In *Propaganda and Communication in World History. Volume 1: The Symbolic Instrument in Early Times,* eds. Harold Lasswell, Daniel Cerner, and Hans Speier, 111-44. Honolulu: University Press of Hawaii, 1979.

Oppenhiem, A. Leo et. al. *The Assyrian Dictionary of the Oriental Institute of the University of Chicago.* Chicago: The Oriental Institute, 1956-.

Oren, E. D. "Esh-Shariʿa, Tell (Tel Seraʿ)." In *Encyclopedia of Archaeological Excavations in the Holy Land. Volume 4*, eds. Michael Avi-Yonah and Ephraim Stern, 1059-69. Englewood Cliffs, NJ: Prentice-Hall, 1978.

———. "Ziglag—A Biblical City on the Edge of the Negev." *Biblical Archaeologist* 45 (1982):155-66.

Otzen, Benedict. "Israel Under the Assyrians." In *Power and Propaganda: A Symposium on Ancient Empires*, ed. Mogens Trolle Larsen, 251-61. Mesopotamia 7. Copenhagen: Akademisk Forlag, 1979.

Pallis, Svend Aage. "The History of Babylon 538-93 B. C." In *Studia Orientalia Ioanni Pedersen*, 275-94. Hauniae: Einar Munksgaard, 1953.

Parker, Richard A. and Waldo H. Dubberstein. *Babylonian Chronology 626 B. C.—A. D. 45*. Studies in Ancient Oriental Civlization 24. Chicago: University of Chicago Press, 1942.

Parrot, Jean. "L'architecture militaire et palatiale des Achéménides a Suse." In *150 Jahre, Deutsches archäologisches Institut 1829-1979*, 79-94. Mainz: Philipp von Zabern, 1981.

Peek, Werner. "Ein Seegefecht aus den Perserkriegen." *Klio* 32 (1939):289-306.

Petersen, David L. *Haggai and Zechariah 1-8: A Commentary*. Old Testament Library. Philadelphia: Westminster Press, 1984.

Pfeiffer, R. H. "Tirshatha." In *The Interpreter's Dictionary of the Bible. Volume 4*, ed. George A. Butterick, 652. New York: Abingdon Press, 1962.

Plöger, Otto. "Reden und Gebete im deuteronomistischen und chronistischen Geschichtswerk." In *Festschrift für Gunther Dehn*, ed. Wilhelm Schneelmelcher, 35-49. Neukirchen: Neukirchener Verlag des Erziehungsvereins, 1957.

Porath, Joseph. "A Fortress of the Persian Period Above Ashdod." *ʿAtiqot* [Hebrew Series] 7 (1974):43-55.

Porten, Bezalel. *Archives from Elephantine: The Life of an Ancient Jewish Military Colony*. Berkeley: University of California Press, 1968.

———. "The Documents in the Book of Ezra and the Mission of Ezra." *Shnaton* 3 (1978-79):174-96 [Hebrew].

———. "The Identity of King Adon." *Biblical Archaeologist* 44 (1981):36-52.

Porter, Bertha and Rosalind L. B. Moss. *Topographical Bibliography of Ancient Egyptian Hieroglyphic Texts, Reliefs, and Paintings. Volume VII. Nubia, The Deserts, and Outside Egypt*. Oxford: Clarendon Press, 1951.

Posener, Georges. *La Prémiere Domination Perse en Égypte: Recueil d'Inscriptions hieroglyphiques*. Bibliotheque d'Étude 11. Cairo: l'Institut francais d'archéologie Orientale, 1936.

Postgate, J. N. "The Economic Structure of the Assyrian Empire." In *Power and Propaganda: A Symposium on Ancient Empires*, ed. Mogens Trolle Larsen, 193-221. Mesopotamia 7. Copenhagen: Akademisk Forlag, 1979.

———. *Neo-Assyrian Royal Grants and Decrees*. Studia Pohl: Series Maior 1. Rome: Biblical Institute Press, 1969.

———. Review of Bustenay Oded, *Mass Deportations and Deportees in the Neo-Assyrian Empire*. *Bibliotheca Orientalis* 38 (1981):635-38.

———. *Taxation and Conscription in the Assyrian Empire.* Studia Pohl: Series Maior 3. Rome: Biblical Institute Press, 1974.

Pritchard, James B., ed. *Ancient Near Eastern Texts Relating to the Old Testament.* Third edition with supplement. Princeton: Princeton University Press, 1969.

———. *Gibeon, Where the Sun Stood Still: The Discovery of the Biblical City.* Princeton: Princeton University Press, 1962.

———. *Tell es-Sa^cidiyeh: Excavations on the Tell, 1964-1966.* University Museum Monograph, 60. Philadelphia: The University Museum, University of Pennsylvania, 1985.

Pritchett, W. K. "The Transfer of the Delian Treasury." *Historia* 18 (1969):17-21.

Purcell, H. D. *Cyprus.* New York: Frederick A. Praeger, 1968.

Raban, Avner. "The Harbor of the Sea Peoples at Dor." *Biblical Archaeologist* 50 (1987):118-26.

von Rad, Gerhard. "Die Nehemia-Denkschrift." *Zeitschrift für die alttestamentliche Wissenschaft* 76 (1964):176-87.

Rahe, Paul A. "The Military Situation in Western Asia on the Eve of Cunaxa." *American Journal of Philology* 101 (1980):79-96.

Rainey, A. F. "The Satrapy 'Beyond the River'." *Australian Journal of Biblical Archaeology* 1 (1969):51-78.

Ranke, Hermann. *Die aegyptischen Personennamen.* Glückstadt: J. J. Augustin, 1935.

Rast, Walter E. *Taanach I: Studies in the Iron Age Pottery.* ASOR Excavation Reports. Cambridge, MA: American Schools of Oriental Research, 1978.

Rawlings, Hunter R., III. *The Structure of Thucydides' History.* Princeton: Princeton University Press, 1981.

———. "Thucydides on the Purpose of the Delian League." *Phoenix* 31 (1977):1-8.

Ray, J. D. "Thoughts on Djeme and Papremis." *Göttinger Miszellen* 45 (1981):57-61.

Redford, Donald B. "Notes on the History of Ancient Buto." *Bulletin of the Egyptological Seminar* 5 (1983):67-101.

Redman, Charles, Edward Curtin, Nina Versaggi and Jeffrey Wanser. "Social Archaeology: The Future of the Past." In *Social Archeology: Beyond Subsistance and Dating,* eds. Charles Redman et al, 1-17. New York: Academic Press, 1978.

Reid, C. I. "Ephorus Fragment 76 and Diodorus on the Cypriot War." *Phoenix* 28 (1974):123-43.

Rendtorff, Rolf. "Esra und des "Gesetz." *Zeitschrift für die alttestamentliche Wissenschaft* 96 (1984):165-84.

Rofé, Alexander. "Isaiah 66:1-4: Judean Sects in the Persian Period as Viewed by Trito-Isaiah." In *Biblical and Related Studies Presented to Samuel Iwry,* eds. Ann Kort and Scott Morschauser, 205-17. Winona Lake, IN: Eisenbrauns, 1985.

Rogerson, John. *Old Testament Criticism in the Nineteenth Century: England and Germany.* Philadelphia: Fortress Press, 1985.

Rose, D. Glenn and Lawrence E. Toombs. "Four Seasons of Excavation at Tell el-Ḥesi: A Preliminary Report." In *Preliminary Excavation Reports: Bab edh-Dhra, Sardis, Meiron, Tell el-Ḥesi, Carthage (Punic),* ed. David Noel Freedman, 109-49. Annual of the American Schools of Oriental Research, 43. Cambridge, MA: American Schools of Oriental Research, 1978.

Rosenthal, Franz. *A Grammar of Biblical Aramaic.* Wiesbaden: Otto Harrassowitz, 1974.

Rössler-Köhler, Ursula. "Zur Textkomposition der naophoren Statue des Udjahorresnet/ Vatikan Inv.-nr. 196." *Göttinger Miszellen* 86 (1985):43-54.

Roux, Georges. *Ancient Iraq.* Second edition. Harmondsworth: Penguin Books, 1982.

Rowley, H. H. "The Chronological Order of Ezra and Nehemiah." In *The Servant of the Lord and Other Essays on the Old Testament,* 135-68. Second edition, revised. Oxford: Basil Blackwell, 1965.

———. "Nehemiah's Mission and Its Background." In *Men of God: Studies in Old Testament History and Prophecy,* 211-45. London: Thomas Nelson & Sons, 1963.

Rudolph, Wilhelm. *Esra und Nehemia samt 3. Esra.* Handbuch zum Alten Testament, 20. Tübingen: J. C. B. Mohr, 1949.

Sack, Ronald. *Amel-Marduk, 562-560 B. C.: A Study Based on Cuneiform, Old Testament, Greek, Latin and Rabbinical Sources.* Alter Orient und Altes Testament Sonderreihe Bd. 4. Neukirchen: Butzon & Beroker Kevelaer, 1972.

———. "Nebuchadnezzar and Nabonidus in Folklore and History." *Mesopotamia* 17 (1982):67-131.

Saggs, H. W. F. *The Greatness That Was Babylon.* New York: Hawthorn Books, 1962.

———. "A Lexical Consideration for the Date of Deutero-Isaiah." *Journal of Theological Studies* 10 (1959):84-7.

———. *The Might That Was Assyria.* London: Sidgwick & Jackson, 1984.

Saley, R. "The Date of Nehemiah Reconsidered." In *Biblical and Near Eastern Studies: Essays in Honor of William Sanford LaSor,* 151-65. Ed. G. Tuttle. Grand Rapids: Wm. B. Eerdmans, 1978.

Salmon, Pierre. *La Politique égyptienne d'Athenes* (VIe *et* V^{e} *siècles avant J.-C.).* Academie Royale de Belgique. Classe des Lettres, Mémoires, t. 57, fasc. 6. Brusselles: Palais des Academies, 1965.

Sancisi-Weerdenburg, Heleen W. A. M. "Medes and Persians: To What Extent Was Cyrus the Heir of Astyages and the Median Empire?" *Persica* 10 (1982):278.

Sanders, N. K. *The Sea Peoples: Warriors of the Ancient Mediterranean, 1250-1150 B. C.* London: Thames and Hudson, 1978.

Sayce, A. H. *The Ancient Empires of the East: Herodotos Books I-III.* London: Macmillan & Co., 1883.

Scharf, J. "Die erste ägyptische Expedition der Athener. *Historia* 3 (1954-55):308-25.

Schepens, Guido. "Historiographical Problems in Ephorus." In *Historiographia Antiqua: Commentationes Lovanienses in Honorem W. Peremans septuagenarii editae,* 95-118. Symbolae. Facultatis Litterarum et Philosophiae Lovaniensis Series A, Volume 6. Leuven: Leuven University Press, 1977.

Schottroff, Willy. "Zur Sozialgeschichte Israels in der Perserzeit." *Verkündigung und Forschung* 19/2 (1974): 46-66.

Schultz, Carl. "The Political Tensions Reflected in Ezra- Nehemiah." In *Scripture in Context: Essays in the Comparative Method,* ed. C. Evans, W. Hallo, and J. White. Pittsburgh Theological Monograph No. 34. Pittsburg: The Pickwick Press, 1980.

Segal, J. B. *Aramaic Texts from North Saqqara with Some Fragments in Phoenician.* Excavations at N. Saqqara: Documentary Series, 4. London: Egypt Exploration Society, 1983.

Sellers, O. R. *The Citadel of Beth-Zur*. Philadelphia: Westminster Press, 1933.

Shanks, Michael and Christopher Tilley. *Social Theory and Archaeology*. Albuquerque: University of New Mexico Press, 1988.

Shennan, Stephen. *Quantifying Archaeology*. Edinburgh: University Press, 1988.

Shiloh, Yigal. *Excavations at the City of David I (1978-1982)*. Qedem: Monographs of the Institute of Archaeology, 19. Jerusalem: Hebrew University of Jerusalem, 1984.

Silberman, Lou H. "Wellhausen and Judaism." *Semeia* 25 (1982):75-82.

Silver, Moses. *Economic Structures of the Ancient Near East*. Totowa, NJ: Barnes & Noble Books, 1986.

Sinclair, Lawrence A. *An Archaeological Study of Gibeah (Tell el-Ful)*. Annual of the American Schools of Oriental Research 34-35. New Haven: American Schools of Oriental Research, 1960.

———. "Bethel Pottery of the Sixth Century B. C." In *The Excavation of Bethel (1934-1960)*, ed. James L. Kelso, 70-6. Annual of the American Schools of Oriental Research 39. Cambridge, MA: American Schools of Oriental Research, 1968.

Skladanek, Bogdan. "The Structure of the Persian State (An Outline)." In *Acta Iranica. Première Serie. Commemoration Cyrus*, 117-23. Leiden: E. J. Brill, 1974.

Smend, Rudolf. "Julius Wellhausen as a Historian of Israel." *Semeia* 25 (1982):11-15.

Smith, H. S., and A. Kuhrt. "A Letter to a Foreign General." *Journal of Egyptian Archaeology* 68 (1982):199-209.

Smith, Morton. "Die Entwicklingen im Judäa des 5. Jh. v. Chr. aus griechischer Sicht." In *Seminar, Die Entstehung der antiken Klassengesellschaft*, ed. Hans G. Kippenberg, 313-27. Suhrkamp Taschenbücher Wissenschaft 130. Frankfurt am Main: Suhrkamp, 1977.

———. "Ezra." In *Ex Orbe Religionum: Studia Geo Widengren, Pars Prior*, 141- 43. Studies in the History of Religions, 21. Leiden: E. J. Brill, 1972.

———. *Palestinian Parties and Politics That Shaped the Old Testament*. New York: Columbia University Press, 1971.

———. "II Isaiah and the Persians." *Journal of the American Oriental Society* 83 (1963):413-21.

Snyder, Francis G. *Capitalism and Legal Change: An African Transformation*. Studies on Law and Social Control. New York: Academic Press, 1981.

von Soden, Wolfgang. *Akkadisches Handwörterbuch*. Wiesbaden: Otto Harrassowitz, 1969-76.

Soggin, J. Alberto. *A History of Ancient Israel*, trans. John Bowden. Philadelphia: Westminster Press, 1984.

Spalinger, Anthony. "Egypt and Babylonia: A Survey (c. 620 B. C.-550 B. C.)." *Studien zur Altägyptischen Kultur* 5 (1977):221-44.

———. "Psammetichus, King of Egypt: II." *Journal of the American Research Center in Egypt* 15 (1978):49-57.

van der Spek, R. J. "Did Cyrus the Great Introduce a New Policy Towards Subdued Nations? Cyrus in Assyrian Perspective." *Persica* 10 (1982): 278-83.

Spiegelberg, Wilhelm. "Der name *Inaros* in ägyptischen Texten." *Recueil de Travaux relatifs à la Philologie égyptienne et assyriennes* 28 (1906):197-201.

Stade, Bernhard. *Geschichte des Volkes Israel.* Allgemeine Geschichte in Einzeldarstellungen Abt. 1 Teil 6. Berlin: G. Grote, 1888.

Stern, Ephraim. "Achaemenian Tombs from Shechem." *Levant* 12 (1980):90-111.

———. "Achaemenid Tombs at Shechem." *Eretz- Israel* 15 (1981):312-30 [Hebrew].

———. "The Archaeology of Persian Palestine." In *The Cambridge History of Judaism. Volume One: Introduction: The Persian Period,* eds. W. D. Davies and L. Finkelstein, 88-114. Cambridge: Cambridge University Press, 1984.

———. "The Earliest Greek Settlement at Dor." *Eretz-Israel* 18 (1985):419-27 [Hebrew].

———. *Material Culture of the Land of the Bible in the Persian Period 538-332 B. C.* Warminster: Aris & Phillips, 1982.

———. "The Persian Empire and the Political and Social History of Palestine in the Persian Period." In *The Cambridge History of Judaism. Volume One: Introduction: The Persian Period,* eds. W. D. Davies and L. Finkelstein, 70-87. Cambridge: Cambridge University Press, 1984.

———. "Seal-impressions in the Achaemenid Style in the Province of Judah." *Bulletin of the American Schools of Oriental Research* 202 (1971):6-16.

———. "The Walls of Dor." *Israel Exploration Journal* 38 (1988):6-14.

———. "Yehud: The Vision and the Reality." *Cathedra* 4 (1977):13-25.

Stern, Ephraim and I. Magen. "A Persian Period Pottery Assemblage from Qadum in the Samaria Region." *Eretz-Israel* 16 (1982):182-97 [Hebrew].

Stronach, David. "The Development of the Fibula in the Near East." *Iraq* 21 (1959):181-206.

Tadmor, Hiyam. "The Campaigns of Sargon II of Assur." *Journal of Cuneiform Studies* 12 (1958):22-41, 77-101.

———. "The Southern Border of Aram." *Israel Exploration Journal* 12 (1962):114-22.

Talmon, S. "Ezra and Nehemiah (Books and Men)." In *Interpretor's Dictionary of the Bible. Supplement,* ed. K. Crim, 317-28. Nashville: Abingdon Press, 1976.

Thucydides. *History of the Peloponnesian War. Volume 1—Books 1 and 2.* Trans. C. Foster Smith. Loeb Classical Library. New York: G. P. Putnam's Sons, 1919.

Toombs, L. E. "The Stratification of Tell Balaṭah (Shechem)." *Bulletin of the American Schools of Oriental Research* 223 (1976):57-9.

Toombs, Lawrence E. and G. Ernest Wright. "The Fourth Campaign at Balatah (Shechem)." *Bulletin of the American Schools of Oriental Research* 169 (1963): 1-60.

Torrey, C. C. *The Composition and Historical Value of Ezra-Nehemiah.* Beihefte zur Zeitschrift für die alttestamentliche Wissenschaft 2. Giessen: J. Ricker, 1896.

Tufnell, Olga. *Lachish III: The Iron Age.* London: Oxford University Press, 1953.

Tuplin, Christopher. "The Administration of the Achaemenid Empire." In *Coinage and Administration in the Athenian and Persian Empires.* Ed. Ian Carradice, 109-66. BAR International Series 343. Oxford: British Archaeological Reports, 1987.

———. "Persian Garrisons in Xenophon and Other Sources." *Achaemenid History* 3 (1988):67-70.

Unger, Eckhard. *Babylon: Die Heilige Stadt nach der Beschreibung der Babylonier.* Berlin: Walter de Gruyter, 1931.

Ussishkin, David. "The Destruction of Lachish by Sennacherib and the dating of the Royal Judean Storage Jars." *Tel Aviv* 4 (1977):28-60.

Unz, Ron K. "The Chronology of the Pentekontaetia." *Classical Quarterly* n.s. 36 (1986):68-85.

van Seters, John. *In Search of History: Historiography the Ancient World and the Origins of Biblical History.* New Haven: Yale University Press, 1983.

de Vaux, Roland. *Archaeology and the Dead Sea Scrolls.* Schweich Lectures, 1959. Revised edition. London: British Academy, 1973.

———. Review of Vogt, *Studie zur nachexilischen Gemeinde in Esra-Nehemia. Revue Biblique* 73 (1966): 602-4.

Vogt, Hubertus C. M. *Studie zur nachexilischen Gemeinde in Esra-Nehemia.* Werl: Dietrich Coelde, 1966.

Wade-Gery, Henry. "Thucydides." In *The Oxford Classical Dictionary,* eds. N. G. L. Hammond and H. H. Scullard, 1067-69. Second edition. Oxford: Clarendon Press, 1970.

Wagner, Max. *Die lexikalischen und grammatikalischen Aramaismen im alttestamentlichen Hebräisch.* Zeitschrift für die alttestamentliche Wissenschaft Beihefte 96. Berlin: Alfred Töpelmann, 1966.

Walker, P. K. "The Purpose and Method of the 'Pentekontaetia' in Thucydides, Book I." *Classical Quarterly* n.s. 7 (1957):27-38.

Wallace, William. "The Egyptian Expedition and the Chronology of the Decade 460-450 B. C." *Transactions of the American Philological Association* 67 (1936):252-60.

Watzinger, Carl. *Denkmaler palästinas: Eine Einführung in die archaeologie des Heiligen Landes. Volume* 2. Leipzig: J. C. Hinrichs, 1935.

Weinberg, J. P. "Das *beit ʾabot* im 6.-4. Jh. v. u. z." *Vetus Testamentum* 23 (1973):400-14.

———. "Probleme der Sozialökonomischen Struktur Judäas vom 6. Jahrhundert v. u. z. bis zum 1. Jahrhundert u. z." *Jahrbuch für Wirtschaftsgeschichte* 1973/I:237-51.

———. "Die Agrarverhältnisse in der Bürger- Temple- Gemeinde der Achämenidenzeit." In *Wirtschaft und Gesellschaft im Alten Vorderasien,* eds. J. Harmatta and G. Komoroczy, 473-86. Nachdruck aus den Acta Antiqua Academiae Scientarum Hungaricae Tom. 22/1-4. Budapest: Akademiai Kiado, 1976.

Weinberg, Saul S. "Post-exilic Palestine: An Archaeological Report." *Proceedings of the Israel Academy of Science and Humanities* 4 (1969):78-97.

Weinfeld, Moshe. "Bible Criticism." In *Contemporary Jewish Religious Thought,* eds. Arthur A. Cohen and Paul Mendes-Flohr, 35-40. New York: Charles Scribner's Sons, 1987.

Weisberg, David B. "Kinship and Social Organization in Chaldaean Uruk." *Jounral of the American Oriental Society* 104 (1984):739-43.

Weissbach, F. H. *Die Inschriften Nebukadnezars II im Wadi Brisa und am Nahr el-Kelb.* Wissenschaftliche Veröffentlichungen der deutschen Orient-Gesellschaft Heft 5. Leipzig: J. C. Hinrichs, 1906.

Wells, Joseph. *Studies in Herodotus.* Oxford: Basil Blackwell, 1923.

Westlake, H. D. "Thucydides and the Athenian Disaster in Egypt." *Classical Philology* 45 (1950):209-16.

Widengren, G. "The Persian Period." In *Israelite and Judean History,* eds. J. Hayes and J. Maxwell Miller, 489-538. Philadelphia: Westminster Press, 1977.

Williamson, H. G. M. "The Composition of Ezra i-vi." *Journal of Theological Studies* n.s. 34 (1983): 1-30.

———. *Ezra, Nehemiah.* Word Biblical Commentary 16. Waco, TX: Word Books, 1985.

———. "Nehemiah's Walls Revisited." *Palestine Exploration Quarterly* 116 (1984):81-8.

Wilson, J. V. Kinnier. *The Nimrud Wine Lists: A Study of Men and Administration at the Assyrian Capital in the Eighth Century B. C.* London: British School of Archaeology in Iraq, 1972.

Wilson, John A. *The Culture of Ancient Egypt*. Chicago: University of Chicago Press, 1956.

Wilson, Robert D. "Tirshatha." In *The International Standard Bible Encyclopedia, Volume 5*, ed. James Orr, 2986-87. Reprint of the 1929 edition. Grand Rapids: Wm. B. Eerdmans, 1957.

Winlock, H. E. *The Temple of Hibis in El Khargeh Oasis. Part I: The Excavations.* Publications of the Metropolitan Museum of Art, Egyptian Expedition, 13. New York: Metropolitan Museum of Art, 1941.

Wiseman, D. J. *Chronicles of the Chaldaean Kings (626-556 B. C.).* London: British Museum, 1961.

Wright, G. Ernest. *Shechem: The Biography of a Biblical City.* New York: McGraw-Hill Book Co., 1965.

———. Review of *The Water System of Gibeon* by James B. Pritchard. *Journal of Near Eastern Studies* 22 (1963):210-11.

Xenophon. *Cyropaedia.* trans. Walter Miller. Loeb Classical Library. Cambridge, MA: Harvard University Press, 1953-60.

———. *Memorabilia and Oeconomicus.* trans. E. C. Marchant. Loeb Classical Library. Cambridge, MA: Harvard University Press, 1953.

Yadin, Yigael, Yohanan Aharoni, Ruth Amiran, Trude Dothan, Immanuel Dunayevsky and Jean Perrot. *Hazor I: An Account of the First Season of Excavations, 1955.* Jerusalem: Magnes Press, 1958.

Yamauchi, Edwin. "The Reverse Order of Ezra/Nehemiah Reconsidered." *Themelios* 5 (1980):7-13.

———. "Two Reformers Compared: Solon of Athens and Nehemiah of Jerusalem." In *The Bible World: Essays in Honor of Cyrus H. Gordon,* eds. Gary Rendsburg, Ruth Adler, Milton Arfa and Nathan Winter, 269-92. New York: KTAV Publishing House, 1980.

———. "Was Nehemiah the Cupbearer a Eunuch?" *Zeitschrift für die alttestamentliche Wissenschaft* 92 (1980):132-42.

Yoyotte, Jean. "Les principautes du Delta au temps de l'anarchie libyenne (Études d'histoire politique)." In *Mélanges Maspero: l'Orient Ancien, Fasc. 4,* 121- 79. Mémoires publiés par les membres de l'institut francais d'archéologie orientale Caire, 56. Cairo: Institut francais d'archéologie orientale, 1961.

Zadok, Ran. "The Nippur Region During the Late Assyrian, Chaldean and Achaemenian Periods, Chiefly According to Written Sources." *Israel Oriental Studies* 8 (1978):266-332.